3. Herbert W Hicks

REFERENCE

7. Vita Studio, Bexhill 1930s

10. W R Stewart

# HIDDEN TALENTS

A Dictionary of
Neglected Artists
Working 1880-1950

Jeremy Wood

Jeremy Wood Fine Art

Published by
Jeremy Wood Fine Art
95 High Street, Billingshurst, West Sussex RH14 9QX

ISBN 0 9522766 0 7

British Library CIP Data
A catalogue record for this book
is available from the British Library

Printed in England by The Marstan Press Limited.
Bexleyheath, Kent DA7 4BJ

# FOREWORD

I have known Jeremy for over 20 years since the days when I was a porter at Bonhams and he had given up a career in accountancy to open a gallery in Cranleigh. In those days he sold Victorian and Modern British paintings by artists such as Stanhope Forbes, Harold Harvey, William Lee-Hankey and Carlton Alfred Smith but as the auction prices for these artists rose at an alarming rate in the late 1970s and 1980s he looked elsewhere for pictures that represented value for money. Over the years he has discovered many talented artists who have been overlooked and who should have been mentioned in the Victorian and Edwardian Art Dictionaries.

This Dictionary is a must for anyone starting to collect pictures at affordable prices and for those wanting to complete their art reference library of Victorian and Early 20th Century artists.

Dendy Easton
Sotheby's

# ACKNOWLEDGEMENTS

I would like to thank all the dealers, museums, libraries and auction houses who have so generously provided me with information over the last eight years. In particular, my thanks are due to John Biggs for his assistance with West Country artists, Grant Waters for sharing his information on Sussex painters and Nick Smith for his research into artists of East Anglia. My thanks to The Royal West of England Academy and the Ipswich Art Club for the use of their catalogues and Anthony Beeson of the Bristol Library for access to his records. Timothy Saxon and Harry Turnbull also supplied me with useful information on several artists. Dendy Easton kindly agreed to write the foreword and provided much help along with his department at Sotheby's Sussex. I would also like to thank my staff at the gallery for their hard work in collating information and reading the proofs. It would have been impossible to compile a dictionary such as this without the assistance of many of the artists' relatives and to them I owe a special debt of gratitude.

# SELECTED BIBLIOGRAPHY AND SOURCES

Royal Academy of Arts (1769-1904). S. R. Publishers Ltd and Kingsmead Reprints (1970).

Royal Academy Exhibitors (1905-1970). E. P. Publishing Ltd (1973).

The Dictionary of British Artists 1880-1940. Antique Collectors Club (1976).

Dictionary of British Artists working 1880-1950. Grant Waters. Eastbourne Fine Art (1975).

Dictionary of Picture Postcards in Britain 1894-1939. A. Y. Cosh. Antique Collectors Club (1981).

Art Sales Index 1970-1992. Art Sales Index Ltd.

Dictionary of British Book Illustrators The Twentieth Century. John Murray (1983).

Who was Who 1897-1980 (7 vols and cumulated index). A & C Black.

Colour Magazine 1913-1931.

The Studio 1893-1950.

The Artist 1931-1950.

Kellys Directories (various counties) 1890-1939.

The Years Art 1885-1940. Hutchinson & Co.

Royal West of England Academy catalogues (1880-1950).

Ipswich Art Club catalogues (1880-1950).

Centenary Exhibition of the Ipswich Art Club catalogue (1975).

Norwich Art Circle catalogues (1885-1910).

Bristol Savages catalogues (1904-1950).

British Watercolour Society catalogues (1921-1935).

Army Officer Art Society catalogues (1925-1939).

Photograh credits: Miss E Chadburn (1, 7, 8), R Farquharson (2), W Hicks (3), Neale Dawe (4), Market Street Gallery, St Helier (5), Onslows Auctioneers (6), I Mcfarlane (9), R Acton (10).

# INTRODUCTION

After 20 years of dealing in paintings, I am often surprised at the many good pictures I find by artists who are not recorded in the reference books. About 10 years ago I started to collect information on 'unrecorded artists' largely for my own interest and then later began to compile this dictionary. Along the way, I came across more information on artists who were recorded and if this added significantly to existing knowledge I felt justified in putting them in the book.

Since much of the information in this dictionary is not readily available, it has meant a new approach to the method of research. I feel that this could only have been undertaken by a member of the picture trade who has the experience of seeing the work first hand. A lot of the data has been gathered from the clues on the pictures themselves and here the back of the picture is often more informative than the front. In an ideal situation there is a label giving the artist's address, but an address alone should be treated with caution as it may be that of an agent or purchaser. Often previous owners have been diligent in inscribing information or attaching an old obituary from a local newspaper. Even if a picture is not in its original frame, artists sometimes inscribed the back of a watercolour or the wooden stretcher of an oil. Where I know that an artist consistently did this, I have noted the fact in the biography as the inscriptions are usually faint and difficult to read.

I have gone to some trouble to establish, where possible, the birth and death dates of the artists listed as their exhibitions may only represent a small part of their working career. For example, if a picture is dated 30 years after the artist's last known exhibition but is within his lifespan then the inscription could be accepted. I have come across several cases of artists who exhibited up to the turn of the century and yet continued to work until the 1940s. Knowing the birth date is useful in establishing that an artist was old enough to have painted a particular dated work. Henry Charles Fox is widely recorded as being born in 1860 but my research proved that he was, in fact, born in 1855. Not perhaps in itself very significant, but it would help to substantiate works dated in the 1870s which might otherwise look improbable.

It is important to understand why so many artists, whose work was competent, are not recorded in the numerous reference books now available. I feel that this is the result of a number of factors.

Firstly, there were the geographical considerations. Artists who did not exhibit in London are less well-known, as many of the existing reference books have been compiled from the London catalogues. London represented an essential shop window for many of the provincial artists. Students at art school were often encouraged to submit work to these exhibitions and, as a result, some artists are only recorded as exhibiting in their student years. The cost of having pictures packed and transported to exhibitions was, perhaps, not so attractive once the artist had created a demand for his work locally.

Secondly, a number of artists did not show work at public exhibitions as they were under contract to dealers or galleries. It they were successful and the work sold quickly, the artist was often under pressure to provide more and the quality declined or the pictures became repetitive. The more discerning galleries would only accept the better pictures and if the artist wanted to sell his lesser works, he was often obliged to sign them with a pseudonym. There must also be other instances where artists have adopted a pseudonym for work that was not of their best but still saleable. A Royal Academician who died in the 1930s, left provision for a colleague to visit his studio after his death and to destroy any work that was not of his best. There can be few artists that have striven to impose such standards for posterity. It has become practice, particularly with the more popular painters, for collectors to assume that the better examples are the artists' work and the lesser ones are copies or fakes. In many instances I am convinced that this is not the case. I have bought several studio collections and these often included examples which were so uncharacteristic or poorly executed that, away from the collection would not have been regarded as the artists' work. Sadly, artists have often not provided for their future and many have painted into old age with failing sight and feel, producing work which was a pale reflection of their true talents.

Thirdly, there were many commercial artists who were employed full-time in the art departments and advertising agencies who never exhibited or sold their work through other outlets. These artists were often very skilled and highly talented and are still, in my opinion, one of the most underrated sectors of the art market. With the advent of three colour printing at the turn of the century many commercial artists, who had previously only worked in black and white, found a big demand for colour illustrations. The work included book illustrations, advertisements, calendars, prints and postcards. Most large printers had their own art department and often employed several full-time artists. Sir Alfred Munnings and Sir William Russell Flint are among those who began their careers working for commercial printers. Many of the commercial artists painted as a hobby but did not exhibit, although J Walter Thompson, the advertising agency, held exhibitions of their artists, entitled 'Weekend Work'.

Lastly, there were the unrecorded artists who for specific reasons used a pseudonym. Sometimes a foreign sounding name on a picture was more in keeping with the subject matter. The watercolour artist Norris Fowler Willatt, who specialised in Dutch canal scenes, found that these sold easier with a Dutch name and thus he signed most of them L Van Staaten. The English artist who signed his French town scenes Pierre Le Boeuff, adopted a further pseudonym, Andrea Vasari, for his Italian subjects. Fritz B Althus, a well-known landscape and marine painter, changed his German name in 1914 and continued to work and exhibit until the 1930s as Frederick B Kerr. A number of very prolific artists, working earlier this century, appear to have used several pseudonyms because they did not want to flood the market with their work. The situation was further confused when several artists were working under a common name. This occurred in the case of A D Bell, where at least three artists who worked for a dealer all used this pseudonym. In this case, fortunately, the artists had their own distinctive styles so the work can be identified.

The 1500 biographies included in this book represent only a small percentage of the unrecorded artists working between 1880 and 1950. I have tried to look at the country as a whole and examine, where possible, the places where the local exhibitions have not been covered in detail in other dictionaries. Some areas where famous groups of artists worked, such as Newlyn in Cornwall and Staithes in Yorkshire have already been the subject of much scrutiny. The Royal West of England Academy at Bristol was an important centre of exhibitions and I have examined their records in detail. Many good West of England artists who did not exhibit in London showed work at the R.W.A. East Anglia is another area which has largely escaped the researchers' attention, but the Norwich Art Circle and the

Ipswich Art Club were active societies with regular exhibitions. The British Watercolour Society, formed in the 1920s, did not have a permanent home but held exhibitions in different provincial towns twice a year. I have not been able to trace a complete set of their catalogues although some of the B.W.S. members are included in this book.

The other main source of information for the biographies apart from the exhibition catalogues are the pictures themselves. Good quality pictures are often appearing on the market by artists who seem to be unrecorded. Over a period of time, as more examples are seen, information can be accumulated as to the subject matter and working dates of the artist. Many date their pictures and this will help to establish their working life. Henry Charles Fox, for example, dated most of his work and as I found no work after 1927, it was a relatively simple task to check the Register of Deaths and discover that he had died two years later. Where an artist has an unusual surname a search of the Public Records or even the telephone directories can put a researcher in touch with the artist's living relatives. When I was looking for details of the talented illustrator W S Bagdatopoulos I discovered the only listing in the telephone directories of that name was the artist's 95 year-old sister – but rarely is the researcher's task so easy. Most surnames are too common to identify the artist or his family with any certainty.

One significant group of lesser known artists were those who died young, particularly those who were killed in the First World War. Harold Stagg was a typical example as he exhibited for only two years from 1912, but his name on the Bromley War Memorial bears testament to why this talented artist is not better known and his work is so seldom seen.

I have always regarded the collecting and updating of biographical information to be a continuous process. Hardly a day passes without someone providing me with information on an unrecorded artist. It is a never ending task to compile a dictionary such as this and since I called a halt I have already collected details of over 300 further artists, who hopefully may form part of an updated or second volume. I would be pleased to hear from anyone who has further information on lesser known painters, whether or not they are included in this book.

To all those who have been so kind in providing information and helping to compile this dictionary, I would like to give my sincere thanks.

Jeremy Wood.
Petworth 1994.

# ART SOCIETIES AND CLUBS

Listed below are some of the principal art societies and clubs featured in this book. With the larger societies it has often been possible to find a complete run of annual exhibition catalogues but with many of the smaller clubs only a few have been traced and there will still be members who are unrecorded.

**The Admiralty Art Club.** First exhibition in June 1921. Around 120 exhibits including works by well-known artists such as Sir John Lavery, Philip Connard, Norman Wilikinson and Charles Pears.

**The Air Force Artists Association.** Founded in 1935. Fourth Annual Exhibition held at the Building Centre, London, in December 1938.

**The Army Officers Art Society.** Founded in 1925 and still active in 1938. Membership was open to past and serving Army Officers and the annual exhibition was held at the R.B.A Galleries in London.

**The Association of Sussex Artists.** Founded in 1928. Annual exhibition held in July, usually in Horsham, open to non-members resident in Sussex. Still active today. John Thoburn McGaw was the first President and then Joseph Powell (q.v.) 1947-1961.

**The Berkshire Art Society.** Founded in 1898. Annual exhibition at Reading also open to non-members residing in the county. Third Annual Exhibition in November 1901.

**The Brighton Arts Club.** Founded c.1905. Exhibitions held for members only, firstly at the club premises at 19 West Street and later at the Brighton Museum and Art Gallery jointly with the Sussex Women's Art Club. The Brighton Museum and Art Gallery had held a spring exhibition of watercolours by local artists and an autumn exhibition of oil paintings since the 1880s.

**The Bristol Savages.** Founded in 1904. Annual exhibition in March for members only. An active club which held weekly sketching meetings. Many of the members were local Bristol artists and included Bartram Hiles, W Evans Linton, F Stuart Richardson and C Brooke Branwhite.

**The British Watercolour Society (B.W.S.).** Founded c.1921. Exhibitions held twice yearly in the leading provincial towns including Hastings (1937), Hereford (1930, 1934, 1940), Kidderminster (1942 and 1944) and Preston (1928). L. Burleigh Bruhl was President and Snow Gibbs was Hon. Secretary of the B.W.S. for many years.

**The Daub Club.** This was a small club of amateur artists that organised watercolour sketching trips in the early 1900s. It appears to have been centred in the South of England although it is not known if any exhibitions were held.

**The Derby Sketching Club.** Founded in 1887. Annual exhibition in January confined to members who were mostly local artists both professional and amateur. Still active in 1940 with a membership of about 100.

**Eland's Art Gallery, Exeter.** (fl. c.1883-1937). Henry Eland established an art gallery in the High Street, Exeter, and from 1894 held the Annual Devon and Exeter Exhibition. These exhibitions were continued into the late 1920s and included many minor artists who did not exhibit elsewhere.

**The Ipswich Art Club.** Founded in 1874. Annual exhibition mostly of members work but also other prominent artists invited to exhibit and some work by non-members from the Suffolk area. In 1975, a Centenary Exhibition was held in Ipswich of 180 works by past and present members. The Club still flourishes today.

**The Leicester Society of Artists.** Founded in 1883. Most the exhibitors were local artists and amateurs. An annual exhibition of members' work was held in the autumn at the City Galleries. Still active in 1939.

**The North British Academy of Arts (N.B.A.).** Founded in 1908. Based at Newcastle-on-Tyne and held annual exhibitions in London and large provincial towns. In 1913 the 7th Annual Exhibition was held in Worcester and in 1914 the 8th Annual Exhibition at the Crystal Palace, London. The Society was still active in 1922.

**The Norwich Art Circle.** Founded in 1885. Two exhibitions of members' work were held annually in the spring and autumn. The members were mostly local artists and the club was still active in the 1940s.

**The Nottingham Society of Artists.** Founded in 1881. A spring exhibition was held at the Museum and Art Gallery of local artists' work including non-members and usually at exhibition of members' work in November. The Presidents in the 1930s were Terrick Williams and Harold Knight.

**The Plymouth Society of Artists.** Founded c.1944. Annual exhibition at the Museum and Art Gallery including work by non-members. Mostly local Plymouth and Devon artists. The 7th Annual Exhibition was held in September 1950.

**The Reading Guild of Artists.** Founded in 1930. Annual exhibition of local artists and craftworkers held at the Reading Museum and Art Gallery. The Guild of Artists still flourishes.

**The Royal Amateur Art Society.** Founded in 1897. Annual exhibition in the spring of members only or their nominees. Still active in 1939. There were also some local branches with exhibitions – Sussex branch, Hove, held annual exhibitions in 1906, 1907, and 1908.

**The Royal West of England Academy (R.W.A.).** Founded in 1844 out of the Society of Bristol Artists. Annual exhibition in the autumn including work by non-members. The principal West Country society with many well-known artists exhibiting.

# ARTIST MONOGRAMS

Individual artist's monograms vary considerably. These are actual examples taken from pictures but should only be regarded as a guide as other variations may exist.

 John F BEE

 Frederick W BIDDER

 J H BOEL

 Isabella M CHARTERS

 Octavious T CLARK

 Clive M DIXON

 Norman DONNELLY

 Rachel M DYER

E John ELSON

 Harry FIDLER

 Reginald W GICK

R Percy GOSSOP

 Florence M GRACE

Evered HOLLAND

 Sidney Yates JOHNSON

 Ethel LARCOMBE

LONGMATE    Ernest LONGMATE

19 ⊞ 27    Charles E MILNES-HEY

℗    George F PENNINGTON

℘    R Noel POCOCK

℗    Elsie K S POWELL

S.J.R 04    Sidney J ROBBINS

NR    Nina ROTHNEY

Ƶ    Zue SAYERS

⋈    Max SINCLAIR

ɼ    Margaret THOMAS

ⱭⱠⱭ    Arthur L WALBANK

*To my sons:*
*Henry and Robbie*
*In the hope that one day*
*they too discover a love*
*of pictures*

# A

## Miss Joan ABBAY (exh. 1903-1906)

Watercolour portrait and landscape painter who was a member of the Ipswich Art Club and showed at least 12 works at their exhibitions 1903-1906. The subjects included local landscapes, portraits in watercolour and some illustrations. She lived at Earl Soham Rectory, near Framlingham, Norfolk.

*W. R. Stewart Acton*        *'Jack and Jill on the Sussex Downs' (w/c)*

## Walter Robert Stewart ACTON (1879-1960)

Painter in oil and watercolour of downland scenes and rural landscapes, who was born in Brighton on 6th July 1879. Stewart Acton was the grandson of the Victorian portrait and figure artist John Stewart, so it is not surprising that he took to painting at an early age. He was educated at the Brighton Grammar School and then followed his father into the antique business in Prince Albert Street, where he specialised as a porcelain restorer. Stewart Acton was a founder member of the 'Pen and Palette Club' and was an active member of the Brighton Arts Club from 1911 until 1925. He had several one-man exhibitions. One at Marshall & Co., Brighton, entitled 'Scenes on the South Downs' in 1909 consisted of 85 local Sussex views and an exhibition at Kent and Lacey's Gallery, Eastbourne, included 40 downland and coastal scenes. His eldest son (Walter) John was also an artist and dealer with a business in Brighton. Stewart Acton was still working after the Second World War and exhibited two Sussex views at the Royal Academy, in 1946 and 1950. He died on 11th August 1960 aged 81. A retrospective exhibition of his work was held at the Canon Gallery, Chichester, in March 1990.

## Miss Albinia M.. ADAMS (fl. 1908)

A student at the Birbeck School of Art, Chancery Lane, London, who in 1908 won the Hardy Prize for painting flowers from nature.

## Edgar T.. ADAMS (exh. 1899-1901)

Painter in oil of landscapes and marines, who lived at Halstead, Essex, and exhibited five works at the Ipswich Art Club 1899-1901. The titles included 'Luccombe, Isle of Wight', 'Evening Spring, River Colne' (both 1899), and 'The Dutchman at Anchor' (1901).

## Miss Emma E.. ADAMS (exh. 1906)

Landscape painter in oil and watercolour who lived at Trimley, Suffolk, and exhibited three works at the Ipswich Art Club Exhibition in 1906. The subjects were 'Totteridge Common' (oil), 'Gulvall Cross' and 'Nanjissel Cove, Cornwall' (watercolours).

## M.. J.. ADAMS (exh. 1935-1937)

Watercolour landscape and figure painter who exhibited with the St Ives Society of Artists in 1935 and 1937. The titles were 'Twenty Years After' (1935), and 'The Hop Pickers' and 'Carpe Diem' (1937).

## Miss Pat ADAMS (exh. 1950)

Painter in oil, watercolour and gouache of figure subjects and landscapes who lived in Plymouth. She exhibited three works at the Plymouth Art Society Annual Exhibition in 1950.

## Percy ADAMS (exh. 1886)

Painter in watercolour of landscapes and architectural subjects who lived in Ipswich and was a member of the Ipswich Art Club. He exhibited three works at the Annual Exhibition in 1866 entitled 'Old Windmill' (watercolour), 'St. Martins Church, Cologne' and 'Tomb of Sir Walter Scott, Dryburgh Abbey' (monochrome sketches).

*W. Avery Adams*        *'Tickenham Church, Somerset' (oil)*

## William Avery ADAMS (exh. 1904-1930)

Painter in oil and watercolour of landscapes, who lived in Bristol. He exhibited regularly at the R.W.A., showing over 40 works 1904-1930. The subjects were mostly scenes of Devon and Cornwall and some local views – 'Spring, Pensford', 'Waning Summer', and 'Sunset, Mullion' (all 1910) are typical titles.

## Miss C.. A.. ADAMSON (exh. 1921)

Miss Adamson exhibited at the Darlington Society of Arts First Annual Exhibition in 1921 and had been a student at the local school of art under Arnold Sharpe.

## Ernest D.. ADCOCK (fl. 1899-1909)

Painter in oil and watercolour who lived in Norwich and was a member of the Norwich Art Circle. He exhibited regularly at the Norwich Art Circle exhibitions, showing 15 works 1899-1909 although there is no record of him after that date.

## John Wilton ADCOCK (1863-1930)

Painter in watercolour of rural landscapes, cottages and beach scenes. He lived in Nottingham and exhibited at the Nottingham Art Gallery in the 1880s. By the late 1920s, he was living at Polegate in Sussex and was a member and exhibitor at the Brighton Arts Club from 1928 until his death in 1930. Some of his lesser works are just signed J Wilton (q.v.).

*A. Allan   'On the Thames' (w/c)   (J Collins and Son)*

## T.. C.. ALDER (fl.c. 1910)

Painter of landscapes and river scenes in watercolour who was probably working about 1910. The subjects included some Yorkshire views in the Goathland area.

## Dorothea A.. H.. ALDWORTH (fl. 1916-1926)

Painter in watercolour of far eastern scenes. She illustrated 'Malayan Memories' (1916) with five colour plates and 'Peeps at the Malay States' (1926) with eight illustrations. Her work has a pleasing, wet, impressionistic style but is often not signed and unlikely to be identified.

## A.. ALLAN (fl. 1920s-1930s)

Painter in watercolour of river landscapes and buildings. The subjects which are well painted include views on the Thames and studies of Oxford and Cambridge Colleges. The work is also signed 'V. Allan' (q.v.) or sometimes just 'Allan'. This does not appear to be the same Allan as the prolific oil painter of Thames views who was working around the turn of the century.

*R. Allan       'Windsor Castle' (oil)       (Sotheby's Sussex)*

## R.. ALLAN (fl. 1900s)

Painter in oil of river landscapes, who was working at around the turn of the century. This prolific artist appears to have signed with other initials and sometimes just 'Allan'. Many of the subjects were Thames views and often painted in pairs. The work is not usually dated, but the title is often inscribed on the reverse. 'Evening on the Thames at Sonning', 'Iffley Lock, Oxford' and 'Windsor Castle' are typical subjects.

## V.. ALLAN (fl. 1920s-1930s)

Painter in watercolour of river landscapes, town scenes and building studies. It seems unlikely that this is the same artist as the painter above although the work is also signed sometimes 'Allan' without an initial. The watercolours are well painted, and include views on the Thames, and studies of Oxford and Cambridge Colleges.

## Mrs Eliza Jane Winifred ALLEN (exh. 1914-1926)

Watercolour landscape painter who lived at St. Andrews Park and, later, at Redland, Bristol. She exhibited regularly at the R.W.A. showing 25 pictures 1914–1926. The subjects were mostly local views and Cornish coastal scenes.

**Miss Geraldine ALLEN A.B.W.S. (fl. 1930s)**
Portrait painter who lived at Leckhampton, Glos. in the 1930s. She was an associate member of the British Watercolour Society.

**H.. G.. ALLSOP (exh. 1921)**
Painter in oil and watercolour who exhibited three works at the Derby Sketching Club in January 1921.

**Ernest AMES (fl. 1900-1930)**
A painter of landscapes and garden scenes in watercolour who had at least two one-man shows in London before the First World War. Graves Gallery held an exhibition of his work in 1910 entitled 'English and Scotch Gardens' consisting of 56 watercolours and including, curiously, four views of Venice. A second exhibition was held at the Modern Gallery of 60 pictures mostly views around St Andrews, Scotland, but also of Suffolk and Southern England. His continental works were studies of Venice and the Italian lakes.

**Capt. David Murray ANDERSON (exh. 1928-1930)**
An officer in the 8th Hussars who exhibited at the Army Officers Art Society Annual Exhibitions in 1928 and 1930. He showed a total of eight watercolours mainly views of India and one of Venezuela. David Anderson lived at Bowhouse, near Dunbar, Scotland.

**G.. A.. ANDERSON (exh. 1915)**
Painter of figure subjects and landscapes who had a one-man exhibition at the Modern Gallery, London, in July 1915. Entitled 'Pictures of India' the exhibition contained 51 works mainly landscapes and market scenes including several of Bombay.

**W.. F.. ANDERSON (exh. 1928-1936)**
An Officer in the Royal Engineers who exhibited a total of 29 works at the Army Officers Art Society exhibitions 1928-1936.

**Miss Cecily M.. P.. ANDREWS (exh. 1917-1926)**
Oil painter of still life and landscapes, lived in London and later at Chesham Bois, Bucks. She exhibited at the Royal Academy in 1917 and 1926, and three works at the First Exhibition of the Admiralty Art Club in 1921.

**Ernest George Henry ANDREWS (1896-1977)**
Painter in watercolour of seascapes and landscapes who was born in Bristol in 1896. He served in the First World War in the Machine Gun Corps. A regular exhibitor at the R.W.A., he showed a total of 28 works 1934-1976 mostly harbour scenes and landscapes in Ireland, Devon and Cornwall. He was also an exhibitor at the Bristol Savages and their President in 1950 and 1970.

**R.. S.. ANGELL (fl. 1906)**
Painter in watercolour of flower still life, who received an hon. mention in The Studio competition in 1906.

**Kenneth M.. ANGUS (exh. 1950)**
Watercolour artist who lived in Plymouth and was a member of the Plymouth Art Society. He showed two watercolours at the Annual Exhibition in 1950, both local views.

**Harcourt S.. ANSON (exh. 1912)**
Watercolour landscape painter who exhibited at the Brighton Arts Club Exhibition of 1912. He exhibited two works, a landscape and a cornfield.

**Walter F.. V.. ANSON (fl. 1912)**
Designer and illustrator of figure subjects. He studied at the Leicester School of Art, and his work was represented at the National Schools of Art Competition in 1912. He signed his work 'ANSON' printed in a box.

**Mrs. M.. ANYON-COOK (exh. 1950)**
Portrait painter in oils who lived and worked in Polperro, Cornwall. She exhibited three works at the Plymouth Art Society in 1950, probably loaned by the sitters as the pictures were not for sale.

**Miss Dorothea APPLEBY (exh. 1930-1933)**
Watercolour artist who lived at Bathwick near Bath and exhibited at the R.W.A. in 1930 and 1933. The works were entitled 'Evening Light' and 'Unemployed'.

**Major J.. B.. ARBUTHNOT (exh. 1930-1939)**
Painter in oil and watercolour who exhibited 18 works at the Army Officers Art Society exhibitions 1930-1939. The subjects included some copies of Old Masters.

**Elizabeth ARMSDEN (exh. 1950)**
Etcher in colour who worked at Studland in Dorset where she shared a studio with A H Berens. Her work was reproduced in The Artist and she exhibited in both London and Paris.

**Miss Evelyn Mary ARNEY (exh. 1900-1903)**
Still life painter in oil and watercolour who lived at Weston-super-Mare and, later, Winscombe, Somerset. She exhibited at the R.W.A. in 1900 'Autumn Fruits' (watercolour) and in 1903 'Apple Blossom' (oil) and 'Auriculas' (watercolour).

*F. Arnold*                                  *'Nightfall' (w/c)*

## F.. ARNOLD (fl. 1920s)

This is a pseudonym for J W Gozzard (q.v.) who worked in the early part of the century as a watercolour artist and illustrator of prints and postcards. The subjects were rural landscapes or moonlight scenes.

## Miss Janet M.. ARNOTT (exh. 1923-1927)

Watercolour landscape painter who lived in Woodbridge, Suffolk, and exhibited 10 works at the Ipswich Art Club exhibitions 1923-1927. The subjects were mostly local views, including Walberswick and Woodbridge.

## J.. M.. ASHBURNER B.W.S. (exh. 1928)

Watercolour landscape painter who was a member of the B.W.S. and exhibited two works at the B.W.S. Exhibition at Preston in 1928.

## Constance ASHBURY B.W.S. (exh. 1928)

Watercolour landscape painter who was a member of the B.W.S and exhibited at their exhibition in Preston in 1928 a picture entitled 'When Spring and Autumn Meet'.

## Mrs. G.. M.. ASHINGTON (exh. 1920-1921)

Watercolour landscape painter who lived at Stoke Bishop, Bristol, and exhibited three works at the R.W.A. in both 1920 and 1921. The subjects were views in Majorca, 'The Turn of the Tide, Tenby' (1920), 'A Flower Stall - Savoy', and 'Blaise Cottages' (1921).

## Miss M.. ASHLEY (exh. 1922)

Painter who lived at Winscombe, Somerset, and exhibited four works at the R.W.A. in 1922.

## Alfred E.. ASKWITH (exh. 1919)

Bradford artist who exhibited at the Local Artists Exhibition in Spring 1919, a work entitled 'The Restless Sea'.

## Mlle Eugenie Olga ASSENMACHER (exh. 1929-1938)

Painter in oils of landscapes, figures and flowers who lived at Aldeburgh, Suffolk, and was a member of the Ipswich Art Club. She exhibited a total of 13 works 1929-1938. The subjects included 'Tulips' (1930), 'The Village Girl' (1935) and 'Helford Village, Cornwall ' (1936).

## J.. W.. ATHERTON (exh. 1921)

Painter of landscapes and still life who exhibited three works at the First Admiralty Art Club Exhibition in June 1921.

## Miss L.. M.. ATKINS (exh. 1900)

Artist who lived at Redland, Bristol, and exhibited two works at the R.W.A. in 1900. The subjects were 'Elizabeth Castle, Jersey' and 'Coombe Dingle' a local landscape view.

## Miss Mary B.. ATKINSON (exh. 1915)

Painter in oil of landscapes and portraits who lived in Clifton and exhibited three works at the R.W.A. in 1915. The subjects were portraits and a view of Strand-on-the-Green.

*Alex Austen*                  *(Sotheby's Sussex)*

*'Threading the Needle' (oil)*

## Alexander AUSTEN (fl. 1900-1910)

Good quality painter in oils of genre, figure subjects and interior scenes often in period costume. 'A Music Recital', 'The Chess Players', and 'The China Mender' being typical titles.

**Reginald Harry AUSTIN (1890-1955)**

Painter in watercolour of landscapes and woodland scenes often featuring birds and animals. R H Austin was apprenticed at the age of 14 at the Royal Worcester Porcelain factory and specialised in painting designs with birds and fruit. He worked at the factory until 1930 when he set up with his brother, Walter, as freelance designers. His watercolours are finely detailed and the quality and subject matter would make them collectable.

**G.. M.. AVONDALE (fl. 1920s)**

Painter in watercolour of marine, beach and coastal scenes. This artist's work is so similar to that of Garmon Morris (q.v.) in size, subject matter, and techniques as to lead the author to presume that they are the same person. The watercolours tend to be small precise fishing boat studies often of a narrow 'portrait' shape. The subjects included West Country views such as St. Michael's Mount and were often signed 'Avondale' without initials.

G M Avondale                                      'Paignton looking towards Harbour' (w/c)

# B

**Ernest H.. BABB (exh. 1950)**

Flower painter in watercolour who lived at Yelverton, Devon, and was a member of the Plymouth Art Society. He exhibited three watercolour still lifes of flowers at the Seventh Annual Exhibition in 1950.

**Miss Florence K.. BABB (exh. 1950)**

Flower and still life painter in watercolour who lived in Plymouth and was a member of the Plymouth Art Society. She exhibited two works in 1950 – 'Pansies' and 'Apple Blossom'.

**Miss Kate Stanhope BADCOCK (fl. 1880s-1910)**

Animal painter who was the daughter of Canon Badcock and sister of the artist Isobel Baynes Badcock. Kate Badcock specialised in painting horses and cattle in landscapes, mostly in oil but some watercolour. She lived in Ripon and died at an early age in 1910.

*W. S. Bagdatopoulos.*        *'Indian Dancer' (w/c)*

**William Spencer BAGDATOPOULOS F.R.S.A. (1888-1965)**

William Spencer Bagdatopoulos was born on the Greek island of Zante on 23rd July 1888. His mother was English and his father Greek, but he spent most of his early childhood in Rotterdam where his father had a successful dried fruit business. At the age of 12 he became the youngest ever student at the Academie van Beeldende in Rotterdam and studied there for the next four years. In 1904, at the still young age of 16, he set out on his first painting tour of the Near East which was to last four years and included Egypt, Palestine and Turkey. He also visited Greece and spent a year at the Academy in Athens. This trip must have given the young Bagdatopoulos his first real experience of painting from life which was to prove so important for his later tours of India and the Far East. About this time he visited London and lived at Hampton Wick while he was studying the more commercial aspects of art at John Hassall's School.

The mid nineteen twenties were to be some of his most productive years with several commissions, advertising work and exhibitions. In November 1924 he was sponsored by the 'Times of India' to paint a series of pictures and his tour of India was to last 18 months. The harsh climate made working conditions difficult but suited his quick sketching style in water and bodycolour. Bagdatopoulos also executed a series of etchings of Indian figure and portrait studies which were of fine quality. His Indian pictures were reproduced in The Studio magazine and in June 1927 a one-man exhibition of his work was held at the Arlington Gallery in New Bond Street.

In 1928 Bagdatopoulos first visited the United States and spent several months touring and painting. From there he travelled to the Far East visiting among other places Japan, China, Siam, Burma, Ceylon and again India. He settled in Hollywood with his mother and two sisters and built a studio at home although for a time he also had an art school in Los Angeles. A number of exhibitions of his work were held in America including an etching exhibition in Los Angeles and watercolour show at the Smithsonian Institution, Washington, in October 1930.

Bagdatopoulos moved to Santa Barbara, California, and lived there until his wife died in 1965. Later that year he came to Praa Sands, Cornwall, to stay with his sisters and he died there aged 77 in December 1965.

**R.. A.. BAGG (fl. 1900s)**

Painter in watercolour of high quality flower and fruit still life studies. This artist does not appear to have exhibited.

**Miss L.. T.. BAGNALL (exh. 1901)**

Painter of landscapes who lived near Chard, Somerset. She was a member of the Berkshire Art Society and exhibited three works at the Third Annual Exhibition in 1901.

*Henry Bailey*     'Calves' (w/c)     (Sotheby's Sussex)

## Henry BAILEY (1848-1933)

Son of a wealthy tea merchant, Henry Bailey was educated at Charterhouse and then trained as a physician but gave up medicine to study art. He began painting in oils, but an allergy to oil paint made him concentrate of watercolours. Bailey exhibited at the major galleries at home and abroad and travelled to Europe painting in France and Italy. He also taught art at the Royal Academy Schools and took the first mixed classes held at the Victoria and Albert Museum.

## S.. C.. BAILEY (fl. 1921)

Painter of coastal scenes and landscapes who exhibited three works at the First Admiralty Art Club Exhibition in June 1921.

## Sir William BAILLIE-HAMILTON (1844-1920)

Watercolour painter of landscapes and river scenes. He had a joint exhibition at the Modern Gallery, London, with Miss Victoria Cholmondeley (q.v.) in March 1906. Baillie-Hamilton showed 35 watercolours at the exhibition– mostly views in Scotland and the South of England.

*Victor Baird*     'Poppa's Chickens (oil)     (Sotheby's)

## Victor BAIRD (fl. 1900s)

Painter in oil of poultry and farmyard scenes. The style suggests that he may have been an illustrator although no evidence could be found.

## Miss E.. P.. BAKER (exh. 1910)

Landscape painter in oil who exhibited two works at the Worthing Art Gallery Summer Exhibition in 1910. One was a view on the Seine and the other a Normandy landscape.

## Miss Ida B.. BAKER (exh. 1901)

Painter in oil of flowers and still life who lived at Southsea, Hants, and exhibited two works at the R.W.A. in 1901. The titles of the works were 'Flowers that Bloom in the Spring', and 'Cape Gooseberries and Sea Holly'.

## Miss Lily A.. BAKER (fl. 1899-1936)

Watercolour landscape painter who lived in Dublin in 1899 and exhibited at the R.H.A. but by the 1930s she had moved to Clifton, Bristol, and exhibited three works at the R.W.A. The subjects were 'Misty Day, Wicklow Mountains' (1933), 'Bally Castle, County Antrim' (1935), and 'Alum Bay, Isle of Wight' (1936).

## Brig.- Gen. W.. BAKER-BROWN (exh. 1928-1939)

Watercolour painter of landscapes and coastal scenes. He exhibited regularly at the Army Officers Art Society exhibitions showing over 50 works 1928-1939. The subjects included Scottish views and West Country scenes. He lived in Sutton, Surrey.

## Maj.-Gen. Thomas Stanford BALDOCK (1854-1937)

Watercolour painter of animals and landscapes. He lived at St. Jude, Cornwall, and exhibited 16 works at the Army Officers Art Society 1928-1931 although he remained a member until 1937. His subjects included West Country views and cattle studies.

## F.. Winifred BALL (fl. 1917-1922)

Book illustrator and watercolour artist who lived at Hexham, Northumberland, and was active from about 1917 until 1922. She painted a series of 15 ink and watercolour illustrations for the Rubaiyat of Omar Khayyam, although the edition may not have been published.

## Dr. G.. D.. J.. BALL (exh. 1950)

Oil painter who lived in Plymouth and exhibited two figure studies at the Plymouth Art Society Exhibition in 1950.

**Miss M.. E.. BALL (exh. 1932-1934)**

Portrait and landscape artist who lived at Weston-super-Mare, Somerset, and exhibited four works at the R.W.A. 1932-1934. The subjects were 'Cottage Porch, Westport' (1932) and three portrait studies.

*Bessie Bamber*       *'Kittens' (oil)*       *(J. Collins and Son)*

**Bessie BAMBER (fl.c. 1900-1910)**

Oil painter of cats and kittens. These fine quality paintings were often small and executed on glass or porcelain. The work was usually signed with initials and dated. Some modern copies of her work exist and can be difficult to tell from the originals.

**Mrs. Mary BANESS A.R.W.A. (exh. 1902-1930)**

Watercolour landscape painter who lived in Bath, Bristol, and from 1923 at Weston-super-Mare, and was an associate member of the R.W.A. She was a regular exhibitor showing over 67 works 1902-1930. Mary Baness also exhibited at a joint woman artists exhibition at the Ryder Gallery, London, about 1905 where she showed 11 watercolours – mostly views of Bristol and Italian landscapes. Some of her work was reproduced as postcards. She signed 'Baness' in a script.

**Miss Florence Whittenham BANTING (exh. 1936)**

Painter in watercolour of flowers who lived at Westbury Park, Bristol, and exhibited two works at the R.W.A. in 1936 – 'Hollyhocks' and 'Pink Asters'.

*G. Barbaro*       *'Ships of the Desert' (w/c)*       *(J. Collins and Son)*

**Giovanni BARBARO (fl. 1900s)**

Painter in watercolour of still life and eastern scenes. The work which is often seen on the market appears identical to that of Arthur Dudley, for whom it was probably a pseudonym. The subjects were usually painted in a long landscape shape, the still life being fruit, and the eastern scenes, street markets or camels in the desert.

**Miss Annie BARBER (fl. 1909)**

A student at the Lambeth School of Art, who won first prize in the National Art Competition in 1909 for a figure composition.

**Miss Constance D.. BARBER (exh. 1926-1927)**

Portrait and landscape painter who lived in Bath and exhibited five works at the R.W.A. in 1926 and 1927. The subjects were two portraits, 'The Quarry' (1926), 'Treasures of the Shore' and 'Wick Rocks' (1927).

*J. Barclay*       *'By the Duckpond' (w/c)*       *(Sotheby's)*

**J.. BARCLAY (fl. 1920s-1930s)**

This was the pseudonym used by the Birmingham artist and illustrator Horace Hammond when working in the 1920s and 1930s. The subjects were rural scenes in watercolour often featuring cottages, figures and animals. Horace Hammond also painted for a local dealer under the name of A D Bell (q.v.). The decorative subject matter and precise style of the 'J Barclay' pictures have resulted in the work becoming increasingly popular.

**Albert G.. BARDSLEY (exh. 1950)**

Painter in oil of landscapes, river scenes and portraits who lived in Plymouth. He was a member of the Plymouth Art Society and exhibited five works at the Annual Exhibition in 1950.

**Maj. The Hon. Maurice BARING (1874-1945)**

Painter of landscapes and allegorical scenes who exhibited seven watercolours at the 'Author and Artist Exhibition' at the Little Art Rooms, London, in 1918. In November 1921 the same gallery held a one-man exhibition showing 49 of his works. These included Russian and Irish landscapes and some war paintings in France.

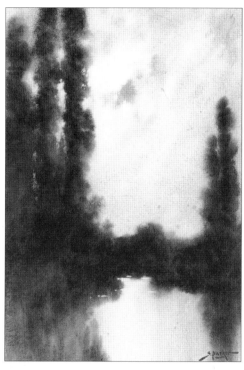

*John Barker*                    *'Moonlight River' (w/c)*

**John BARKER** B.W.S. (fl. 1920s)

Painter in watercolour of moonlight river landscapes. This artist appears to have been a member of the British Watercolour Society and exhibited there in the 1920s.

**Reginald BARKER (exh. 1926-1927)**

Landscape artist who lived in Bristol and exhibited five works at the R.W.A. in 1926 and 1927. All the exhibits were continental views – 'Lake Maggiore', 'Lake Thun' and 'Above Sion' (1926), and 'Old Bridge, Lucerne' and 'Chillon' (1927).

**Mrs. D.. H.. BARLOW (exh. 1912)**

Watercolour painter who exhibited two works at the Winchester Art Society in 1912 – a wharf scene and a Fenland view.

**Mrs. M.. J.. BARNARDISTON (exh. 1930-1948)**

Watercolour landscape painter who lived in Woodbridge and was a member of the Ipswich Art Club. She exhibited a total of 20 works 1930-1948. The subjects were mostly Scottish including Perthshire, Invernesshire and the Orkneys, but there were also some views in British Columbia (1931-1934).

**Miss G.. Lilian BARNES (exh. 1927-1933)**

Painter of flowers in oil and watercolour who lived at Melton in Suffolk and was a member of the Ipswich Art Club. She exhibited 14 works at the Ipswich Art Club 1927-1933, 'A Summer Bunch' (watercolour) and 'Familiar Wild Flowers' (oil) are typical titles.

**G.. R.. BARR (fl. 1880-1886)**

Painter in oil of flowers and still life. It is curious that this good quality artist does not appear to have exhibited. Most of the subjects are flower studies and are dated from the 1880s, although he may also have painted some marines.

*G. W. Bartlett*                    *'L.M.S. Express, 1923' (w/c)*

**G.. W.. BARTLETT (fl. 1923-1928)**

Painter of train and ship portraits in pencil and watercolour. This competent artist does not appear to have exhibited, but may have been connected with the railways as some of his surviving sketches are on Southern Railway Company paper. The style of the work suggests that the artist may have worked as an illustrator or for postcards.

**Henry George BARWELL (c. 1829-1898)**

Former President of the Norwich Art Circle and watercolour artist. A memorial exhibition of his work was held by the Norwich Art Circle in May 1899 consisting of 51 landscapes, mostly English, but some Breton and Italian views. The pictures were loaned by his daughter Miss Louisa Barwell (q.v.) and were not for sale. Henry Barwell was a wine merchant in a local family business and died on 9th July 1898 aged 69.

**Miss Louisa Mary BARWELL (exh. 1900-1906)**

Daughter of H. G. Barwell (q.v.). Watercolour painter who lived in Norwich and was a member of the Norwich Art Circle. She exhibited regularly at their exhibitions from 1900 to 1906 showing a total of 15 works, mostly gardens and landscapes, but with some foreign views.

**Stanley W.. BARWELL (exh. 1903-1911)**

Oil painter, watercolour and black and white artist who lived at Sheringham in Norfolk. He was a member of the Norwich Art Circle and exhibited over 25 pictures 1903-1911. Many of his pictures were marines or coastal scenes – 'Incoming Tide' (oil), 'Clew Bay, Ireland' (oil) and 'Preparing for Sea' (watercolour) are typical titles. He also painted horses and hunting scenes.

A. D. Bastin          'Rats' detail (oil)          (Sotheby's Sussex)

**Alfred Dickman BASTIN (1849-1913)**

Still life and genre painter in oil and watercolour who exhibited widely in London and the provinces. Alfred Bastin was born in London in 1849 and worked from various addresses in West London, although by the 1880s he was living at Egham, Surrey, and around 1900 he moved to Worthing, Sussex, where he died in 1913. The work is of good quality and the popular subject matter has meant that the better examples can command high prices. He signed his work A D Bastin in a printed script.

**J.. BATE (fl. 1921-1934)**

Painter in watercolour of moorland landscapes and West Country views in the style of Charles Brittan. The artist does not appear to have exhibited but the pictures are often dated and span from 1921 to 1934.

**Margaret BATTAMS (1881-1974)**

Painter in oils of animals, particularly horses and dogs. Margaret Battams was born on the 27th March 1881, the youngest daughter of Robert Battams, a farmer at Brampton Ash in Northants. She studied

art at the School of Animal Painting in London under W Frank Calderon. Many good artists received their training at Calderson's School and one of her fellow students at that time was Lionel Edwards. Despite her considerable talent, Margaret Battams did not exhibit although she painted a number of commissions of horses and dogs in both oil and pencil. A highly creative person, she also made wooden models of farm animals and jigsaw puzzles. Her paintings are not often seen on the market but the quality and subject matter would make them collectable. Margaret Battams died on 3rd May 1974 at the age of 93.

**Miss E.. Dora BATTISCOMBE (exh. 1911)**

Miniature painter who exhibited a work entitled 'A Dear Brave Heart' at the Coronation Exhibition, London, in 1911. She was a member of the Society of Miniaturists.

**James Francis BAWN (exh. 1900-1930)**

Landscape artist and sculptor who lived in Bristol and exhibited five works at the R.W.A. 1900-1930. These were mostly sculpture and two landscapes entitled – 'Tilly Whim Caves, Dorset' and 'Bit of Leigh Woods' (both 1900).

Henry Bayfield          'The Duckpond' (w/c)          (Angela Hone)

**Henry BAYFIELD (1859-1929)**

Watercolour painter of rural scenes and cottages. Henry Bayfield was an art teacher by profession, being Headmaster of the Saffron Hill School of Art (1890-1896) and Headmaster of the High Wycombe School of Art (1900-1911). Henry Bayfield later lived at St Leonards-on-Sea and died on 15th September 1929.

**Dorothy BAYLEY (exh. 1935-1937)**

Painter in oil and watercolour of landscapes and still life. She exhibited at the St Ives Society of Artists Exhibitions in 1935 and 1937, mostly landscapes in oil.

*P. A. Beale    'Plymouth Fishing Boats' (w/c)    (J. Collins and Son)*

## P.. A.. BEALE (exh. 1923-1925)

Artist who lived at Paignton, Devon, and later in Plymouth, and exhibited at the R.W.A. in 1923 and 1925. The oil exhibited in 1923 was entitled 'The Trawler, Cattewater, Plymouth'.

## Charles Philip BEAUCHAMP A.R.I.B.A.
## (exh. 1933-1947)

Architect and watercolour landscape painter who lived at Bristol in 1933, Bath in 1939 and finally moved to Tunbridge Wells, Kent, in the 1940s. He exhibited five landscapes at the R.W.A. 1933-1947, which included local views – 'Avon, Sea Mills', and 'Shirehampton' (1933). He also was a regular exhibitor with the Bristol Savages showing a total of 28 works 1934-1945, mostly West Country landscapes and some views of Wells and Ely.

## Arthur BEAUMONT (born 1879, exh. 1913-1915)

Painter in oil of landscapes and coastal scenes who was born in Bradford, Yorks, in 1879. Arthur Beaumont studied art under Julius Olsson in St Ives and he painted there for some years. His work is of good quality but he did not exhibit widely although he did show 'A Summer Sea' at the R.W.A. in 1913. Two views of St Ives were illustrated in The Studio magazine in 1915, where he was praised as a young talent upholding the traditions of the St Ives school. After the First World War, Arthur Beaumont appears to have moved to the U.S.A. , as he is recorded as living at Stapleton, New York, in the 1920s.

## Miss Elfreda Gertrude BEAUMONT (1891-1987)

Landscape and figure painter in oil, watercolour and tempera. Born in London on 1st March 1891, she was the niece of the artist Frederick Samuel Beaumont and the sister of Helen Beaumont (q.v.). She studied art at Goldsmiths College and first exhibited at the Royal Drawing Society in 1906. Elfreda Beaumont exhibited at the Royal Academy in 1916 and then again in the 1930s having moved to Rimpton in

Somerset. Her last Academy picture in 1941 'I had a little Nut Tree' was bought for the permanent collection of the Russell-Cotes Art Gallery in Bournemouth. Her work was reproduced in Colour Magazine and the Illustrated London News.

*Helen M. Beaumont    'Life Class, 1916' (w/c)    (H. Merewether)*

## Miss Helen Marion BEAUMONT (1896-1987)

Painter in watercolour of figure subjects and illustrator who was born on 24th September 1896 and was the niece of Frederick Samuel Beaumont and sister of Elfreda Beaumont (q.v.). She studied art at Goldsmiths College under Edward J. Sullivan but gave up a promising career after her marriage in the 1920s.

## John Francis BEE (born 1895, fl. 1922-1945)

Illustrator, designer and poster artist who was born in Wolverhampton in 1895. John Bee first trained to be a schoolmaster but with the advent of the First World War, he joined up and served for three years on the Western Front before being invalided out in 1917. In 1922 John Bee took up commercial art after a brief period as a stage designer and by 1931 he had moved to London and was working as a freelance artist. During the 1930s he moved his studio to Norfolk and concentrated on poster work including commissions for the G.W.R. and L.N.E.R. Railways. In the Second World War, John Bee continued to work as an artist on propaganda posters and war illustrations for The Graphic. His work was reproduced in The Artist magazine and the subject of an article in 1946. John Bee signed with a monogram (see index).

## Cecil BEECHING (exh. 1909)

A student at the School of Animal Painting under W. Frank Calderon. He exhibited some black and white drawings at the First Exhibition of the Calderon Art Society in June 1909.

*S. J. Beer*       *'Falmouth Harbour' (w/c)*       *(J. Collins and Son)*

## Sidney James BEER (1875-1952)

Painter in watercolour of coastal scenes and landscapes who was born in Paignton, Devon, in 1875, the son of James Dodderidge Beer, a carver and gilder. Sidney Beer moved to Cornwall in 1906 and set up his studio in Church Lane, Falmouth. At first he was listed in the local trade directories as a picture framer, later as a picture dealer and by 1928 as 'The proprietor of Beer's Art Gallery'. Although the quality of the work varies, some of the harbour scenes are attractive and would be of local interest. Around 1940, Sidney Beer moved to Carharrack near Redruth, where he died aged 77 in 1952.

*W. Andrew Beer*               *(Sotheby's Sussex)*
*'Scotch Express and Blue Prince'*

## William Andrew Edward BEER (1862-1954)

Painter in oil and watercolour of landscapes, coastal scenes and bird studies, illustrator and postcard artist. Andrew Beer was born in Exmouth, Devon, on 18th July 1862 the son of William Beer, a photographer. A self-taught artist, he worked as an illustrator in the art department of Harvey Barton & Co. who were commercial printers in Bristol. Many of his Devon landscapes and coastal scenes were published as postcards, often in sepia and then hand

tinted, while some were published in book form such as 'Gems of Dartmoor' containing 15 local views. Andrew Beer's most collected work is his portrait studies of racing pigeons, painted early this century. He was a racing pigeon enthusiast and acted as a judge at many shows. Pigeons were sent by rail to Bristol for him to paint and the finished pictures were offered as prizes at the shows. The pictures were often inscribed with the bird's name and racing achievements. Andrew Beer died in Bristol at the age of 92 on 2nd October 1954. He usually signed Andrew Beer or sometimes W A Beer on early works.

## Cdr. H.. H.. G.. BEGBIE R.N. (exh. 1932-1935)

Landscape painter in watercolour who lived at Little Sodbury, near Bristol, and exhibited seven works at the R.W.A. 1932-1935. The titles of the work included 'Bude' (1932, 1933), 'Old Corn Market' and 'Loading Rubble' (1935).

*A. D. Bell*       *'Off Beachy Head' (w/c)*       *(J. Collins and Son)*

## A.. D.. BELL (fl. 1920s-1950s)

At least two different artists painted under the pseudonym of A D Bell, mostly in the inter war years, for Arthur Joseph, a dealer from Brierley Hill, Birmingham. The most prolific was Wilfrid Knox (q.v.) who specialised in portraits of clipper ships, harbours, coastal scenes and some landscapes. Some of the pictures are dated with an earlier (pre-war) date and when the works are found in the original frame often have a fictitious biography of the artist printed on the reverse.

The other artist working under this pseudonym was Horace Hammond, a Birmingham landscape painter, whose watercolour landscapes were in the style of Birket Foster. These are also signed J Barclay (q.v.) and often feature figures and animals outside cottages. There may have been a third artist who used the pseudonym A D Bell as some of the work is unlike the style of either Hammond or Knox, but this has not been substantiated.

Lilian M. Bell                        *'Artist's Garden, Algiers' (w/c)*

*Godwin Bennett*               *'The Lanes, Brighton' (oil)*

### Miss Lilian Margaret BELL (fl. 1890-1898)

This is the maiden name of L M Dixon (q.v.) used on her watercolours up to her marriage to Clive M Dixon (q.v.) in 1898. The subjects included some landscapes in North Africa.

### Miss M.. BELOE (exh. 1912)

Watercolour painter who exhibited two works at the Winchester Art Society Exhibition in 1912. She painted landscapes and some continental views.

### Basil BENGER (1883-1958)

Painter in watercolour of landscapes and coastal scenes, who lived at Bosham, Sussex. Basil Benger was the younger son of the artist W Edmund Benger and brother of Berenger Benger. Although he did not have a formal art training, he would probably have received tuition from his talented family. Basil Benger was a member of the Society of Sussex Painters and exhibited 20 works 1932-1935. Most of the subjects were Devon coastal views but also some landscapes of Arundel and Bosham. The titles included 'The Ness, Teignmouth', 'Ottery St. Mary' and 'Seaton Cliff' (all 1933).

### F.. BENI (fl. 1920s-1940s)

Painter in watercolour of coastal and moorland scenes, particularly in the West Country. The work is very similar to that of F Parr (q.v.) for whom it may be a pseudonym. Dartmoor scenes signed F.. Beni were published as postcards in the 1940s by Francis Frith & Co.

### Godwin BENNETT (born 1888, fl. 1920-1950)

Painter in oil and illustrator of landscapes and coastal scenes who was born in Brighton in 1888. He lived in Croydon for a number of years and exhibited two Sussex downland views at the Royal Academy in 1951 and 1952. Godwin Bennett also painted Cornish harbour and beach scenes and some were published as postcards by J Salmon Ltd.

### Vincent BENNETT (exh. 1950)

Painter in oil of landscapes and figures who lived in Plymouth. He was a member of the Plymouth Art Society and exhibited four works at the Annual Exhibition in 1950.

### William A.. BENNETT A.R.W.A. (exh. 1922-1927)

Landscape painter in oil who lived near Portishead, Somerset, and later at High Ackworth, near Pontefract, Yorks. He was an associate member of the R.W.A. and exhibited six works 1922-1927. The titles included 'Autumn in the Lambourne Valley' (1922), 'Spring in Suffolk' and 'A Wood near Walberswick' (1927).

### Wallace BENNETTO (fl. 1897)

Watercolour artist who lived at Newquay, Cornwall, and was recorded in the local trade directory for 1897.

### Miss Hetty Muriel BENTWICH (fl. 1910)

A student at the Royal Academy Schools in 1910 where she won a prize for a decorative design of a hunting scene.

### John BERRY (fl. 1945)

Painter of portraits and landscapes including some war illustrations. His work is reproduced in The Artist magazine in 1945 and in John Bull in the 1950s.

*Paul Bertram*       *(David James Gallery)*
*'Dutton, Bucks' (w/c)*

## Paul BERTRAM (fl. 1900s)

Painter in watercolour of rural landscapes. Paul Bertram was the brother of Charles Pigott and the son of the Sheffield artist W H Pigott. Paul Bertram does not appear to have exhibited in London but he did show three works at Elands Art Gallery, Exeter, in 1907. A shepherd and sheep in a country lane is a typical subject and the style shows the influence of his father's work.

## Miss Merrie BEVERLEY (exh. 1902-1905)

Painter in oil and watercolour of landscapes and still life. Merrie Beverley lived in Norwich and was a member of the Norwich Art Circle where she exhibited 16 works 1902-1905. Most of her work was oil still life and flower studies but she also painted landscape views in Brittany.

## E.. A.. BHIWANDIWALA (fl. 1930s)

Painter of portraits in oils who studied art at Heatherley's School in London. He was known as the 'Orpen of India' and executed many fine portraits in this country in the 1930s, as well as many of Indian nobles. His work was reproduced in The Artist magazine in 1933.

## Miss Grace E.. BIBBING (exh. 1900)

Artist who lived in Bristol and exhibited 'Primrose Time' at the R.W.A. in 1900.

## Frederick William BIDDER (1862-1938)

Painter in watercolour and occasionally oil, of landscapes, seascapes and still life. Frederick Bidder was born in Hammersmith in 1862 and studied art at the South Kensington School, but followed his father into a more secure profession as a civil engineer. He qualified as a member of the Institute of Civil Engineers and was awarded the Telford Gold Prize in 1901. One of his professional achievements was his involvement in the design of the London Underground system in the late 1920s.

Frederick Bidder first worked and married in Nottingham and while there, he exhibited at the Nottingham Art Gallery in 1892 and 1893. He moved to Wimbledon in about 1900 and he lived there until his death in 1938. Frederick Bidder was not a professional artist but he always wanted to be and his work, like many others, has slipped into obscurity. His artistic talent was however passed to the next generation as his daughter M Joyce Bidder is a respected sculptress and miniature painter. He signed his work with a monogram (see index).

## Miss Lavinia BILLINGS (fl. 1909)

A student at the Birbeck School of Art who won the Hardy Prize in 1909 for still life painting in oils.

## Phylis BINET (fl. 1950s)

Artist in pastel of dog and cat portraits who was working in the 1950s. She lived in West Sussex for a number of years and also gave private tuition locally.

*H. H. Bingley*       *(J. Collins and Son)*
*'Breakers at Coverack, Cornwall' (w/c)*

## Herbert Harding BINGLEY A.B.W.S. (fl. 1927-1933)

Painter in watercolour of marines, coastal scenes and, particularly, West Country views. Some of the artist's work is inscribed and dated and he was certainly active 1927-1933. His work is quite well painted although the subject matter, such as empty seas and coasts, can lack interest and has kept his prices down in auction. H H Bingley did paint some detailed marines and attractive cottage scenes and these are more popular.

**Emily Houghton BIRCH (1869-1944)**

Painter, mostly in watercolour, of landscapes and coastal scenes. She was the wife of S J Lamorna Birch and the mother of Joan (q.v.) and Elizabeth 'Mornie', who were also artists. The work of Emily Birch is more precise than that of her daughters, often detailed studies of rocks and trees. She exhibited some work locally including two landscapes at the St Ives Society of Artists Summer Exhibition in 1935.

**Joan Houghton BIRCH (born 1909)**

Painter in oil and watercolour of landscapes and coastal scenes. She was the younger daughter of S J Lamorna Birch and Emily Houghton Birch (q.v.). Joan was not a prolific artist and most of her work was done in the 1920s and 1930s prior to her marriage. She showed some work at local exhibitions and in 1934 exhibited an oil at the Royal Academy entitled 'April, Penberth, Cornwall'. In 1946, she emigrated to Australia, where she now lives.

**W.. H.. BIRCH (fl. 1920s-1933)**

A student at the Goldsmith's College School of Art in 1920. A colour design for a showcard by the artist is reproduced in The Studio magazine of that year. He was the Principal of the Epsom School of Art in 1933.

*Evelyn Bishop          (J. Collins and Son)*
*'Bull Point, Ilfracombe' (w/c)*

**Evelyn BISHOP (exh. 1907)**

Painter in watercolour and bodycolour of West Country coastal scenes in a style similar to F J Widgery. This is thought to be a pseudonym used by Frank Dobson when he was working in Cornwall in the early 1900s. A picture entitled 'A Path to the Sea' was exhibited by 'Evelyn Bishop' at Elands Art Gallery, Exeter, in 1907. The work which is colourful and quite well executed would probably have been sold locally to tourists.

**S.. B.. BLADEN (fl. 1928)**

A Sheffield artist who studied by correspondence course at the Press Art School under Percy Bradshaw. A figure study in pencil by him was reproduced in The Studio in 1928.

**Aubrey A.. BLAKE (fl. 1897-1906)**

Painter in oil of landscapes who lived in Norwich and was a member of the Norwich Art Circle. He exhibited two works in 1897 and remained a member until 1906 but did not exhibit in the later years.

**Miss M.. M.. BLAKE (exh. 1900-1901)**

Watercolour landscape painter who lived at Sprowston near Norwich, and was a member of the Norwich Art Circle. She exhibited a total of six works in 1900 and 1901, and after that date she is recorded in her married name – Mrs G T Carré, but did not exhibit.

**Miss Ruth BLAND (exh. 1890-1896)**

Landscape painter in oil who lived in Ipswich and was a member of the Ipswich Art Club. She exhibited a total of 37 works at the Ipswich Art Club 1890-1896. The subjects were mostly local landscapes and the titles include "A Sketch near Norwich' and 'On the Orwell - Low Tide' (1893).

**H.. C.. BOARD (exh. 1917-1922)**

Artist who lived in Bristol and, later, Portishead, Somerset. He exhibited two works at the R.W.A. in 1917 and 1922, both oils, entitled 'Summer' and 'Coast Scene'.

**Miss Frances I.. BOBBETT (exh. 1915-1925)**

Landscape painter in watercolour who lived at Redland, Bristol, and later at nearby Chew Magna and exhibited three works at the R.W.A. 1915-1925. The titles included a 'View of Westbury on Trym' and 'Rydal Water'.

*J. H. Boel          'Landing the Catch' (oil)*

**J.. H.. BOEL (fl. 1889-1910)**

Painter in oil and occasionally, watercolour of landscapes, figures and coastal scenes. This artist is catalogued as both J H Boel and H B Joel as the signature is monogrammed with the initials (see index) and difficult to read. He was a prolific artist and the work is often seen on the market. The earlier examples from the 1890s are usually dated. (Illus. p.15)

**Lt. Col. John BOIS (1881-1941)**

Officer in the Kings Own Royal Regiment who lived in Lancaster and painted watercolour landscape and figure subjects. He exhibited more than 40 works at the Army Officers Art Society 1928-1938. The subjects include English landscapes and some sketches abroad such as Omdurman in the Sudan.

**Fred E.. BOLT (1868-1944)**

Landscape painter in oil and watercolour who was born in Bristol in 1868. He was a regular exhibitor at the R.W.A. showing over 40 works 1889-1920 – mostly watercolour landscapes of local scenes and Devon and Cornwall views. Fred Bolt also exhibited at the Paris Salon 1907-1914 and he was a member of the Bristol Savages where he showed over 200 works 1910-1945. He was made a life member of the Bristol Savages in 1934. The Bristol City Art Gallery has examples of his work.

**Frederick George BOND (exh. 1881-1899)**

Painter in oil and watercolour of landscapes and coastal scenes who lived in Ipswich and was a member of the Ipswich Art Club. He was a regular exhibitor showing 29 works 1881-1899. Most of the subjects were local views but also some scenes in Cornwall and Yorkshire. The titles included 'Walberswick' and 'On the Blythe' (both oils, 1888) and 'Whitby Harbour' and 'Old Houses, Whitby' (watercolours, 1899).

**Lt. Col. Reginald Copleston BOND (1866-1936)**

Landscape painter in oil who lived at Clare in Suffolk and exhibited two works at the Ipswich Art Club in 1934. The titles were 'Head Waters of the Stour' and 'After the Storm, Caldy Island'.

**W.. K.. BOND (exh. 1900-1923)**

Watercolour landscape and marine painter who lived in Ipswich and was a member of the Ipswich Art Club. He was a regular exhibitor showing at least 51 works 1900-1923. Most of the subjects were local landscapes or marines. The titles included 'The Wake of the Steamer' (1903), 'Walberswick Bridge' and 'Blakenham Mill' (both 1919).

**Alfred BONHEUR (exh. 1907-1927)**

Watercolour landscape painter who lived at Clifton, Bristol, and exhibited four works at the R.W.A. 1907-1927. The titles were 'Autumn' (1907), 'Haunt of the Pheasant' (1925), 'Reynards Hunting Ground' (1926) and 'Sunshine and Shadow' (1927).

**Miss Marie L.. BONNOR (exh. 1903)**

Artist who lived in Bristol and exhibited two works at the R.W.A. in 1903. The titles were 'A Pink Sunset' and 'A Common in the Forest of Dean' (oil).

*J. Bonny     'Berkshire Meadows, Newbury' (oil)     (Hampshire Gallery)*

**J.. BONNY (fl. 1890-1910)**

Painter in oil and watercolour of rural landscapes who was working around the turn of the century. The pictures are quite well painted and the pleasing subject matter has made them popular with collectors. The artist does not appear to have exhibited. Typical titles include 'A Summer Landscape', 'A Sunlit River' and 'The Village Lane'.

**Alfred H.. BOOL (fl. 1909-1918)**

Artist who lived in Wimbledon and is listed in the local directories as working from 1909 to 1918. He may have been related to Charles Bool (q.v.).

*Charles A. Bool     'Through Hill and Dale' (w/c)     (Martin Boyce)*

## Charles A.. BOOL (fl. 1900s)

Painter in watercolour of waterfall scenes and coastal subjects. Charles Bool does not appear to have exhibited but his work was used by J Salmon Ltd for postcards, including views of the Isle of Wight. He may have been related to Alfred Bool (q.v.) who is also unrecorded. The surname is often misread by auction rooms and catalogued as 'Boot'. (Illus. p. 16).

## Miss F.. E.. BOORNE (exh. 1919-1936)

Painter in watercolour of landscapes and coastal scenes who lived at Redland, Bristol, and exhibited 28 works at the R.W.A. 1919-1936. Most of the subjects were local scenes but also included Cornwall, Dorset, Hampshire and Isle of Wight views, and a landscape in Italy.

## Mary Firth BOOTH (fl. 1907)

An artist who lived in Wigan and in 1907 won second prize in The Studio competition for a portrait study in pencil of an old lady.

## Maj. Gen. Sir George Deane BOURKE (1852-1936)

Painter in watercolour of landscape and still life. Late of the Royal Army Medical Corps, he exhibited 13 works with the Army Officers Art Society 1928-1932. The subjects included still life and landscape views in France and Switzerland.

## W.. H.. BOW (exh. 1888-1891)

Watercolour and landscape painter who lived in Bristol and exhibited seven works at the R.W.A. 1888-1891. The subjects were local views and included 'Nailsea Station' (1888) and 'The River Avon at Saltford' (1890). The Bristol City Art Gallery Exhibition of 1979 'Within Living Memory' included two local views by this artist.

## Capt. C.. E.. BOWDEN (exh. 1930-1936)

Watercolour landscape painter who lived in Northfield, Birmingham, and exhibited 14 works at the Army Officers Art Society 1930-1936. The subjects include West Country views of Porlock and the Teign.

## H.. BOWDEN-SMITH (exh. 1912)

Watercolour artist who exhibited two eastern scenes at the Winchester Art Society in 1912.

## Frank T.. BOWEN (exh. 1916)

Plymouth artist who exhibited at the the R.W.A. in 1916, a watercolour entitled 'Bickleigh Dale, Devon'.

*L. Bowing*     *'A Moorland Stream' (w/c)*     *(J. Collins and Son)*

## L.. BOWING (fl.c. 1910)

Painter in watercolour of moorland landscapes and river scenes who was working early in this century. The work is heightened with bodycolour and is similar in style and colour to that of Ivy Stannard.

## Miss B.. M.. BOWKER (exh. 1922-1924)

Watercolour artist who lived in Bath, and exhibited at the R.W.A. in 1922 and 1924, two works entitled 'The Chestnut' and 'Pultney Bridge, Bath'.

## Miss Edith BOWKER (exh. 1900)

Artist who lived at Winchester, Hants, and exhibited two works at the R.W.A. in 1900 entitled 'White Iris' and 'Artist's Tools'.

## Percy Noel BOXER (born c. 1886)

Landscape painter in oil, watercolour and pencil and also an etcher. Percy Noel Boxer was the assistant teacher at the Blackheath School of Art and Goldsmith's College, New Cross. He exhibited three works at the Royal Academy 1911-1914 but does not appear to have shown work elsewhere. A series of fine quality pencil studies of buildings by him were reproduced in The Studio – 'Sketches of Old Rye' (1912) and 'Views of Greenwich' (1916). Percy Noel Boxer had settled in Switzerland in 1913 perhaps for his poor health from which he had suffered for many years.

## W.. J.. BOYES (exh. 1919)

A Bradford artist who exhibited landscapes at the Local Artists Exhibition at the Cartwright Hall in 1919.

## Vernon Carr BOYLE (1895-1954)

Watercolour landscape and marine artist. Vernon Boyle was born in Bideford, Devon in 1895, educated at the Bideford Grammar School and Exeter University. After the First World War he taught at the Poole Grammar School and, from 1929, at Perse, in Cambridge. Vernon Boyle returned to Devon in the 1940s and ran the Buckleigh laundry until 1946. His local watercolour views are collected in the Bideford area.

**E.. BRADDON (exh. 1924)**

Watercolour landscape painter who exhibited 'The Road to Bratton Castle' at the B.W.S. Exhibition in Cheltenham in 1924.

**Miss M.. J.. BRADDON (exh. 1910-1936)**

Watercolour landscape painter who lived in Bath and exhibited 19 works at the R.W.A. 1910-1936. The subjects were mostly Cornish views with some Sussex and Bath scenes and, in 1934, two views in the Pyranees.

**Charles Smith BRADLEY (1866-1929)**

Born in Hampstead and educated at Eastbourne College, Charles Bradley was originally intending to follow his father into a medical career. He volunteered in the First World War as a gunner and, later, held a commission in the First Sussex Volunteer Regiment. Charles Bradley studied art under Charles Johnson R.I. and exhibited several works in London and at the Brighton Arts Club. In 1925 the Hove Art Gallery held an exhibition of 34 watercolours by him, mostly Sussex landscapes and downland views. He lived at Keymer, near Ditchling, in Sussex for many years.

*Stanley O. Bradshaw*     *'Avro 504' (w/c)*     *(Richard Riding)*

**Stanley Orton BRADSHAW (1903-1950)**

Watercolour painter and illustrator of aeronautical subjects. Stanley Bradshaw was born on 2nd February 1903 and educated at Clarks College, after which he joined his father's clothing manufacture business. Always interested in aeroplanes, he learnt to fly at the London Aeroplane Club and qualified as a pilot in 1926. At the outbreak of War, unable to fly with the R.A.F., he joined the Air Transport Auxiliary and flew over one thousand hours in this capacity. In 1947, he became editor of 'The Light Plane' and did much to promote the private flying movement. He

was tragically killed in a flying accident on April 7th 1950. Stanley Orton Bradshaw's pictures have that rare quality of being both technically accurate and artistically pleasing. They capture a feeling of the period which is lacking from the work of some of his contemporaries. A collection of his paintings are in the R.A.F. Museum at Hendon.

**Miss A.. R.. BRAMSTON (exh. 1912)**

Watercolour landscape painter who was a member of the Winchester Art Society. She exhibited four works, all French landscapes, at the Winchester Art Society Annual Exhibition 1912.

**Catherine BREBNER B.W.S. (exh. 1928)**

Watercolour landscape painter who was a member of the B.W.S. and exhibited at their Autumn Exhibition at Preston in 1928 a watercolour entitled 'A Canal at Bruges'. She may have been related to Elizabeth Brebner, a flower and landscape painter, who lived in Putney and was working up to the 1920's.

**Ralph Herbert BRENTNALL A.R.I.B.A. (1901-1980)**

Landscape painter in watercolour, pastel and charcoal who was an architect by profession. Ralph Brentnall was a bomb disposal officer in the Royal Engineers during World War II and was awarded the M.B.E. for bravery. He was a member of the Bristol Savages and exhibited a total of 62 works 1935-1978 – mostly Cornish landscapes and also some French views. He was President of the Bristol Savages in 1945 and 1964, and was elected a life member in 1977. Ralph Brentnall was an occasional exhibitor at the R.W.A. showing work in 1935 and 1936. He died on 30th July 1980.

**Harris BRETT (fl. 1900s)**

Painter in watercolour of Eastern desert and Nile scenes who was active in the early years of this century. The work is quite competent, but the artist does not appear to have exhibited. The pictures are often in a long landscape form as befits the subject and usually signed H Brett, or Harris Brett with a date. 'On the Nile, nr Luxor – 1906' is a typical title.

**Henry BRIDGEMAN (exh. 1890-1893)**

Painter of landscapes in oil who lived at Sudbury, Suffolk, and was a member of the Ipswich Art Club. He exhibited a total of five works 1890-1893, the subjects being local views including 'River Stour, near Sudbury', 'View near Southwold', and 'St Olave's, near Lowestoft' (1893).

## E.. W.. BRIERLEY (exh. 1934-1936)

Artist who lived at Westbury on Trym, Somerset, and exhibited five works at the R.W.A. 1934-1936. The subjects were local landscapes and views of Lacock and Mousehole in Cornwall.

*W. T. Brocklebank*       *'China Clay Works, St Austell' (w/c)*

## William Thornton BROCKLEBANK (1882-1970)

Painter in oil, and sometimes watercolour, of landscapes, coastal scenes and flower still life. William Thornton Brocklebank grew up in Kendal, was educated at the Royal Grammar School, Lancaster, and Cambridge University where he read Music and Religion. He served with the Royal Army Medical Corps in the First World War and in the early 1920s, moved to Newlyn in Cornwall. There he met and married Winifred Snell, who also worked as an amateur artist. Many of his subjects were oil landscapes and coastal scenes in Cornwall and Devon. He was a member of the Plymouth Art Society and exhibited there in the 1950s and 1960s. Brocklebank had moved from Newlyn to Plymouth and he continued to paint until his death in 1970. The pictures are usually signed W T Brocklebank, sometimes with a date, but some of the work is just signed 'W Thornton' (q.v.). The contents of his studio were sold by Bonhams in Honiton in February 1991.

## Mrs Winifred BROCKLEBANK (1893-1963)

Amateur painter of portraits, figures and landscapes in oil and watercolour. Winifred Snell was the daughter of a monumental mason from Newlyn who married the artist William Brocklebank (q.v.) in 1926. She was a member of the Plymouth Art Society and exhibited in the 1950s. The contents of her studio were sold by Bonhams in Honiton in February 1991.

## W.. S.. BROOK (fl.c. 1900)

A good quality painter in oil who copied works by many of the leading artists of his day such as Lucy Kemp-Welch and Messonier. The pictures were often large and usually unsigned. W S Brook lived at Upper North Street in Brighton, and sold most of his work through the local shops.

## Maj. E.. A.. P.. BROOKE (exh. 1928-1934)

Landscape painter in oil and watercolour who lived at Llandudno in North Wales. An officer in the Queen's Own Cameron Highlanders, Maj. Brooke was a regular exhibitor at the Army Officers Art Society showing 21 works 1928-1934. The pictures included oil landscapes of Wales and Scotland and watercolours of Deeside.

## John H.. BROOKES (fl. 1912)

Student of the Leicester School of Art whose work was represented in the National Schools of Art Competition in 1912. A watercolour still life study was reproduced in The Studio magazine.

## Miss Dorothy BROWN (exh. 1919-1926)

Painter in watercolour of landscapes, portraits and miniatures who lived in Salisbury and exhibited at the R.W.A. 1919-1926. Some of her local Salisbury views were published as postcards by J Salmon and Co in the 1920s.

## F.. Peter BROWN (fl. 1906)

A student of the Rochester School of Art, whose colour print designs were shown at the National Schools of Art competition in 1906.

*Lilian Brown*       *'Time to get up' (oil)*       *(Fairhurst Gallery)*

## Lilian Susan Clara BROWN (fl. 1928-1940)

Painter in oil of figures, interiors and still life. Very little information has been found on this highly competent artist working between the Wars. A small exhibition of work from her studio was held at the Fairhurst Gallery, London SW6, in October 1987.

**M.. Hilda BROWN (exh. 1896-1937)**

Painter in oil and watercolour of flowers and still life who lived at Teignmouth in Devon and exhibited at Birmingham and the Royal Academy in 1912. She also showed an oil and watercolour of flowers at the St Ives Society of Artists Winter Exhibition in 1937.

**Miss A.. E.. BROWNE (exh. 1886)**

Artist who lived at Colchester, Essex, and was a member of the Ipswich Art Club. She exhibited an oil entitled 'Rabbits' at their Annual Exhibition in 1886.

**J.. J.. BROWNSWORD A.R.C.A. (fl. 1894-1928)**

A student at the Royal College of Art from 1894 who in 1897 won a Gold Medal for a drawing of animals at the National Schools of Art Competition. He later lived in Hull and was Principal of the Hull School of Art from c. 1920-1928.

**Edward P.. BRYAN (fl. 1908)**

Pen and ink artist who lived at High Broughton, Manchester. He won first prize in The Studio competition for an illustration from the Arabian Nights.

**Miss Constance C.. BUCKNALL (exh. 1908-1913)**

Miniature painter who lived at Clifton, Bristol, and exhibited five works at the R.W.A. 1908-1913. The subjects were all portrait miniatures. She also exhibited a portrait at the Royal Academy in 1911.

**Miss M.. P.. BUCKWORTH (exh. 1899-1903)**

Watercolour painter of figures, flowers and genre who lived in Norwich and was a member of the Norwich Art Circle. She exhibited 13 works at their exhibitions 1899-1903, mostly watercolours of figures, flowers and landscapes.

**Miss Rosa A.. J.. BUDD (exh. 1897-1901)**

Watercolour painter of landscapes, buildings and flowers. She lived at Somerton Rectory, Great Yarmouth, and was a member of the Norwich Art Circle exhibiting 12 works 1897-1901. Several of her watercolour landscapes were views of the Broads.

**C.. BULGIN (exh. 1907)**

Painter in watercolour who exhibited two works at the Elands Art Gallery Exhibition entitled 'Pictures by West Country Artists' in Exeter in 1907. The subjects were both views of Exeter.

**Claude BULL (exh. 1933-1937)**

Painter in oil of still life who lived in Ipswich and exhibited four works at the Ipswich Art Club 1933-1937.

**Miss Helen Constance BULL (exh. 1932-1938)**

Watercolour landscape artist who lived at Levington, Suffolk, and was a member of the Ipswich Art Club. She exhibited at the Ipswich Art Club in 1932 and 1938, the titles of the work being 'View from Levington', 'Broke Hall Farm' (1932) and 'Cortina, Italy' (1938). She was related to Richard Bull (q.v.).

**Richard H.. BULL (exh. 1932-1934)**

Painter of birds in watercolour who lived at Levington, Suffolk, and was a member of the Ipswich Art Club. He exhibited at the Ipswich Art Club in 1932 – 'Pigeon' and 'Sheldrake', and in 1934 'Jay' and 'Grouse'. He was related to the artist Helen C Bull (q.v.).

**Emma BUNT (exh. 1911-1937)**

Painter in oil of flowers and still life, who lived at Falmouth in Cornwall and exhibited at the Royal Academy in 1911. Later, Emma Bunt showed oils of still life at the St Ives Society of Artists in 1935 and 1937.

**Arthur T.. BURBERY (exh. 1950)**

Artist in watercolour and pencil who lived at Peverell, Plymouth, and exhibited at the Plymouth Art Society in 1950. He showed two watercolour landscapes of local views and a pencil study.

**Mrs. A.. M.. BURCHILL (exh. 1927-1938)**

Flower and still life painter who lived in Bristol. She exhibited seven works at the R.W.A. 1927-1938, mostly flower studies.

**Miss Ethel M.. BURCHILL A.R.W.A.**
**(exh. 1917-1928)**

Landscape painter in watercolour who lived in Redland, Bristol, and later moved to Cardiff. She was an associate member of the R.W.A. and exhibited 27 works 1917-1928. Many of the subjects were local views in Bristol, with some of York, and her later exhibits included Venice and Lake Como.

**Elsie BURRELL (exh. 1914)**

Painter of portraits in watercolour. An exhibition of her work was held at the Dudley Gallery in London in March 1914, consisting of 39 portraits.

**Miss Sermonda BURRELL (exh. 1900-1901)**

Painter in oil and watercolour of portraits and landscapes who was a member of the Ipswich Art Club and exhibited in 1900 and 1901. The titles were 'Flower Field near Haarlem' and 'Eilenroc, Corsica' (watercolours 1900) and 'Rt. Hon. Lord Gwyder' and 'The Countess of Lindsey' (oils 1901).

**Mrs. M.. E.. BURROWES (fl. 1920s)**

Watercolour painter of landscapes, continental views and town scenes who lived at Charlton Kings and exhibited at the 1924 Cheltenham Group of Artists Exhibition. Her exhibits were 22 watercolours of Venice and 25 views of Bordighera and Mentone. Previously she studied on the continent where she exhibited under her former name of Mrs. M E Clisset.

**W.. B.. BUSH (exh. 1936-1938)**

Landscape painter who lived at Keynsham, Bristol, and exhibited four works at the R.W.A. 1936-1938. The subjects were foreign views including 'A Street in Florence' and a view of Kandy, Ceylon.

*William Busk*                    *'Rothenburg, Bavaria' (w/c)*

**William BUSK** A.R.C.A. **(1861-1942)**

Watercolour painter and art teacher. He exhibited two figure subjects at the Royal Academy in 1889 and 1892 but does not seem to have exhibited elsewhere. William Busk left Horsham about 1890 and moved to Dorset. From 1897-1913 he was Principal of the Bridport and Dorchester Schools of Art. He died at Leighton Buzzard on 16th July 1942 at the age of 81.

**Miss M.. A.. BUTCHER (exh. 1927-1935)**

Landscape artist who lived at Frampton Cotterell, near Bristol, and exhibited 10 works at the R.W.A. 1927-1935. The subjects included views of St Ives, Staithes, Stokesay Castle and scenes in Germany and Switzerland.

**Miss Elizabeth Field BUTLER (exh. 1881-1894)**

Artist who lived at Ipswich and then later Felixstowe and was an active member of the Ipswich Art Club. She exhibited a total of 30 works 1881-1894.

**Miss Carolyn G.. BUXTON (exh. 1901-1911)**

Watercolour painter of landscapes and garden scenes who lived in Norwich and later at Whissonsett Hall near Dereham. Carolyn Buxton was a regular exhibitor at the Norwich Art Circle, showing 33 pictures 1901-1911. Most of her work was landscape and garden scenes, but she also painted some French views.

**Dudley BUXTON (fl.c. 1905-1910)**

An illustrator who exhibited two works at the Prosser Gallery Exhibition around 1905 entitled 'Leading Motorists and their Cars'. Some of his work was published as comical motoring postcards by C W Faulkner and others around 1910.

**Mrs. E.. G.. BUXTON (exh. 1890s-1911)**

Watercolour artist who lived in Norwich and exhibited at the Norwich Art Circle from the 1890s until 1911. Her pictures were mostly landscapes and garden scenes.

**Miss Theresa BUXTON (exh. 1900-1906)**

Watercolour flower and landscape painter who lived at Buckhurst Hill and was a member of the Norwich Art Circle. She exhibited 17 pictures 1900-1906, mostly landscapes including some local views.

**Miss ... BYNG (exh. 1886-1899)**

Watercolour landscape and coastal painter who lived in Ipswich and exhibited at the Ipswich Art Club. She showed work in 1886 entitled 'A Cornish Cross' and in 1899 'The Cornish Coast – North'.

**E.. M.. BYWATERS (fl. 1897)**

Landscape artist who lived in Brighton, Sussex, and won second prize for a pen and ink landscape in The Studio competition in 1897.

# C

## Dorothy CADMAN (fl. 1914-1922)

Painter in oil of still life, figures and interiors who lived in London and was working from 1914 until the early 1920s. A small exhibition of her work was held at the Fairhurst Gallery, London, in October 1987.

*Dorothy Cadman*      *(Fairhurst Gallery)*
*'Portrait Study' (oil)*

## Florence Blanche CAINS (exh. 1932-1947)

Painter, illustrator and designer who lived at St Georges, Bristol, and was working in the 1930s. She exhibited four works at the R.W.A. 1932-1947 which included landscapes and flowers.

## M.. R.. CAIRD (fl. 1918-1921)

Poster artist and illustrator who established a studio in Edinburgh in 1921 with a fellow poster artist W R Lawson. He specialised in decorative poster design and his work was reproduced in The Studio.

## J.. CALLINGHAM (fl. 1909-1914)

Painter in oil of marines and coastal scenes. This competent artist does not appear to have exhibited but small canvasses, often dated, are seen on the market. The subjects include battleships and many have titles inscribed on the reverse such as 'Shipping off the Coast of Calais'.

## M.. Eleanor CALLIS B.W.S. (exh. 1928)

Watercolour landscape painter who was a member of the B.W.S. and exhibited 'The Old Barn, Herts' at their 1928 Preston Exhibition.

*A. Calvert*      *'Camels in the Desert' (w/c)*

## A.. CALVERT (fl.c. 1920s)

This prolific artist specialised in small watercolours of eastern scenes, usually Bedouins and camels in the desert. He also painted under the name of Otto Tilche (q.v.) and the pictures are often in pairs and sometimes just signed with initials.

## Miss Katherine CANN (exh. 1900)

Still life painter in oil who lived at Crediton, Devon, and exhibited two works at the R.W.A. in 1900 – 'Fruit' and 'Orange and White Lilies'.

## Mrs Florence Emma Matilda CAPES (1868-1956)

Painter in watercolour of landscapes, rivers and harbour scenes. Although most of the work was watercolour, she did paint some oils and red chalk figure studies. The subjects include views on the Thames and Cornish harbour scenes. The later work is signed F Capes, whereas the early pictures are signed with her maiden name Florence Furneaux (q.v.).

## Miss Agnes M.. CAPON (exh. 1891-1894)

Landscape and still life painter in oil who lived at Manningtree, Essex. She was a member of the Ipswich Art Club and exhibited four works 1891-1894. The titles included 'Barns at Flatford, East Bergholt', 'Stutton Mill from Mistley Cliff' (1893) and 'A Basket of Apples' (1894).

## Gunnar CARLSON (exh. 1927-1933)

Landscape painter who lived at Clifton, Bristol, and exhibited 11 works at the R.W.A. 1927-1933. The subjects included Polperro, Chipping Campden, Bruges (1927), and three views of Brittany (1930).

## Dorothy Comyns CARR (1849-c.1919)

Painter of landscapes and flower still life in oil and watercolour. Dorothy Carr exhibited widely in London and the provinces from 1901 until her death around 1919. A retrospective exhibition of her work was held at Walkers Gallery, London, in October 1919. It consisted of 51 watercolours and two oils, mostly landscape scenes in the South of England but also some Dutch and Alpine views and some still life of flowers.

## Norman S.. CARR (fl. 1913)

Illustrator and mural painter in oils, who at one time worked for Royal Doulton Potteries producing decorated ceramic tiles. Norman Carr had no formal art training but he worked with W J Neatby and was influenced by his style. Much of his work was marine painting – he painted murals for the Armada Room at the Imperial Hotel, London, and a study of The Victory at Trafalgar for Portsmouth. Norman Carr also produced illustrations for several nautical books and yachting papers.

## Wilson CARR (fl.c. 1870-1910)

This was a pseudonym adopted by Paul H Ellis, the landscape painter who lived at Handsworth, Birmingham, and later at Rhyl, North Wales. He was a regular exhibitor at the Royal Birmingham Society of Artists, showing over 50 works, he also exhibited in London and the provinces. Most of the subjects were rural landscapes and those signed 'Wilson Carr' are often watercolour sketches. Paul Ellis does not appear to have exhibited as 'Wilson Carr' but he may have shown a few works as 'Ellis Carr'.

## Sidney CARTER (died 1917)

Black and white artist and illustrator, who was killed in action on 23rd March 1917.

## Miss Mabel CARWARDINE (exh. 1902-1915)

Painter in oil and watercolour of animals and landscapes who lived at Brislington, near Bristol, and exhibited 12 works at the R.W.A. 1902-1915. The subjects included poultry and some dog portraits.

## Mrs Maud CASH-REED (1864-1953)

Painter in watercolour of landscapes, figures and interiors. Born Maud Higham in Plymouth in 1864, she was the youngest of four children and brought up by her mother, as her father had left to find fortune in Australia. She was educated privately and in 1886 married Dr William Cash-Reed who had a practice in Plymouth. In the 1900s Dr Cash-Reed sold the practice and moved to Liverpool. Initially Maud Cash-Reed had no formal art training although she did attend life classes at the Westminster School of Art in the 1930s. She travelled widely and painted abroad in France, Germany and Belgium while accompanying her husband, as well as Italy, Portugal, Malta, Hungary and Jamaica.

Maud Cash-Reed held small exhibitions of her work usually abroad, where the pictures were sold at modest prices. She often gave them away to friends. She died at Lisborn in 1953 at the age of 89.

## Leonard CASLEY (exh. 1920-1929)

Landscape painter who lived at the Lizard, Cornwall, and was probably the son of William Casley who lived there in the 1890s. Leonard Casley was a regular exhibitor at the R.W.A. in the 1920s. Most of the subjects were coastal scenes – 'Kennack Sands, Cornwall' (1927), 'Grey Rocks and Grey Sea' and 'Needles, Isle of Wight' (1928) are typical titles.

## Barry CASTLE (exh. 1912)

Landscape painter in oil who exhibited at the Worthing Art Gallery Summer Exhibition in 1912.

## Mrs Annie E.. CASTLEY (exh. 1932-1935)

Watercolour landscape painter who lived at Little Stonham, Suffolk, and was a member of the Ipswich Art Club, where she exhibited eight works 1932-1935. The subjects were mostly local views and rural scenes – 'The Garden Gate', 'An Autumn Tangle', and 'Through the Barn Doors' (1934) are typical titles.

## Miss K.. E.. CASWALL (exh. 1901)

Painter who lived at Binfield, Berks, and was a member of the Berkshire Art Society. She exhibited three works in 1901 – two local landscapes and a French Chateau.

M. Cash-Reed     'In the Tower' (w/c)

F. Catano     'Italian Lakescene' (w/c)

**F.. CATANO (fl. 1880s-1920s)**

The distinct style of this artist's work suggests that it is probably a pseudonym for the painter who usually signs 'E. St John' (q.v.). The subjects are often Italian lake views and Eastern desert scenes. He does not appear to have exhibited. (Illus. p.23).

**Miss Violet M.. R.. CAUDWELL (exh. 1913)**

Artist who lived at Coggershall, Essex, and exhibited two works at the R.W.A. in 1913. The titles were 'A Grey Morning' and 'An Orchard in Spring'.

**Nicolas CAVANAGH (born 1867)**

Marine artist who was born at Waterford in Ireland and brought up in London. He stowed away on a liner to New York while a teenager and worked there before returning to England in 1887. From 1887 until 1933 he spent much of his time at sea, working for shipping lines and these voyages gave him the opportunity and inspiration for his painting.
A one-man exhibition of this self-taught artist was held at the Little Burlington Galleries in London in 1936. The exhibition consisted of 60 pictures of shipping and the sea and the catalogue contained a very enthusiastic forward written by Paul Nash. The subjects include 'Reefed Topsail', 'Full on the Quarter', and 'The Lower Thames'. He also painted some portrait studies of sailors.

M. E. Chadburn                'In the Stable' (w/c)

**Miss Mary Elizabeth CHADBURN (born 1915)**

Painter in oil of horses and equestrian subjects. She was born at Ollerton, near Newark, in 1915, and moved to Bexhill-on-Sea in the 1920s. She was educated locally and first studied art at the Vita Studio in Bexhill. In 1937, Miss Chadburn went to Bushey and

studied animal painting under Margaret Frobisher who had taken over the school from Lucy Kemp-Welch. Miss Frobisher made all her students exhibit at the principal exhibitions. Although she did not have her work hung at the Royal Academy, Miss Chadburn did exhibit at the Society of Women Artists, The Royal Cambrian Academy and later at the Paris Salon.

In 1958, after working as a cook for Sir Alfred Munnings in exchange for tuition, she bought an old mill in Essex which she converted into a studio for her painting. Four years later she travelled to Morocco and painted there extensively – the pictures forming an exhibition at the Medici Galleries, London, on her return in 1963. Miss Chadburn now lives in retirement in France.

**Oswald CHAMBERS (fl. 1894)**

Artist who lived at Peckham, and won second prize for a portrait study in ink, in The Studio competition of 1894.

**Miss L.. M.. CHANIN (exh. 1927)**

Landscape painter who lived at Minehead, Somerset, and exhibited at the R.W.A. in 1927. The titles were 'The Old Yarn Market, Dunster' and 'The Torridge, Low Tide'.

**Miss Winifred G.. CHANNON (exh. 1924-1926)**

Painter in watercolour of landscapes and miniatures and an etcher. She lived in Cheltenham and exhibited with the Cheltenham Art Group 1924-1926 showing a total of 21 works. These were mostly etchings of street scenes and watercolour landscapes, but also four portrait miniatures.

**Francis Forbes Wolferstan CHANTER
(exh. 1900-1901)**

Landscape painter in oil who lived at Redland, Bristol, and exhibited at the R.W.A. in 1900 and 1901. The works were entitled 'Evening, Mounts Bay', and 'Summer Day, Scilly Isles'.

**Miss M.. CHARLESWORTH (exh. 1889)**

Watercolour landscape artist who lived at Bickley, Kent, and was a member of the Ipswich Art Club. She exhibited in 1889 an 'Italian Courtyard' and a 'Farmhouse at Wool, Dorsetshire'. In 1890 a Miss C Charlesworth of the same address exhibited two garden scenes and this could be the same artist or perhaps a sister.

*I. M. Charters*        *'Spring Flowers' (w/c)*

## Miss Isabella M.. CHARTERS (exh. 1894-1936)

Painter in watercolour and illustrator of flowers and landscapes who lived in Leicester and was a member of the Leicester Society of Arts. She also exhibited in the 1890s at Liverpool, Nottingham, and the Society of Women Artists. Isabella Charters was an art mistress by profession who found time to illustrate a large number of books and manuals on flower subjects and had work published in Amateur Gardening and The Garden. Her fine quality flower pictures earned her Silver and Bronze Medals at the Royal Horticultural Society. In October 1936, after her retirement from teaching, an exhibition of her work was held at the Burton-on-Trent Art Gallery. This consisted of 68 watercolours mostly flower studies but also some landscapes. The landscapes included views in Sussex, Norfolk, Wales and Scotland, and some Italian studies of Florence and Bordighera. The flower studies and illustrations are often signed with a monogram (see index).

## E.. Gordon CHASE (exh. 1926)

Painter of figures and landscapes who exhibited 14 works at the 'Ten Man Show' at Gieves Gallery, London, in 1926.

## Leopold Alfred CHENEY (1882-1928)

Illustrator, cartoonist and black and white artist, who died on 29th September 1928 at the age of 46. Some pen and ink cartoons by Leo Cheney are illustrated in 'The Art of Pen Drawing' by G M Ellwood (1927).

## Arthur Leonard CHERRY (fl. 1906-1941)

Etcher and occasional painter in oil, watercolour and pastel of landscapes and marines who was working from about 1910 until 1940. The family owned a successful photographic studio and framing business in St Albans, Herts, and this would have given Arthur the opportunity to display his work. It is not known if he was actively involved in the family business but he is recorded as living in the town from 1906 until 1941. Many of Arthur Cherry's works were small etchings of London buildings and river scenes, but he also painted some marines in oil and some views around St Albans. This talented artist does not appear to have exhibited.

## Miss M.. CHIDSON (fl. 1909)

A student at the Lambeth School of Art who received an 'Hon. Mention' for a fairy tale illustration in the National Schools of Art Competition in 1909.

## Nora CHITTY (fl. 1900s)

Painter in oil of flowers and moonlight landscapes. She lived in Lion Street, Chichester, Sussex, and was working in the early part of this century. She was the sister of Sybil Chitty (q.v.).

## Sybil Sedgwick CHITTY (1885-1982)

Painter of flowers and still life in oil who lived in Chichester, Sussex, and was the sister of Nora Chitty (q.v.). The flower paintings are of good quality and are usually signed 'Sybil Chitty' with a date.

## Miss Victoria CHOLMONDELEY (exh. 1906)

Landscape painter in watercolour, who had a joint exhibition at the Modern Gallery in March 1906 with Sir William Baillie-Hamilton (q.v.). She exhibited 31 works, mostly continental views, including scenes in Madeira, Rome and Bruges.

## Arnold CHRISTIEN (exh. 1905)

Oil painter of landscapes and rural scenes. He showed four landscapes at an exhibition of local artists at the Merehall Art Gallery, Bolton, in 1905.

## Frank H.. CHUBB (exh. 1950)

Watercolour landscape artist who lived at Paignton, Devon, and exhibited with the Plymouth Art Society in 1950. He showed three watercolours all Devon views.

H. Church    'Windsor Castle' (oil)    (Roger Hurlin)

## H.. CHURCH (fl.c. 1890)

Painter in oil of landscapes and river scenes who was active at the end of the 19th century. His work was competently executed and included views on the Thames. Usually signed 'H Church' printed in red.

## Walter CHURCHER (fl. 1900-1914)

Landscape painter in oil and watercolour and illustrator, who was a founder member and the Hon. Secretary of the London Sketch Club 1901-1911. A watercolour landscape by Walter Churcher and a caricature portrait of him by H M Bateman were illustrated in The Studio in 1913.

## Miss D.. A.. CHURCHMAN (exh. 1923-1937)

Watercolour flower painter who lived at Melton near Woodbridge, Suffolk. She was a member of the Ipswich Art Club and exhibited 37 works 1923-1937, mostly flower studies.

## Miss Anna CHURCHYARD (1832-1897)

Painter in oil and watercolour of landscapes and still life who lived in Woodbridge and was a member of the Ipswich Art Club. She was the daughter of the well-known Woodbridge artist Thomas Churchyard and sister of Harriett and Laura (q.v.) who were also members. Anna Churchyard was a regular exhibitor showing a total of 85 works 1884-1896. The subjects were mostly local views in watercolour, 'Warren Hill, Woodbridge' and 'The Deben' (1895) are typical titles. She also painted a number of flower still lifes.

## Miss Harriett CHURCHYARD (1836-1927)

Painter in watercolour of figure subjects and genre who lived at Woodbridge, Suffolk, and was a member of the Ipswich Art Club. She was the daughter of Thomas Churchyard, and sister of Anna and Laura (q.v.) who were also members. Harriett Churchyard exhibited a total of seven works 1884-1890, mostly genre subjects. 'A Rustic Figure' (1885), 'Fishing' (1886) and 'First Lessons' (1890) are typical titles.

## Miss Laura CHURCHYARD (exh. 1884-1890)

Landscape painter in watercolour who lived in Woodbridge and was a member of the Ipswich Art Club. She was the daughter of Thomas Churchyard and sister of Anna and Harriett (q.v.) who were also members. Laura Churchyard exhibited a total of 37 works 1884-1890. The subjects were mostly local landscapes 'At Brightwell', 'Wilford Bridge' and 'Little Bealings Church' (all 1886) are typical titles.

## Miss E.. Percival CLARK (exh. 1900)

Artist who lived in Chiswick, London, and exhibited an oil at the R.W.A. in 1900 entitled 'The Lake, Kew Gardens'.

O. T. Clark
'Stepping Stones near Arundel, Sussex' (oil)

## Octavious Thomas CLARK (1851-1921)

Painter in oil of rural landscapes and cottages. This prolific Victorian landscape artist did not appear to exhibit but his work is frequently seen on the market. The pictures are often dated and the larger canvasses are usually signed in full whereas the smaller pictures tend to be monogrammed (see index). O T Clark was born in London, and died aged 70 at Romford, Essex, in 1921.

## Samuel Joseph CLARK (fl. 1874-1918)

Painter in oil of landscapes, animals and farmyard scenes. The artist's work shows some points of similarity to that of O T Clarke (q.v.) and they may have been related. S J Clark's paintings are usually of finer quality and command higher prices but he also does not appear to have exhibited his work.

## Alfred CLARKE (exh. 1916-1936)

Watercolour landscape painter who lived at Bristol and exhibited 37 works at the R.W.A. 1916-1936. The subjects included local views and scenes of Dorset, Scotland, Lake Lugano and Switzerland.

## E.. E.. CLARKE (exh. 1921)

Watercolour artist who was a member of the Derby Sketching Club and exhibited there in 1921.

## James Bosworth CLARKE (1838-1920)

Painter in oil and watercolour of landscapes and coastal scenes. James Clarke was born at Worcester in 1838 and at the age of 14 started as a gilding apprentice at the Royal Worcester Porcelain factory and worked there for about 15 years. In the 1880s, James Clarke had moved to Liskeard in Cornwall, and by 1893 he was living in Plymouth, being listed in the local directories as an artist.

In 1889, he exhibited two landscapes in oil at the Plymouth Arts Club and most of his work was local Devon and Cornwall views. James Clarke continued to live in Plymouth, teaching art and painting, until his death in 1920.

## Miss Emily A.. CLAYDEN (exh. 1880-1915)

Landscape painter in oil and watercolour who lived in Ipswich and was a member of the Ipswich Art Club. She was a regular exhibitor showing a total of 66 works 1880-1915. The subjects included local landscapes, Devon, Scottish, and Dutch views and some flower studies. The titles included 'In the Trossacks' (oil, 1881), 'Dutch Interior' (1902) and 'Beer Street' (watercolour, 1910).

## Dorothy E.. CLAYTON (exh. 1919)

A Bradford landscape artist who exhibited four works at the local artists exhibition at the Cartwright Hall, Bradford, in 1919. The subjects were all local Yorkshire views.

## J.. M.. CLAYTON (fl.c. 1920)

Painter in watercolour of landscapes and rural scenes. The subjects include working horses and are well painted, although the artist did not exhibit.

## Miss Ada Louise CLENCH (exh. 1911-1913)

Miniature portrait painter who exhibited at the Coronation Exhibition in London in 1911. She lived in Bristol and showed a work at the R.W.A. in 1913. Ada Clench was a member of the Society of Miniaturists.

W. B. Clibborn        'The Slipway' (w/c)

## William Barclay CLIBBORN (1878-1967)

Painter of landscapes and marines in gouache, watercolour and oil, who was born in Birkenhead in 1878. An accountant by profession he did however work as a commercial artist producing posters and calendars for shipping lines and railway companies. His clients included the Cunard and Waverley Shipping lines and the London and North Eastern Railway Company. Most of the work was painted in the 1950s and included Devon and Cornwall coastal scenes, shipping subjects and landscapes in Suffolk, where he lived in later life. Many of the pictures are watercolour heightened with bodycolour in an attractive bold style. The work is usually signed W B Clibborn, or sometimes W B C on small sketches.

Olive Cliffe        'Red Setters' (oil)

## Olive Estelle Minna CLIFFE (1884-1968)

Painter in oil of dogs and other animals who was the youngest daughter of William Perring Hollyer (q.v.) a landscape artist. Three of her sisters painted – Eva Hollyer (1865-1948), Maud Hollyer (1867-1970) and Edith de Chair (1869-c.1955). Her brother, Gregory (1871-c.1950s) who emigrated to America was also an artist but only Olive Cliffe attended art school. She was most active in the 1920s when she painted many dog portraits on commission. Olive Cliffe also did some illustration work including magazines, childrens books and pictures for 'Who's Who at the Zoo'. By the 1930s commissions were less frequent but she found work decorating leather goods with dogs, horses and foxes for a firm in Piccadilly. She continued to paint after the war, most of the work being small oil studies of dogs heads on board. She signed her work O Cliffe, often indistinctly, with a flourish on the C and sometimes a date. (Illus. p.27).

Ina Clogstoun            'Irises, Rome, 1905' (w/c)

Frank Clifford                    (Sotheby's Sussex)
'Upper Pool from London Bridge, 1921' (w/c)

## Frank CLIFFORD (fl. 1916-1921)

Painter in watercolour of marines including Pool of London scenes and clipper ships. The work appears to be identical in both style and colour to William M Birchall and it seems probable that Frank Clifford was a pseudonym. Examples of work signed Frank Clifford have been seen dated from 1916 to 1921.

## Brig.-Gen. Walter Rees CLIFFORD (1866-1947)

Watercolour landscape painter who showed a total of 12 works at the Army Officers Art Society exhibitions 1928-1930. The subjects were mostly Spanish and Italian views.

## Mrs. M.. E.. CLISSET

Former married name of Mrs M E Burrowes (q.v.), when she was living and exhibiting on the continent.

## Miss Ina CLOGSTOUN (1869-1909)

A good quality painter in watercolour of landscapes, flowers and garden scenes. This talented artist had three one-woman exhibitions at the Fine Art Society, London, in February 1904, March 1906 and May 1909, entitled 'Watercolours of the Italian Spring and the English Summer'. The exhibitions contained a total of 110 watercolours and most of these were landscapes or garden scenes. Her style and colour was similar to the work of Ella Du Cane. Sadly, Ina Clogstoun had died before the start of the 1909 exhibition, after a long illness, at St Remo in Italy and this catalogue contained an obituary as a supplement.

Arthur Clough                    'The Dee Estuary' (w/c)

## Arthur CLOUGH (fl.c. 1890-1920)

This good quality watercolour artist painted rural landscapes, often depicting working horses. He does not appear to have exhibited and there is no indication as to where he lived, although he may have been related to Tom Clough of the North Wales family of artists. Arthur Clough's work is seldom seen on the market, although the quality and subject matter would make it collectable. (Illus. p.28).

## R.. CLOUGH (exh. 1883-1886)

Painter in oil and watercolour of landscapes and still life who lived at Lowestoft, Suffolk, and was a member of the Ipswich Art Club. He exhibited a total of 21 works at their exhibitions 1883-1886. Most of the subjects were local landscapes. 'Christmas Day, Covehithe – 1884' (oil), 'The Ferry, Reedham' (watercolour), both 1885 exhibits, are typical titles.

## Charles CLOWES (died c.1900)

A Memorial Exhibition of the work of Charles Clowes was held by the Norwich Art Circle in May 1900. The exhibition consisted of 27 oils and watercolours and nine black and white studies. The subjects were mostly local landscapes and also some views of Germany.

*S. W. Clutten*     *'Cley Mill, Norfolk' (w/c)*     *(J. Collins and Son)*

## Samuel William CLUTTEN (fl. 1904-1921, died c.1952)

Painter in watercolour of landscapes and occasionally flowers who was working earlier this century. Samuel Clutten lived in Finchley, North London, and worked for an insurance company. Most of his painting was confined to holidays and the subjects included West Country and Norfolk views. He signed his work S W Clutten in printed letters and sometimes with a date.

## Mrs Walter CLUTTERBUCK (exh. 1897-1911)

Painter in watercolour, and sometimes oil, of landscapes, flowers and gardens. She lived in Norwich and later in London and was a member of the Norwich Art Circle. Mrs Clutterbuck was a regular exhibitor with the Norwich Art Circle, showing 58 works 1897-1911. Most of the works were watercolours of flowers, gardens and local views, but also some landscapes of Kashmir and a number of oils of Italy.

*W. C. Cluett*     *'Royal Navy Warship – 1898' (w/c)*     *(N. R. Wood)*

## William Charles CLUETT (1868-1958)

Painter in watercolour and gouache of ship portraits who was born at Portsea, Hants, in 1868. Many of his pictures were small finely detailed studies of Naval vessels and are usually titled and dated on the reverse. W C Cluett does not appear to have exhibited but he probably found a market for the work locally.

*J. Coad*     *'On the Oakement, Dartmoor' (w/c)*     *(J. Collins and Son)*

**James COAD (fl.c. 1930s)**

West Country painter of moorland scenes with a similar style to F J Widgery. He does not appear to have exhibited but probably sold his work locally. (Illus. p.29).

**Wilfred R.. COAST (exh. 1924)**

Watercolour landscape and marine painter who exhibited at the B.W.S. Annual Exhibition at Cheltenham in 1924. He showed two works 'Building the Rick, Chatham' and 'Trawlers, Ramsgate'.

**Joseph William COBB (exh. 1907-1912)**

Painter of landscapes and still life who lived at Tilehurst, Reading, and exhibited seven works at the R.W.A. 1907-1910. The titles include 'Fruit' and 'Curfew Tolls the Knell of Parting Day' (both 1910). He also exhibited two landscapes at the Worthing Art Gallery Summer Exhibition in 1912.

**Mrs B.. K.. COBBOLD (exh. 1887)**

Painter in oil of figures and landscapes who lived at Dedham in Essex and was a member of the Ipswich Art Club. She exhibited two works in 1887 entitled 'Sir Gareth' and 'Archway at Hyères'.

**Miss Florence COBBOLD (exh. 1884-1885)**

Landscape painter in oil who lived in Ipswich and exhibited at the Ipswich Art Club in 1884 and 1885. The titles were 'A Silver Birch' and 'Capel Hall, Trimley' (1884) and 'China' (two works, 1885).

**H.. C.. COBBOLD (exh. 1933-1934)**

Painter in oil and watercolour of landscapes and rural scenes, who lived in Ipswich and was a member of the Ipswich Art Club. He exhibited six works in 1933 and 1934 including 'Burgh Mill, Norfolk', 'Cattle Sense' and an interior.

**Mrs J.. Patteson COBBOLD (exh. 1901-1909)**

Watercolour landscape painter who lived in Ipswich and was a member of the Ipswich Art Club. She exhibited nine works at the Ipswich Art Club Exhibition in 1901 and eight in 1909, the subjects being mostly continental landscapes. The titles included 'Day at Syracuse', 'Vesuvius, Sunset', 'Early Morning, Kashmir', and 'In Mogul Garden' (all 1909).

**A.. COCHRANE (exh. 1935)**

Landscape painter in oil, who exhibited two coastal scenes at the St Ives Society of Artists Summer Exhibition in 1935.

**Miss Iris COCHRANE (exh. 1913)**

Animal painter who was a student at the Calderon School of Animal Painting. In 1913 she exhibited a portrait of a dog at the exhibition of the Calderon Art Society.

**Taka M.. COCHRANE (exh. 1935-1937)**

Watercolour artist who exhibited a still life at the St Ives Society of Artists Summer Exhibition in 1935 and also at their Winter Exhibition in 1937.

**Miss E.. E.. COCKLE (exh. 1923-1925)**

Painter in oil who lived at Clifton, Bristol, and exhibited three works at the R.W.A. 1923-1925. The subjects were a church interior and two views of Mevagissey harbour.

**Alfred COE (exh. 1905-1948)**

Painter in oil and sometimes watercolour of still life and landscapes who lived in Ipswich and was a member of the Ipswich Art Club. He was a prolific exhibitor showing at least 211 works 1905-1948. Most of the subjects were local views and flower still life. The titles included 'A Sketch – Dedham', (1905) and 'Sweet Peas', 'Violets' and 'Cromer Cliffs' (all 1927).

*N. Pine Coffin      'A Faithful Friend, 1916' (w/c)*

**Nora Pine COFFIN (fl. 1914-1916)**

Painter in watercolour of landscapes and animals, who lived at Exmouth in Devon. She exhibited once at the Royal Academy in 1914, a picture entitled 'The Call of the Wild'.

*L. Colborne*                    *'The Conqueror' (oil)*

### Laurence COLBORNE (fl.c. 1920)

Painter in oil and watercolour of marine and figure subjects, often in period costume. Curiously this good quality artist does not appear to have exhibited but he is known to have worked as an illustrator of comic postcards. He signed his work 'L Colborne'.

### Miss M.. D.. COLE (fl. 1925)

A member of the 'New Autumn Group' of painters who were based in St John's Wood. A delicate book illustration by the artist was reproduced in The Studio in 1925.

### Henry COLLER (born 1886, fl. 1936-1950)

Black and white artist and magazine illustrator who wrote a series of articles for The Artist magazine in 1936 and 1937 entitled 'Approach to Story Illustration'. Henry Coller's illustrations included work for Home Journal. His post-war work included some illustrations for John Bull magazine.

### Miss Joan COLLER (exh. 1926-1929)

Watercolour painter who lived in Ipswich and was the daughter of Edward H Coller. She exhibited three works at the Ipswich Art Club 1926-1929, entitled 'Burford', 'Bird Study' and 'Interior'.

### Rev. A.. M.. COLLETT (exh. 1885)

Landscape artist who lived in Ipswich and was a member of the Ipswich Art Club. He exhibited two monochrome studies in 1885 – 'Sketch at Sproughton' and 'Bramford'.

### William Valken COLLETT (1871-1916)

Artist and illustrator who lived at Westbury Park, Bristol, and was probably the son of W Vizor Collett (q.v.). A series of Christmas postcards were published of his work. He died in Bristol in 1916 at the age of 45.

### William Vizor COLLETT (fl. 1897-1905)

Etcher and postcard artist who lived in Bristol and was probably the father of W Valken Collett (q.v.). He exhibited five etchings at the R.W.A. in 1903.

*H. Collier*                    *'The Huntsman' (w/c)*

### H.. COLLIER (fl. 1930s)

A good quality watercolour artist who was probably working around the 1930s. The artist has a pleasing technique of detailed pencil drawing overlaid with coloured washes. The subjects include horse portraits.

### Miss Blanche COLLINS A.R.W.A. (exh. 1901-1914)

Painter in oil and watercolour of landscapes, portraits and still life who lived in Bath and was an associate member of the R.W.A. She exhibited over 14 works at the R.W.A. 1901-1914, which included Devon views, portraits and flower still life. The titles include 'The Orange Seller' (1902), 'A Little Cottage Maid' (1904), and 'The Chieftain's Daughter'.

### F.. C.. COLLINS (exh. 1919)

Painter of river and moorland landscapes who lived at Bingley, Yorks, and exhibited three works at the Bradford local artists exhibition in 1919.

### Frank COLLINSON (exh. 1919)

Painter who lived at Oakenshaw near Bradford and exhibited two landscapes at the Bradford local artists exhibition in 1919.

## Frederick N.. COLWELL (exh. 1935-1964)

Painter in oil and watercolour of landscapes and still life. In 1935 he exhibited 10 works at the French Gallery, London. The exhibition was for J Walter Thompson's Industrial Artists and entitled 'Weekend Work'. He also exhibited three landscapes and a still life at the Royal Academy 1937-1964. Frederick Colwell lived in London and later at Ashtead in Surrey.

*W. E. H. Condon*      *'Nanga Parbet, 1926' (w/c)*

## Brig.-Gen. William E.. H.. CONDON (born 1886)

Painter in watercolour of landscapes, mostly West Country views or scenes in India and Kashmir. He was born in Cawnpore, India, in 1886, the son of a doctor, educated and brought up in England and studied art under George Hutchinson in Bristol.

William Condon returned to India on being commissioned in the Indian Army. Most of his exhibiting over the next 35 years was in India and largely based on sketches he made in Kashmir and on the North West Frontier. In 1925 he exhibited seven works at the Army Officers Art Society First Annual Exhibition in London. The subjects were all scenes of Devon and India.

William Condon retired as a Brigadier and took a farm in Devon but he continued to paint and became President of the Exeter Art Society.

## Miss Emily CONNAL (fl. 1908)

A student at the Birbeck School of Art, London. She was painting around 1908 and the subjects of her work include shipping on the Thames.

## Miss E.. N.. CONNOLLY (exh. 1927)

Watercolour artist who lived at Clifton, Bristol and exhibited at the R.W.A. in 1927 – 'The Cliff at Bude, Cornwall'.

## Harold CONNOLLY (fl. 1930s-1956)

Illustrator and commercial artist in watercolour. In the 1930s Harold Connolly was an active commercial artist and produced some stylish illustrations of sports cars for the M.G. car brochures of the period. He later illustrated for Ford and other car companies and also did some work for the Autocar. After the War he lived in Brighton and was a member of the Brighton Arts Club 1950-1953. Harold Connolly also showed some work at the R.A.C.'s Exhibition of Motoring Art in 1956.

*G. Hamilton Constantine*      *'Scarbro' (w/c)*      *(Cdr. J. Morton-Lee)*

## George Hamilton CONSTANTINE (1875-1967)

Painter in watercolour, and sometimes in oil, of rural landscapes, beach and harbour scenes. He was educated at the Sheffield Central School and the Sheffield College of Art, where his fellow pupils included David Jagger and Stanley Royle. Although G H Constantine is probably best known for his rural scenes in watercolour of horses ploughing or collecting wrack on beaches, he also painted landscapes in oil.

George Constantine did not need to exhibit his work widely as there was a steady demand for it from dealers in this country and New York. He did, however, exhibit once at the Royal Academy in 1916 and also held exhibitions in Huddersfield and Rotherham. He was Hon. Secretary of the Sheffield Society of Artists throughout the 1930s.

The fine quality of G H Constantine's work, and the appealing subject matter, have helped to make his pictures as popular today as they were in his lifetime.

## A.. B.. K.. COOK (exh. 1912)

Watercolour artist who exhibited two views of Venice at the Winchester Art Society Exhibition in 1912.

## Miss Kathleen M.. C.. COOK (exh. 1926-1927)

Artist who lived at Weston-super-Mare and, later, Brockhampton, Glos. She exhibited at the R.W.A. in 1926 and 1927 works entitled 'Lauterbrunnen Chasm' and 'Bath Court, Reading'.

## Miss May COOK (exh. 1912)

Watercolour painter of figures and interiors who exhibited two works at the Winchester Art Society Exhibition in 1912.

## Arthur Stanley COOKE (1852-1919)

Painter, illustrator and author who lived in Brighton and was an early member of the Brighton Arts Club. A S Cooke was the author of 'Southdown Songs and Idylls' (1909) and 'Off the Beaten Track in Sussex' (1911) to which he contributed over forty pen and ink illustrations. He died in Brighton on 31st July 1919 at the age of 67.

## C.. J.. F.. COOMBS (exh. 1929-1931)

Artist who lived at Clifton, Bristol, and specialised in bird studies. C J F Coombs exhibited six works at the R.W.A. 1929-1931, all birds, including 'Crows', 'Rooks' and 'Golden Eagle'.

Henry Cooper     'The Farm Pond' (oil)     (Sotheby's)

## Henry COOPER (fl. 1910-1935)

Painter of highland scenes and rural landscapes in oil and, occasionally, watercolour. This prolific artist appears regularly at auction but the quality of his work is variable and this affects the prices. He painted some Devon scenes such as 'Cockington Mill', and 'On the River Dart', as well as views of South East England and highland landscapes. He does not seem to have exhibited any works.

R. Cooper     'A Wayside Inn' (w/c)     ( J. Collins and Son)

## Reginald COOPER (fl. 1930s)

Painter and illustrator in watercolour and bodycolour of rural scenes and cottages. Much of the work of this prolific artist was reproduced as prints and postcards and thus tends to be bright in colour. The colour and style is similar to J W Gozzard (q.v.) but the quality is usually not quite so fine. Reginald Cooper's best work is attractive and becoming more collectable. He signed his pictures R. Cooper or sometimes just with initials.

## A.. COPSEY (exh. 1884-1885)

Painter in oil of buildings and rural landscapes who lived at Sudbury in Suffolk and was a member of the Ipswich Art Club. He exhibited a total of six works 1884-1885 and the subjects, mostly local scenes, included 'The Old Lodge, Pentlow, Essex' and 'A Cottage at Gestingthorpe, Essex'.

## Lt.-Col. E.. F.. CORBETT (exh. 1928-1939)

Watercolour landscape painter who lived at Tavistock, Devon, and exhibited 25 works at the Army Officers Art Society exhibitions 1928-1939. The subjects were mostly local Devon views and some studies of Dartmoor ponies.

## Miss N.. CORDINGLEY (exh. 1932-1934)

Artist who lived at Clifton, Bristol, and exhibited at the R.W.A. in 1932 and 1934 – 'Warehouses, Bristol Docks' and 'The Mouth of the Avon'.

## C.. B.. CORE (fl. 1910-1940)

Painter in watercolour of rural landscapes who was working between 1910 and 1940 and by the later date was living at Dulwich Village, London. He does not appear to have exhibited.

**Frank Robert CORNISH (born 1868, exh. 1923-1937)**

Painter, mostly in watercolour, of landscapes who lived at Felixstowe and was a member of the Ipswich Art Club. He exhibited a total of 65 works 1923-1937. The subjects included views on the Thames, Devon, and Bordighera in Italy but were mostly local scenes in the Ipswich area.

**W.. R.. CORNISH (exh. 1921-1926)**

Painter who lived in Bristol and exhibited five works at the R.W.A. 1921-1926. The subjects were mostly local landscapes.

**Arthur N.. COTTERELL (exh. 1918-1921)**

Painter in oil and watercolour of landscapes who lived in Bristol and exhibited 10 works at the R.W.A. 1918-1921. The subjects were mostly views in France and some local scenes. Arthur Cotterell was still painting in the early 1970s.

A. J. Couche      'Exmouth from Battery' (w/c)      (J. Collins and Son)

**Arthur J.. COUCHE (fl. 1907-1939)**

Watercolour painter who exhibited three works at the annual Devon and Exeter Artists Exhibition at Elands Art Gallery, Exeter, in 1907. The subjects were all local Exmouth views. He was still listed as a working artist in Exeter in 1939.

**Constance J.. D.. COULSON (fl.c. 1910)**

Watercolour painter and illustrator of Far Eastern scenes. She painted a series of six watercolours which were used by A & C Black as colour plates in 'Peeps at Korea' (1910) and also some plates in 'Peeps at the Far East'.

**J.. COULSON (fl. 1920-1927)**

Oil painter of Middle Eastern and desert scenes. Typical titles of his work are 'Bedouins by the Pyramids', 'A Meeting in the Desert', and 'Water Carriers by the Nile'. The pictures painted in the 1920s are usually dated. The artist does not appear to have exhibited.

**Fred COUPE (born 1875)**

Painter of industrial landscapes in oil and watercolour who was born in Burnley in 1875. He studied at the Burnley School of Art and exhibited widely in the provinces. An article on his industrial landscape painting appeared in The Studio magazine in 1928. Fred Coupe lived in Manchester for a number of years.

**Roy W.. A.. COURTICE (exh. 1932-1933)**

Landscape and portrait painter who lived at Brislington, Bristol, and exhibited a total of four works at the R.W.A. in 1932 and 1933. The subjects were portraits and local Bristol views.

**Miss Bertha COWELL (exh. 1895-1903)**

Watercolour landscape painter who lived in Ipswich and was a member of the Ipswich Art Club. She exhibited six works 1895-1903 and the titles included 'On the Sure, Yorkshire' (1902) and 'Silvern Memories' (1903), and two views of Christchurch.

**Miss Florence COWLEY (exh. 1900)**

Artist who lived in Bristol and exhibited at the R.W.A. in 1900 a work entitled the 'Old Manor House, Easton'.

**Cecil COWPER (exh. 1924)**

Watercolour painter of landscapes and figure subjects who exhibited three works at the B.W.S. Annual Exhibition at Cheltenham in 1924.

**Miss Octavia S.. COX R.W.A. (exh. 1889-1938)**

Landscape painter in watercolour and sometimes in oil who lived at Clifton, Bristol, and was a member of the R.W.A. She was a regular exhibitor for almost 50 years showing a total of 73 works 1889-1938. Most of the works were watercolour landscapes of local views and scenes in Norfolk, Wales, Devon and Cornwall. She also painted some flower studies.

**Eric H.. CRADDY (exh. 1932-1950)**

Painter in watercolour and oil of landscapes, marines and still life who lived in Bristol. He exhibited eight works at the R.W.A. 1932-1950 and a total of 51 works at the Bristol Savages from 1937. The landscapes and marines were mostly watercolours and the still life paintings were oils.

**V.. P.. CRAIG (fl.c. 1920)**

Watercolour landscape painter who was working in the early part of the century and painted some views in the Rye area of Sussex.

**Miss Helen CRAVEN (exh. 1900-1901)**

Painter of still life in oil who exhibited at the R.W.A. in 1900 and 1901, works entitled 'Autumn Leaves and Berries' and 'Roses'.

**Miss E.. Mercy CREED B.W.S. (fl. 1924-1934)**

Watercolour painter of portraits, flowers and landscapes who exhibited three works at the B.W.S. Exhibition at Cheltenham in 1924. The subjects were 'Roses in France', 'April in England' and 'Portrait'. In the early 1930s she was living at Bexhill-on-Sea, Sussex.

*Clara Cripps*                          *'St Nicholas Church, Brighton' (w/c)*

**Miss Clara CRIPPS (exh. 1886-1887)**

Painter in oil and watercolour of portraits, figures and landscapes. She lived in Worthing and exhibited at the Brighton Art Gallery Annual Watercolour (May) and Oil (October) Exhibitions in 1886 and 1887, mostly portraits and figure subjects. The titles included 'Old Houses, West Tarring' (1886) and 'A Dear Little Girl' and 'Study of a Head' (1887).

**Sylvester CROOK (exh. 1905)**

Oil landscape painter who lived in Bolton and exhibited at the Local Artists Exhibition at Bolton in 1905.

**William CROSLEY (fl. 1908)**

Landscape and still life artist in pencil. He was an engineer by profession, but his travel on work to Panama, the West Indies, and the Gold Coast gave him the opportunity to sketch. His work included detailed studies of flora and fauna, and some was reproduced in The Studio magazine in 1908.

**Miss E.. Mary CROSS (exh. 1904-1911)**

Watercolour painter of rural landscapes, who lived at Postwick, and later at Swainsthorpe, Norfolk, and exhibited at the Norwich Art Circle 1904-1911. She showed over 25 works, mostly landscape views.

**Joseph A.. CROSTON (exh. 1905)**

Painter of fruit and still life who lived at Westhoughton and exhibited two works at the Local Artists Exhibition at Bolton in 1905.

**T.. S.. C.. CROWTHER (1862-1903)**

Illustrator and black and white artist who worked for The Graphic magazine. He died on 3rd October 1903 at the age of 41.

**Miss P.. P.. CRUMP (exh. 1915)**

Bristol artist who exhibited two works at the R.W.A. in 1915 entitled 'St Mary, Redcliffe' and 'A Study'.

**Harry Edmunds CRUTE (1888-1975)**

Painter in watercolour and oil of landscapes, harbours and flowers who was born on 18th July 1888. He was a self-taught artist and a friend of the Devon painters Wycliffe Egginton and Thomas Binmore. A pottery decorator and designer by profession, he worked for the Whatcombe Pottery, Torquay, in the early 1920s before setting up in partnership as the Daison Art Pottery. Finally he left to join the Dartmouth Potteries around 1930. Harry Crute was a prolific artist who painted coastal and harbour scenes which were sold in local shops to the tourist trade. Other subjects included oil paintings and watercolours of flowers, village scenes and Dartmoor landscapes as well as paintings on glass. Harry Crute died in Torquay at the age of 87 in 1975. The work is usually signed H Edmunds Crute or sometimes with initials.

**Miss Mabel CULLEY (exh. 1901-1909)**

Painter in oil and watercolour who lived at Thorpe Hamlet, Norfolk. She was a member of the Norwich Art Circle and exhibited 26 pictures 1901-1909. The oil paintings were still life and landscapes but most of her pictures were Norfolk and Devon views, interiors and beach scenes in watercolour.

**Mrs. M.. E.. CULVERWELL (exh. 1925-1927)**

Landscape artist who lived at Clifton, Bristol, and exhibited at the R.W.A. in 1925 and 1927. The subjects were both beach scenes at Tintagel, Cornwall.

*R. H. Neville Cumming*      *'Oceana' (w/c)*      *(Sotheby's)*

## R.. H.. Neville CUMMING (fl. 1889-1911)

Painter in watercolour of marines and ship portraits. His work is usually inscribed and dated – 'Dreadnought at Sea' (1905) and 'The Nile Boat, Scarborough' (1911) being typical titles. The artist was quite prolific and the popular subject matter makes the pictures collectable. A series of postcards were published of his work.

## Florence T.. CUNDALL (exh. 1900-1901)

Watercolour still life painter who lived at Redland, Bristol, and exhibited a total of four works at the R.W.A. in 1900 and 1901. The works were 'Daffodils', 'Primroses', 'Apple Blossom' and 'Gentians'.

## Miss K.. B.. CURTIS (exh. 1917-1918)

Portrait painter and sculptor who lived at Stoke Bishop, Bristol, and exhibited three works at the R.W.A. 1917-1918. These were a portrait bust, a medallion and an oil painting of a lady.

## Miss S.. J.. CURTIS (exh. 1931-1936)

Artist who lived at Westbury Park, Bristol, and exhibited at the R.W.A. in 1931 and 1936. The subjects were 'Bristol Central Library' and a portrait 'Joyce'.

## A.. Margaret CUTTING (exh. 1930-1932)

Painter of flowers and still life who lived at Stoneham Aspal, near Stowmarket, Suffolk. She was a member of the Ipswich Art Club and exhibited six works 1930-1932. 'Dahlias' and 'Lilac Time', both watercolours, shown in 1931, are typical titles.

# D

### Frederick DADE (1874-1908)

Watercolour artist who was born in Scarborough on the 6th August 1874 and was a younger brother of Ernest Dade. His father, a photographer and portrait painter, had died before he was born and his mother was left to bring up seven children. Frederick Dade painted coastal scenes and marines similar to those of his elder brother, but his work is less common. He was ill for several years and died of tuberculosis at the age of 34 on 2nd December 1908.

*Fred Dade        'Shipping off the Coast (w/c)        (Sotheby's Sussex)*

### Alice Sophia DAINTREY (1851-1936)

Painter of landscapes, flowers and figures who lived at Petworth, Sussex, and was exhibiting from the 1880s until 1913. She was the younger sister of Constance Daintrey (q.v.) who was also an artist. Alice Daintrey exhibited at the London Salon 1910-1913, at the Society of Women Artists and in Liverpool. She died on 23rd April 1936 at the age of 85.

### Miss Constance M.. DAINTREY (1845-1916)

Watercolour painter of English landscapes and Continental views who lived in Petworth, Sussex, and was working around the turn of the century. Constance Daintrey had several solo exhibitions in London. She showed 74 works at the Continental Gallery in February 1900, mostly views of England, France, Italy and Norway. The Doré Gallery held two exhibitions – 'Boats and Gardens' (59 works) and 'Venice, Como and the New Forest' (72 works). Her last exhibition was probably 'Northern Mists and Southern Gardens' at The Graves Gallery around 1910. She died on 24th November 1916, aged 71.

### Miss Edith M.. DALE-GLOSSOP (exh. 1912)

Painter in oil of landscapes and portraits who exhibited three works at the Worthing Art Gallery Summer Exhibition in 1912. The subjects were two portraits and a landscape.

### Charles Frederick DALLEY (1878-1943)

Painter in oil of Jersey landscapes and coastal scenes who was born in St. Helier in 1878. He worked from a studio in St. Helier and at one time taught painting. Charles Dalley died in Jersey in 1943 at the age of 65.

### Percival G.. DALTON (exh. 1950)

Landscape and marine painter in oil who lived at St. Austell, Cornwall, and exhibited at the Plymouth Art Society Exhibition in 1950. He showed five works, two oils of Cornish views and three miniature ship portraits.

### P.. S.. DAMANT (exh. 1902-1903)

Landscape and still life painter in oil who lived in Colchester, Essex and was a member of the Ipswich Art Club. He exhibited 'A Summer Afternoon' and 'Still Life' (1902) and 'A Lane in Cheshire' (1903).

### Mrs. J.. L.. (Sophie) DANIELL (exh. 1904-1920)

Watercolour landscape painter who lived in Bristol and exhibited over 17 works at the R.W.A. 1904-1920. Most of the subjects were local views, also some Kent and Sussex scenes and a view of Switzerland.

### Miss H.. DARBYSHIRE (exh. 1935-1937)

Artist who lived at Redland, Bristol, and exhibited two works at the R.W.A. in 1935 – 'Roofs at Bristol' and 'The Gardener'.

*J. F. Darley        'Loading Coasters' (w/c)        (Bourne Gallery)*

### James Frederick DARLEY (1847-1932)

Painter in oil and watercolour of figures and rural landscapes. James Darley was a Chartered Accountant by profession and lived first in London, then at New Haw, Surrey, and later at Woking. He was a regular exhibitor at the R.B.A. showing a total of 73 works 1886-1908. In 1900, James Darley was elected a Member of the R.B.A. and the next eight years were to be his most prolific as he showed over 60 pictures. The subjects included some watercolour figures such as 'The Young Anglers' and 'Peppino' (both 1902) but most were rural landscapes in oil such as 'Harvesting on the South Coast' (1903), 'The Oatfield' (1904) and 'An Old Thatched Cottage' (1905). He painted many local views in Surrey as well as scenes in Sussex, Kent and Essex. An exhibition of his work was held at Jeremy Wood Fine Art, Petworth, Sussex, in June 1991.

*George Davey*                    *'Prehistoric Games' (lithograph)*

## George DAVEY (1882-1944)

Freelance commercial artist, illustrator and journalist, also landscape painter in oil and watercolour, cartoonist and etcher. George Davey lived at Golders Green, London, and contributed daily cartoons to the 'Westminster Gazette' and humorous drawings for comics such as 'Lot o' Fun'. His work was much in demand in the 1920s and 1930s. George Davey worked as a postcard artist, with commissions for Valentines, Misch and Stock, and J. Mandel & Co, which included comic cards, Christmas cards and calendars. He was also a freelance journalist and a member of the London Press Club. Most of his painting was in the South of England and the coastal resorts but he also sketched in Belgium and Holland. By the 1930s the regular commercial work was becoming less frequent but George Davey continued to paint and sell landscapes up until his death in 1944.

## Miss Kate H.. DAVEY (exh. 1919-1929)

Watercolour landscape painter who lived at Clifton, Bristol, and exhibited 11 works at the R.W.A. 1919-1929. Most of the exhibits were Cornish scenes including four views of Tintagel.

## Miss W.. DAVEY (exh. 1900)

Artist who lived at Clifton and exhibited at the R.W.A. in 1900. The work in the Professionals Section was entitled 'Rye from the Marshes'.

## K.. M.. DAVIDSON B.W.S. (exh. 1928)

Watercolour landscape painter who was a member of the B.W.S. and exhibited a view of Newquay, Cornwall, at their Autumn Exhibition at Preston in 1928.

## Brig.-Gen. K.. M.. DAVIE (exh. 1928-1935)

Watercolour painter who exhibited 25 works at the Army Officers Art Society Exhibitions 1928-1935. His subjects appear to be mostly watercolour landscapes.

## Maj. G.. B.. DAVIES (exh. 1928-1929)

Etcher, often of Indian scenes, who exhibited at the Army Officers Art Society Exhibitions of 1928 and 1929. An officer in the Bombay Pioneers, he lived at Bransgore, Hants.

## Mrs. A.. Mollie DAVIS (exh. 1918-1929)

Painter in oil and watercolour of landscapes and coastal scenes who lived in Bristol and exhibited 10 works at the R.W.A. 1918-1929. Most of the subjects were coastal scenes and sunsets – 'Summer Sea, Newquay' (1924) and 'Singing Waves' (1928) being typical titles.

## Lt. G.. M.. O.. DAVY (exh. 1928-1933)

An officer in the Royal Horse Artillery who exhibited 15 works with the Army Officers Art Society 1928-1933. The subjects were Venice views and some English landscapes in watercolour.

## Alice Georgiana DAWE (1879-1977)

Watercolour artist and miniature painter who was the daughter of the artist Frank Rawlings Offer (q.v.). She studied at the Southampton School of Art but it was not until 1929 that she started to sell her work. Her commissions were mainly portrait miniatures and she did exhibit one at the Royal Academy in 1955. Most of her landscape work was done in Canada and she died in Unionville, Ontario, in June 1977.

*J. Dawkins*                    *'The Valhalla' (oil)*

## J.. DAWKINS (fl.c. 1900)

Painter in oil of marines. The work of this competent artist who was painting around 1900 is occasionally seen on the market, although he does not appear to have exhibited. (Illus. p.38).

## R.. J.. DAY (fl. 1908)

A student at the Birbeck School of Art, London, who was awarded the A W Mason prize for still life painting in 1908.

## F.. DEAKIN (fl. 1911)

Painter in oils of animals working prior to the First World War, possibly as an illustrator. The work is of good quality, but the artist does not appear to have exhibited.

## William Osmond DELLIS (1896-1987)

Painter in watercolour, and occasionally pastel, of landscapes and cottage scenes. William Dellis was born in New Brighton, Lancs, on 28th October 1896. His family moved to Liverpool, and the young William Dellis served with the Liverpool Scottish Regiment in France throughout the First World War. From 1919, he worked as a printer and stationer but painting was his abiding interest. Although he had no formal art training, William Dellis was a competent painter and his work shows the influence, in both colour and technique, of his friend David Woodlock. He did not sell his pictures but some were given to friends and could eventually appear on the market. William Dellis was also a Life Member and Past President of the Mahatma Circle of Magicians in Liverpool – he gave many magic shows in the 1930s. He died at the age of 90 on 18th January 1987.

## Miss Katherine DENNES (exh. 1922-1926)

Painter who exhibited with the Darlington Art Society 1922-1926. The subjects were genre and allegorical paintings.

## Alexander DENNY (exh. 1900-1903)

Landscape artist in pastel who lived in Norwich and was a member of the Ipswich Art Club. He exhibited a total of 22 works 1900-1903. 'Early Morning', 'Sunrise', 'Golden Evening' and 'Moonlight' all from 1903 are typical titles.

## Mrs. Ernest DENNY (exh. 1906)

Watercolour painter who exhibited 16 works as part of a joint exhibition at the Modern Gallery, London, in December 1906. The subjects were all views of Swiss mountains and lakes.

## Miss P.. M.. DENTON (exh. 1922-1932)

Painter of landscapes, genre and still life, who lived in Bristol and later at Stratton St Margaret, Wilts. She exhibited 11 works at the R.W.A. 1922-1932 including figure subjects and flower studies.

G. De Paris                'Rodmell Church, Sussex, 1905' (w/c)

## George J.. DE PARIS (1828/9-1911)

Painter in watercolour of architectural subjects, often old Sussex buildings and churches. George De Paris lived at Hove and much of his work was sold locally where it is still mostly found today. He exhibited at the Brighton Art Gallery Annual Exhibition from 1880-1887. The subjects were Sussex churches and also included studies at Shrewsbury, Cambridge, Peterborough and Gloucester. He continued to work into his old age, showing two watercolours of old houses at the Sussex Artists Exhibition in Brighton in 1909. The Horsham Museum has a view of the Carfax, Horsham, by him. His pictures are well painted and of historical interest, but much of the subject matter is no longer fashionable. George De Paris died in Brighton at the age of 82 in 1911.

## Arthur DE TIVOLI (fl.c. 1920)

Painter in oil of landscapes and coastal scenes who was probably working around the 1920s. The subjects are usually views in the Bournemouth area including Poole Harbour and Christchurch. He does not appear to have exhibited.

## F.. J.. DICKINS (fl. 1921)

Watercolour landscape painter who was active in the early 1920s but does not appear to have exhibited. The work includes some English coastal views and also Continental town and lake scenes.

## Joseph DIPLOCK (fl. 1896)

Artist and illustrator who lived in Brighton and was a Member of the Brighton Arts Club. In 1896 he won first prize in The Studio competition for a design. Joseph Diplock had eight landscape views in pen and ink posthumously published in 'Off the Beaten Track in Sussex' by Arthur S Cooke in 1911.

**B.. DISNEY-ROEBUCK (exh. 1950)**

Flower painter in watercolour who lived at Budleigh Salterton and exhibited two works at the Plymouth Art Society in 1950.

**Clive Macdonnell DIXON (1870-1914)**

Painter in oil and watercolour of historical genre, figures, horses and landscapes. He was also an illustrator, pastel and woodcut artist. Clive Dixon was born on the 10th February 1870 and was educated at Rugby and then went to Sandhurst where he was commissioned into the Queens Lancers. He saw active service on the North West Frontier and later in the Boer War where he was A.D.C. to Sir George White and was besieged at Lady Smith. At this time Clive Dixon wrote and illustrated a humorous picture book of his experiences entitled 'The Leaguer of Lady Smith'.

In 1898 he married Lilian Margaret Bell (q.v.), herself a talented amateur artist, and they lived at Great Ayton, and later Stokesley in Yorkshire. At the outbreak of War in 1914 Clive Dixon rejoined his Regiment and he was killed in action on the 5th November 1914 near Ypres, at the age of 44.

Clive Dixon's work is of fine quality, but is seldom seen on the market. The subjects include some large historical genre scenes and some fine studies of arab horsemen painted in North Africa. He exhibited five oils at the Royal Academy 1908-1911, mostly historical genre, and two works at the Walker Art Gallery, Liverpool. The larger works are usually signed in full, but smaller works often with initials or a monogram (see index).

**Mrs. C.. W.. DIXON (exh. 1933-1936)**

Landscape artist who lived at Shirehampton vicarage, Bristol, and exhibited seven works at the R.W.A. 1933-1936. The subjects were mostly local scenes, 'The Vicarage Garden', 'Dunkery' and also some Cornish views.

**Lilian Margaret DIXON (1875-1963)**

Painter in watercolour of landscapes, gardens and some figure subjects. She was born Lilian Margaret Bell on the 16th September 1875 in Algiers, the daughter of an ironstone master from Saltburn in Yorkshire. Lilian Dixon painted throughout her life, including scenes in Norway, France, Spain, Algeria and South Africa where she lived while her husband was serving in the Boer War. Lilian Bell married Clive Dixon in 1898 and thereafter her pictures were signed with her married name. She never exhibited except locally with the Cleveland Sketching Club. Her eldest daughter Margaret, born in India at the turn of the century, married the talented equestrian artist and illustrator Geoffrey Sparrow.

**Frank DOBBS (1872-1906)**

Watercolour landscape painter, who lived in West Kensington and died on 2nd January 1906.

**Philip DOLAN (fl. 1870s)**

Fine quality genre, interior and still life painter in watercolour. The work of this artist does not appear on the market very often and may explain why he has escaped the attention of most of the current dictionaries of painters. 'Dressing her Hair' and 'Cupboard Love' which depicts a cat on a table being stroked by a girl, a subject he painted several times, are typical of his genre painting. He also painted still lifes of birds nests on a mossy bank in the manner of William Hunt.

**Percy N.. DOLLERY (exh. 1950)**

Oil painter who lived in Plymouth and exhibited four works at the Plymouth Art Society Exhibition in 1950. These included a beach scene, a caricature portrait, and a painting of a horse sale.

W. Anstey Dollond          (Sotheby's Sussex)
'A Roman Beauty' (detail) (w/c)

## William Anstey DOLLOND (1858-1929)

A fine quality painter of neo-classical scenes in watercolour and occasionally oil. He lived in London, Deal in Kent and later at Pewsey in Wiltshire. He exhibited widely in London and the provinces. William Dollond died on 8th December 1929 at the age of 71. (Illus. p.40).

## H.. DOLLOND-HULKE (fl.c. 1920-1930)

Painter in watercolour of West Country coastal scenes and landscapes. The artist does not appear to have exhibited but probably sold the work locally.

## Vere G.. F.. DOLTON (exh. 1935-1937)

Watercolour landscape painter who exhibited at the St Ives Society of Artists Exhibitions in 1935 and 1937. The titles were 'After Rain, Zennor' and 'Ballans' (1935) and 'Beddgelert' and 'Old Cottage, Selworthy' (1937).

## Norman DONNELLY (fl. 1937)

Painter in oil of landscapes who lived at Thornton, Lancs, and was working in the late 1930s. The subjects were often local views and he sometimes signed with his initials monogrammed (see index).

## Frederick K.. DOREY (exh. 1932-1936)

Landscape and interior painter who lived at Keynsham, Bristol, and exhibited seven works at the R.W.A. 1932-1936. The subjects were local views and Dorset landscapes including Wool and Studland.

## James DORIA (exh. 1950)

Oil painter who lived at Tintagel, Cornwall, and was a member of the Plymouth Art Society. He exhibited three oils at their 1950 Exhibition – all Swiss landscape views.

## John C.. DOUGLAS (exh. 1935-1937)

Landscape painter in oil who exhibited at the St Ives Society of Artists Exhibitions in 1935 and 1937. The titles were 'Trevail and Wicca' and 'Autumn Gold' (1935) and 'Alpine Afterglow' and 'Coast Study' (1937).

## Miss Ethel DOUGLAS-WILLAN (exh. 1900-1901)

Watercolour painter who lived at Lamberhurst in Kent and was a member of the Norwich Art Circle. She exhibited four works with the Circle in 1900 and 1901 – watercolour landscapes and cottage scenes.

## Miss E.. DOWDING (exh. 1905)

Painter in oils who exhibited several works at the Bath Society of Artists Second Annual Exhibition in 1905.

*A. S. Dowes*          *'Tudor Cottage, Prinsted, Sussex' (w/c)*

## Mrs. A.. S.. DOWES (exh. 1935-1937)

Landscape painter in oil and watercolour who lived at Southsea, Hants, and was a member of the Portsmouth and Hampshire Art Society. She was a regular exhibitor showing at least 12 works 1935-1937. Titles included 'A Hampshire Village', 'Old Mill, Bosham' and 'Harvest, Chidham' (all 1935).

## T.. H.. DOWLING (exh. 1950)

Watercolour painter who lived in Plymouth and exhibited two works at the Plymouth Art Society Exhibition in 1950, both local landscapes.

## Miss K.. Thornton DOWN (exh. 1933)

Watercolour landscape artist who lived in Ipswich and was a member of the Ipswich Art Club. She exhibited four works in 1933 – all views on the Norfolk Broads – 'Weyford Bridge', 'Horsey Mere . .' (pair) and 'Horsey Church'.

*H. Cecil Drane*          *'The Star Inn, Rusper, Sussex – 1901' (oil)*

## Herbert Cecil DRANE (1862-1932)

Painter in oil of rural landscapes particularly around Dorking, Surrey, where he lived. Herbert Cecil Drane had an unusual manner of applying the paint which make his works easy to identify. He exhibited widely in London and the provinces but sold much of his work locally. He died in 14th July 1932 aged 70.

**Arthur DREW (fl. 1900s)**

Painter in watercolour of continental town scenes. This was probably a pseudonym for the artist who usually signs 'Pierre Le Boeuff' and was, in fact, Thomas E. Francis.

**J.. E.. DREW (exh. 1901)**

Landscape painter who lived in Reading and showed four works at the Berkshire Art Society Annual Exhibition in 1901. The pictures were local views including the Kennet and Mapledurham Mill.

**Miss Nora L.. DREW (exh. 1907)**

Watercolour landscape painter who exhibited in 1907 at Elands Art Gallery, Exeter, a work entitled 'Spring, . . . Dunster'.

**Capt. Algernon DRUMMOND (exh. 1928-1931)**

Watercolour painter who exhibited 10 works at the Army Officers Art Society Exhibitions 1928-1931. The subjects included a garden scene and some continental views.

**Capt. F.. B.. H.. DRUMMOND (exh. 1928-1939)**

Landscape painter in watercolour who lived at Winchester and exhibited nine works at the Army Officers Art Society Exhibitions 1928-1939.

**The Hon. Mrs. DRUMMOND (exh. 1912)**

Watercolour artist who showed two Scottish landscapes at the Winchester Art Society Exhibition of 1912.

**Jack M.. DUCKER (fl.c. 1910-1930)**

Painter in oil of Highland and Scottish loch scenes. A prolific artist similar in subject and quality to F. E. Jamieson, but he does not seem to have exhibited.

**I.. N.. DUCKETT (exh. 1928-1929)**

Artist who lived at Shirehampton, Bristol, and exhibited at the R.W.A. in 1928 and 1929, works entitled 'The Kings Head, Chiswell' and 'The Drawbridge, Bishops Palace, Wells'.

**Lewis DUCKETT A.R.C.A. (born 1892, exh. 1950)**

Landscape painter in oil and watercolour who was born in Sunderland in 1892. He was Principal of the Northampton School of Art from c. 1927-1933. In 1950, he exhibited five works at the Plymouth Art Society when he was living at Yelverton, Devon. The subjects included a horse portrait and some watercolour views of Dartmoor.

**Mrs. M.. M.. DUCKETT (exh. 1928-1932)**

Artist who lived in Zanzibar and from 1930 at Coombe Down, near Bath. She exhibited four works at the R.W.A. 1928-1932, all views of Zanzibar, including 'An Arab Doorway', and 'In the Bazaar'.

**Alan DURMAN (1905-1963)**

Artist who was born in Weymouth, Dorset, and trained as a photographer. He exhibited eight works at the R.W.A. 1934-1949, mostly landscapes, and he also showed work with the Bristol Savages, where he was elected President in 1946. He decorated several buildings in Saltford and Clifton with his murals, and also worked as a poster artist. Alan Durman lived at Saltford and died there on 14th May 1963 at the age of 58.

*Wilfred Dutton*       *(J. Collins and Son)*
*'Too Dear!' (w/c)*

**Wilfred DUTTON (fl. 1934)**

Illustrator and commercial artist who was active in the mid 1930s but does not appear to have exhibited. He had a competent technique and his style suggests that the work may have been used for postcards or story illustration.

**Miss Rachel M.. DYER (exh. 1924)**

Watercolour landscape painter who lived in Hampstead, London, and exhibited at the Society of Women Artists in 1924. Her subjects included town scenes in Northern France, and she signed her work with initials in a monogram (see index).

*W. H. Dyer*     *'Fingle Bridge, Dartmoor' (w/c)*     *(J. Collins and Son)*

### William Henry DYER (fl.c. 1890-1930)

Painter in watercolour and sometimes oil, of Devon coastal and moorland scenes. He lived for most of his life in Babbacombe, Devon, and his brother Charles Dyer was an amateur artist. William Dyer does not appear to have exhibited regularly but he did show a view of Torbay at an exhibition of West Country artists at the Graves Gallery, London, around 1900. His work is often found in the West Country so presumably he found a market for it locally.     He

travelled widely and visited Switzerland, Italy, India and Egypt where he did some sketches of the tombs. William Dyer also had his work published as postcards by J. Salmon of Sevenoaks. These were mostly West Country views, particularly Dartmoor scenes, and date from the 1920s.

### Miss Beatrice DYKE (exh. 1900)

Artist who lived at Easton, Bristol, and exhibited a landscape, 'The Old Mill at Stapleton', in the Professionals Section at the R.W.A. in 1900.

### Fred DYMOND (1902-1981)

Painter in watercolour and sometimes oil of landscapes and cottages who was born at Parr, Cornwall, in December 1902. He lived in London, Torquay, St Ives and finally Clovelly, where he died on 18th December 1981. He signed his work 'DYMOND', in capitals, without an initial.

### R.. J.. D.. DYMOND (exh. 1930-1947)

Commercial artist, designer, pastel and watercolour painter who lived at Redland, Bristol, and exhibited nine works at the R.W.A. 1930-1947. The subjects were mostly studies of buildings and churches in Bristol.

# E

### Sir William EAMES (1821-1910)

Painter of marines and landscapes in watercolour. William Eames was brought up and educated in County Cork, Ireland. In 1844 he entered the Royal Navy as an engineer, by 1870 he was Chief Inspector of Machinery and from 1869 to 1881 was Chief Engineer to Chatham Dockyard. William Eames invented a ventilation system adopted by all Navy ships in the 1870s. He served in the Crimean War in 1855 and while there painted a number of landscapes and marines. A watercolour of Sebastopol is in the National Maritime Museum Collection, Greenwich.

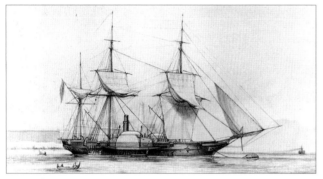

W. Eames                    'Paddle Tug in Valetta Harbour''

### Mrs. Kate EARL (exh. 1912)

Painter in watercolour of flowers who exhibited a work at the Worthing Art Gallery Summer Exhibition in 1912.

### M.. Peploe EARLE B.W.S. (exh. 1924-1928)

Landscape painter who exhibited two works at the B.W.S. Exhibition at Cheltenham in 1924. She also showed two West Country views at the B.W.S. Preston Exhibition in 1928.

### Edwin EARP (fl. 1900s)

The most prolific of the Earp family who painted coastal, river and lake scenes. He does not appear to have exhibited but may also be the same artist who paints under the name of L.. Lewis (q.v.)

### Miss E.. M.. EARP (fl. 1906-1922)

Watercolour painter and art teacher who lived at York Villas, Brighton, and was related to the better known artist Henry Earp. She exhibited at the Royal Amateur Art Society Exhibition at Hove in 1906.

### Miss M.. EARP (exh. 1906)

Another member of the Brighton family of artists who showed a watercolour of Lewes Castle at the Royal Amateur Society Exhibition in 1906.

### W.. A.. EARP (fl.c. 1880-1900)

This member of the Earp family painted mostly coastal scenes in the Brighton area. Many of his watercolours are studies of the old Chain Pier.

W. H. Earp                    'Fishing off the Beach' (w/c)

### W.. H.. EARP (fl. 1900s)

Painter in watercolour of landscapes, loch and coastal scenes who was one of the Brighton family of artists. The pictures were often painted in pairs in a long landscape or tall 'portrait' format. Works by this prolific artist are frequently found in the South of England.

### H.. EAST (fl.c. 1890-1920)

Painter in oil of landscapes and rural scenes who was active around the turn of the century. This prolific artist did not exhibit but the work is often seen on the market and good examples command high prices. The subjects of the pictures include river scenes in North Wales such as 'On the Llugwy' and 'Church Pool, Bettws-Y-Coed' and some rural landscapes such as 'Near Gomshall' and 'Driving Sheep'. The style of the work is similar to that of Daniel Sherrin (q.v.).

### W.. ECCLES (fl. 1941)

Painter in watercolour of landscapes and rural scenes who was working in the early 1940s. The work is of good quality and includes some haymaking scenes.

### Philip L.. EDEN B.W.S. (exh. 1928)

Watercolour landscape painter who was a member of the B.W.S. and exhibited at their Autumn Exhibition at Preston in 1928. He showed two pictures, an architectural study and a moonlight scene.

## Francis John Harris EDGCOMBE (1849-1922)

Painter in oil of landscapes, rivers and coastal scenes who was born at Gosport, Hants, on 27th January 1849. He first trained as a domestic servant but once his artistic talent was recognised he was given a formal art training and took to painting full time. He lived in Plymouth for many years and had a studio there where he taught painting to supplement his income. His landscapes were often coastal or village scenes in Devon and his pleasing style and popular subject matter have made the work collectable. The oil paintings are simply signed F.H.E. and with a date.

## Roland W.. EDMONDS (exh. 1900-1901)

Landscape painter who lived at Heavitree near Exeter, Devon, and exhibited at the R.W.A. in 1900 and 1901. The subjects were 'A Cottage, Countess Weir, Exeter' and 'A Cottage at St Petrock Minor, Cornwall'.

## Mrs. Elsie G.. ELDRIDGE A.C.T. (exh. 1923-1948)

Painter in oil and watercolour who lived at Stowmarket and Eye in Suffolk and was a member of the Ipswich Art Club. She exhibited a total of 28 works at their exhibitions 1923-1948, mostly landscapes, still life and animal studies. The titles included 'Roses' and 'Feeding Time' (both oils, 1923), and 'Eye Church Tower' and 'Dutch Barge, Rotterdam' (both 1937).

## R.. Granville ELIOT (fl. 1890s-1920s)

Oil painter of genre and figure subjects who lived at Slinfold, near Horsham, Sussex. He exhibited once at the Royal Academy in 1891 and at the Conduit Street Galleries in 1897, otherwise most of his work was shown locally. 'Picking Summer Flowers' and 'Washing Day' are typical titles, the latter being painted at Tintagel, in Cornwall.

*James Elliott*                    *'Sheep on the Clifftop' (w/c)*

## James ELLIOTT (fl.c. 1880-1920)

Landscape painter in watercolour, pen and ink illustrator and postcard artist who lived at Newquay, Cornwall. James Elliott illustrated J C Oliver's 'Illustrated Guide to Newquay' in 1884 with 15 pen and ink studies of local views. He had his watercolours reproduced as postcards, depicting views in the Newquay area, and also gave sketching lessons. James Elliott signed his work 'Elliott – Newquay', probably to differentiate himself from the better known Manchester artist of the same name who was exhibiting at the Royal Academy and elsewhere from the 1880s.

## Maj. P.. W.. ELLIOTT (exh. 1930)

Painter who exhibited at the Army Officers Art Society from 1930.

*Gordon Ellis*          *'S.S. American Veteran, Westbound, North Atlantic, Force 10' (oil)*

## Gordon ELLIS (1920-1978)

Marine painter in oil. Gordon Ellis was born in Liverpool on 17th July 1920. As a boy he was always fascinated with the sea and spent many hours wandering around the docks and watching the ships. Gordon Ellis was educated at the Merchant Taylors School, where he received art training from Claude Fisher, and at the age of 17 had paintings of a sailing ship reproduced in colour in The Tatler. After leaving school he worked briefly for the Liverpool Printing Company before joining John Brown's shipyard at Clydebank, where he worked for nearly 12 years as a naval architect. In his spare time he painted marines for shipowners but it was not until 1948 that Gordon Ellis took up painting professionally and the family moved to Lowick in Northumberland.

Gordon Ellis received commissions from shipowners and companies in America, Canada and throughout Europe. He had a one-man exhibition of his work in Guernsey, mostly of local subjects, and also one at the Boydell Gallery, Liverpool in 1968. Apart from marines, Gordon Ellis painted landscapes, children and horses.

Because so much of his work was commissioned and many of these from abroad his pictures are seldom seen on the market. However, the fine quality of the painting and the popular subject matter would make them collectable.

Gordon Ellis died at the age of 58 in 1978.

## Miss H.. G.. Venn ELLIS (exh. 1928-1938)

Landscape artist who lived at Woodbridge, Suffolk, and was a member of the Ipswich Art Club. She exhibited a total of 19 works 1928-1938, including views in Sussex and Cornwall.

*John Ellis    'Clovelly' (w/c)    (J. Collins and Son)*

## John ELLIS (1854-1919)

Painter in watercolour, and sometimes pastel, of landscapes, street scenes and portraits. John Ellis was born in Peterborough, Nottingham, in 1854 and studied at the Nottingham School of Art. He first visited Clovelly, Devon, in the 1870s and he married a local girl there in 1900, setting up a studio at the White Cottage. Many of his watercolours were views of Clovelly High Street which he sold to visitors but he also painted some portraits, mostly of his family. He was not a frequent exhibitor, but did show one work at the Royal Society of British Artists, London, in 1884. He signed his work J Ellis with the J and E monogrammed and followed by the date.

## Ernest John ELSON (1901-1959)

Watercolour and pastel artist and art teacher who was born in Birmingham in 1901. He studied art locally and then as a young man went to live in Canada for 12 years. Later, John Elson returned to Birmingham and worked as an engineer until he emigrated to New Zealand in 1949. He settled in

Napier and taught art there, as well as in Hastings. He was a member of the Hawkes Bay and East Coast Art Society from 1952. John Elson died in New Zealand on 28th February 1959 at the age of 57. He sometimes signed his work with a monogram (see index).

## Ambrose ELTON (exh. 1913-1918)

Landscape painter in oil who lived at Bradford-on-Avon and exhibited 10 works at the R.W.A. 1913-1918. The titles included – 'Doone Country', 'Pippet Street, Bradford-on-Avon' and 'Harvest in the Auvergne' (all 1917).

## Maj.-Gen. Henry Strachan ELTON (1841-1934)

Watercolour landscape and bird painter who exhibited 14 pictures at the Army Officers Art Society 1928-1930. The subjects were mostly landscape views in Southern India and Burma and bird studies such as 'Pink Headed Duck, Orissa' (1930). He lived in London and later at Sidmouth, Devon.

## A.. EMENY (exh. 1920-1924)

Landscape painter in oil and watercolour who lived in Ipswich, and was a member of the Ipswich Art Club, exhibiting at least 12 works 1920-1924. The subjects were mostly local views, such as 'Martlesham Creek' and 'On the Orwell, Pin Mill' and also some foreign views 'Chanak Harbour, Asia Minor' (1924). J. Emeny (q.v.), exhibited from the same address.

## J.. EMENY (exh. 1920-1925)

Landscape painter in oil who lived in Ipswich and was a member of the Ipswich Art Club, exhibiting at least 17 works 1920-1925. The subjects were mostly local views – 'The Banks of the Orwell' and 'Cornfield near Hadleigh' (1925) were typical titles. A. Enemy (q.v.) exhibited from the same address.

## Bertha Lillie ENDACOTT (1885-1952)

Painter in watercolour and postcard artist of Devon views. She was born Lillie Haydon in Exeter in 1885 and married the artist Sidney Endacott (q.v.) in 1903. Her husband taught her to paint and after his death, Worths Art Gallery in Exeter published a series of her work as postcards. About 16 postcards, all views of Clovelly, were published which were printed in half tone and hand tinted. Lillie Endacott died on 22nd February 1952 and was buried in Exeter Cemetery beside her husband, in a grave adorned with an artist's palette.

*S. Endacott*          *'New Inn, Clovelly' (w/c)*

## Sidney ENDACOTT (1873-1918)

Painter in oil and watercolour of portraits and landscapes, postcard artist, sculptor and wood carver. Sidney Endacott was born on 14th June 1873 at Ashburton in Devon, the fifth of seven sons. He attended Ashburton Grammar School and gained a scholarship to Blundells School in 1885. In 1893 Sidney Endacott went to Kansas, U.S.A., where he stayed for a year and completed an extensive wood carving commission for a wealthy patron. On his return to Exeter he worked as a sculptor, carver and stained glass artist for J Wippell & Co. In 1903 Sidney Endacott married Bertha Lillie Haydon (q.v.) and for a while worked as a teacher at the Exeter School of Art before taking up painting full time. Most of his work was sold through Worths Art Gallery in Exeter who also published over 140 postcards of the paintings. These cards, in half tone and then hand tinted, were mostly local views in Exeter and some Devon villages.

During the Great War, Sidney Endacott put his artistic talents to good use by making technical drawings of military vehicle parts for operating manuals. After several years of poor health, Sidney Endacott died on 3rd November 1918.

Sidney Endacott's work is not often seen on the market but the quality and the popular subject matter would make it collectable.

## Miss Daphne K.. ENGLAND (exh. 1912)

A member of the Winchester Art Club who exhibited four watercolours at their Annual Exhibition in 1912. The subjects were landscapes – two views at Seaton, Devon, and two at Dinant in France.

*H. English*          *'Evening on the Stour' (w/c)*

## H.. ENGLISH (fl.c. 1890-1920)

Painter in watercolour of rural landscapes, river and coastal views. The subjects include South of England and West Country scenes and are often inscribed with the location on the reverse. The work is of good quality but the artist does not seem to have exhibited.

## E.. A.. R.. ENNION (exh. 1937)

Painter in watercolour of birds who had a one-man exhibition at the Greatorex Gallery, London, in April 1937 of 'Gamebirds, Ducks and Various'. The exhibition consisted of 41 watercolours and included birds of the Fenlands, Scotland and Iceland.

## F.. EVANS (fl. 1900s)

Painter in watercolour and occasionally oil of garden scenes and landscapes. The pictures are competently painted but are not inscribed or dated. The artist does not seem to have exhibited.

## Vivien EVANS (fl. 1905-1924)

Animal painter in oil who specialised in cat paintings and some portraits of dogs. 'A Tabby on the Wall', 'The Green China Cat' and 'The Marmalade Cat' are typical titles and these pictures were often dated. The artist's clear and precise style may suggest that he worked as an illustrator.

## Dorothy EVERARD (exh. 1935-1937)

Painter of portraits in watercolour who exhibited two works at the St Ives Society of Artists Summer Exhibition in 1935 and also a portrait of 'Jimmie Limpot' at the Winter Exhibition in 1937.

*Edward Eyres    'St Columb, Cornwall' (pen and ink)*

## Edward EYRES (fl. 1897-1920s)

Artist and illustrator in pen, pencil and watercolour. The work is finely executed and it is curious that this artist does not appear to have exhibited. The subjects include Cornish harbours and street scenes and also some Norfolk views.

## J.. W.. EYTON (fl.c. 1890-1910)

Painter in watercolour of marines who was working at the turn of the century. This competent artist does not appear to have exhibited. The subjects are often fishing boats and known examples include 'Trawlers off the Eddystone Lighthouse' – 1897.

# F

**Miss Ena H.. FABIAN (exh. 1920-1928)**

Landscape artist who lived at Redland, Bristol, and exhibited three works at the R.W.A. 1920-1928. The titles were – 'Pouty', 'Castle of Chillon' and 'Dungeon Keep, Berkeley Castle'. She was the daughter of the artist Ernest Fabian (q.v.).

**Ernest Fuller FABIAN** R.W.A. **(1867-1931)**

Art teacher, portrait painter and modeller who lived at Durdham Down, Bristol, and exhibited six works at the R.W.A. 1895-1921, mostly portraits, head studies and terracottas. Ernest Fabian was a teacher by profession and taught modelling at the Municipal School of Art, Bristol, for 37 years. He was also a member of the Bristol Savages where he exhibited seven works 1907-1915 and was later made a life member. Born in Winchester, Hants, in 1867, he lived most of his life in Bristol, and died there after a long illness in April 1931.

**Frank R.. FAINT (exh. 1950)**

Oil painter who lived at Plymouth, and exhibited four works at the Plymouth Art Society in 1950. The subjects were landscapes and a flower still life.

**Miss Mary FAIRCLOUGH (exh. 1938-1948)**

Portrait, landscape, lino-cut artist and potter who lived at Keynsham, Bristol, and exhibited at the R.W.A. in 1938 and 1948. The subjects were 'Pine Trees' and a portrait.

**F.. A.. FAIRLIE (fl. 1930s)**

Painter in gouache and tempera of landscapes, who has a very similar style and technique to Cecil Arthur Hunt. He lived at Beldorny, Nairn, Scotland and was probably working in the 1930s.

**John T.. FAIRS (fl. 1930)**

Artist who lived at Kew, London, and was working around 1930.

**Mrs. Mary L.. FANING (exh. 1936-1945)**

Watercolour landscape painter who lived at Bildeston, Suffolk, and was a member of the Ipswich Art Club. She exhibited five works 1936-1945 and the titles included 'The Courtyard, Swan Inn, Lavenham' (1936) and 'Misty Morning, Lake Como' (1938).

A. C. Fare        'The Ship Inn, Porlock' (w/c)        (J Collins and Son)

**Arthur Charles FARE** R.W.A. **(1876-1958)**

Painter in watercolour of landscapes and architectural subjects who was born in Bath in 1876. Arthur Fare was a member and regular exhibitor at the R.W.A., showing 106 works 1922-1956. He was also a member of the Bristol Savages and their President in 1927. Arthur Fare exhibited over 200 works with the Bristol Savages 1922-1958. In addition to West Country village and harbour scenes, he painted in France, Italy and Spain. Work by Arthur Fare is in the Bristol City Art Gallery.

C. W. Farley                'Canteen Counter' (oil)

**Charles W.. FARLEY (fl. 1935-1960s)**

Painter in oil of landscapes and portraits who lived at Richmond, London, later East Molesey and then Cheltenham in the 1960s. He exhibited in London from 1935, including two portraits at the Royal Academy 1938-1943 and after the war he was a member of the Cheltenham Arts Society. Work by him was reproduced in The Artist magazine.

## John FARQUHARSON (1865-1931)

Painter in watercolour of landscapes and coastal scenes. The only son of the artist David Farquharson, John was educated at Watson College, Edinburgh, and then at the Edinburgh School of Art. He had an active military career serving in the Sudan, in South Africa in the Boer War and then in The Great War in France. While serving under General Kitchener in the Sudan he had a series of drawings published in The Graphic. In the early 1900s John Farquharson moved to Sennen, near Penzance in Cornwall, having lived for a time in London. He exhibited at the Royal Scottish Academy regularly in the 1890s but does not appear to have shown work in London. John Farquharson's watercolour landscapes are of fine quality and his work has not yet received the true recognition that it deserves.

## R.. N.. FARRER (exh. 1919)

Watercolour painter of marines who lived in Huddersfield and exhibited four works at the Yorkshire Union of Artists Exhibition in 1919. The titles included 'Rough Sea off Whitby' and 'French Coast near Boulogne'.

## Jack Merville FAULKS (born 1899)

Illustrator and commercial artist. Born at Edmonton, London in 1899, Jack Faulks was educated at Mercers College where at an early age he showed a talent for art. On leaving school he joined the Royal Naval Air Service and qualified as a pilot, seeing active service in the Mediterranean. After the First World War Jack Faulks studied art at a Polytechnic where he was taught by H G Theaker and Harry Watson.

At the age of 22 he received his first commission for the 'Penny Pictorial' to which he was to contribute many further works. In the 1940s his work was much in demand with commissions from the 'Illustrated London News', 'Womans Illustrated' and 'Wife and Home' as well as designs for book jackets. An article on his work appeared in The Artist magazine in May 1945.

## Miss C.. M.. FEILDEN (exh. 1900-1907)

Watercolour artist who lived at Swaffham, Norfolk, and was a member of the Norwich Art Circle. She exhibited a total of 11 works 1900-1907 mostly portraits, flowers and an Italian garden scene.

## Gwendoline FELLOWES B.W.S. (exh. 1928)

Watercolour landscape painter who was a member of the B.W.S. and exhibited a view of St Ives, Cornwall, at the B.W.S. Preston Exhibition in 1928.

R. Fenson          'A Country Lane' (oil)          (Philip Parker)

## R.. FENSON (fl. 1898-1911)

Painter in oil of landscapes and rural scenes. This artist is variously catalogued as Robin or Robert Fenson but usually signed just R Fenson, in red, often with a date. This was a pseudonym for Henry Maidment (q.v.) and he also sometimes signed A Wynne (q.v.). Typical titles include 'On a Country Lane' and 'A Summer Landscape' and dated examples have been seen spanning from 1898 until 1911. The quality of the work and the decorative subject matter have made the paintings increasingly collected in recent years.

## Arthur FERRIER (born 1891, fl. 1920-1936)

Cartoonist, illustrator and figure painter who was born in Scotland in 1891. After the First World War, he came to London and worked as a freelance illustrator for magazines and national newspapers. Arthur Ferrier also worked in pastel, drawing portraits and figure subjects. He wrote and illustrated a series of articles on painting technique for The Artist magazine in 1935 and 1936.

H. Fidler          'Feeding the Bees' (oil)

## Harry FIDLER (1856-1935)

Painter in oil, and sometimes watercolour, of rural life and farming subjects. He was born on 22nd January 1856, the ninth of 10 children, the son of William Fidler, a Yeoman farmer. Much of his early life was spent helping his elder brother James to manage the family farm at Teffont Magna, Wilts. Harry Fidler leased an old Methodist Chapel in Teffont as a studio which he used until about 1906. In the 1890s he studied at the Herkomer School in Bushey, and it was probably there that he met Laura Clunas (1868-1936), later to become his wife. Harry Fidler exhibited 31 works at the Royal Academy 1891-1935 and also showed work at the Paris Salon, R.B.A., R.O.I. and the New English Art Club. In 1930 a one-man show was held of his work at the Grundy Art Gallery, Blackpool, which still retains some of his paintings. Many of his subjects were farming scenes often featuring heavy horses. Typical titles included 'Going to the Harvest Field', 'The First Furrow', 'The Apple Cart' and 'New Corn from Old Fields'. Other subjects featured bees - 'A Swarm in June' and chickens - 'The Poultry Run'. Harry Fidler died on 10th May 1935 at Stoke by Andover, aged 79. A Memorial Exhibition was held of both of his and Laura's work at the Arlington Gallery, London, in 1936. His early work – black and white studies, rustic portraits and farming scenes – are usually signed with his 'Fid' monogram (see index), whereas the later more impressionistic pictures are usually signed 'H Fidler'. (Illus. p.50).

## Arthur FIELD (exh. 1883-1895)

Landscape painter in watercolour who lived at Ipswich and was a member of the Ipswich Art Club. He was a regular exhibitor showing 36 works 1883-1895. Most of the subjects were local views, typical titles being 'Boathouse on the Stour', 'Sproughton' (1885) and 'Old Maltsters Arms, Ipswich' and 'Easton, Suffolk' (1886).

## Miss Violet FIELD (exh. 1935-1937)

Watercolour landscape and marine painter who lived at Felixstowe, Suffolk and was a member of the Ipswich Art Club. She exhibited nine works 1935-1937, including a view of 'Rye, Sussex' and a French harbour scene.

## Sidney FILMORE (fl. 1913)

Watercolour painter of landscapes, including some French views. This competent artist does not seem to have exhibited.

## Bessie FINCH (fl. 1903)

Student of the Lambeth School of Art who showed designs in pen and ink at the National Competition for Schools of Art in 1903. Her work was reproduced in The Studio magazine.

*W. H. Finch      'At Fordingbridge, Hants' (w/c)      (J. Collins and Son)*

## W.. H.. FINCH (fl.c. 1900-1930)

Watercolour painter of village scenes and rural landscapes. The pictures are usually inscribed on the reverse and the subjects are often Sussex villages. The colour and style of painting is similar to George Whyatt of whom he may have been a pupil or admirer.

*W. C. Fisher      'A Chat in the Cornfield' (oil)*

## W.. C.. FISHER (fl.c. 1880-1910)

Painter in oil and watercolour of landscapes, rivers and rural scenes. The artist does not appear to have exhibited, although the work is quite competent and the appealing subject matter would make the pictures collectable. The work is sometimes signed with initials and often painted in oil on paper.

*Fish-hawk*        *'The Crossbill' (w/c)*

## 'FISH-HAWK'

This was the pseudonym adopted by the talented bird artist David Knightly Wolfe Murray (q.v.).

## George Green FISKE (1847-1932)

Landscape painter in oil who lived at Hintlesham and Needham Market, Suffolk, and was an early member of the Ipswich Art Club. He was a regular exhibitor showing at least 88 works 1876-1929. Most of the subjects were local landscape views and the titles included 'Cromer' and 'The Street, Hintlesham' (1880) and 'Spring Farm, Coddenham' (1890). The Ipswich Museum has an oil by George Fiske of 'Willie Lott's Cottage'.

## W.. G.. FISKE (exh. 1885-1895)

Watercolour landscape painter who lived at Bildeston, Suffolk, and was a member of the Ipswich Art Club. He exhibited 17 works 1885-1895, mostly portraits and figure studies. The titles included 'The Village Blacksmith' (oil, 1886) , 'In Distress' and 'The Ostrich' (both oils, 1887) and 'Thinking' (watercolour, 1890).

## Miss Kathleen M.. FISON (exh. 1930-1934)

Watercolour landscape and figure painter who lived at Felixstowe, Suffolk, and was a member of the Ipswich Art Club. She exhibited a total of 12 works 1930-1934. The subjects included figure studies, buildings and landscapes in Italy and Switzerland.

## F.. W.. FITCH (fl. 1900s)

Painter in watercolour of rural scenes, cottages, and hunting subjects who was active at the turn of the century. The artist painted in a slightly primitive manner but the pictures have considerable charm.

## Edward Hubert FITCHEW (1851-1934)

Illustrator, of books and magazines in black and white and watercolour, and art editor. Edward Fitchew was born in Brighton in 1851. He moved to London to study art and then joined the staff of the recently founded Black and White magazine. After working for Cassells, Edward Fitchew joined Harmsworth Magazine as the art editor and was responsible for editing 'Sixty Years a Queen' in 1897. Much of his illustration work prior to 1900 was in monochrome but he was equally competent working in colour and produced illustrations for A & C Black including six plates for 'Peeps at Korea' in 1910.

His daughter, Dorothy Fitchew, became an artist and illustrator of some distinction. Edward Fitchew lived in Bromley, Kent, in his later years and died there on 6th November 1934.

## Miss Evangeline Esther May FITCHEW A.R.W.A. (born 1887, exh. 1920-1950)

Artist who was born in Brighton in 1887 and moved to Bristol in the 1920s where she became art mistress at Redland High School. She was an associate member of the R.W.A. and exhibited nine works 1920-1950. The subjects were figures in watercolour and an etching.

## V.. FITZGERALD (exh. 1938)

Aviation artist and portrait painter who exhibited seven works at the Air Force Artists Association Annual Exhibition in December 1938.

**Cyril D.. FITZROY (1861-1939)**

Watercolour painter of architectural subjects and country houses and, in particular, studies of St Paul's Cathedral. Cyril Fitzroy was Registrar of the Royal College of Art and exhibited four works at the Royal Academy. He died in Chelsea on 9th July 1939.

**Mrs. Winifred J.. FLEMING A.R.W.A.**
**(exh. 1929-1947)**

Painter of flowers and still life who lived in Bristol. She was an associate member of the R.W.A. and a regular exhibitor showing a total of 36 flower paintings 1929-1947.

**Ernest W.. P.. FLEXEN (exh. 1918-1925)**

Watercolour landscape painter who lived in Bath and later at Stratton, Glos. He exhibited eight works at the R.W.A. 1918-1923 which included wartime views in France and some local scenes. In 1923 Ernest Flexen moved to Cirencester and joined the Cheltenham Group of Artists. He exhibited 12 watercolours at Cheltenham in 1924 and nine works in 1925, mostly local views. Ernest Flexen also designed and exhibited jewellery.

**Mrs. Ernest FLEXEN (exh. 1924)**

Landscape painter in watercolour. She was the wife of Ernest Flexen (q.v.) and exhibited with the Cheltenham Group of Artists in 1924 – a watercolour landscape and a still life.

**Miss Elizabeth Gill FLIGHT (exh. 1908-1925)**

Landscape painter in oil and watercolour who lived in Bristol. She was a regular exhibitor at the R.W.A., showing over 20 works 1908-1925. The subjects included local views, Devon and Cornwall landscapes and two miniatures of Westminster. She was also a member of the Royal Drawing Society.

**H.. FLORANCE (exh. 1950)**

Painter in watercolour who lived at Plympton, Devon, and exhibited two works at the Plymouth Art Society Exhibition in 1950.

*Alfred Flowers*          'Full Sail'          (Robert White)

**Alfred FLOWERS (fl. 1907-1924)**

Painter in watercolour and oil of marines who lived in Falmouth, Cornwall, and was working in the 1920s. This good quality artist does not appear to have exhibited but his paintings of clipper ships are seen on the market and have become collectable.

**Donald Henry FLOYD (1892-1965)**

Painter in oil of landscapes and rural scenes. Donald Floyd was born in Plymouth and studied for five years at the Plymouth School of Art. He first exhibited in 1913 and was preparing for a solo exhibition in Bond Street the following year when the War interrupted his plans. During the First World War, he joined the Devonshire Regiment and he served in Palestine and the Middle East. Donald Floyd was a regular exhibitor at the Royal Academy showing a total of 13 works 1920-1950.

In the late 1940s, he went to Ceylon where he was commissioned by the Government to paint pictures of the island. As a result of illness in the early 1950s, Donald Floyd lost the use of his right arm but he continued to work, teaching himself to paint with his left hand. He moved to Tintern, Mon., in 1940 and lived there until his death at the age of 73 in 1965.

**Mrs. E.. FLOYD (exh. 1950)**

Oil portrait painter who lived in Plymouth and exhibited two portraits at the Plymouth Art Society Exhibition in 1950.

**J.. F.. M.. FLOYD (exh. 1923-1928)**

Watercolour landscape and still life painter who lived in Bath and exhibited 10 works at the R.W.A. 1923-1928. The subjects were mostly flower gardens and still life and also some views of Scotland and Sussex.

**John FOLLETT (exh. c.1910)**

Watercolour landscape painter who had a joint exhibition at the Doré Gallery, London, with Agnes Rupert Jones in about 1910. John Follett showed 38 watercolours, all landscapes, and the subjects included views on the Thames and in Scotland, France, Tangiers and India.

**Leonard L.. FOOTE (exh. 1923-1926)**

Artist who lived at Newport, Mon., and exhibited four works at the R.W.A. 1923-1926. The titles included 'The Pool of London' (1923) and 'Down with the Tide' (1926).

*Leyton Forbes*                    *(Images in Watercolour)*
'Near Trewerry, Cornwall' (w/c)

## Leyton FORBES (fl. 1900-1920s)

Painter in watercolour of cottage scenes and gardens. This artist has become increasingly popular over the last few years, partly due to the appeal of his subject matter. An old label on one of his pictures states that he was a 'Silver Medallist at the Walker Art Gallery, Liverpool' and that his pictures have been 'Purchased by HM the Queen'. He lived and worked in the West Country and many of his subjects were Cornish cottages.

## Mrs. M.. FORESTER (exh. 1927-1928)

Artist who lived in Bristol and exhibited at the R.W.A. in 1927 and 1928. The works were entitled 'Monte Legnone' and 'Mind the Steps'.

## Robert FORMAN (fl. 1946)

Artist in pen and ink who wrote and illustrated a series of articles in The Artist magazine in 1946 entitled 'Drawing Architectural Subjects'.

## Miss C.. M.. FORSTER (exh. 1901)

Artist who lived at Wokingham and was a member of the Berkshire Art Society. She exhibited two works at their 1901 Exhibition in Reading, both rural landscapes.

## Harold FORSTER (born 1895)

Illustrator and commercial artist. Harold Forster was born in London in 1895 and educated at Watford Grammar School before going to the Watford School of Art. There he became a pupil of Fred Taylor who realised Harold Forster's talent and sent him to the Birbeck School of Art in London. During the First World War he joined the Yeomanry and saw active service in Gallipoli, Syria and Palestine. He produced a large number of war sketches at this time. In the 1920s and 1930s Harold Forster returned to his magazine illustration, in particular work for Woman's Journal and The Strand Magazine. His work was featured in The Artist magazine in 1934.

## Capt. F.. C.. W.. FOSBERY (exh. 1928)

Artist who was a member of the Army Officers Art Society and exhibited six pictures in 1928.

## Walter C.. FOSTER A.R.C.A. (fl. 1919-1930)

Watercolour landscape painter and art teacher who lived at Bingley, Yorks, and exhibited two works at the Bradford Local Artists Exhibition in 1919. The titles were 'A Winter Afternoon' and 'October Morning'. Walter Foster was the Headmaster of the Bingley School of Art in 1920 and then Headmaster of the Shipley School of Art from about 1925 to 1930.

## Miss M.. FOWELL (exh. 1895-1906)

Landscape painter in oil and watercolour who lived at Birkenhead, Cheshire, and was a member of the Ipswich Art Club. She was a regular exhibitor showing 53 works 1895-1906. Most of the subjects were local views but she also painted in Switzerland. The titles included 'Pin Mill' and 'Erwarton Hall' (both oils, 1901) and 'Brienz Lake, Switzerland' and 'Jungfrau from Interlaken' (watercolours, 1906).

*Alice Fowler*          'The Well at Baveno' (w/c)

## Miss Alice Maud Levine FOWLER (1861-1949)

Painter in watercolour of landscapes, buildings and rural scenes. This talented artist did not exhibit except for a joint exhibition with Frank Fowler at Walkers Gallery, London, in October 1903 entitled 'Watercolours at Home and Abroad'. It consisted of 57 of her watercolours, mostly sketches from the English home counties, but also of Varenna and Menaggio in Italy and some landscapes of Ceylon. Alice Fowler lived at Brimpton, Berks, and died at the age of 88 on 11th November 1949.

## Henry Charles FOX R.B.A. (1855-1929)

Henry Charles Fox was born in London in 1855. In 1880, he had his first picture accepted at the Royal Academy and then was to show another 20 works there up until 1913. By this time he was a well established artist and did not exhibit any more although he continued to paint and sell his work locally to within a couple of years of his death. H C Fox is best known for his rural landscapes in watercolour but he also painted in oil and had a series of large etchings published by Gladwell Brothers, London, in the 1880s. Gladwells also held an exhibition of his work entitled 'Rural London – Sketches and Drawings' in 1885. By the 1920s Henry Charles Fox had moved to Billingshurst in Sussex and he died at Horsham on the 30th April 1929.

## John T.. FOXELL (exh. 1924-1925)

Watercolour landscape painter who lived at Felixstowe, Suffolk, and was a member of the Ipswich Art Club. He exhibited a total of 12 works 1924-1925. Most of the subjects were local views, including 'Middle Bridge, Dedham', 'On the Stour, Dedham' and 'Christchurch Park, Ipswich' (1925).

## Miss Mabel FOXWELL (exh. 1901-1911)

A landscape painter in oil and watercolour who lived in Norwich and exhibited with the Norwich Art Circle. She showed 17 works 1901-1911, mostly local landscape views.

## Thomas Edward FRANCIS (fl. 1900s)

London landscape painter in oil and watercolour who exhibited mostly in London in the first decade of this century. The artist appears to have painted under a number of pseudonyms, particularly 'Pierre Le Boeuff' (q.v.), 'Arthur Drew' (q.v.) and 'Andrea Vasari' (q.v.).

## Mary FRANK (1806-1906)

Miniature painter who was the sister of W A Frank (q.v.).

## William Arnee FRANK (1808-1897)

Although essentially an artist of the first half of the 19th century, W A Frank was active into his eighties and was still showing work at the R.W.A. in 1891. Little is known about his early life although he did teach drawing in Clifton and published a series of lithographs of local Bristol views in 1831. His watercolour landscapes are well painted usually in strong colours which give them a distinctive appearance. The subjects are mostly views around Bristol, the Wye Valley and North Wales.

## Lt.-Col. Cecil FRASER (1885-1951)

Watercolour landscape painter who lived in London and exhibited with the Army Officers Art Society 1928-1934. He showed a total of 25 works including views in Egypt and some Scottish landscapes.

*F. G. Fraser*                    *'A Bend in the River'* (w/c)

## Francis Gordon FRASER (exh. 1907)

F G Fraser was probably the most prolific, yet least recorded, member of the famous Huntingdonshire family of landscape painters. It appears likely that he was the second son of Robert Winchester Fraser born on 6th November 1879. He painted river landscapes in the typical Fraser style in watercolour but the quality of his work is variable and this has affected its value. F G Fraser did not exhibit in London but did show two works at the Devon and Exeter Annual Exhibition at Elands Art Gallery, Exeter, in 1907. The subjects were typical river scenes – 'The Thames near Oxford' and 'On the Mole'.

## James D.. FRASER (exh. 1881-1907)

Landscape painter in oil who lived at Ipswich and was a member of the Ipswich Art Club. He was a regular exhibitor showing at least 38 works 1881-1907. The subjects were mostly oil landscapes and the titles included 'Harwich Harbour' (1890), 'Arran from Cumbrae' (1900) and 'Gateway, Carisbrooke Castle' (1902).

*William Freeman*                    *'On the Beach'* (w/c)

**William Edward FREEMAN (1853-1935)**

Landscape painter in watercolour who was born in Camberwell, in 1853. William Edward Freeman studied at the National Art Training School, South Kensington, and on his marriage around 1870 he moved to Surbiton where he opened a shop selling artists materials. He was a member of the Thames Valley Art Club but never made a great effort to sell his work which may explain why this talented artist is not better known. After the First World War the family moved to Teddington where he continued to paint until a few weeks before his death in 1935. William Freeman painted in a bold, impressionistic style and his subjects included beach scenes, Thames views and London streets. (Illus. p.55).

*Fred French*          *'Faithful Companions' (oil)*

**Frederick FRENCH (fl. 1884-1902)**

Oil painter of dogs and cats who lived at Leamington, Warks., and was active from the 1880s until the early 1900s. He does not appear to have exhibited but he is listed in the local trade directories so he probably worked on commissions and sold his pictures locally. Frederick French's animal portraits are well painted and would be collectable but the work is not often seen on the market. He usually signed Fred French and with a date.

**Geoffrey Maurice FRENCH (exh. 1934-1941)**

Landscape painter in watercolour who lived in Felixstowe and was a member of the Ipswich Art Club. He exhibited at least 18 works 1934-1941. The subjects included studies of old buildings in South Wales (1935) and views of Canterbury (1936).

**B.. FRINGES (exh. 1904-1906)**

Etcher, landscape and figure painter who was French by birth but lived and worked in Bristol at the turn of the century. He exhibited 24 works at the Bristol Savages Exhibitions 1904-1906 including etchings – mostly figure subjects and river scenes.

**George Lewis FROST (fl. 1930s)**

Illustrator, particularly of motoring subjects, who worked for the Carlton Studios in London. He wrote and illustrated a series of articles for The Artist magazine entitled 'Automobile Illustration' in 1935 and 1936.

**Edward Ransome FRY (exh. 1919-1938)**

Artist in pencil and chalk of architectural subjects and landscapes who lived in Bury St Edmunds, Suffolk, and was a member of the Ipswich Art Club. He exhibited at least 18 works 1919-1938, mostly pencil and chalk studies of buildings. The titles included 'Windmill, Delft' and 'Lacock, Wilts' (both 1930) and 'Rothenberg' and 'Abbeville' (both 1938).

**Miss Priscilla A.. FRY (exh. 1900-1901)**

Watercolour landscape painter who lived in Bristol and exhibited five works at the R.W.A. 1900-1901. The subjects were views in Norway and the Pyrenees. The titles included 'Morterash Waterfall' and 'Near Flatmark, Norway' (1900) and 'Pyrenees in May' (1901).

**J.. V.. FULLER (exh. 1921)**

Painter of marine subjects who exhibited three works at the First Admiralty Art Club Exhibition in 1921. The titles of the pictures were 'Barges', 'Yachts' and 'Off Greenhythe'.

**Dr. G.. FULLER-ENGLAND (exh. 1912)**

Watercolour painter who was a member of the Winchester Art Society and exhibited three works at the 1912 Exhibition, all Devon coastal scenes.

**Florence Emma Matilda FURNEAUX (1868-1956)**

Florence Furneaux studied at the Crystal Palace School of Art in the 1890s and a few works, mostly figure studies, are known to exist. Later, she painted watercolour landscapes under her married name of Florence Capes (q.v.).

# G

**Horace C.. GAFFRON (fl.c. 1920-1950)**

Illustrator, commercial artist and art teacher. Horace Gaffron was born in Aberdeen and was a student at the Grays School of Art before training as a lithographer at Mugiemoss in Scotland. During the First World War he served with the Gordon Highlanders on the Western Front where he was seriously wounded and lost a leg.

After the War, Horace Gaffron taught art but still managed to contribute drawings to The Daily Graphic and other publications, before moving to a studio in London. From 1927 to 1930 he worked in America and returned as a freelance director of an American agency. Horace Gaffron then took a studio at Lincolns Inn where he worked until the 1950s. He contributed illustrations to many magazines including Ladies Journal and Good Housekeeping and was the subject of a special article in The Artist magazine in 1949.

**Patience GALLOWAY (exh. 1939)**

Etcher and colour woodcut artist who exhibited at the Society of Graver Painters in Colour and was an associate member. A series of articles on colour woodcuts in The Artist magazine featured her work in 1940.

**Edith GARDINER (exh. 1924)**

Watercolour painter who exhibited two pictures at the B.W.S. Annual Exhibition at Cheltenham in 1924. The titles were 'Evening, Bosham' and 'Tidal Mill at Lancieux'.

**Theo Lucifer GARDINI (exh. 1939)**

Landscape painter in oil who exhibited at the Archer Gallery, London, in 1939. A view in South Devon by the artist was illustrated in The Artist magazine.

**G.. GARDNER (fl. 1926)**

A student at the Royal College of Art in 1926, whose work – 'The Railway Station' was reproduced in The Studio that year.

**James GARDNER (fl. 1936)**

A commercial illustrator, who worked for the Carlton Studios. A colour illustration 'The Locomotive Shed' was reproduced in The Artist magazine in 1936.

**Miss N.. GARDNER (exh. 1914)**

Painter who lived at Clifton, Bristol, and exhibited two works at the R.W.A. in 1914.

**Miss Elsie GARRETT (exh. 1895-1896)**

Landscape and portrait painter in oil and watercolour who lived in Ipswich and was a member of the Ipswich Art Club. She exhibited a total of nine works 1895-1896. The subjects included local views such as 'On the Gipping' (1895, watercolour) and 'Willie Lott's House, Flatford' (1896, oil).

**Arthur W.. GARRINGTON (exh. 1887-1900)**

Landscape painter in oil and watercolour who lived in Bristol and exhibited 24 works at the R.W.A. 1887-1900. The subjects included figures, local landscapes and Devon views.

**Brig.-Gen. Alfred Allan GARSTIN (1850-1937)**

Watercolour painter who lived at Guildford, Surrey, and exhibited with the Army Officers Art Society 1928-1933. He showed a total of 26 works mostly local Surrey scenes but also some views in Spain.

**Capt. Charles de Lisle GAUSSEN (1896-1971)**

An officer in the Royal Engineers who exhibited 16 works with the Army Officers Art Society 1928-1933. The subjects included buildings in Exeter and a Copenhagen bridge.

*Arthur W. Gay*   *'Pintails' (w/c)*   *(Michael Webb)*

**Arthur Wilson GAY (1901-1958)**

Watercolour painter of still life, birds and landscapes and, later, portrait and figure painter. He lived in Bristol and exhibited 17 works at the R.W.A. 1925-1949 – mostly portraits and some landscapes. In 1928, he was elected a member of the Bristol Savages and exhibited there for 30 years. Arthur Gay died at Redland, Bristol, in June 1958.

## Lt. Col. Edward Anthony Sydney GELL (born 1875, exh. 1928-1938)

Watercolour painter who lived in Highgate, London, and exhibited with the Army Officers Art Society 1928-1938. He showed a total of 35 works mostly watercolour views in France and Italy.

## Miss Hilda K.. GENGE (exh. 1921-1922)

Portrait and figure painter who lived at Clifton, Bristol, and exhibited at the R.W.A. 1921-1922. The subjects were 'The Orange Seller' and a portrait.

## Miss Stella GENGE (exh. 1913-1922)

Portrait painter who lived at Clifton, Bristol, and exhibited five works at the R.W.A. 1913-1922. The subjects were all portrait studies in oil.

## Harold K.. GEORGE (exh. 1935-1965)

Painter in watercolour and etcher who exhibited at the French Gallery, London, in 1935. The exhibition was of 'Weekend Work' by industrial artists employed by J Walter Thompson Ltd. He showed three watercolours, a landscape of Rye and two views of Allerford, Somerset, and also an etching. Harold George also exhibited an etching at the Royal Academy in 1937. He lived at Wembley, but after the War moved to Berkshire and continued to exhibit at the Royal Academy showing 11 works 1954-1965.

## Miss Ethel GERITY (exh. 1900-1901)

Landscape painter who lived in Bristol and was probably the sister of Miss K M Gerity (q.v.). She exhibited two works at the R.W.A. – 'At Symonds Yat, on the Wye' (1900) and 'Wickham Bridge, Stapleton' (1901).

## Miss K.. M.. GERITY (exh. 1900-1901)

Landscape painter, who lived in Bristol, and was probably the sister of Ethel Gerity (q.v.). She exhibited two works at the R.W.A. – 'At Portishead, Eventide' (1900) and 'Fishponds Church' (1901).

## N.. J.. GIBB (exh. c. 1900)

Marine artist and painter of architectural subjects who held a joint exhibition at the Ryder Gallery, London, c.1900. He showed 40 pictures, mostly Pool of London scenes and studies of London buildings.

## Reginald W.. GICK (fl. 1920s)

Portrait painter in oils. Reginald Gick was a dentist by profession and lived at Beech Street, Liverpool in the 1920s. His portraits were of good quality but he does not appear to have exhibited. The work is usually signed with a monogram (see index) and dated.

## Charles Lovett GILL F.R.I.B.A. (1880-1960)

Painter in watercolour of landscapes. Charles Gill was born at Harberton Ford, Devon, and was educated at Newton College, before attending the Royal Academy Schools in London. He became a distinguished architect, in practice with Professor A E Richardson up until the Second World War and then on his own. Charles Gill was a keen amateur watercolour painter and painted landscapes in France and Spain as well as local views. He lived for many years at Odiham, Hants, and died on 23rd March 1960.

## Edmund Ward GILL (1820-1894)

Painter of landscapes in oil, particularly waterfalls, which gained him the nickname of 'Waterfall Gill'. He was the eldest son of the artist Edmund Ward Gill (1794-1854), and brother to William Ward and George Reynolds Gill (q.v.). Edmund Ward Gill exhibited widely in London and in the provinces. An exhibition of the Gill family was held at the Hereford Public Library in 1888 and also as part of an Exhibition of Deceased Herefordshire Artists at the Museum and Art Gallery in 1928.

*G. R. Gill*        *'The Waterfall' (oil)*

## George Reynold GILL (1827-1904)

Painter of landscapes, waterfalls, town and architectural views, who was born in Hereford the youngest son of Edmund Ward Gill. In 1841 he studied at the School of Design, Somerset House, and subsequently followed the more secure career of teaching and became a Master at the School of Art, Truro. Five works by George R Gill were shown at the Exhibition of Deceased Herefordshire Artists at the Museum and Art Gallery in 1928.

**Marion GILL (fl. 1903)**

Artist who lived at Newcastle-on-Tyne and won first prize for The Studio Pencil Portrait Competition in 1903.

**William GILL (exh. 1879-1890)**

Landscape painter in watercolour who lived at Colchester, Essex, and was a member of the Ipswich Art Club. He exhibited 60 works 1879-1890, mostly local views. The titles included 'Malting Farm, Lexden, Colchester', 'Sleepen Bridge, Colchester' and '. . . Brightlingsea, Essex' (1890).

W. W. Gill    'Tumbling Waters' (oil)    (Sotheby's)

**William Ward GILL (1823-1894)**

Painter in oil of landscapes, town scenes and occasionally still life. William Ward Gill was the second son of Edmund Ward Gill and was born in Bridgnorth on 1st May 1823. He started painting mainly in watercolour but by the early 1840s, following a tour of the Lake District, he concentrated on oil painting. William Gill exhibited in London, including six works at the Royal Academy, and in Liverpool. 10 of his pictures were included in the Exhibition of work by Deceased Herefordshire artists at the Hereford Museum and Art Gallery in 1928. William Ward Gill's work is of good quality and he is probably one of the more underrated members of the family. Often he signs very finely with initials and his work can pass unrecognised in sales as a result.

**Walter GILLIARD (exh. 1925-1928)**

Landscape artist who lived in Bristol and exhibited three works at the R.W.A. – 'A Quiet Nook' (1925), 'Near Keynsham' (1926) and 'A Glimpse of the Avon' (1928). He was the father of Claude Gilliard, the commercial artist, who was born in 1906.

**Marian GLEB (fl. 1944-1950)**

Illustrator of figure subjects and animals who wrote a series of articles in The Artist magazine entitled 'Pencil Drawing'. Her earlier work appears to be signed Marian Kratodrust.

**Miss W.. Doris GOAMAN (exh. 1928-1934)**

Landscape and figure painter who lived at Clifton, Bristol, and exhibited 16 works at the R.W.A. 1928-1934, including views in Brittany and Newlyn, Cornwall. In 1935, she moved to London.

**Miss Amelia GODDARD (exh. c. 1890)**

Painter in oil, watercolour and pastel who lived at Christchurch, Hants, and held a joint exhibition with her sister Eliza at the Doré Gallery, London, in about 1890. The exhibition was entitled 'The Knot of Grass' and featured scenes from gypsy life and other New Forest subjects. Amelia Goddard exhibited 15 oils, two watercolours and two pastels and most of the subjects were gypsy scenes, figure and portrait studies and rural landscapes. The title picture in oil – 'The Knot of Grass' was priced at 200 guineas, far in excess of the other exhibits, depicted the old gypsy custom of marking the way for fellow travellers.

**Walter W.. GODDARD (fl. 1892)**

Painter in oil of landscapes and river scenes who was working in the 1890s. The work was of good quality but he does not appear to have exhibited.

**Miss L.. C.. GODWIN (exh. 1904-1913)**

Watercolour artist of cottages and landscapes who lived at Stoke Bishop, Bristol, and exhibited five works at the Leeds Art Gallery Exhibitions of 1904 and 1905. She also exhibited a watercolour entitled 'Venice' at the R.W.A. in 1913.

**Ruth GOLDNEY (1894-1989)**

Painter in watercolour and pastel of landscapes, flowers and miniatures. She was born in Saxmundham, Suffolk, where her father was Vicar and married Major P C Goldney who served in India 1926-1937. While in India she painted extensively and also later during visits to Canada, Norway, East Africa and Bermuda. Although essentially an amateur artist, Ruth Goldney painted all her life and to within a few weeks of her death in December 1989.

**Edward C.. GOODDY (exh. 1902)**

Landscape painter in oil and watercolour who lived at Eye, Suffolk, and was a member of the Ipswich Art Club. He exhibited three works in 1902, entitled 'The Carnian Alps . . . Carinthia' (oil), 'The Mouth of the River Conway, North Wales' (oil) and 'Eye.Suffolk' (watercolour).

**Marjorie J.. GOODGE (exh. 1950)**

Painter who lived at Polruan, Cornwall, and exhibited two works at the Plymouth Art Society in 1950. The subjects were a harbour scene and an oil painting of Johannesburg.

**Thomas H.. GOODING (exh. 1932-1935)**

Landscape painter in oil who lived in Ipswich and was a member of the Ipswich Art Club. He exhibited a total of 14 works 1932-1935. The subjects were mostly rural landscapes and the titles included 'Spring in the Meadows', 'A Suffolk Lane' and a 'Wayside Cottage' (all 1935).

**Miss GOOSE (exh. 1878-1896)**

Painter in oil of flowers, still life and landscapes who lived in Ipswich and was a member of the Ipswich Art Club. She was a regular exhibitor showing a total of 32 works 1878-1896. Most of the exhibits were still life subjects 'Wild Flowers', 'Meadow Daisies', and 'Peaches' being typical titles.

**Jack GORDGE (exh. 1921)**

Artist and illustrator in black and white and watercolour, who was a former student of the Polytechnic School of Art. In October 1921, Jack Gordge had a joint exhibition with Marchant Smith at the Harlequin Cafe in Beak Street, London. Two works from the exhibition were illustrated in The Studio magazine.

*Arthur Gordon        'Kew from the Island' (w/c)        (Sotheby's)*

**Arthur GORDON (fl. 1891-1909)**

This was a pseudonym used by the artist whose real name was Gordon Arthur Meadows. He was a prolific artist in oil and watercolour of Thames scenes – 'Kew from the Island' (1897), and 'On the Thames at Mortlake' (1903) are typical titles. His work is usually dated and inscribed with the location on the reverse.

**F.. GORDON (fl. 1900s)**

This was a pseudonym used by Francis Gordon Fraser (q.v.) for some of his watercolour river landscapes. The majority of his work was signed in full F G Fraser.

**Harold GORDON (exh. 1906-1907)**

Watercolour painter of river and coastal scenes who exhibited in 1906 and 1907 at the Annual Devon and Exeter Exhibition at Elands Art Gallery in Exeter. The works were entitled 'A Cornish Sea', 'Half a Gale', and 'The Squall'.

**Miss Constance Frederica GORDON-CUMMING (1837-1924)**

Watercolour landscape painter, author and traveller who exhibited 1882-1902. She showed three works at the Royal Scottish Academy 1882-1883, while living at Crieff in Scotland. Miss Cumming travelled widely and was the author of several books including 'Two Happy Years in Ceylon' and 'At Home in Fiji', published in 1901. A large exhibition of her foreign landscapes was held at the Brighton Art Gallery in 1902. This consisted of 127 views of Ceylon, 48 of Fiji and 15 sketches of New Zealand.

**D.. GORE-BROWNE (exh. 1912)**

Painter of landscapes and flowers who was member of the Winchester Art Society and showed three works at the Annual Exhibition in 1912.

**Edward GOSLING (exh. 1936)**

An armless artist who painted with the brush held between his toes. His work was exhibited at the Reeves 'Goya' Exhibition in 1936. A fine quality work entitled 'A Welcome Rest' of horses is illustrated in The Artist magazine.

**R.. Percy GOSSOP (fl. 1898-1900)**

Artist in pencil. A fine quality illustration of a street scene was reproduced in The Studio magazine in October 1900. He signed his work with a monogram (see index).

**Miss Alice L.. GOWER (exh. 1907-1919)**

Painter in oil and watercolour of landscapes who lived in Colchester, Essex, and was a member of the Ipswich Art Club. She was a regular exhibitor showing 24 works 1907-1919. The subjects include some continental views 'Bruges', 'Mennagio' (oils) and 'A Dutch Lane' (watercolour, all 1919).

## Albert R.. GOWERS (exh. 1885-1893)

Landscape painter in oil who lived in Ipswich and was a member of the Ipswich Art Club. He exhibited 20 works 1885-1893 and the titles included 'The Gipping near Bramford' (1889) and 'The Road by the River' (1890). He was related to Arthur Gowers (q.v.).

## Arthur GOWERS (exh. 1883-1898)

Landscape painter in oil who lived in Ipswich and was a member of the Ipswich Art Club. He was a regular exhibitor, showing 65 works 1883-1898. Most of the subjects were local landscapes and marines and the titles included 'A Morning in the Channel' (1890), 'On the Thames – Morning' (1894), and 'Mill on the Broads' (1898).

## Percival B.. GOWERS (exh. 1919-1945)

Painter in oil and watercolour of landscapes who lived in Ipswich and was a member of the Ipswich Art Club. He exhibited 23 works 1919-1945. The titles included 'A Path to the Sea' (oil, 1928), 'Clearing after Rain' (watercolour, 1928) and 'Where the Waves Gently Pass' (1945).

## Miss Marjory GOW-STEWART (exh. 1910-1913)

Painter in oil and watercolour of landscapes and figure subjects who lived at Clifton, Bristol, and exhibited four works at the R.W.A. 1910-1913. These included figure subjects and a view of Grenada.

*J. W. Gozzard*    *'The Close of the Day' (w/c)*    *( J. Collins and Son)*

## James Walter GOZZARD (1888-1950)

Painter and illustrator in oil and watercolour of rural landscapes. Born in Lichfield, Staffs in 1888, J W Gozzard was a prolific illustrator whose work was reproduced as both prints and postcards. He produced a series of Scottish views in watercolour that were published by Valentines in Dundee, some street scenes published by William McKenzie and some rural landscapes published by Philco in London. In addition to the postcards, a large number of prints were made of his work in both black and white and colour that were available up to the First World War.

J W Gozzard does not appear to have exhibited either in London or the provinces. His watercolour was often heightened with bodycolour and his precise style made the work very suitable for reproduction. His larger works were usually signed in full whereas the smaller studies were often initialled. Some of the work was signed with a pseudonym 'F Arnold' (q.v.).

## Miss Florence M.. GRACE (exh. 1884-1936)

Painter in oil and watercolour of landscapes and still life. Florence Grace was a regular exhibitor at the R.W.A. showing over 88 works 1884-1936. Many of the subjects were West Country views including Newlyn and St Ives, also local scenes, Scottish views and of Bruges. The titles include 'Interior of a Cornish Net Loft' and 'Old Dutch House, Bristol' (1903), and 'Yealmton Village' (1907). She signed her work with a monogram (see index).

## Ben GRAHAM (fl. 1907-1930s)

This was a pseudonym used by Douglas H Pinder (q.v.) on some of his moorland landscapes when he was living at Horrabridge, Devon, until the 1930s. Under this name he exhibited three Dartmoor views at Elands Art Gallery, Exeter, in 1907 at an exhibition entitled 'Pictures of the West Country by Devon Artists'. These were painted in gouache in the manner of F J Widgery, who was a popular painter of the time.

## Miss Ellen L.. GRANT (exh. 1912)

Landscape painter in watercolour who exhibited two works at the Worthing Art Gallery Exhibition of 1912. The subjects were both Swiss views.

## Miss M...W.. GRANT (exh. 1923-1924)

Watercolour landscape painter who lived at Bromeswell, Suffolk, and was a member of the Ipswich Art Club. She exhibited four works 1923-1924, which were views of Bromeswell and Wissington, in Suffolk, and a landscape at Beddgelert in Wales.

## F.. GRAYSON (fl.c. 1900)

Marine painter in watercolour. The work, in the style of F J Aldridge, appears identical to W.. Stewart (q.v.), for whom it was probably a pseudonym. The artist also appeared to sign J.. Hill (q.v.).

## A.. E.. GREATEREX (exh. 1931-1938)

Painter in oil who lived at Bures, Suffolk, and was a member of the Ipswich Art Club. He exhibited seven works 1931-1938, mostly portraits in oil.

## Miss E.. M.. GREEN (exh. 1930-1935)

Artist who lived at Westbury on Trym, Somerset, and exhibited eight works at the R.W.A. 1930-1935. The subjects were mostly rural scenes, landscapes and some still life.

## Henry G.. GREEN (fl. 1901)

Watercolour painter who lived at Reading and was a member of the Berkshire Art Society. In 1901, he exhibited two works at the Annual Exhibition in Reading entitled 'A Misty Morning' and 'A Backwater'.

## I.. F.. GREEN (exh. 1910)

Watercolour landscape painter, who had an exhibition of English and continental views at St Georges Gallery, London, in December 1910.

## Mrs. T.. W.. M.. GREEN (exh. 1932-1933)

Artist who lived at Redland, Bristol, and exhibited at the R.W.A. 1932-1933. The titles of the work were 'Old Mill, Coombe Dingle' and 'Brixham, South Devon'.

## Miss Taylor GREENE (fl. 1903)

Portrait painter who was educated in Paris. By 1903, she was establishing a reputation for portraits and one of her works was reproduced in The Studio magazine that year.

## Lt. Col. A.. D.. GREENHILL-GARDYNE (exh. 1928-1931)

Landscape painter, late of the Gordon Highlanders, who exhibited 15 pictures at the Army Officers Art Society 1928-1931. The subjects were landscapes, mostly views in North Africa.

## Bertie GREENWOOD (fl. 1897)

Figure and portrait artist who lived at Willesden Green, London, and won first prize in The Studio magazine competition for a study of a head, in 1897.

## Miss Lydia D.. GREENWOOD (exh. 1917-1932)

Painter in watercolour of buildings and landscapes, who lived at Weston-super-Mare, Flax Bourton in Somerset and at West Town near Bristol. Lydia Greenwood exhibited two watercolours of buildings at the Royal Academy in 1917 and showed 27 works at the R.W.A. 1919-1932. The subjects included figures, local landscapes and views in Cornwall and Northern France.

## Victor A.. GREGORY (exh. 1950)

Oil painter of landscapes and harbour scenes who lived at Tavistock, Devon, and exhibited two works with the Plymouth Art Society in 1950.

## Sidney GREY (fl. 1900s)

Painter in watercolour of interior scenes, in the manner of GG Kilburne, with figures in costume dress. This artist's work is of good quality but he does not appear to have exhibited.

## Miss S.. D.. GRIBBLE (exh. 1919-1920)

Watercolour landscape painter, who lived at Clifton, Bristol, and exhibited four works at the R.W.A. 1919-1920. The subjects were two views of St Ives, Looe in Cornwall and Minehead in Somerset.

*Dorothy Griffiths*      *'A Moroccan Girl' (w/c)*

## Mrs. Dorothy B.. GRIFFITHS (fl. 1920-1939)

Painter in watercolour, pastel and etcher of figures and landscapes who was working from 1920 to 1939. Dorothy Griffiths was the daughter of George Cochrane Kerr, a well known Victorian marine artist. She was a frequent traveller, often sketching and painting passengers on board ship, and visiting among other places, Gibraltar, Tangier and Malta.

In April 1924, Dorothy Griffiths was the first woman to travel into the Atlas Mountains of Morocco during the Riff War. Accompanied only be a native guide she took her camping and painting equipment on a donkey sketching portraits of people and landscapes as she went.

## Leslie GRIMES (1898-1983)

Painter in oil and watercolour of landscapes, illustrator and political cartoonist. Leslie Grimes started a formal art training but this was cut short with the outbreak of War in 1914, and at 16 he joined up and served in the infantry and then as a pilot in the R.F.C. After the War, Leslie Grimes worked for Douglas Motorcycles as a technical illustrator before joining the Daily Star as a political cartoonist. He produced a series of political cartoons called 'All my own Work', which ran for many years and in over 800 editions. Leslie Grimes also painted landscapes in oil and in 1944 exhibited a view of Kensington at the Royal Academy. He lived in Haslemere, Surrey, later London and after the Second World War he lived in Ibiza but later returned to England where he died in 1983.

## Miss GRIMSEY (exh. 1882-1888)

Watercolour landscape painter who lived in Ipswich and was a member of the Ipswich Art Club. She exhibited six works, mostly local scenes 1882-1888.

## Marian GROTOWSKI (exh. 1942-1944)

Portrait, figure and still life painter in oil who exhibited five works at the Ipswich Art Club 1942-1944. The titles included 'Lady with a Straw Hat' (1942), 'The Lost Button' (1943) and 'Roses' (1944).

## W.. J.. GROVE (exh. 1932-1937)

Artist who lived at Eastville, Bristol, and exhibited nine works at the R.W.A. 1932-1937. The subjects were mostly views of Chipping Campden, Glos, also one of Warwick and Conway, North Wales.

## Mrs. M.. E.. GULLEY A.R.W.A. (fl. 1915-1931)

Artist who lived at South Petherton, Somerset, and was an associate member of the R.W.A., exhibiting four works 1924-1929. She may have been related to Cathy Gulley, the Bristol watercolour figure painter, who also exhibited at the R.W.A.

## Col. Clarence Preston GUNTER (born 1873, exh. 1928)

Watercolour landscape painter who exhibited four works at the Army Officers Art Society Exhibition in 1928 including some views of Burma and India. He lived at Budleigh Salterton, Devon.

## Miss Katherine (Kit) B.. GUNTON A.R.W.A. (exh. 1920-1958)

Landscape painter and miniaturist who lived at Cotham, Bristol, and was an associate member of the R.W.A. She was a regular exhibitor showing 58 works 1920-1958. Katherine Gunton travelled widely and many of the landscapes were views in France, Italy, Spain, Portugal and Norway. She also exhibited linocuts, and some portrait miniatures in the 1920s. Katherine Gunton moved to the Bournemouth area around 1970.

## Miss Agatha GURNEY (exh. 1900-1905)

Watercolour painter of animal subjects who lived at Keswick Hall, Norwich, and was a member of the Norwich Art Circle. She exhibited 11 works 1900-1905, mostly horse portraits and animal studies.

## Gerard H.. GURNEY (fl. 1898-1911)

Watercolour landscape painter who lived at Keswick Hall, Norwich, and was a member of the Norwich Art Circle. He was probably the brother of Agatha and Helen Gurney (q.v.). Gerard Gurney exhibited 14 pictures 1900-1911, mostly local landscapes. The titles included 'River at Keswick' and 'Landscape at Wexford' (both 1900).

## Miss Helen GURNEY (exh. 1897-1911)

Watercolour painter of flowers, garden scenes and landscapes who lived in Norwich and was a member of the Norwich Art Circle from 1898. The most active member of the Gurney family, she exhibited over 40 works 1897-1911, and may also have been working later. Most of the subjects were watercolour garden and flower paintings, but she also painted some local views.

## Miss Judith E.. GUTCH (exh. 1926-1934)

Artist in oil and etcher of landscapes and figure subjects who lived in Ipswich and was a member of the Ipswich Art Club. She exhibited a total of 17 works 1926-1934. The subjects were figures, local landscapes and some foreign views including Majorca and Switzerland. The titles included 'The Windmill' Walberswick (1930), 'Alms House, Doyen' (1926), 'Sunlight on Majorca' (1927) and 'Loch Rannock' (aquatint, 1927).

## D.. L.. GUY (exh. 1925-1928)

Artist who lived in Bristol and exhibited seven works at the R.W.A. 1925-1928. These were all pen and ink decorations.

## Henry Coulton GUYATT (1857-1939)

Landscape painter in oil and watercolour who lived at Long Ashton, Bristol, and was a member of the Bristol Savages. He was a regular exhibitor showing over 150 works 1907-1938. The subjects were mostly landscape views of the West Country, North Wales and Berkshire. He also showed 19 works at the R.W.A. 1918-1934 mostly West Country views.

# H

**Miss M.. V.. HACKSLEY (exh. 1915-1916)**

Landscape and figure painter who lived in Bristol, and exhibited four works at the R.W.A. 1915-1916. The titles were 'The Goose Girl', 'Hollyhocks', and 'Bude Haven' (1915), and a black and white study 'Newlyn' (1916).

**Miss E.. Maud HALE (exh. 1900)**

Landscape painter in oil, who lived at Swindon, Wilts, and exhibited two works at the R.W.A. in 1900 – 'A Courtyard, Normandy', and 'Still Waters'.

**Albert HALL (exh. 1908-1915)**

Landscape painter who lived in Bristol and exhibited four works at the R.W.A. 1908-1915. The titles were 'Gloucestershire Lane' (1908), 'Old Cottages' and 'Near Almonsbury' (1910), and 'A Devonshire Lane' (1915).

**Mrs. E.. M.. HALL (exh. 1920-1933)**

Watercolour landscape painter who lived at Clifton, Bristol and exhibited 25 works at the R.W.A. 1920-1933. The subjects were Welsh views and several foreign landscapes including views in Switzerland, Austria, Venice and Tangier.

*S. E. Hall          'Lulworth Cove' (w/c)          (J. Collins and Son)*

**S.. E.. HALL (fl.c. 1910-1930)**

Painter in watercolour of river and coastal scenes, landscapes and cottages. The colour and style of this artist's work is very similar to that of John Lynas-Gray and is sometimes catalogued as this artist, although there is no firm evidence to substantiate this. The quality of S E Hall's work is more variable, and the wider subject matter includes some Venetian views and scenes on the Nile. S E Hall watercolours usually have a printed label on the reverse proclaiming them to be an original work by the artist.

**Miss Hylda F.. C.. HALLETT (exh. 1912)**

Watercolour landscape painter who exhibited a view of Ditchling Beacon, Sussex, at the Worthing Art Gallery Summer Exhibition in 1912.

**Beamish HAMILTON (fl. 1891)**

Painter in watercolour of landscapes and coastal scenes. This good quality artist does not appear to have exhibited, although he was active in the early 1890s and did some work in the Tenby area of South Wales.

**C.. F.. HAMILTON (exh. 1909)**

Artist who exhibited at the Second Exhibition of the New Society of Painters and Sculptors at the Rowley Gallery, London, in 1909.

**G.. H.. HAMMERSLEY (exh. 1920-1924)**

Watercolour figure and portrait painter who lived at Clifton, Bristol, and exhibited four works at the R.W.A. 1920-1924. The subjects were three portraits and 'Dartmouth Fair' (1920).

**C.. Eaton HAMMOND (exh. 1884-1889)**

Watercolour landscape painter who lived at Newmarket, Suffolk, and was a member of the Ipswich Art Club. He exhibited seven works at their exhibitions 1884-1889, and the titles included 'In the City of York' and 'Burnham Beeches' (1884).

**Miss R.. HAMMOND (exh. 1887-1890)**

Watercolour landscape painter who lived at Newmarket, Suffolk, and exhibited three works at the Ipswich Art Club 1887-1890. The titles included 'Lincoln Minster' and 'St Marys Church, Beverley' (1890).

*C. P. Hancock-Neate          'Turkeys' (w/c)*

**Mrs. Christine P.. HANCOCK-NEATE (exh. 1934-1940s)**

Painter in watercolour of landscapes and rural scenes who lived in Brighton and exhibited from 1934 including two works at the Royal Academy. The pre-war pictures were signed C P Hancock, whereas her later works were signed with her hyphenated surname. The subjects included landscape views in Sussex and Dorset and some scenes in France and Italy.

## Capt. Thomas Henry Herbert HAND
## (born 1870, fl. 1909-1921)

Painter in watercolour of marine subjects who lived at Southsea, Hants, and was working early this century. This competent artist does not appear to have exhibited at the major exhibitions but may have found a market for his work locally. The subjects include studies of battleships, lifeboats and fishing vessels as well as some estuary scenes. Many of the pictures are dated and known works span dates between 1909 and 1921.

## T.. H.. HANDOLL (exh. 1930-1931)

Artist who lived at Fishponds, Bristol, and exhibited at the R.W.A. 1930-1931. The subjects were 'Old Roman Bridge' and 'Ducks'.

## Henry HANFORD B.W.S. (exh. 1928)

Watercolour landscape painter who was a member of the B.W.S. and exhibited at their 1928 Preston Art Gallery Exhibition. The picture was entitled 'Beside the Lock, Teddington'.

## Col. A.. F.. P.. HARCOURT (exh. 1901)

Landscape painter who lived at Streatley on Thames and was a member of the Berkshire Art Society. He exhibited four works at the 1901 Exhibition in Reading, including local landscape views.

## Miss B.. M.. HARDING (exh. 1923-1930)

Artist who lived in Bath and exhibited three works at the R.W.A. 1923-1930. The subjects included a view at Mousehole, Cornwall, and 'The Old Manor Farm'.

## F.. A.. HARDING (exh. 1927-1928)

Artist who lived at Bishopston, Bristol, and exhibited three works at the R.W.A. – two tree studies (1927) and 'Bristol from Kellaway Avenue' (1928).

## Miss M.. J.. HARDING (exh. 1929-1931)

Artist who lived at Redland, Bristol, and exhibited four works at the R.W.A. 1929-1931. The subjects were 'Little Comberton, Worcs', 'A Country Inn', 'The Creek, Faversham' and 'Looe, Cornwall'.

## M.. L.. HARDING (exh. 1927)

Watercolour landscape painter who had a one-man exhibition at the Modern Gallery, London, in November 1927. The exhibition consisted of 62 watercolours, mostly views in England, Scotland and France.

S. A. Harding          'A Breton Street' (w/c)          (N. & J. Taylor)

## Samuel Alfred HARDING (1868-1941)

Painter mostly in watercolour of landscapes, old buildings and street scenes. He exhibited six works at the Royal Academy 1924-1935, mostly French views and a still life. Samuel Harding also had one-man exhibitions at Walkers Gallery, London, in 1926 and again in 1936 entitled 'Watercolour Drawings of Malaya, Java, Bali and the Home Countryside'. A friend of S J Lamorna Birch, they travelled to France by car on a painting trip in 1923. Samuel Harding lived at Leatherhead, Surrey, and later at Pulborough, Sussex, where he died on the 15th July 1941.

Cyril Hardy          'An Eastern Gateway' (w/c)          (Howes Gallery)

## Cyril HARDY (fl.c. 1900-1940)

Watercolour painter of North African town and market scenes. The work bears a striking resemblance to that of Noel Harry Leaver but is usually not of such quality, although he may have been a pupil or admirer. The pictures are usually heightened with bodycolour and the style suggests that the artist may have been an illustrator. 'A Moorish Street, Old Arabia' and 'A Courtyard in the East' are typical titles.

**Miss Mary L.. HARDY (exh. 1923)**

Watercolour landscape painter who lived at Chalfont St Peter, Bucks, and was a member of the Ipswich Art Club. She exhibited two works in 1923 entitled 'Beanfield, Hollesley' and 'Shingle Street from Hollesley'.

**Alfred HARFORD R.W.A. (1848-1915)**

Landscape painter in oil who lived at Redland, Bristol, and exhibited 49 works at the R.W.A. 1885-1915. The subjects included landscapes in Devon, Scotland and Wales and some foreign views including Bruges and Venice.

*Gordon Hargrave*        *'Kentmere under Snow' (w/c)*

**Gordon HARGRAVE (fl.c. 1890-1920)**

Painter in watercolour of landscapes and cottages who was working at the turn of the century. Gordon Hargrave is listed in the trade directories for Sussex in the 1890s, when he was living at Midhurst. In 1912 he held a joint exhibition at the Dudley Gallery, London, with his son John who was showing illustrations for Treasure Island. Gordon Hargrave exhibited 38 watercolour landscapes, mostly cottage and river scenes, including several views on the River Chess in Bucks.

**Joseph HARKER (fl. 1912)**

Scenic artist who was an early member of the London Sketch Club and their President in 1912.

**Thomas Howard HARKER (1842-1926)**

Painter in oil and watercolour of railway subjects, landscapes and genre who was born in Sunderland on 29th April 1842. After spending some time in the Merchant service and the Army he came to Bristol about 1874 and worked for the Bristol and Exeter Railway as a station inspector. Later, he joined the Great Western Railway as a passenger guard and retired in the late 1890s. Thomas Harker exhibited 11 works at the R.W.A. 1884-1891 including landscapes, figures and some early railway subjects. Titles

include 'The Flying Dutchman at Sea' (flooded main line between Durston and Bridgewater) 1884 and '. . . . the Train passing through Willow Vale, Frome' 1886. His exhibit of 1891 'A Great Western Railway Guard' could perhaps have been a self portrait. A view of Bristol station was purchased by the City Art Gallery but appears no longer to be in their possession. Thomas Harker's work is not often seen on the market but the early railway pictures would be the most collectable.

**Miss E.. T.. HARLE (exh. 1920-1927)**

Artist who lived at Falfield, Glos, and later at Filleigh, near Barnstaple, Devon. She exhibited five works at the R.W.A. 1920-1927, the titles included 'Homeward Bound' (1921) and 'Noontide' (1922).

**Mrs. H.. HARLOCK (exh. 1884)**

Landscape painter in watercolour who lived at Brandon, Suffolk, and was a member of the Ipswich Art Club. She exhibited three works in 1884 – 'Languard Fort . . . .', 'Hunstanton Cliffs', 'A Sketch – Feltwell'.

*Edith Harms*        *'Denne Park, Horsham' (w/c)*        *(Reid Gallery)*

**Edith Margaret HARMS (1870-1943)**

Painter in watercolour of flowers and landscapes who was born on 28th May 1870. Little is known of her early life, but her father was a builder at Horsham, Sussex, and she first exhibited from there in 1897. The colour and style of her early work show a distinct similarity to that of Charles J Adams who was also living in the town, so it is likely that she was a pupil of this well known landscape painter. Edith Harms exhibited watercolours at the major exhibitions during the next 35 years including three works at the Royal Academy – 'A Halt by the Wayside' (1900), 'Sweet Williams' (1916) and 'Rue des Cordeliers, Dinan' (1932). She taught art for many years at the Horsham School of Art and local schools and was also a founder member of the Association of Sussex Artists in 1928. Edith Harms spent her holidays painting in France and Northern Italy and in the 1930s visited the St Ives Summer School where she studied oil painting and sketched the children of local fishermen. As a teacher, Edith Harm's work is not as plentiful as some artists but her pictures are still found in the Sussex area and the Horsham Museum have four of her local landscape views.

*H. Harmsworth   'Cottages at East Hoathly, Sussex' (w/c)*

## H.. HARMSWORTH (fl.c. 1900)

Painter in watercolour of landscapes and cottages who worked in Sussex and lived in Brighton. This good quality artist may have been related to J Harmsworth who was living nearby and working at the same time.

## Maud HARMSWORTH (fl.c. 1900)

Painter in watercolour of rural landscapes who was working at around the turn of the century. Despite the quality of the work she does not appear to have exhibited.

## T.. Laurence HARPER (exh. 1950)

Painter in watercolour and gouache of coastal scenes and landscapes. He lived in Plymouth and exhibited three works at the Plymouth Art Society in 1950.

## E.. R.. HARRINGTON (exh. 1921)

Painter of shipyard scenes who exhibited two works at the First Admiralty Art Club Exhibition in June 1921.

## George HARRIS (fl. 1880s-1900s)

Painter in oil of landscapes who was a younger brother of Henry Harris (q.v.). He was born at Cullompton, Devon, around 1847, but lived and worked for much of his life in Bristol. He was a member of the Bristol Savages and did show some work at the R.W.A. George Harris painted local views in the Bristol area, although the pictures were not usually of such good quality as his brother's work or command the same prices. He does not appear to have exhibited widely and probably sold most his work locally.

*Henry Harris                    (J Collins and Son)*
*'A Woodland Stream' (oil)*

## Henry HARRIS (1852-1926)

Painter in oil, and occasionally watercolour, of landscapes and rural scenes. Henry Harris was born at Cullompton, Devon, in 1852, the son of a miller, and one of 15 boys. One of his brothers, George (q.v.) was also to become an artist. By 1872, Henry Harris had moved to Bristol, married, and was working as a house painter and decorator. By 1875 he was working full time as an artist and the next three decades were to be his most productive period. Most of his landscapes were local views, but he also painted in Wales including views of Chepstow and Tintern Abbey. The work varies in quality but the subject matter and location make the good examples collectable. He had his own distinctive style, particularly in the painting of trees, which helps to make the work easy to recognise. Henry Harris continued to paint well into this century and after a short illness, died in Bristol in 1926.

## Henry HARRIS (of Clifton) (exh. 1870-1880)

This artist is not the better known Henry Harris, brother of George, but a separate painter of the same name who was working in the area at the same time. He often signed his work Henry Harris Clifton, because, presumably, there was also confusion when they were working. Henry Harris of Clifton was a regular exhibitor at the R.W.A. showing a total of 44 works 1870-1880. The subjects were mostly views in Cornwall, North Wales and Scotland and also some Irish landscapes.

## Miss Josephine M.. HARRIS (exh. 1950)

Figure and landscape painter in watercolour who lived at Saltash, Cornwall, and exhibited three works at the Plymouth Art Society Exhibition of 1950.

## A.. D.. HARRISON (exh. 1900-1903)

Landscape painter in oil who lived in Bristol and exhibited four works at the R.W.A. 1900-1903. The subjects were Scottish lochs and a castle in North Wales.

*Brook Harrison    'Wells, Somerset' (w/c)    (J. Robbins)*

## Brooking Alfred Wrankmore HARRISON (1860-1930)

Painter in watercolour of landscapes, marines and harbour scenes who lived for many years at Shoreham in Sussex. Brook Harrison was a good quality artist who was active from about 1879 and did occasionally exhibit in London, showing work at the R.B.A. 1885 and at the Goupil Gallery 1925. The majority of his work was local Sussex scenes and he

exhibited with the Brighton Arts Club 1905 and with the Society of Sussex Artists 1929. Other subjects included views of Bruges and Northern France as well as scenes in Dorset, Somerset and Cornwall. Brook Harrison died on 24th February 1930 at the age of 69. A Memorial Exhibition was held at the Marlipins Museum, Shoreham.

## Frank W.. HARRISON (exh. 1932-1933)

Landscape painter in watercolour who lived at Felixstowe, Suffolk, and later at Esher, Surrey, and was a member of the Ipswich Art Club. He exhibited four works 1933-1934 including some local views. The titles were 'Farmyard, Capel Hall, Fakenham' and 'Farm Buildings, Trimley' (1933) and 'Brockweir, Wye Valley' and 'A Surrey Pool' (1934).

*J. Clifford Harrison    'On the Italian Lakes' (pen & ink)*

## John Clifford S.. HARRISON (1847-1903)

Artist in watercolour and pen and ink, musician and poet. Clifford Harrison specialised in highly detailed studies of English and continental buildings and landscapes and much of his work was done in his later years despite failing health. He held two exhibitions at the Graves Gallery, London around 1900 and both contained over 80 of his works. In 1904, the Graves Gallery held a Memorial Exhibition to Clifford Harrison and showed 142 of his pen and ink, and watercolour landscapes. He signed his work 'Clifford Harrison'.

## Claude Montague HART (1870-1952)

Painter in oil and watercolour of seascapes and coastal scenes. Son of the artist Thomas Hart, Claude Montague Hart was born at the Lizard, Cornwall in 1870 – his elder brother Sydney and Tracy were also to become artists. 'Monty', as he was known, studied painting in Antwerp but returned to the Lizard which was to provide the subjects for many of his seascapes. He exhibited eight works at the North British Academy 1914-1918 and two at the R.W.A. 1929 with the typical titles of 'Sea Fog Clearing' and 'Atlantic Breakers, The Lizard'. Many of his pictures were sold locally to visitors but by the 1940s the demand had dropped and he ceased painting. He was deeply involved with the lifeboat service and for 39 years he acted as secretary for the local Lizard rescue boat. The early works are usually signed Claude M Hart, whereas the later ones are signed just C M Hart.

*T. Dyke Hart*     *'Towarne Head, Newquay' (w/c)*     *(J Collins and Son)*

## T.. Dyke HART (fl.c. 1900-1920)

Painter in watercolour of coastal scenes who was working in the West Country in the early years of this century. The artist is thought to be one of the children of Thomas Hart (1830-1916) a coastal scene painter who lived in The Lizard, Cornwall. Several of his children painted and Tracy D Hart was probably the artist featured here. The work is attractive and well painted and is signed T. Dyke Hart in a printed script.

## G.. Garstin HARVEY (exh. 1905)

Tempera artist, who exhibited at the Tempera Exhibition at the Carfax Gallery in 1905. G Garstin Harvey was a member of the Tempera Society that was formed in 1901 to encourage the use of this medium. One of his Carfax Gallery exhibits 'St Vitus's Dance' was illustrated in The Studio magazine.

*A. Haselgrave*     *'The Village Pond' (w/c)*

## A.. HASELGRAVE (fl.c. 1890-1920)

Painter in watercolour of haymaking scenes and rural landscapes. The work of this prolific artist is often seen on the market and although the quality is variable the pleasing subject matter has made the work increasingly popular. Titles of known works include 'Haymaking' (1893), 'A Surrey Common', 'The Sussex Downs', 'Harvesting near Lustleigh' and 'Evening near Redruth'. The artist's name is thought to be Albert, although he is frequently catalogued as, and confused with, Adelaide L Haslegrave despite the different spelling of the surname. He signed his work 'A Haselgrave' sometimes with a date.

## Violet M.. HASWELL (exh. 1911)

Miniature portrait painter who exhibited at the Coronation Exhibition, London, in 1911. She was a member of The Society of Miniaturists.

## Miss Dora J.. HATCHARD (exh. 1928-1936)

Etcher who lived at Cotham and later Knowle, Bristol, and exhibited 18 works at the R.W.A. 1928-1936. The exhibits were mostly etchings and included building studies in Bristol and landscape views in Cornwall and Yorkshire.

## E.. A.. Ashford HATHERLEY (exh. 1935-1936)

Watercolour landscape painter who lived at Redland, Bristol, and exhibited a total of four works at the R.W.A. 1935-1936. The works were entitled 'Portcullis Inn, Hillesley, Glos', 'Longa Quies', 'On a Cotswold Farm' and 'Ebb Tide'.

## Charles Greaves HATTERSLEY (born c. 1854)

Eldest of the three Hattersley brothers, who studied at the Sheffield School of Art in 1870 and was later listed in the local trade directories as a gilder, artist and picture restorer.

F. W. Hattersley    'On the Beach, Harlech' (w/c)    (Reid Gallery)

## Frederick William HATTERSLEY (born 1860)

Painter in watercolour of landscapes and beach scenes. Frederick William Hattersley was born in Sheffield in 1860 and his father was a stove and fender manufacturer in the city. It looks likely that the family business diversified, as Frederick is recorded as a carver and gilder in the 1880s and from 1896 the local trade directories list him as an artist. This talented and much collected painter has largely escaped the attention of the writers of the reference books since he did not exhibit in London. Unlike his brothers, Frederick apparently had no formal art training although he did exhibit with the Sheffield Society of Artists c. 1870-1890. His work has a distinctive style and the subjects are often figures on a windswept hill or beach. The Sheffield Museums Department has six local views by the artist.

## George Pearson HATTERSLEY (born c. 1858)

Elder brother of F W Hattersley (q.v.), George Pearson Hattersley studied at the Sheffield School of Art and exhibited with the Sheffield Society of Artists in the 1870s. The Sheffield Museums Department has a local view in oil by him dated 1882.

W. S. Hatton    'On the Ishmail Canal, Cairo' (w/c)

## W.. Scarlett HATTON (fl.c. 1900-1920)

Painter in watercolour of landscapes who was working in the early part of the century. His subjects were mostly English landscapes and some middle eastern scenes. This competent artist does not appear to have exhibited.

## Ernest Binfield HAVELL (1861-1934)

Watercolour painter and sculptor, who was born in Reading, Berks, in 1861. In 1896, Ernest Havell held a joint exhibition with Mrs Jopling at the Clifford Gallery in London. He showed mostly views in Italy, including Venice and Capri, where he had spent much time. Ernest Havell also exhibited two sculptures at the Royal Academy 1890-1891 while he was at the School of Arts at Madras, India.

## Miss Joyce HAVELL (exh. 1920-1921)

Landscape and still life painter in watercolour who lived at Felixstowe, Suffolk, and was a member of the Ipswich Art Club. She exhibited four works 1920-1921 entitled 'Harwich Harbour', 'Cushion Cover', 'Spring Morning' and 'Summer Evening'.

## Mrs Ethel HAVERS (exh. 1896-1911)

Painter in watercolour of landscapes, figures and miniature portraits. She lived in Norwich and was a member and regular exhibitor at the Norwich Art Circle. Ethel Havers showed a total of 23 pictures 1896-1911, in the first year exhibiting under her maiden name of Ethel Buckingham. Many of her exhibits were portrait miniatures, but she also showed watercolour landscapes, beach scenes and interiors.

## Gladys Mary HAVERS (fl. 1931-c. 1954)

Painter in watercolour who lived at Ewhurst, Surrey, and was working from the early 1930s. Her subjects included some far east views and a study of Chinese Junks by her was exhibited posthumously at the Royal Academy in 1954. She signed G Havers in printed letters.

## W.. O.. HAWES (exh. 1921)

Painter of still life and landscapes who exhibited five works at the Admiralty Art Club's First Exhibition in 1921.

## Violet E.. HAWKES (fl. 1908)

A student at the Liverpool School of Art who won a Gold Medal at the National Schools of Art Competition in 1908 for a figure study.

## H.. L.. HAWKINS (exh. 1935)

Industrial artist, employed by J Walter Thompson, who exhibited at the exhibition of 'Weekend Work' at the French Gallery, London, in 1935. He showed two still life oil paintings.

*E. Stretton Hawley*      *' Dignity and Impudence' (w/c)*

### E.. Stretton HAWLEY (exh. 1905)

Painter in oil and watercolour of animals and rural scenes who was working in the early part of this century. It is curious that this good quality artist is not better known or recorded. He did, however, have a joint exhibition with George Hawley at the Bruton Galleries, London, in November 1905. This consisted of 20 works, all rural scenes, and the titles included 'The Wool Waggon', 'Cart, Mare and Foal', 'The Hennery', 'The Duck Pond', 'Unloading' and a horse portrait. The work is not often seen on the market but is occasionally found in East Sussex where he lived.

### Miss Winifred HAXELL (fl. 1908-1909)

A student at the Lambeth School of Art who received an Hon. Mention at the National Schools of Art Competition in 1909 for an oil portrait. She also painted still life in watercolour.

### Elaine HAXTON (exh. 1935)

Painter in oil and watercolour of landscapes and still life. She exhibited five pictures at an exhibition of 'Weekend Work' by Industrial Artists at the French Gallery, London, in 1935. The subjects were mostly oil landscapes and a watercolour view in France.

### Mrs. G.. R.. HAYES (exh. 1921)

Painter of portraits who exhibited four pictures at the First Admiralty Art Club Exhibition in 1921.

### Miss Ruby G.. HAYWARD (exh. 1930-1931)

Painter in oil of figures and landscapes who lived at Woodbridge, Suffolk, and was a member of the Ipswich Art Club. She exhibited a total of six works 1930-1931, the titles included 'The Dinner Hour', 'The Doll's Trousseau' and 'The Paper Chase'.

### Basil HEAD (fl. 1912)

Black and white artist and illustrator, probably of books and magazines, who was working prior to the First World War. His work included some motoring subjects.

### Miss R.. HEADING (exh. 1923-1924)

Landscape artist who lived at Redland, Bristol, and exhibited at the R.W.A. 1923-1924. The titles were 'Autumn in the Downs' (1923) and 'Ideford, Devon' (1924).

### Edward HEALEY (1842-1916)

Landscape painter who lived in Bradford, Yorks, and was working before the First World War. A landscape by him was exhibited at the Bradford City Art Gallery in 1951, in an exhibition of work by past and present local artists. He died on 20th September 1916.

### Miss Mary HEALEY ((1885-1923)

Watercolour artist who lived in Bradford, Yorks, and was the daughter of Edward Healey (q.v.). The Bradford City Art Gallery showed four of her works at their Exhibition of Local Artists in 1951, which included an oil portrait and some watercolour views of Canada.

### Miss B.. Lanta HEAP A.R.D.S. (fl. 1927-1934)

Landscape painter and art teacher who was an associate member of the Royal Drawing Society 1927-1934 and worked from a studio in Chelsea. In the early 1930s Lanta Heap organised sketching classes in London and Surrey.

*H. Percy Heard*     *'Bideford Bridge, North Devon' (w/c) (J Collins and Son)*

## Hugh Percy HEARD (1866-1940)

Painter in oil and watercolour of marine and coastal scenes. Hugh Percy Heard was born in Bideford, Devon, on January 2nd 1866. Few details exist of his early life but it appears that he painted from an early age and after living in London and Swansea for a time returned to Bideford in 1911. Hugh Heard ran the Westward Ho! Art Club and was Headmaster of the Bideford School of Art from 1910 until the 1930s. He was not a frequent exhibitor but did show two works at the R.A. and also exhibited at the R.B.A. and in Liverpool. Hugh Heard was a keen actor and play producer, and later in his life these interests took over from his painting. His work is of good quality and many of the views are of Bideford and the surrounding area. (Illus. p.71).

## Jessica F.. HEATH (exh. 1935-1937)

Painter in oil of landscapes and coastal scenes. Jessica Heath exhibited an oil of 'Rocks and Sea' at the St Ives Society Summer Exhibition in 1935 and two similar works at their Winter Exhibition in 1937, entitled 'Sunshine and Storm' and 'Tregiffian Cliffs'.

## Sidney HEATH (fl. 1896)

Landscape artist and illustrator. Examples of his work were reproduced in The Studio in 1896 – eight pen and ink landscape studies for 'Bideford-on-Avon as a Sketching Ground'.

## Arthur HEATHCOTE (exh. 1914-1918)

Artist who lived in Kensington, London, and exhibited 14 works at the North British Academy 1914-1918.

## Miss Ethel HEAVISIDE (exh. 1914-1918)

Artist who lived in Torquay, Devon, and exhibited 5 works at the North British Academy in 1914. She was probably the daughter of Fred Heaviside.

## Miss Alice HEELAS (exh. 1901)

Painter of figure subjects who lived at Wokingham, Berks, and exhibited two works at the Berkshire Art Society Exhibition of 1901. The titles were 'Home Life' and 'The Fisherboy'.

## J.. Allister HEIR (exh. 1909)

Landscape artist, who exhibited at the Gilbert Garrett Sketch Club Exhibition in March 1909, a work entitled 'Trees and Sunshine'.

E. Hellicar                    'The Harbour' (w/c)

## Evelyn A.. HELLICAR (1862-1929)

Painter in watercolour of marines, buildings and landscapes, born in 1862, the son of the vicar of Bromley. An architect by profession, he exhibited six architectural designs at the Royal Academy 1891-1909, mostly local subjects such as 'The Public Library, Bromley, Kent' (1906) and 'The Hall at Ralston, Bromley' (1891). He was a member of the Bromley Sketching Club and his watercolour subjects included Thames views and scenes in Belgium and France. He died at Hambleton, Yorks, in 1929.

## Herbert HELPS (1893-1959)

Landscape and marine painter in watercolour, etcher and commercial artist. Herbert Helps was born at Westbury Park, Bristol. After serving in the Royal Worcester Yeomanry in the First World War he worked as a freelance commercial artist. He joined E S & A Robinson of Bristol and later Mardon, Son & Hall, commercial printers, and specialised in cigarette cards. Herbert Helps was a regular exhibitor with the Bristol Savages showing over 100 works 1912-1959. These works included etchings and watercolours and the subjects up until the 1930s were mostly rural scenes and West Country landscapes. From the mid 1930s, Herbert Helps specialised in marines, particularly studies of sailing ships. 'HMS Victory', 'The Golden Hind' (1949) and 'Entrance to Portsmouth Harbour' (1951) are typical titles. He does not appear to have exhibited elsewhere although some of his sketches were published by Punch. Herbert Helps died on 29th September 1959.

## Miss E.. HEMPSON (exh. 1889-1890)

Landscape painter in oil who lived at Manningtree, Essex, and was a member of the Ipswich Art Club. She exhibited a total of 12 works 1889-1890. The titles included 'The Stour, Mistley' and 'Harvest Time' (1889).

## Miss K.. HEMPSON (exh. 1889-1890)

Landscape painter in oil who lived at Ramsey, near Harwich, Essex, and was a member of the Ipswich Art Club. She exhibited a total of eight works 1889-1890. The titles included 'A Bit of the Stour' and 'Mistley from the Cliff' (1889). She was probably related to Miss E Hempson (q.v.) who lived nearby and exhibited similar works.

## Miss L.. HEMSWORTH (ex. 1888-1892)

Watercolour landscape painter who lived at Bacton, Suffolk, and was a member of the Ipswich Art Club. She exhibited five works 1888-1892, mostly views near Carlisle and in Scotland. The titles included 'Established Church, Lochgilphead', 'Distant view of Carlisle Castle - sunset' (both 1888) and 'Raworth Castle, Near Carlisle' (1890).

## Capt. Richard HENNESSEY (1876-1953)

Painter in oil and watercolour of landscapes and coastal scenes who lived at Harleston, Norfolk. He exhibited 29 works with the Army Officers Art Society 1928-1937. These included Dorset coastal scenes in oil and some French views in watercolour. Among the titles were 'Brownsea Castle, Poole Harbour' and 'Old Town, Grasse' (both 1930).

## Miss L.. M.. HERIZ-SMITH (exh. 1926-1938)

Painter in oil of landscapes and rural scenes who lived at Ruan Minor, Cornwall, and was a member of the Ipswich Art Club. She was a regular exhibitor showing 19 works 1926-1938. The titles included 'The Old Pent House, Cadgwith' and 'The Village Street, Cadgwith' (1934) and 'Morning Sunshine' and 'Evening Calm' (1936).

## H.. Z.. HERRMANN (fl. 1890s)

A good quality painter in watercolour of landscapes and rural scenes who was working at the end of the last century. These pictures are sometimes attributed to the German oil painter Hans Herrmann but the subject matter and style appear to be different. H Z Herrmann often painted cottage scenes and harvesting subjects.

J. Heseldin          'A Cornish Harbour' (w/c)

## James Marshall HESELDIN (1887-1969)

Painter in watercolour of landscapes, Cornish street and harbour scenes who was born in Leeds in 1887. Little is known about this competent artist as he does not appear to have exhibited although he lived in Cornwall and his pictures are mostly found in the West Country. The Cornish street scenes are among his most attractive work. James Heseldin died at St Austell, Cornwall, on 12th January 1969 at the age of 81.

## Robert J.. HEWITT (fl. 1905-1921)

Painter in watercolour of rural landscapes and moorland scenes who lived in Essex. This competent artist often painted windswept landscapes and his subjects included West Country and Essex views. He was a regular prize winner of The Studio magazine drawing competitions (1905-1911) when he was living at Brentwood and Warley, Essex. Although Robert Hewitt does not appear to have exhibited, one of his watercolours, 'Wind in the Dunes', was reproduced in Colour Magazine in April 1921.

## Catherine M.. HIBBS (fl. 1911)

A student at the Torquay School of Art, whose design for a colour print of a cottage was reproduced in The Studio magazine in 1911.

*H. W. Hicks*                    *'Yes Tor, Dartmoor' (w/c)*

*E. D. Hill*                    *'Bedroom Interior, 1928' (oil)*

## Herbert William HICKS (1880-1944)

Painter in watercolour and gouache of moorland and coastal scenes, who was born in Exeter in 1880. A self-taught artist, 'Herbie' Hicks was a prolific painter of West Country views in the style of F J Widgery. Many of the subjects were local Devon views and were usually inscribed with the location on the reverse. Much of his work was sold through C Samuel's Gallery, in Fore Street, Exeter. He was friend of the Exeter artist, Frederick Parr (q.v.) and they sometimes painted together in an attic studio. A fall in demand for the pictures in the 1930s forced Hicks to abandon painting and concentrate on his hairdressing business.

## Victor HICKS (fl. 1935)

Humorous illustrator, cartoonist and commercial artist. He wrote and illustrated a series of articles on 'Humorous Illustration' for The Artist magazine in 1935.

## Frank HIDER (1861-1933)

Painter in oil and sometimes watercolour of coastal scenes and rural landscapes. This artist was very prolific and his work is frequently seen on the market – the beach scenes in oil being the most common. The oils were often inscribed with the title and location on the reverse. Typical titles include 'Off the Cornish Coast', 'Bringing in the Catch' (1910) and 'Seagulls Haunt' (1916). Frank Hider's style and colour are similar to S Y Johnson (q.v.) but he usually painted with a broader technique. There are also some similar oils signed George Hider (q.v.) and he may have been related. Frank Hider lived at Forest Gate, Essex, for a number of years and died on 29th November 1933.

## George HIDER (fl.c. 1900)

Painter in oil of landscapes who was working around the turn of the century. The style and subject matter was similar to that of Frank Hider (q.v.) who may have been related.

## Eleanor Deane HILL (1882-1972)

Oil painter, illustrator in ink and watercolour, poet and amateur authoress. Eleanor Hill (née Matthews) studied art in London and in Florence. She had a studio for a time in Bedford Gardens but spent much of the year at her villa in Florence. Apart from oil interiors, some of her best work was her book illustration done in the early years of this century. She did a series of illustrations for George Meredith's 'The Shaving of Shagpat', but it is not known if they were published. Eleanor Hill lived for many years at Whitchurch, Hants, and died in Italy on 24th January 1972.

## J.. HILL (fl. 1920s)

Watercolour marine artist whose work is similar in style to F J Aldridge. The same artist also signs W Stewart (q.v.) and was probably a pupil or imitator of the Worthing marine painter. The popular subject matter of these works have made them increasingly collected.

## Mrs. Nina HILL (1877-1970)

Painter in oil of flower still life, portraits and landscapes. This is the married name of the artist Nina Rothney (q.v.) and appears on her work after 1910. Most of her later exhibits were flower still life, including five at the Royal Academy 1927-1936 and also two at the Paris Salon 1934 and 1936. In the late 1930s, she separated from her husband and moved with her son to the USA. Nina Hill died on 21st February 1970 aged 92 at Southern Pines, North Carolina. A retrospective exhibition of her work was held at Jeremy Wood Fine Art, Cranleigh, Surrey, in November 1979. Her large flower still life painted in the 1930s, are among the most decorative of her work and are signed Nina Hill in capitals.

*H. D. Hillier     'The Derwent, Grange, Borrowdale' (w/c)     (Sotheby's)*

## H.. D.. HILLIER (fl.c. 1880-1920)

Painter in oil and watercolour of highland scenes and river landscapes. The work is thought by many to be that of Henry H Parker, who is best known for his large river scenes. No address has been found for H D Hillier nor does he appear to have exhibited.

## Frank HINE (fl.c. 1920)

Watercolour landscape painter who was probably working in the early part of this century. His work is competent but he does not appear to have exhibited.

## Frank Robert HINKINS (fl. 1930-1934)

Artist who lived at Clayton, near Hassocks, Sussex, and was listed in the local trade directories as working in the early 1930s.

## Phil HIPS (fl. 1930s)

This is another pseudonym of the highly productive artist who usually signed his work F E Jamieson. The subjects are usually Scottish loch scenes or highland river landscapes in oil and they are often inscribed with the location on the reverse.

## Mrs. H.. C.. M.. HIRST (exh. 1921-1935)

Landscape painter who lived at Westbury on Trym and exhibited 12 works at the R.W.A. 1921-1935. The subjects were Cornwall and Devon coastal scenes and two Swiss landscapes.

## Mrs. Laura S.. HITCHCOCK (exh. 1905-1908)

Painter in oil and watercolour who lived at East Bergholt, Suffolk, and was a member of the Ipswich Art Club. She exhibited a total of 12 works 1905-1908 mostly scenes around Flatford but also some Devon views including 'New Bridge, on the Dart'. She also exhibited at the Society of Women Artists in 1908. Laura Hitchcock was the wife of H F Hitchcock also a member of the Ipswich Art Club.

## C.. I.. HOBSON (fl. 1912)

A pupil at the New School of Colour Printing whose work was illustrated in The Studio in 1912.

## Lilian HOCKNELL (exh. 1925)

Portrait artist in pen and ink who had an exhibition of 14 child studies at the Sporting Gallery, Covent Garden, in November 1925. She signed her work with initials.

## Charles Martin HODGES (1858-1916)

Painter in oil of genre, portraits and landscapes. He lived in Bath and was a regular exhibitor at the R.W.A. showing 20 works 1887-1915. The subjects were portraits, figure studies and landscape views in Devon and Scotland.

## W.. W.. HODGES (exh. 1878)

Landscape painter who lived at Clifton, Bristol, and exhibited four works at the R.W.A. in 1878. The subjects were studies of streets and buildings in Bristol. A view of 'Wickham Bridge, Stapleton' by W W Hodges is in the Bristol City Art Gallery.

## Winifred HODGKINSON (fl. 1910)

Watercolour artist who lived at Thornton Heath, Surrey. She won second prize for a watercolour still life in The Studio Competition of 1910.

## Mrs. Beatrice Prudence HOLDEN R.W.S. (1920-1988)

Painter in oil and watercolour of portraits, figures and still life. This is the married name of Beatrice Johnson (q.v.), the wife of Douglas Hamilton Holden (q.v.). Most of her work was signed with her maiden name, but she did also exhibit (including three works at the Royal Academy) in the early 1950s under her married name of Holden.

## Douglas Hamilton HOLDEN R.W.S. (1919-1972)

Watercolour landscape painter who was the son of the artist Harold Henry Holden (1885-1977). Douglas Hamilton Holden studied at the Birmingham College of Art and at the Royal College of Art in London. He was Head of Department of Foundation Studies at St Martin's School of Art and a member of the R.W.S. He married Beatrice Johnson (q.v.) the portrait and landscape artist.

## Carl HOLDER (died c. 1900)

Oil painter who was the son of Edward Henry Holder, brother of Edith Holder (q.v.) and worked under the name of Paul Romney (q.v.).

**Miss Edith HOLDER (fl. 1920s-1930s)**

Watercolour painter, decorator and art teacher who lived in Reigate, Surrey, and taught art at St. Davids School. She was the daughter of the artist Edward Henry Holder and sister of Carl Holder (q.v.). Edith Holder was a prolific artist who supplemented her income by selling her work which included painted silk scarves for Liberty's.

**Miss A.. L.. HOLDING B.W.S. (fl. 1924-1932)**

Watercolour painter, who exhibited three works at the B.W.S. Exhibition in Cheltenham, in 1924. The titles were 'Temptation', 'Most Delicious' and 'In Lilac Time'. She was also a member of the Paul Brinson Art Club in 1932.

**Evered HOLLAND (fl. 1929-1935)**

Painter in watercolour of landscapes who lived at Watersfield, Sussex. His work, often painted on 'Cox Paper', has a distinct sombre palette similar to the Littlehampton artist Edwin Harris. He was a member of the Society of Sussex Painters and exhibited 13 landscapes at their Exhibitions 1933-1935. Many of his works were local views – 'A Sussex Lane' and 'The Old Farm' being typical titles. He signed his work with a monogram and often a date (see index).

W. P. Hollyer                                    (Sotheby's)
'Highlanders' (oil)

**William Perring HOLLYER (1834-1922)**

Painter in oil of landscapes and animals. William Perring Hollyer specialised in highland landscape views often featuring cattle, a subject popular in the late nineteenth century. Most of the scenes were Scottish but he also painted some Welsh views and his titles included 'Morning in the Highlands', 'Welsh Ponies, Capel Curig' and 'Startled' (a study of a stag,

dated 1884). He also painted some domestic animals and there are some surviving examples of the artist's pets. Five of his ten children were to become artists of whom Eva Hollyer was probably the best known, but Maud Hollyer, Edith de Chair, Gregory Hollyer and Olive Cliffe (q.v.) all showed talent in their particular fields. Many of William Perring Hollyer's works were large and impressive and the best examples command high prices. He signed his work W P Hollyer sometimes with a date and often inscribed on the reverse.

**R.. W.. HOLMAN (fl.c. 1920)**

Painter in watercolour of moorland landscapes who was probably working in Devon around the 1920s. The paintings are similar in colour and style to Charles E Brittan Jnr. and include some views of Dartmoor. The subjects often include sheep or cattle and are painted in a precise manner and usually heightened with bodycolour. He signed R W Holman and sometimes with a date.

Gerald Holmes                              'Ullswater' (w/c)

**Gerald HOLMES (fl. 1920s-1940s)**

Painter in watercolour of landscapes and coastal scenes. This competent artist was quite prolific but does not appear to have exhibited. The subjects include views of the West Country and in the Lake District.

**Harold J.. HOLMES B.W.S. (exh. 1928)**

Watercolour landscape painter who was a member of the B.W.S. and exhibited a Sussex view at their Autumn Exhibition in Preston in 1928.

**Miss Margaret HOLMES (exh. 1898-1911)**

Watercolour landscape painter who lived in Norwich and was a member of the Norwich Art Circle. She exhibited a total of 21 works 1898-1911, mostly local scenes and some Thames Valley views, including Windsor. She also painted some interiors.

## Wilfred HOLMES (fl.c. 1900)

Painter in watercolour of cottages and garden scenes. This good quality artist has a style similar to that of Arthur Claude Strachan although he does not appear to have exhibited. His subjects include cottages in Surrey and Warwickshire.

## Miss Emily F.. HOLSNER (fl. 1930)

Artist who lived in Brighton and is recorded in the local trade directory as working around 1930.

## Miss Emily G.. HOME A.R.W.A. (exh. 1875-1928)

Watercolour landscape and still life painter who lived at Clifton, Bristol, and was an associate member of the R.W.A. She was a regular exhibitor, showing over 58 works 1875-1928. The subjects were rural landscapes, figures and still life and the titles included 'The Travellers Joy' (1900), 'A Country Lass' and 'Homeward' (1907) and 'End of the Summer' (1908).

## Lt. Col. John R.. H.. HOMFRAY (1868-1944)

Artist who exhibited at the Army Officers Art Society in 1930.

## Miss May HONY (exh. 1914)

Artist who lived at Clifton, Bristol, and exhibited two pictures at the R.W.A. in 1914.

*Eileen Hood*       *'Carthorse' (Postcard)*

## Miss Eileen K.. HOOD (born c. 1893, fl. 1915-1925)

Painter in watercolour and illustrator of horses and dogs who lived at Stanmore, Middlesex. Eileen Hood took to drawing at an early age and in 1904 she won the G F Watts Prize at the Royal Drawing Society for an animal study. She exhibited occasionally in London at the R.I. but much of her work was animal illustrations reproduced as postcards. She painted a series of watercolours of horses published by Geographia Ltd and some dogs for Hodder and Stoughton. Her work is not well known as it is seldom seen on the market but the quality and subject matter would make originals collectable.

## E.. Horace HOOPER (fl. 1890s)

Painter in oil and watercolour of rural scenes and river landscapes. The style and subject matter suggest some family connection with John Horace Hooper, whose work is well known. Some Thames Valley views exist, including 'A Cornfield near Sonning, Berks'.

## Mrs. Millicent L.. HOOPER (exh. 1925-1950)

Painter of portraits and flower subjects who lived at Ipswich and was a member of the Ipswich Art Club. She exhibited nine works 1925-1950, mostly portraits and figures but also some flower paintings such as 'Marigolds' (1946).

## Miriam Mabel HOOPER (1872-1953)

Painter of landscapes and rural scenes in watercolour. Miriam Hooper was born in Redhill in 1872 and studied at the Croydon School of Art, where Charles Shannon was the visiting tutor. Her brother Vincent married Tatton Winter's daughter and that Reigate artist thus became her tutor and a great influence on her painting style. The family ties were further strengthened when her brother, who was an architect, formed a partnership with Tatton Winter's son, Cecil. Miriam Hooper exhibited widely both in London and in the provinces, including two works at the R. A. 'Middleburg, Holland' (1915) and 'A Bridge over the Arun' (1926). She travelled abroad and spent most of her holidays painting in Holland, France, Italy and Spain. Her nephew, George Hooper, also became a respected landscape painter in oil and watercolour.

## Miss D.. K.. E.. HOPE (exh. 1920)

Artist who lived at Clifton, Bristol, and exhibited two black and white sketches at the R.W.A. in 1920, these were studies of Clifton College.

## Reginald (Rex) Frederick HOPES (1890-1982)

Painter in watercolour of landscapes, flowers and still life. He was born in Bristol and educated locally. After serving in the Great War in France, he moved to London to study art at the Slade School. Rex Hopes returned to Bristol in the early 1930s and was a regular exhibitor at the R.W.A. showing some 32 works 1932-1976. He was an active member of the Bristol Savages and exhibited over 180 works 1933-1978. The subjects were mostly flowers and landscapes. Rex Hopes was a life member of the Bristol Savages and President in 1946, 1957 and 1967. He moved from Bristol to Longlevens, Glos, and died aged 92 on 26th February 1982.

*Nöel Hopking*       (*Mill House Antiques*)
*'Nuthatches' (w/c)*

## Nöel Hubert HOPKING (1883-1964)

A fine quality painter in watercolour of birds and animal subjects who was born in London in 1883. He exhibited in London from 1920 including two works at the Royal Academy. After the Second World War, Nöel Hopking moved to Horsham, Sussex, where he continued to paint and sell his work locally. Much of his work was done for illustration as cards and prints. His pictures are seldom seen on the market but the quality and the subject matter would make them collectable.

## Francis Powell HOPKINS (1830-1913)

Painter in oil and watercolour of golfing scenes and also an author on golf and fishing subjects. Francis Powell Hopkins was born in Cambridge, educated at Rugby School and after an army career retired to Bideford in North Devon. He was a keen fisherman and with the proximity of the course at Westward Ho!, became an enthusiastic golfer. Francis Hopkins probably had no formal art training, but his competent style and the sought after subject matter have made his golfing pictures highly collectable. An exhibition of 17 of his golfing pictures was held at Burlington Galleries, London, in July 1988. Francis Hopkins also wrote articles on golf for The Field and in 1893 a book 'Fishing Experiences' which he also illustrated. His oils, which are rare, were signed F P Hopkins or with initials, whereas the watercolours were signed under a pseudonym 'Major S' or 'Shortspoon' (q.v.)

## G.. C.. HOPKINS (fl.c. 1920)

Painter in watercolour of marines who was working early this century. His subjects include fishing boats in the Red Sea.

## Miss M.. HOPPER (exh. 1931-1934)

Artist and illustrator who lived at St. Andrews, Bristol, and exhibited nine works at the R.W.A. 1931-1934. The subjects were flowers, landscapes, figures and a bookplate design. The titles included 'The Tired Puppet' (1931), 'Silver Birch' (1932), 'Christmas Roses' and 'St. Giles Fair, Oxford' (both 1933) and 'Crantock' (1934).

*Fred Horley*       *'West Horsley, 1909' (w/c)*

## Frederick Richard HORLEY (1872-1944)

Painter in watercolour of cottage scenes and landscapes. Fred Horley lived in East Sheen, Surrey, and worked in London at his printing business. At weekends he cycled into the Surrey countryside and painted landscapes in the company of other artists. Fred Horley did not make any effort to sell his work during his lifetime and until recently most of his output had remained with his family. A quiet, retiring, family man Fred Horley was tragically killed during an air raid on 31st July 1944.

## Miss A.. HORSTMANN (exh. 1919-1936)

Miniature, flower and landscape painter, who lived at Bath and exhibited 25 works at the R.W.A. 1919-1936. The subjects were mostly portrait miniatures and also some flowers and landscapes.

## Stanley HOUGHTON (fl. 1945)

Artist in pen and ink, whose series of sketches of the Eighth Army in Italy were reproduced in The Artist magazine in March 1945.

## Stanley R.. HOUNSELL (exh. 1950)

Painter who lived in Plymouth and exhibited two tempra pictures at the Plymouth Art Society Annual Exhibition in 1950.

### Miss Ethel Lilley HOVENDEN (1873-1953)

Miniature portrait painter in watercolour who was born in Brixton, London, on 26th October 1873. Little is known of her early life but she was a friend and pupil of William Tatton Winter. She exhibited at the Royal Academy in 1899 and at the Society of Miniature Painters but after her marriage in 1903 did not show any work until 1915. Her later work was exhibited under her married name of Ethel Lilley Robertson (q.v.).

### Jamison HOWELL (exh. 1950)

Landscape painter in oil and watercolour who exhibited three works at the Plymouth Art Society Annual Exhibition in 1950.

### George HOWELL-BAKER A.R.W.A., N.B.A. (exh. 1912-1916)

Artist who lived at Bridgend, Glamorgan, and was a member of the N.B.A. and an associate of the R.W.A. He exhibited seven pictures at the R.W.A. 1912-1916, mostly views of churches.

### Frederick Walter HOWELLS (born 1885, exh. 1925-1936)

Landscape painter who lived at Filton near Bristol, and later, Brosley in Shropshire. He exhibited 25 works at the R.W.A. 1925-1936. The subjects were mostly local scenes, landscapes and coastal studies.

*Kate Howes*                    *'Old Barn, 1912' (w/c)*

### Miss Kate A.. HOWES (fl. 1894-1900)

Watercolour painter of landscapes and flowers who lived at Ryde on the Isle of Wight, and, later, Southampton. She was the daughter of Frederick Howes who was a portrait and figure painter. In 1894, Kate Howes received an Hon. Mention in The Studio card design competition but does not appear to have exhibited. She did belong to the local art society called the 'Daub Club'.

### S.. F.. HOWITT (exh. 1889-1894)

Landscape and portrait painter who was a member of the Norwich Art Circle and exhibited 17 works 1889-1894. The subjects were mostly local landscapes, a few portraits and some views in Germany.

### Maria A.. HOYER (exh. 1912)

Watercolour landscape painter who, although not a member, exhibited three pictures at the Winchester Art Society Annual Exhibition in 1912. These were watercolour landscape views, including a French scene.

### Mrs. Stanley S.. HOYLAND (exh. 1885-1888)

Painter in oil of landscapes who lived at Ipswich, Suffolk, and was a member of the Ipswich Art Club. She exhibited a total of four works 1885-1888, the titles included 'At Bealings' and 'Near Shrubland' (both 1885).

### H.. HUBNER (exh. 1913)

Artist who won first prize in the Gilbert Garrett competition – Animal Painting Section – for a study of Polar bears, in 1913.

### Miss Alfreda T.. HUDD (exh. 1917-1918)

Watercolour artist who lived in Bristol and exhibited at the R.W.A. 1917-1918. The titles were 'Chrysanthemums' and 'Balgdon'. She was probably the sister of D A Hudd (q.v.).

### Miss D.. A.. HUDD (exh. 1915-1917)

Landscape painter in watercolour who lived in Clifton, Bristol, and was probably the sister of A T Hudd (q.v.). She exhibited four works at the R.W.A. 1915-1917. The titles included 'Moonlight – Hyde Park' (1916) and 'Cortebelle' (1917).

### Cyril A.. HUDSON (exh. 1926)

Artist who exhibited six landscapes at a 'Ten Man Show' at the Gieves Gallery, London, in 1926. The subjects were views in England and France.

### M.. U.. HUDSON (fl. 1900s)

Painter in oil of portraits and figure subjects. This good quality artist does not appear to have exhibited.

### Rose K.. HUGH-JONES (exh. 1930)

Oil painter, watercolourist and wood engraver who had an exhibition of her work at the Brook Street Gallery, London, in 1930. The exhibition consisted of 58 works mostly oils and watercolours and four wood engravings. The subjects included landscape views in North Wales, Italy, Capri, Mexico and South Carolina.

**Madeline HUGHES (fl.c. 1900)**

Painter in watercolour of figures and landscapes, who often depicted fisherfolk on the shore. She appears also to have painted under the name of A Poisson (q.v.) and much of her work was signed in this manner.

*H. Hughes-Richardson    'Blashford, Hants' (w/c)    (J. Collins and Son)*

**H.. HUGHES-RICHARDSON (fl.c. 1920s)**

This prolific watercolour artist had a most accomplished free technique of painting landscapes, similar in style to Wilfrid Ball. It is curious that an artist of this quality does not appear to have exhibited. The subjects include river landscapes, rural scenes and some views of Venice.

**A.. E.. HUITT (exh. 1921)**

Landscape painter who exhibited three pictures at the First Admiralty Art Club Exhibition in June 1921.

**Claude HULK (fl. 1900s)**

Painter in watercolour of landscapes and some hunting scenes. His landscape subjects include Devon and Cornwall coastal scenes.

**E.. HUMPHRIES (exh. 1920-1924)**

Artist who lived in Gloucester and exhibited four works at the R.W.A. 1920-1924. The titles included 'At Anchor' (1920) and 'The Black Barque' (1924).

**Miss Annie Lucy HUNNIBELL (exh. 1885-1890)**

Painter in oil of landscapes who lived in Ipswich and was a member of the Ipswich Art Club. She exhibited 21 works 1885-1890, mostly local views. The titles included 'Cottages at Long Melford', 'Playford Hall' and 'Melford Green' (all 1888).

**Charles Frederick HUNNIBELL (exh. 1884-1897)**

Painter in oil of figure subjects who lived in Ipswich and was a member of the Ipswich Art Club. He exhibited nine works 1884-1897, mostly portraits and figure studies. Miss Annie Hunnibell (q.v.) also exhibited from the same address.

**F. C. W.. HUNNIBELL (exh. 1912)**

Painter in oil of landscapes who exhibited two works at the Worthing Art Gallery Summer Exhibition in 1912.

**Miss Mary H.. HUNNYBUN (exh. 1890-1892)**

Painter in oil of landscapes who lived in Colchester, and was a member of the Ipswich Art Club. She exhibited in 1890 and two works in 1892 – 'Haybarn Cottage, East Bergholt' and 'Flatford'.

**Harry Millson HUNT (fl. 1875-1891)**

Painter in oil of Middle Eastern and desert scenes and occasionally English landscapes and marines. His work is of good quality and dates from the last quarter of the nineteenth century. The oils are usually inscribed on the reverse – 'Old Cairo from the Nile' (1886) and 'Returning to a Bedouin Camp, Mount Sinai' (1890) are typical titles.

**Miss Jessie HUNT (exh. 1910)**

Watercolour artist who exhibited a church interior study at the Worthing Art Gallery Summer Exhibition in 1910.

**Henry HURLSTONE (exh. 1922-1923)**

Watercolour landscape painter, who lived at Stratton-on-the-Fosse, near Bath, and exhibited three works at the R.W.A. 1922-1923. The titles were – 'Wind in the Hill', 'March Sunshine' (1922) and 'Evening Gold' (1923).

**Maj. Edgar E.. HUSEY (exh. 1928-1930)**

Watercolour landscape painter who exhibited eight works at the Army Officers Art Society 1928-1930. The subjects included views in Siam and the Far East.

**Albert S.. HUTCHINGS (exh. 1935-1936)**

Landscape painter who lived at Portishead, Bristol, and exhibited four works at the R.W.A. 1935-1936. The subjects were all Cornwall and Devon coastal scenes – 'Castle Rock, Lynton' and 'The Incoming Tide' were typical titles.

**Mrs. H.. R.. M.. HUTT (exh. 1904-1908)**

Watercolour landscape and interior painter who lived at Dulverton, Somerset, and was a member of the Norwich Art Circle. She exhibited six works 1904-1908, which were watercolour landscapes and a church interior.

George Hyde                    (Bourne Gallery)
              'St Pauls from Fleet  Street''

## George HYDE (fl. 1900s)

This was a pseudonym for George Hyde-Pownall,
who specialised in painting small London street
scenes in oil.  He also painted some river landscapes
and coastal scenes.

# I

## Frank INGALL (fl.c. 1920)

Painter in watercolour and pastel of dogs who was probably working in the 1920s. This competent artist does not appear to have exhibited but his work is seen on the market and the subject matter has made it collectable. He signs Frank Ingall in a printed script.

## C.. F.. INGERSON (fl. 1912)

Etcher and colour printer who was a pupil at the School of Colour Printing in 1912. An example of his work was reproduced in The Studio magazine in that year.

## Miss. M.. Leslie INGLIS A.R.W.A. (exh. 1929-1939)

Landscape and still life painter who lived at Clifton and later at Chew Stoke, Bristol, and was an associate member of the R.W.A. She exhibited 19 works at the R.W.A. 1929-1939, mostly local views, alpine scenes and some flower still life. The titles include 'The Village Fair' Chew Stoke' (1933), 'The Dairy Yard' (1934) and views of Heidelberg, and the Tyrol (1936).

*Leslie Ingram*      *(Marble Hill Gallery)*
*'Low Tide, Whitby, 1920' (w/c)*

## Leslie INGRAM (fl.c. 1920)

Painter in watercolour of landscapes and harbour scenes who was working in the early 1920s. This good quality artist certainly worked in the Whitby area but does not appear to have exhibited.

## Miss M.. INGRAM (exh. 1933-1936)

Artist who lived at St Andrew Park, Bristol, and exhibited at the R.W.A. a work each year from 1933 until 1936. The titles were 'Norman Archway, Haughmond Abbey', 'Dundry Church', 'Caravans' and 'Long Ashton Church'.

## Jessie M.. ISAAC A.R.W.A. (exh. 1898-1933)

Painter in watercolour of landscapes, still life and miniatures who lived in Bristol and was an associate member of the R.W.A. She was a regular exhibitor showing over 55 works 1898-1933. The subjects included views of Chipping Campden (1920), The Lake District (1921) and the Cotswolds (1928 and 1929). She was also a craftworker, decorating china and brooches, and some of these were exhibited at the Cheltenham Arts Exhibition in 1924.

## W.. ISBELL (exh. 1900-1901)

Watercolour landscape painter who lived at Clifton, Bristol, and exhibited five works at the R.W.A. 1900-1901. The subjects included local views and scenes in Hereford and North Wales. 'The Oat Harvest, Shirehampton' (1900) was a typical title.

## Eileen IZARD (exh. 1956)

Painter of flower still life in oil who exhibited at the St Ives Society of Artists Summer Exhibition in 1956. The pictures were entitled 'Tulips' and 'Freesia'.

# J

### Brig. Gen. Evan Maclean JACK (1873-1951)

Watercolour landscape painter who exhibited 10 pictures at the Army Officers Art Society Exhibitions 1928-1930. Most of the subjects were landscapes including views in Wales, Shropshire and French harbour scenes. He lived in Southampton and died on 10th August 1951.

### Maud Howland JACKSON (fl.c. 1900)

Artist in pastel who lived at Ringwood, Hants. Her work included some French town scenes.

### R.. D.. JACKSON (exh. 1924)

Watercolour painter who exhibited three views of Jersey at the B.W.S. Annual Exhibition at Cheltenham in 1924.

### Mrs. A.. E.. JAMES (exh. 1924-1938)

Flower painter who lived at Chilcompton, near Bath, and exhibited 11 works at the R.W.A. 1924-1938. The exhibits were all flower studies, including four of Roses.

### Rev. H.. L.. JAMES (exh. 1884-1889)

Watercolour landscape painter who lived at Walberswick, Suffolk, and later Everton, Liverpool. He was a member of the Ipswich Art Club and exhibited 33 works 1884-1889. The titles included 'Golf Tower, Bawdsey Ferry', 'The Quay, Walberswick' and 'Easton Broad, Suffolk' (all 1885).

### Mrs. S.. S.. JAMES (exh. 1886-1889)

Painter in watercolour of flowers and still life, who lived at Walberswick, Suffolk, and, later, Everton, Liverpool, and was the wife of the Rev. H L James (q.v.). She was a member of the Ipswich Art Club and exhibited 15 works 1886-1889. The titles included 'The Deserted Nest' and 'A Study of Roses' (both 1888).

### F.. E.. JAMIESON (fl.c. 1910-1940)

Painter in oil and watercolour of highland landscapes and coastal scenes. The work of this highly prolific artist is curious since the oils and watercolours have two quite distinctive styles and subject matter. The oil paintings are most frequently seen and these are highland landscapes or loch scenes – sometimes they appear to be signed with pseudonyms such as 'W Richards' (q.v.) and 'Phil Hips' (q.v.). – the location is usually inscribed on the reverse. The watercolours are often coastal scenes with boats and figures on a shore, painted in a more traditional Victorian style, and possibly pre-date the oils. F E Jamieson's beach scenes were published as postcards around 1920 by G Ajelli & Co of London on a textured card to give the appearance of an oil. Jamieson is known to have travelled widely in the South of England between the wars selling his work but does not appear to have exhibited.

### Dudley JARRETT (fl. 1930s)

Illustrator and commercial artist who married the artist Marcia L Foster. They often jointly worked on commissions, sometimes both painting parts of the same figure.

### Miss Mabel JARRETT (exh. 1900-1901)

Still life and flower painter who lived at Eastville, Bristol, and exhibited at the R.W.A. 1900-1901. The titles were 'Marguerites and Virginia Creeper' and 'Still Life'.

### Miss Eleanor V.. JAUNCEY (exh. 1919-1920)

Watercolour artist who lived in Ipswich and was a member of the Ipswich Art Club. She exhibited a total of five works at their exhibitions in 1919 and 1920, the titles included 'Submarine Telegraph Station', and 'Nelson's Column from Whitehall' (both 1919).

F. E. Jamieson      'A Highland Loch' (oil)      (Philip Parker)

Florence Jay      'On Guard' (oil)      (Sotheby's)

**Miss Florence JAY (exh. 1926-1927)**

Painter of animals in oil and watercolour who had two exhibitions of horses and dogs at the Sporting Gallery, London, 1926 and 1927. The first consisted of 66 paintings and the second 63, both oil and watercolour. Some of the works were commissioned portraits of animals which had been lent back for the exhibition by the owners. Florence Jay's paintings do now appear on the market and the dog oils, in particular, are collectable. She signed her work Florence Jay in a printed script. (Illus. p. 83).

**Mrs. E.. Maud JEENS (exh. 1924-1925)**

Watercolour and pen and ink artist who lived in Gloucester and exhibited a total of 13 works at the Cheltenham Art Society Exhibitions of 1924 and 1925. Most of the pictures were studies of cathedrals and other buildings, but there were also some Egyptian views.

*G. H. Jenkins*                *'On the Tamar looking towards Cremyll' (w/c)*

**George Henry JENKINS (1843-1914)**

Painter in oil and watercolour of coastal, beach and moorland scenes. G H Jenkins lived in Plymouth and much of his subject matter was taken from that part of Devon. He exhibited locally at the Society of Western Artists, at the Plymouth Arts Club and also at the R.W.A. in Bristol. He showed a total of 20 works at the R.W.A. 1892-1895 at the Annual and Winter Exhibitions. These included Welsh views such as 'On the Lledr, North Wales' (1895) and Cornish scenes such as 'King Arthur's Castle, Tintagel' (1892). George Jenkins did not exhibit regularly in London, but he did show 'Trawlers entering Plymouth Sound' at the Doré Gallery in an exhibition of West Country Artists c. 1900. He also showed work at Elands Art Gallery, Exeter, including two Dartmoor views in 1907. Raphael Tuck published some postcards for the 'Picturesque Devon' series but these were signed G. H. Jenkins Jr.

**Miss Mary JERVIS-WHITE-JERVIS (exh. 1902-1947)**

Landscape painter who lived at Felixstowe and later at Melton, Suffolk, and was a member of the Ipswich Art Club. She was the daughter of Herbert Jervis-White-Jervis who was President of the Ipswich Art

Club in 1910. She was a regular exhibitor showing 45 works 1902-1947 and the subjects were mostly local landscapes and some Italian views. The titles included 'Felixstowe Cliffs', 'After Sunset, Hollesley Heath' and 'A Venetian Bridge' (all 1910).

**Mrs. Edmund JERVOISE (exh. 1912)**

Watercolour painter who was a member of the Winchester Art Society and exhibited a garden scene in 1912.

*Edith Jezzard*                *'A Kentish Farmyard' (w/c)*

**Edith JEZZARD (fl.c. 1930)**

Painter in watercolour of landscapes and rural scenes. This artist had a distinctive and appealing style with the work drawn in soft pencil and then heightened with coloured washes. She does not appear to have exhibited but did work at one time in Kent.

**Miss Hilda JILLARD (1899-1975)**

Painter in oil and watercolour of figures, landscapes, and animals. Hilda Jillard was born on 16th October 1899 near Godalming, Surrey. She studied at the Farnham School of Art, later at the Slade under Henry Tonks, and also at Frank Calderon's School of animal painting. Hilda Jillard exhibited regularly with the Guildford Art Society, and in 1939 had an exhibition of oils at the Wertheim Gallery in London. In 1942, she moved to St Ives, Cornwall, and stayed there for 12 years, exhibiting with the local art society and at nearby Newlyn. There are works by Hilda Jillard in the permanent collection of the Imperial War Museum, London, and at the Newlyn Orion Art Gallery, Penzance.

**H.. B.. JOEL (fl.c. 1890-1910)**

Painter in oil and occasionally watercolour of landscapes, figures and coastal scenes. This artist is catalogued as both H B Joel and J H Boel (q.v.) as the signature is monogrammed with the initials and is difficult to read. There is some evidence that Joel was his actual name. He was a prolific artist and the work is often seen on the market. The earlier examples painted in the 1890s are usually dated.

Beatrice Johnson                    'Reading' (w/c)

### Beatrice Prudence JOHNSON R.W.S. (1920-1988)

Painter in oil and watercolour of portraits, figures, and still life. Beatrice Johnson studied art in Birmingham, and at the R.C.A., London, before teaching at the Croydon School of Art. She first exhibited in London in 1938, and showed six works at the Royal Academy 1950-1960, mainly portraits. Although married to the artist Douglas Hamilton Holden (q.v.), she mostly continued to exhibit under her maiden name.

### Sidney Yates JOHNSON (fl. 1890-1926)

A prolific painter of landscapes in oil who was working from about 1890 until around 1926. His work has a distinctive style and is similar to that of Frank Hider (q.v.). The subjects are often in pairs and usually Cornish coastal scenes, beach scenes, highland landscapes and cottages in a rural setting. The artist did not often inscribe the work with the location, but it was usually dated, with the signature S Y Johnson scratched in the wet paint. He sometimes signed with a monogram (see index).

### Miss G.. D.. JONES (exh. 1927)

Miniature painter who lived at Chagford, Devon, and exhibited three portrait miniatures at the R.W.A. in 1927.

### R.. B.. Hooper JONES (exh. 1932-1955, died c. 1961)

Painter in oil, watercolour and pastel of figure subjects and landscapes who lived at Redland, Bristol, and worked as a commercial artist for E.S.&A. Robinson. He was a member of the Bristol Savages and exhibited a total of 67 works at their exhibitions 1934-1955. These were mostly views of Bristol and the South of England but also some foreign landscapes including Italy and Yugoslavia. He showed two works at the R.W.A. in 1932 and 1936. R B Hooper Jones also worked as a poster artist and his work included Air Raid Precaution poster designs in 1939. He did little work after the mid 1950s due to failing health and he died about 1961.

### Miss Winifred J.. JONES A.R.W.A. (exh. 1913-1928)

Painter in oil and watercolour of landscapes, flowers and figure subjects who lived in Bristol and was an associate member of the R.W.A. She was a regular exhibitor showing over 38 works 1913-1928. The subjects included flower studies, landscapes, portraits and some old master copies.

### Miss Phyllis Tiel JORDON (exh. 1928-1935)

Painter in watercolour of landscapes and still life who lived in Darlington, Co. Durham, and exhibited 1928-1935. She exhibited a still life of roses at the Royal Academy in 1928 and two watercolours – 'Rocks, Kennack Sands' and 'Porthmeor Beach, St Ives' at the St Ives Society of Artists Summer Exhibition in 1935.

### Miss Ruth JOY (exh. 1912)

Watercolour landscape painter who exhibited four works at the Winchester Art Society Exhibition in 1912. The subjects were market scenes, a view of Concarneau in Brittany, and a view of Bruges.

### Miss Annette JUMP (exh. 1919)

Landscape and figure painter who lived in Ipswich and was a member of the Ipswich Art Club. She exhibited four works in 1919 – 'In the Chantrey Garden', 'Chantrey Hall', 'In Mr Notcutt's new Garden' and 'Lady Warwick and Children'.

# K

## John KEENAN R.W.A. (1904-1971)

Painter of landscapes and flowers who was born in Carlisle and moved to Bristol in 1929. He worked in the artists department of Mardon Son and Hall, a local commercial printers, until his retirement. He specialised in watercolour studies of flowers, local landscapes and architectural subjects. Many of his flowers studies were used as illustrations for cigarette cards by W D & H O Wills in the 1930s. A regular exhibitor at the R.W.A., he showed 66 works at their exhibitions 1929-1971, mostly West Country landscapes and flowers but also some foreign views including Dinan, Paris and Venice. John Keenan exhibited over 90 works with the Bristol Savages 1947-1968, again mostly landscapes and flowers. He was President of the Bristol Savages in 1956 and 1965 who own examples of his work. He died in Westbury on Trym, Bristol, in 1971.

John Keenan                    (R. McFetrich)
*'A Bristol Backstreet' (w/c)*

## Miss N.. KEER (exh. 1887)

Landscape painter in oil who lived at Ipswich and was a member of the Ipswich Art Club. She exhibited two works in 1887, entitled 'Orford Church' and 'Morning, up the Gipping'.

## Walter D.. KELLAR (exh. 1927-1932)

Artist who lived in Bristol and exhibited seven works at the R.W.A. 1927-1932. The exhibits were mostly West Country landscapes, but other subjects included 'Stratford on Avon' (1930) and 'The River at Pitlochery' (1931).

S. E. Kelly        *'Babbacombe Bay, Devon' (w/c)*        ( J. Collins and Son)

## Samuel E.. KELLY (fl. c. 1920s)

Painter in watercolour and sometimes oil of coastal scenes who lived and worked around Torquay, Devon. This artist's work is not often seen on the market but the quality and pleasing subject matter would make the pictures collectable. One of his most popular subjects was Babbacombe Bay, Devon. Samuel Kelly also painted bay scenes in oil on pottery dishes and these were probably made for the tourist market.

## Miss I.. A.. KENDAL (exh. 1925-1927)

Still life painter who lived at Coniston, Lancs, and exhibited three works at the R.W.A. 1925-1927. The titles included 'Basket of Lilacs' (1926) and 'Primroses and Violets' (1927).

## Miss May KENNAWAY (exh. 1911-1930)

Painter of miniatures, flowers and still life who lived at Teignmouth, Devon, and later at Bath. She exhibited at the R.H.A. and the London Salon 1911-1916 while living at the Devon address and later was a regular exhibitor at the R.W.A. showing 11 works 1926-1930. The subjects, including miniatures, were mostly flowers and also two studies of church fonts.

## Col. C.. KENNEDY (exh. 1924)

Pen and ink artist of architectural views who exhibited four works at the Cheltenham Art Group Annual Exhibition in 1924.

*A. Kennett-Barrington*          *'Church Street, Witley' (w/c)*

## Lady Alicia Georgette KENNETT-BARRINGTON (1848-1905)

Born in 1848, Alicia Georgette Sandeman was the daughter of George Sandeman of the famous port company. She lived at Westfield on Hayling Island and at Hyde Park Gardens, London. In 1878 she married Vincent Kennett who was involved with first aid and relief work with the St John's Ambulance Association and she assisted him with his work for the National Aid Society later to become the Red Cross. Vincent received a Knighthood in 1886 and Alicia was made a Lady of Grace of the Order of St John of Jerusalem in 1889. Sir Vincent died in 1903, as a result of a ballooning accident, and Alicia in 1905. She was a competent watercolour artist and her sketches were often landscapes and cottage scenes in the South of England.

## Fred Ritre KERLY (exh. 1901)

Reading artist who exhibited two landscapes at the Berkshire Art Society Exhibition in 1901. The subjects were Mapledurham Mill and a view at Burnham, Somerset.

*Alfred Kerr*          *'Ombres et Lumiere, Seine' 1950 (oil)*

## Alfred KERR (exh. 1950-1952)

Landscape painter in oil who lived in London in the early 1950s and exhibited three paintings at the R.O.I. 1950-1952. The subjects were all French landscapes – 'Ombres et Lumiere, Seine', 'The Grand Palais, Paris' and 'Les Andeleys, Normandy'.

## Mark KERR (exh. 1938)

Artist who exhibited eight works with the Air Force Artists Association in December 1938. The subjects were mostly warships but also some aeroplanes.

## Miss Annie I.. KETTLEWELL (exh. 1916-1917)

Artist who lived at Fishponds, Bristol, and exhibited at the R.W.A. in 1916 and 1917. The titles were a 'Study of a Tiger' and 'Coombe Dingle' – both black and white drawings.

## Lt. Col. W.. KEYWORTH (exh. 1928-1937)

Watercolour landscape painter who lived at Teignmouth, Devon, and exhibited 14 pictures with the Army Officers Art Society 1928-1937. The subjects were mostly English and Continental landscape views.

*S. L. Kilpack*          *(Bourne Gallery)*
*'A Rocky Coast' (oil)*

## Sarah Louisa KILPACK (1839-1909)

Painter in oil of coastal scenes, marines and occasionally landscapes. The pictures tend to be small and painted on card and the subjects are usually views of Jersey, but also some views in Guernsey and Northern France. Sarah Louisa Kilpack was the daughter of Thomas Kilpack and was born at Covent Garden, London, on the 15th December 1839. Although most of her working addresses were in London she was a frequent visitor to Jersey, often staying with friends in St. Saviours. She exhibited regularly at the Society of Women Artists showing a huge total of 119 works 1867-1909. Sarah Kilpack died in London on 25th October 1909. She often signed her small studies S L Kilpack or S L K in orange.

## George A.. KING (fl. 1889-1905)

Landscape painter in oil and watercolour who lived in Norwich and was a member of the Norwich Art Circle. Although a member in 1889, he did not exhibit until 1901. George King showed a total of 10 pictures 1901-1905, mostly local landscapes in both oil and watercolour.

## Maj. Gerald Hartley KING (1882-1940)

Artist who lived at Weybridge, Surrey, and exhibited seven works with the Army Officers Art Society 1928-1935.

## Miss M.. KING (exh. 1932-1935)

Sculptor and flower painter who lived in Bristol and exhibited five works at the R.W.A. 1932-1935. These were three sculptures and flower paintings of 'Marguerites' (1934) and 'Roses' (1935).

## Miss V.. A.. KING (exh. 1925-1929)

Landscape artist and etcher who lived at Horfield, Bristol, and from 1929 at Chippenham, Wilts. She exhibited at the R.W.A. 'A Farmhouse' (1925), 'The Docks, Bristol' (1926) and 'The Frome at Stapleton' (1929) – these were probably etchings as a number of etchings of local views are known to exist.

*Thos Kingston*  (J Collins and Son)
*'A Farmstead in Somerset, 1919' (w/c)*

## Thomas KINGSTON A.R.W.A. (1863-1929)

Bristol born painter in oil and watercolour of landscapes, flowers and marines. He was a founder member of the Bristol Savages and a regular exhibitor 1905-1930. He was also an associate member of the R.W.A. and exhibited regularly 1898-1928. Many of the subjects were local landscapes, flower and garden scenes and, from 1924, mostly Italian views including Venice and Lake Maggiore. The Bristol City Art Gallery has an oil painting by him.

*Mabel A. Kingwell*    *'Working Horses' (w/c)*    *(Sotheby's Sussex)*

## Mabel Augusta KINGWELL (1890-1924)

Painter in watercolour of animals, particularly Dartmoor ponies, who was born at Totnes, Devon, in 1890. Mabel Kingwell was paralysed as a result of a childhood accident, but despite her disability became a successful painter. She did not exhibit widely but did show a work 'Study on the Beach, Weston-super-Mare' at the Royal Academy in 1914 and exhibited at the Walker Art Gallery, Liverpool. Despite her short life, Mabel Kingwell was quite prolific and her work is often found in the West Country. The subject matter and the pleasing style have helped to make her paintings increasingly popular in recent years. The pictures are usually signed 'Mabel A Kingwell', sometimes with a date. Mabel Kingwell lived at North Huish, near Ivybridge, Devon, and later in Plymouth. She died at Exeter on 24th May 1924 at the age of 33.

## Francis Joseph 'Wiggs' KINNAIRD (1875-1915)

Painter in watercolour and occasionally oil of river landscapes and rural scenes. Francis Joseph Kinnaird was born in London on the 16th March 1875. He was the second son of Francis H Kinnaird and brother to Henry who was some years his senior and a respected landscape artist. Wiggs Kinnaird, as he became known, was plainly influenced by Henry but his colours tend to be softer and the style not quite so precise. He exhibited widely, mostly in the provinces, at Birmingham, Glasgow, Liverpool and Manchester 1895-1911 and first lived in London, later Cornwall and Gillingham in Dorset. Wiggs Kinnaird was commissioned in the South Stafford Regiment in 1907 and became an Instructor of Musketry, he was promoted to Captain in 1910. He went to France with his Regiment in March 1915 and was wounded in action at Richebourg in May. He was brought back to London and died of his wounds on 10th June 1915, at the age of 40. Had he lived and continued to paint Wiggs Kinnaird may have become as well known as his brother, for whom he is sometimes mistaken.

## 'E.. P..' (Patrick Russell Edmund) KINSELLA (1874-1936)

Painter and illustrator of theatre subjects, theatrical posters and also a comic postcard artist. This versatile Irish artist worked in England and towards the end of his life lived at Shoreham, Sussex, where he died on the 8th May 1936. Although he is probably best known by the postcard collectors, his theatre paintings of dancing girls are occasionally seen on the market and can command high prices. He signed his work 'E. P. Kinsella'.

## Katherine KINSELLA (fl. 1900s-1935)

Painter of landscapes, flower and garden scenes. She had an exhibition entitled 'Paintings of Italy' at the Brook Street Gallery, London, in May 1935. It consisted of 38 pictures mostly landscapes and buildings but also some flower and garden studies.

## T.. C.. KIRK (exh. 1924-1929)

Landscape artist, who lived at Wootton-under-Edge, Glos., and exhibited 10 works at the R.W.A. 1924-1929. The titles included 'The Sunny Wall, San Tropez, France' and 'La Rue Droite, France' (both 1927).

## Dawson KITCHINGMAN (exh. 1929-1934)

Painter of landscapes and coastal scenes who lived at Langford, near Bristol, and exhibited 13 works at the R.W.A. 1929-1934. The subjects were mostly West Country views – 'Polperro', 'The Lizard' (1931) and 'Cottages at Looe' (1933) are typical. He also painted some flower studies.

## Ethel M.. KITSON (exh. 1919)

Bradford landscape painter, who exhibited three works at the Local Artists Exhibition in 1919. The titles included 'Road to Baslow, Derbyshire' and 'Glimpse of the River'.

## Miss Bertha W.. KNIGHT (exh. 1911)

Miniature painter who exhibited a work entitled 'Starting Out' at the Coronation Exhibition of 1911 in London. She was a member of the Society of Miniaturists.

*Frank H. Knight        'Unloading at the Wharf' (w/c)    (J Collins and Son)*

## Frank H.. KNIGHT (fl. 1930s)

Painter in watercolour of landscape and harbour scenes who lived at Upper Beeding, Sussex, and was working in the mid-1930s. It is surprising that this competent artist does not appear to have exhibited. He may have sold his pictures locally.

## Wilfrid KNOX (1884-1966)

Painter in watercolour, gouache and occasionally oil, of marines and landscapes who was born in Handsworth, Birmingham, in 1884. Little is known of his early life although Wilfrid Knox had worked as a engineer and served in the Royal Flying Corps during the First World War. He painted under contract for Frost and Reed but much of his work was painted for a local Birmingham dealer under the pseudonym of A D Bell (q.v.). The subjects were mostly clipper ships, harbour scenes and landscapes with views in the West Country, Scotland, Ireland and Venice. Some early works of First World War fighter planes are known to exist but the Venice views, in the manner of Frank Wasley, are among his most decorative and collectable work. At least one other artist painted under the pseudonym of A D Bell – Horace Hammond – but these pictures were mostly in the style of Birket Foster and quite easily distinguished from Knox. Wilfrid Knox also used the pseudonym R MacGregor (q.v.) and most of these pictures were clipper ships. A fictitious printed biography often found on the old frames of A D Bell paintings have for many years helped to hide the artists' true identities. Wilfrid Knox died on 30th October 1966 at the age of 82. An exhibition of over 50 of his works was held by Harper Fine Paintings, at Poynton, Cheshire, in November 1987.

# L

## Miss Caroline H.. LACON (exh. 1880-1884)

Landscape and portrait painter who lived at Ipswich and was a member of the Ipswich Art Club showing 28 works 1880-1884. The subjects were portraits, local scenes and building studies in France and Spain. The titles included 'Fuentarabia, Spain' and 'Laon Cathedral, France' (both 1881), and other studies of Paris, Pau and Rouen.

## Leonard LACY (exh. 1894-1907)

Landscape painter in oil and watercolour who lived in Ipswich and was a member of the Ipswich Art Club. He exhibited a total of 47 works at the Ipswich Art Club 1894-1907, mostly local scenes. The titles included 'On the Meadows, Dedham', 'By the Waterside' and 'Dedham Brook' (all oils, 1901).

## C.. de Wynter LANE (exh. 1935-1937)

Landscape painter in watercolour who exhibited four works at the St Ives Society of Artists Exhibition in 1935 and 1937. The titles were 'The Goddess Kwang Ywan', 'In Bluebell Time' (1935) and 'Kettata Sand' and 'Early Morning' (1937).

## Miss Joan LANGFORD-REED (fl. 1937)

Student at the St John's Wood School of Art whose painting 'At Art School' was reproduced in The Artist magazine in January 1937.

*William Langley*     *'Highland Cattle' (oil)*     *(Sotheby's Sussex)*

## William LANGLEY (fl. c. 1890-1920)

Painter in oil of rural landscapes and coastal scenes who was working in the early 1900s. The subjects of this prolific artist included views in Cornwall, the South of England, Wales, Scotland and Ireland. Among the titles of known works are 'On the Lledr', 'Wee Bridge, Killarney', 'In the Glen' and 'Sunshine after Rain, a Village in the Thames'. The work shows a distinct similarity to that of several artists working at the time and the signature could possibly be a pseudonym. The pictures are often large and decorative and have become increasingly popular in recent years.

## Ethel LARCOMBE (fl. 1905)

Painter in watercolour of figures and landscapes, illustrator, and card designer. Ethel Larcombe was a prize winner in The Studio magazine design competition of 1905, when she was living in Exeter. Some postcards of her work were published by E W Savory of Clifton, Bristol, in the early 1900s. She sometimes signed with a monogram (see index).

## George LARNER (fl. 1938-1940)

Painter of portraits, figures and animals who lived at Irby, on Merseyside, and was working in the late 1930s. He exhibited at the Walker Art Gallery, Liverpool, in 1938.

*Molly Latham*     *'Horse Study' (oil)*

## Molly Maurice LATHAM (c. 1900-1987)

Painter and illustrator in oil and watercolour of equestrian subjects. Her talent for art showed at an early age when she won a Royal Drawing Society prize at school in 1914. In the 1920s Molly Latham worked as an illustrator but her real interest was in painting horse subjects and she concentrated on this from the 1930s. A series of limited edition hunting prints were published by Eyre and Spottiswood in 1930 and in 1933 she illustrated the cover of the special hunting edition of The Field. In 1934 Molly Latham had a one-woman exhibition in Horsham of horse portraits and hunting scenes and then in 1938 a similar show at Ackermanns Gallery in London. She continued to work after the war, exhibiting in the 1950s at the Brighton Arts Club and the Sussex Womens Art Club.

Molly Latham died in 1987 and her studio sale was held at Graves, Son and Pilcher auction rooms in Hove, Sussex in January 1988.

**Denys Maurice Orlando P.. LAW (1907-1981)**

Painter in oil of landscapes, rivers and coastal scenes particularly Cornish views. Denys Law was born on 9th November 1907 at Pangbourne, Berks, his father was an architect and his mother an amateur watercolour artist. He started in a career as an electrical engineer, but after the Second World War took up painting full time and settled in Lamorna in 1946. Denys Law originally painted with his mother but once in Cornwall came under the influence of Stanley H Gardiner. His technique was to paint a small 10" x 8" sketch on location and work up a finished picture in his studio. One of his favourite subjects was a river in a wooded landscape much in the manner of S J Lamorna Birch and these pictures are sometimes now wrongly attributed. Denys Law found a ready market for his work locally and did not exhibit in London at the major exhibitions. He was however a member and exhibitor with the St Ives Society of Artists.

**Sydney LAWRENCE (fl. c. 1880-1910)**

Watercolour landscape painter who was working at the turn of the century and appears to be the same hand as E St John (q.v.) and F Catano (q.v.). The subjects were usually Italian lakeside towns with figures and boats painted in a precise and colourful style often heightened with bodycolour. The artist does not appear to have exhibited but the competent style and pleasing subject matter have made the work popular.

**Miss Edith LEACH (exh. 1912)**

Oil painter who was a member of the Winchester Art Society and exhibited two works at their 1912 Exhibition, entitled 'A Passage' and 'Timeworn Timber'.

**F.. LEATHER (fl. 1898)**

Artist who lived in Wandsworth and was a prize winner at The Studio magazine sketching competition in 1898.

**M.. K.. LEATHES B.W.S. (exh. 1928)**

Painter in watercolour of flower subjects who was a member of the B.W.S. and exhibited a flower study at their Autumn Exhibition at Preston in 1928.

*Pierre Le Boueff*     *'The Market Square' (w/c)*     *(Reid Gallery)*

**Pierre LE BOUEFF (fl. 1900s-1920s)**

This was a pseudonym of Thomas Edward Francis (q.v.) which he often signed on his French landscapes and town scenes. The oil paintings are mostly inscribed on the reverse and the subjects include town scenes in Normandy and Belgium. The French and Belgium views are usually signed Le Boueff because the use of a foreign artist's name made the subject easier to sell. The town scenes in particular are most attractive and can command high prices.

**Frank H.. LEE (exh. 1921)**

Still life painter in oil who exhibited two paintings at the Derby Sketching Club Exhibition of 1921.

**Norman LEE (fl. c. 1930)**

Watercolour landscape painter who lived in Bolton, Lancs. The style and colour of his lake scenes show a similarity to the work of the Tucker family who may have been an influence on him. He signed his work with flourishes on the first letters.

**R.. H.. LEEFE (fl. 1925)**

Illustrator and theatrical designer who was a member of the New Autumn Group. His work was reproduced in The Studio magazine in 1925.

*Rowley Leggett*     *'The Meet' (oil)*

**Miss Rowley LEGGETT (1878-1945)**

Painter in oil, and occasionally watercolour, of horses, rustic scenes and still life. The rustic subjects and thick impasto paint have a similarity to Harry Fidler's work but her patchwork use of bright colours give her pictures a style and character all of their own. Little is known of her early life but she was the youngest of three sisters and probably studied art in Paris around 1900. Her first exhibition entitled 'Field and Farm Life' was held at the Continental Gallery, London, in May 1903. It consisted of 23 oils, mostly rural scenes, including views in Northern France and

Sussex. From 1904, she exhibited regularly in London and the provinces at major exhibitions until 1919 and also showed work at the Paris Salon. She lived near Cranleigh, Surrey, for several years and then moved to Fittleworth, Sussex, where she remained until her death in 1945. Rowley Leggett's distinctive style and appealing subject matter should make the work increasingly collectable.

## Henry J.. LEIGH (exh. 1901)

Painter of beach and coastal scenes who lived at Caversham, Reading, and exhibited two works at the Berkshire Art Society Exhibition in 1901. The titles were 'A Lonely Shore', and 'Sand Dunes, Skegness'.

## George William LEIGHTON (exh. 1895-1898)

An architect by profession who lived in Ipswich and exhibited seven works at the Ipswich Art Club 1895-1898. The subjects were all architectural designs for houses in Felixstowe.

## Miss Helen LEIPNER (exh. 1885-1894)

Painter in oil of portraits, genre and rural life scenes who lived at Redland, Bristol, and exhibited 20 works at the R.W.A. Annual Exhibitions 1885-1894. The subjects were mostly portraits and some landscapes and street scenes. The titles included 'Old Betsy of St Ives' (1892) and 'Farm Life in Cornwall' and 'Cornish Interior' (1893). She also exhibited 25 sketches at the Winter Exhibitions of the R.W.A. 1887-1893, these being mostly portraits and lamplight scenes. Helen Leipner does not appear to have exhibited in London, but she did exhibit two works in Birmingham in 1893.

## Mrs. M.. C.. I.. LEITH (fl. 1908)

Watercolour artist and author who wrote and illustrated 'Peeps at Iceland' published by A & C Black in 1908. The book illustrated six of her landscapes in colour, but she appeared to know her limitations as further illustrations with figures were painted by M A Wemyss.

## Miss Hilda LENNARD (fl. 1909-1910)

Painter in oil of marines and portraits who studied at the Royal Academy School of Art in 1909 and 1910. Hilda Lennard was runner-up for the Turner Gold Medal and Scholarship for marine painting. She exhibited a portrait in oil at the Royal Academy in 1910.

## Edward A.. LEONARD A.R.W.A. (exh. 1877-1936)

Watercolour landscape painter who lived at Redland, Bristol, and was an associate member of the R.W.A. He was a regular exhibitor, showing over 77 works at the Annual Exhibitions of the R.W.A. 1877-1936 and 53 works at the Winter Exhibitions. The subjects were local landscapes, West Country, Welsh and Scottish views. He travelled widely and his continental

landscapes included views of Switzerland, Norway and Venice.

## Mrs. K.. M.. LEWCOCK (exh. 1931-1950s)

Landscape and flower painter in watercolour who lived at Ipswich and was a member of the Ipswich Art Club. She was a regular exhibitor, showing at least 88 works 1931-1950. The subjects were local landscapes, views of Cornwall and Yorkshire and still life of flowers. The titles included 'Boats at Pin Mill', 'The River at Ely' and 'Anemones' (all 1933) and 'Mousehole, Cornwall' (1941).

F. G. Lewin                    'Just Married' (w/c)

## Frederick George LEWIN (1861-1933)

Painter in watercolour, illustrator, cartoonist and black and white artist who was born in Bristol in 1861. He was the son of Frederick Lewin, a sea captain, and was educated locally before taking a job as a reporter for the Western Daily Press. F G Lewin was an able writer but it was soon apparent that his real talents were as an illustrator and cartoonist. A self-taught artist, he was soon contributing cartoons to Punch, Zig Zag, Magpie and other magazines. For more than 50 years he illustrated for the Bristol local newspapers including cartoons for the Evening Times and a series on inns for the Evening Post. F G Lewin designed comic postcards for J Salmon and others for E W Savory, a local Bristol publisher. He was a regular exhibitor at the R.W.A. showing over 60 works 1903-1916, mostly watercolours and pen and ink cartoons but also a few oils. He was elected a member of the R.W.A. in 1906. F G Lewin illustrated a number of books, mostly of a humorous nature, prior to 1914 and also 'Bristol' a record of the city, published in 1922.

Frederick George Lewin was a highly versatile and talented artist, who like so many illustrators has not yet received the true recognition that he deserves. He died at home in Redland, Bristol, on the 14th October 1933 at the age of 72.

**Miss Ada I.. LEWIS (fl. 1913)**

A student of the Bristol School of Art who exhibited an etching at the National Competition of Schools of Art in 1913.

**Alfred LEWIS (exh. 1887-1891)**

Painter in watercolour of landscapes who lived at Weston-super-Mare and exhibited five works at the R.W.A. 1887-1891. The subjects were all landscapes and included scenes in Yorkshire, Surrey and Rouen in France.

*J. Lewis*        *'Richmond Old Bridge' (oil)*

**James Isiah LEWIS (1860-1934)**

Painter in oil of river landscapes who lived in Richmond, Surrey, and was working from the end of the nineteenth century. James Lewis was a prolific artist and painted mostly views on the Thames at Richmond and Kew. The work, often commissions, varied in quality, but the better examples are decorative and are collected in the Richmond area. A retrospective exhibition of his work was held at the Orleans House Gallery in October 1984. He signed J. Lewis, sometimes with a date, and dated examples exist spanning the years 1895-1925.

*L. Lewis*     *'On the Beach, 1898' (w/c)*     *(Sotheby's)*

**L.. LEWIS (fl. c. 1890-1910)**

Painter in watercolour of coastal scenes, marines and landscapes who was working around 1900. The subjects were often painted in pairs and were mostly beach scenes with figures and boats. The work is sometimes wrongly attributed to Lennard Lewis, a landscape and architectural painter who was working at the same time. The watercolours of L Lewis are very similar to the work of W H Earp (q.v.) and if not a pseudonym, the artist may have been related to the Brighton family of painters. The work is usually signed L Lewis and dated.

**Lowry LEWIS (1850-1913)**

Marine painter in oil and watercolour who was born in Falmouth and later moved to Bristol. He was a member of the R.W.A. and a founder member of the Bristol Savages. He exhibited at the R.W.A. 1890-1914 and at the Bristol Savages – 89 works 1905-1913. The subjects were mostly Cornish marine and coastal scenes but there were also views of Guernsey (1905 and 1906), Switzerland (1910) and the Gower Peninsula (1912). Lowry Lewis died in June 1913 at the age of 63. After his death, the Bristol City Art Gallery bought 'The Bay of Sorrento, from Naples' and 'Sennen Cove, Cornwall'.

**Lt. Col. L.. C.. LEWIS (exh. 1928-1939)**

Watercolour landscape painter who lived in London and later Hampton, Middx, and exhibited over 30 works with the Army Officers Art Society 1928-1939. The subjects included London views and paintings of Bruges and Bermuda.

**Percy LEWIS (exh. 1913-1915)**

Watercolour artist who lived in Bristol and exhibited three works at the R.W.A. 1913-1915. The titles included 'Santa Maria, Della Salute' (1913) and 'Rio Della Pallada, Venice' (1915).

*Alfred Leyman*       *(J Collins and Son)*
*'The Butterwalk, Dartmouth' (w/c)*

**Alfred LEYMAN (1856-1933)**

Painter in watercolour of street scenes and landscapes particularly of the Devon area where he lived. Alfred Leyman was born in Honiton on 27th September 1856. He started as an artist but turned to the more secure profession of teaching and was Art Master at Allhallows School from 1893 until the 1930s. Although he did not exhibit in London, Alfred Leyman did show his work locally, including 16 pictures at the Annual Devon and Exeter Exhibition at Elands Art Gallery in 1906. 'The Guildhall, Exeter', 'The Street, Clovelly' and 'The Butterwalk, Dartmouth', are typical titles.

The topographical nature of the subject matter combined with an appealing style have made Leyman's work very collectable in recent years particularly around his home town of Honiton. (Illus. p.93).

F. Leyton                              'Newquay, Cornwall' (w/c)

**F.. LEYTON (fl. c. 1930s)**

Painter in watercolour of beach and coastal scenes. Most of the subjects were views of Devon and Cornwall and were probably painted for the tourist market.

**Capt. Arthur LILLIE (exh. 1886-1888)**

Painter in watercolour of marines and landscapes who lived in Kensington, London, and was a member of the Ipswich Art Club. He exhibited a total of seven works at the Ipswich Art Club Exhibitions in 1886 and 1887, and the titles included 'Passage of Boats . . Britanny' and 'Roscoff' (both 1887). He also exhibited at the Dudley Gallery, London, in 1888.

**The Hon. Constance LINDLEY (fl. 1899-1908)**

Watercolour painter of landscapes who lived at East Carleton, Norfolk, and was a member of the Norwich Art Circle. She exhibited 25 pictures with the Norwich Art Circle 1899-1908, mostly watercolour landscapes. The subjects included views of Rye and landscapes painted in Holland, Venice and Japan.

**Wilfred J.. Esmond LINEHAM (exh. 1905-1914)**

Watercolour landscape and marine painter who lived at Lee, Kent, and was a member of the Ipswich Art Club. He was a regular exhibitor showing 34 works 1905-1914. The subjects included the South of England and many continental views. Typical titles included 'Dordrecht Boats', 'Near Rotterdam' and 'Zaandam, Holland' (all 1905).

**George LINGFORD (exh. 1900-1909, died 1933)**

Landscape painter in oil and watercolour who lived in Bristol and was educated at Dace's School. He studied art in Bristol under Henry E Stacey and then went to Liverpool before returning to take a studio in Corn Street. George Lingford married the sister of Ernest Elhers R.W.A. a fellow Bristol artist. He was a founder member of the Bristol Savages and exhibited four landscapes 1905-1909. He also showed three watercolours at the R.W.A. 1900-1903 including Scottish Loch views. In the 1920s, George Lingford left Bristol for London and later went to British Columbia where he died in 1933.

**W.. LINSLEY (1860-1944)**

This was a pseudonym adopted by the Yorkshire artist Walter Linsley Meegan (q.v.). and signed on some of his pictures. He was best known for his moonlight landscapes and harbours in the style of Atkinson Grimshaw. He lived at Leeds and Scarborough but also owned a cottage on Merseyside. He exhibited once from a Liscard address in 1904 at the Walker Art Gallery, Liverpool, as 'W Linsley'. Most of the work is signed with the artist's full name.

**William Henry Bernard LINTOTT (1865-1950)**

Landscape painter in oil who lived at Horsham, Sussex. He was a friend and pupil of Jose Weiss and his style shows the influence of that Amberley artist. His work was usually small impressionistic landscapes on panel, often not signed but inscribed 'Bernard Lintott' on the reverse. He exhibited at the Association of Sussex Artists Exhibitions in Horsham. His elder sister Kitty Lintott also painted and exhibited in the 1890s.

**Norman LITTLE (fl. 1905-1916)**

Painter in watercolour and black and white illustrator who was working between 1905 and 1916. Norman Little exhibited a watercolour at the Royal Academy in 1907 from a South Kensington address entitled 'In the Clouds' and also showed some work at the London Salon. This versatile and talented artist worked as an illustrator and cartoonist but he also painted portraits, figure studies and rural scenes in watercolour. Some war sketches in France of 1916 exist and he is thought to have been killed later on active service. He signed his work Norman Little often with a date. (Illus. p.95).

*Norman Little*        *'The Bandsman' (w/c)*

## Miss P.. M.. A.. LITTLEWOOD (exh. 1920-1923)

Landscape and figure painter who lived in Monmouth and exhibited four works at the R.W.A. 1920-1923. The titles included 'The Harbour, Newlyn' and 'French Sailors' (both 1923), and 'St. Mary Redcliff from the Docks' (1922).

## Stanley LLOYD (1881-1954)

Painter of landscapes, portraits, figure subjects and illustrator of children's books. He was a founder member of the Bristol Savages and a regular exhibitor, showing 83 works 1906-1923. He painted a wide variety of subjects, including landscapes, portraits, interiors and hunting scenes. The landscapes were views in Cornwall, France and the Canary Islands. Stanley Lloyd exhibited once at the Royal Academy in 1922, an oil entitled 'Milking Time'. The Bristol City Art Gallery have a painting by him of the Savages First Annual Dinner and the Savage Club also have a number of his works. In the 1920s Stanley Lloyd lived at Paul, near Penzance, Cornwall, and later at Knowle, Bristol.

## Conway LLOYD-JONES (exh. 1880-1889)

Landscape painter in watercolour who lived in London and, later, Wimborne, Dorset. He was a member of the Ipswich Art Club and exhibited 61 works 1880-1889. Many of the subjects were West Country views – 'On the Dart, Holme Chase' and 'On the Shore, Lynmouth' (both 1880) were typical titles.

## C.. F.. LOCK (fl. 1928-1930)

Painter of landscapes and figure subjects who exhibited 15 works with the Army Officers Art Society 1928-1930. The subjects included a figure study and some Egyptian scenes.

## Miss Lucy LOCKWOOD (fl. 1925-1927)

Painter in oil of horses and figures who lived at Melrose, Scotland, and was working in the 1920s. This good quality artist specialised in painting horse subjects and curiously only appears to have exhibited one work, at the Royal Scottish Academy in 1927. Her known works include a portrait of a lady on a hunter (1925), a study of a grey mare and horses and carts on a quarry road. The work is not often seen on the market but the quality and subject matter would make it collectable.

*W. Lockwood*        *' Penzance Harbour, Cornwall' (w/c)*

## W.. LOCKWOOD (fl. c. 1900s)

Painter in watercolour of marines and harbour scenes who was working around 1900. This good quality artist does not appear to have exhibited. The watercolours have a pleasing wet style and are signed 'W Lockwood' printed.

## Miss Margaret LONG (exh. 1903-1908)

Painter in oil of flowers and still life who lived at Bramford, Suffolk, and was a member of the Ipswich Art Club. She exhibited a total of nine works 1903-1908, mostly flower studies and some still life.

## Miss L.. R.. LONGE (exh. 1890-1893)

Watercolour landscape painter who lived at Folkestone, Kent, and exhibited at the Ipswich Art Club. She showed six works 1890-1893 which included 'A Lane at Brockenhurst', 'Christchurch Priory, Hants', and some Suffolk views.

## Arthur LONG-HOLLOWAY (exh. 1925-1937)

Watercolour landscape painter who lived at Lewisham, South London, and was a member of the Ipswich Art Club. He was a regular exhibitor showing 26 works 1925-1937. The titles included marines, such as 'Anchored off Greenwich' (1925), but most of the subjects were landscapes including 'Burghfield Mill' (1930) and 'The Giants Castle' (1927).

## Edith May LONGMATE (1892-1983)

Painter in watercolour and oil of flowers, landscapes and miniature portraits. She was the wife of Ernest Longmate (q.v.). She exhibited three works at the Royal Institute of Painters in Watercolour in 1925 and 1926 but painted, mostly as an amateur, flower studies and portrait miniatures of the family. Edith Longmate later lived in Deal, Kent, and died 2nd February 1983, aged 90.

Ernest Longmate          (Hugh Merewether)
'The Sunshade' (w/c)

## Ernest LONGMATE (1900-1983)

Watercolour painter of portraits and figure studies, miniaturist and commercial illustrator, who was born 13th May 1900.

Much of Ernest Longmate's early career was devoted to working as an illustrator. His most famous work was a poster for Brooke-Bond Oxo circa 1927, for which his daughter was the sitter. He exhibited at the major exhibitions in the 1920s and 1930s showing work at the Royal Academy and the Royal Institute. He also exhibited at the Paris Salon 1925-1928 and one of these works was reproduced on the front cover of the Illustrated London News. The later works of Ernest Longmate was mostly portraits and miniatures commissioned through Harrods. He signed with a monogram (see index).

## Col. William LORING (1872-1935)

Artist who exhibited five works at the Army Officers Art Society Exhibitions 1928-1931. He lived at Chandlers Ford, Hants.

## Miss B.. J.. F.. LOTHIAN (exh. 1931-1935)

Artist who lived at Compton Martin, near Bristol, and exhibited at the R.W.A. in 1931 'Twisted and Leaning Columns' and in 1935 'Marigolds'.

A. V. Lovegrove          'Church End Farm, Haddenham' (oil)

## Albert Vernon LOVEGROVE (1899-1971)

Landscape painter in oil who lived in Reading, Berks, and was born on 11th March 1899. He was a founder member of the Reading Guild of Artists, which was established in 1930, and showed regularly at their exhibitions. Many of his subjects were local views in the Thames Valley and he also painted in Shropshire. An exhibition including 15 oils by A V Lovegrove was held at the Roland Goslett Gallery, Richmond, in June 1989. He signed his work 'A Vernon Lovegrove', printed, usually with a date.

## Maj. E.. H.. LOVELL (exh. 1929)

Artist who exhibited with the Army Officers Art Society from 1929.

## John LOVELL (exh. 1883-1889)

Painter in oil of marines and coastal scenes who lived in Bristol, and later Bath, and exhibited 10 works at the R.W.A. 1883-1889. The subjects were coastal or beach scenes – 'An Old Oyster Bed on Whitstable Beach . . .' (1884) and 'Wind and Rain on the Cornish Coast' (1889) are typical titles.

**Miss Lydia Priscilla LOWE (exh. 1900-1934)**

Painter of landscapes and river scenes, who lived in Bristol and exhibited 12 works at the R.W.A. 1900-1934. She exhibited in two phases 1900-1910, river and harbour scenes, and then 1927-1934 mostly local views and a still life. 'On the Frome, Frenchay' (1903), 'Ansteys Cove, Torquay' (1927) and 'Iffley Mill, on the Thames', are typical titles.

**Miss May LOWNDS (exh. 1909)**

Watercolour landscape painter who had an exhibition of 56 pictures at the Doré Gallery, London, in April 1909. The subjects were mostly landscapes in Kent, Devon and East Anglia and a number of views of Whitby. May Lownds lived in Kensington.

**Samuel Joseph LOXTON R.W.A. (1856-1922)**

Illustrator, pen and ink artist and etcher who lived at Redland, Bristol, and was a member of the R.W.A. He exhibited at least 15 works 1893-1913, mostly local architectural subjects. Samuel Loxton was an architect by profession with a Bristol firm but by 1910 he was listed in the local directories as an artist. He illustrated several books on architecture and articles for the Bristol Observer and Bristol Evening News. The Bristol Central Reference Library has a collection of his work.

**Miss Mina LOY (fl. 1910-1912)**

An exhibition of her work was held at the Carfax Gallery in October 1912, where The Studio magazine described her as being a 'gifted colourist'. She was married to the artist Stephen Haweis.

**Capt. E.. W.. LOYD (exh. 1928-1939)**

Watercolour painter who was a regular exhibitor at the Army Officers Art Society 1928-1939 showing a total of 53 pictures. The subjects were mostly rural landscapes and some London scenes, such as 'Lots Road Power Station' and views of Chelsea.

**Miss C.. Vera Pryce LUCAS (exh. 1918-1935)**

Painter in oil and watercolour of portraits and landscapes who lived in Bristol and exhibited 12 works at the R.W.A. 1918-1935. These exhibits include five portraits, local landscapes and views in Britanny.

**Miss Mary Sophia LUDLOW (exh. 1892-1913)**

Painter in oil and watercolour of landscapes, flower studies, figures and portraits. She was a member of the R.W.A. and exhibited over 30 works 1892-1913. The subjects were mostly local landscapes and some French views. Mary Ludlow was living at a Paris address when she exhibited at the London Salon in 1908 and 1909.

**W.. H.. LUDLOW (fl. 1929-1944)**

Painter in oil of still life, landscapes and coastal scenes. This artist had a pleasing impressionistic style and was quite prolific but did not seem to exhibit. The landscapes included views in France and Spain and were often inscribed and dated.

R. J. Lugg          'A Dartmoor Stream' (w/c)          (J Collins and Son)

**Robert James LUGG (1877-1951)**

Painter in gouache and illustrator of Devon moorland scenes who was born at Okehampton, Devon, in 1877. His father had started a photographic business in the town and after serving as an engineer in the First World War, Robert Lugg returned to Okehampton and kept the studio and gallery in the Arcade. He sold his local moorland views to tourists along with landscapes by F J Widgery, a popular artist of the time. R J Lugg did not exhibit widely but did sell work through Elands Art Gallery in Exeter. His work was also reproduced as half tone hand tinted postcards by Francis Frith & Co., including Dartmoor views and some of Surrey. Robert Lugg died at Okehampton on 1st February 1951 aged 73. He signed his work R J LUGG in capitals with a flourish on the L.

**Victor LUMMIS (exh. 1950)**

Oil painter of landscapes who lived in Plymouth and exhibited two paintings at the Plymouth Art Society in 1950.

**Miss E.. M.. LUTON (exh. 1928-1930)**

Landscape artist who lived in Bath and exhibited five works at the R.W.A. 1928-1930. The subjects included views in the Lake District, Shrewsbury and Zermatt, Switzerland.

**Hugh Fownes LUTTRELL (exh. 1916-1917)**

Landscape painter in oil who lived at Bere Alston, Devon, and exhibited three works at the R.W.A. 1916-1917. The titles were 'The Gatehouse, Dunster Castle' (1916) and 'The Banks of the Tamar' and 'Druids Combe, West Somerset' (both 1917) – the latter title priced at a surprising £400.

**Ethel Mary LYNCH (c. 1885-c. 1969)**

Painter in oil and watercolour and art teacher who was born in Rochester, Kent, around 1885. She was a member of the National Society of Art Masters and taught art at the Rochester Grammar School and later in the 1930s at the Camberwell School of Art. Ethel Lynch painted mostly watercolours and the subjects included still life, flowers and landscapes including views on the Medway and at Reculver near Herne Bay. She lived at Rochester, Swanley and Otford in Kent and later retired to Bournemouth.

**Harry Stanton LYNTON (fl. 1886-1904)**

Painter in watercolour and occasionally oil of eastern and desert scenes who was working between 1886 and 1904. H S Lynton's work gained popularity with the increased interest in the Middle Eastern subjects – 'On the Nile', 'Bedouins by an Oasis' and 'Near Cairo' being typical titles. The work varies in quality but at its best could be mistaken for A O Lamplough his more famous contemporary. Other subjects include views on the Rhine and Venice.

# M

## R.. MACAULEY (fl. c. 1900)

Painter in watercolour of marines who was working around 1900. The artist does not appear to have exhibited but the work shows a similarity to that of A Ramus (q.v.) and there is a possibility that one artist used several names. The work was competently painted and often featured fishing boats in squally seas.

F. McAllister                    (J Collins and Son)
'At Buckhaven, Fife' (w/c)

## F.. McALLISTER (fl. 1910-1946)

Painter of street scenes and rural landscapes in watercolour. This competent artist lived in Glasgow, and painted in Yorkshire as well as his native Scotland. The pictures were often large, usually signed in red and inscribed on the reverse. The artist had a pleasing style with strong colours and a wet impressionistic technique.

## Col. Montague W.. H.. McCHEANE (1872-1955)

Artist who exhibited three works at the Army Officers Art Society Exhibition in 1932. He lived at Sevenoaks, Kent.

## Jessie Ferguson McCONNEL (fl. 1903-1909)

Artist and illustrator who was a student at the Lambeth School of Art in 1903. A book illustration by her entered for the National Competition for Schools of Art was reproduced in The Studio magazine in that year.

## Lt. Gen. Sir Frederick W.. N.. McCRACKEN (1859-1949)

Watercolour landscape artist who lived at Sanderstead, Surrey, and exhibited 51 works at the Army Officers Art Society 1928-1938. Most of the pictures were watercolour views of the West Indies, Spain and South Africa. Many of the pictures were not for sale and presumably painted for the artist's pleasure.

## John MACDIARMID B.W.S. (exh. 1928)

Landscape painter who was a member of the B.W.S. and exhibited three works at the B.W.S. Autumn Exhibition at Preston in 1928. The subjects included Scottish views.

## Miss Gertrude McDONALD (exh. 1910-1927)

Watercolour landscape artist who lived at Clifton, Bristol, and exhibited five works at the R.W.A. 1910-1927. The subjects were mostly local views 'In Leigh Woods' (1910), 'The Severn Valley' (1919) and 'Ruins, Old Bishop's Palace – Bristol' (1927) are typical titles.

## Lt. Col. R.. J.. MACDONALD (exh. 1928-1934)

Watercolour painter of military subjects and landscapes who lived at Windsor, Berks, and exhibited with the Army Officers Art Society 1928-1934. He showed a total of 18 watercolours mostly regimental uniforms and landscapes.

W. Alister Macdonald                    ( Johnston Fine Art)
'Vauxhall Bridge at Low Tide' (w/c)

## William Alister MACDONALD (1860-1956)

Painter in watercolour of landscapes, coastal and river scenes who was the son of a Scottish Free Church Minister, John Macdonald, of Clyne, Sutherland. William Alister Macdonald exhibited in London 1892-1936, including two works at the Royal Academy – 'Doubtful Weather – Loch Hourn' (1892) and 'Her Palaces and Towers' (1893) when he had a studio in North London. He married Lucy Winifred Cary, a miniature painter and daughter of the artist William H Cary, who was a manageress of the Arlington Galleries in Bond Street, London. William Alister Macdonald had two exhibitions at the Arlington Galleries – in 1935 'Among the Islands of the South Seas... Impressions in Watercolour' and in 1936 'Prewar Wanderings: Watercolours at Home and Abroad'. The Guildhall Art Gallery, London, have a collection of London views which were purchased at the second exhibition. He travelled widely, particularly in the South Pacific, and he lived at one time in Gaugin's house in Tahiti.

His watercolour landscapes are of good quality and the London views in particular are collected. He is sometimes confused with William Macdonald, an oil landscape painter who lived at Bushey and later, Edinburgh, and was working at the same time. William Alister Macdonald died at the age of 96 at Pao Pao, Ile de Moorea, French Oceana, on the 11th August 1956. (Illus. p.99).

## Lt. Col. J.. B.. MacGEORGE (exh. 1930)

Artist who exhibited five works at the Army Officers Art Society Exhibition in 1930.

## Helen MACGREGOR (fl. 1937)

Animal painter, who was a pupil of Frank Calderon at the School of Animal Painting. She specialised in painting horses and dogs 'at the studio or in the owners home'. In the late 1930s, she was the principal of a School of Art with Miss Cottel in Adam and Eve Mews, London W8.

## R.. MacGREGOR (fl. 1930s-1940s)

Watercolour painter of marine subjects, in particular clipper ships. This is another pseudonym adopted by the artist Wilfrid Knox (q.v.). The pictures are often bright in appearance and heightened with bodycolour. 'Yacht Offshore', 'Stiff Breeze' and 'On the High Seas' are typical titles.

## J.. McINNES-MILLAR (exh. 1926)

Painter in oil, watercolour and pen and ink of landscapes, portraits and still life. He lived at Burton-on-Trent and was an active member of the Derby Sketching Club. In 1926, McInnes-Millar had a one-man exhibition entitled 'Here and There' at the Burton-on-Trent Art Gallery consisting of 65 oil paintings, watercolours and miniatures, many of the works being local views.

## Miss MACK (exh. 1906)

Landscape and figure painter in watercolour who lived at North Walsham, Norfolk, and exhibited three pictures at the Norwich Art Circle Annual Exhibition in 1906. The subjects were views of the Broads and a study of a fisherman.

## Miss D.. I.. McKAIG (exh. 1936)

Flower painter who lived at Weston-super-Mare, Somerset, and exhibited two works at the R.W.A. in 1936 entitled 'Wallflowers' and 'Asters'.

## Miss Margery MACK-SMITH (exh. 1915-1924)

Watercolour landscape artist who lived in Bristol and exhibited six works at the R.W.A. 1915-1924. The titles included 'View of the Quantocks', 'Ashton Court' and 'On the Moor' (1919).

## Annie McLEISH (fl. 1898-1902)

Illustrator and designer who studied under Fred Burridge at the Mount Street School of Art, Liverpool, in 1898. Her entry for the National Competition for Schools of Art 'The Blind Beggar's Daughter' was illustrated in The Studio magazine in June 1902.

## Phoebe McLEISH (fl. 1903-1905)

Illustrator, stained glass artist, designer and sculptor. Probably related to Annie McLeish (q.v.) she was also a student at the Liverpool School of Art under David Muirhead, and Herbert MacNair. In 1904, she held the City Scholarship and later was awarded the Travelling Scholarship. Her work was reproduced in The Studio magazine in 1905.

## Mary MACLEOD (exh. 1920)

Watercolour landscape painter who in 1920 had an exhibition of Chinese pictures at the Grafton Galleries, London. The subjects were mostly watercolour landscapes but there were also some architectural studies.

*Bertha McNish*                    *'Kittens at Play' (oil) - detail*

**Bertha McNISH (fl. 1895-1902)**

Painter in oil of figures, animals and birds who was working around 1900. The subjects of the animal paintings included cats, dogs and horses. The pictures were competently painted although the artist does not appear to have exhibited. The work was usually signed in full and dated. (Illus. p.100).

**Miss Irene McPHERSON (exh. 1913-1916)**

Painter and sculptor who lived at Redland, Bristol, and exhibited three works at the R.W.A. 1913-1916. These included a portrait bust sculpture and a painting of a chapel interior. She also exhibited in 1914 at the North British Academy.

**Isabel L.. MACPHERSON (exh. 1935-1937)**

Landscape painter who exhibited at the St Ives Society of Artists Exhibitions in 1935 and 1937. The works were entitled 'Spring in Gloucestershire', 'Bishop Rock, Newquay' (1935) and 'Lamorna Cove', 'Watergate Bay, Newquay' (1937).

**C.. W.. MAGGS (exh. 1913-1914)**

Artist who lived at Melksham, Wilts, and exhibited at the R.W.A. in 1913 and 1914.

*Henry Maidment*     *'A Country Lane' (oil)*     *(Sotheby's Sussex)*

**Henry MAIDMENT (fl. 1889-1914)**

Painter in oil of rural landscapes who was working prior to the First World War. His work was well painted and this combined with the popular subject matter have made the pictures keenly collected. Henry Maidment also worked under the pseudonyms of R Fenson (q.v.) and A Wynne (q.v.). Many of the subjects were views in Essex but he also painted in Wales, Warwickshire, Kent, Surrey and Sussex. Typical titles include 'A View near Braintree' (1893), 'A Wayside Cottage' and 'On the River Lluwy, Bettws-y-Coed' and dated examples have been seen from 1889 to 1914.

**Sir George MAKGILL** Bt. **(1868-1926)**

Painter of landscapes and coastal scenes who lived at Walberswick, Suffolk and later at Aldbury, Herts, and was a member of the Ipswich Art Club. He exhibited 12 works in 1911 and the titles included – 'On the River Blyth' and 'Southwold Quay' (both oils).

**Col. L.. N.. MALAN (exh. 1930)**

Artist who exhibited seven works at the Army Officers Art Society Exhibition in 1930.

**Miss Thalia MALCOLM (exh. 1930s)**

Painter of landscapes, portraits, still life and flowers who lived at Milford, Surrey. In October 1930, she had an exhibition of 25 pictures at the French Gallery in London. The subjects were mostly views in France, The Dolomites and Cortina in Switzerland, but there were also some still life of fruit and flowers and a portrait.

*J. M. Mallenda*     *'Harvest Moon' (oil)*

**J.. M.. MALLENDA (fl. c. 1900)**

Painter in oil of landscapes and coastal scenes who was probably working around 1900. There is no evidence that the artist exhibited but the work was of good quality and the subjects, often small landscapes, were painted on board.

**Wilfrid T.. MALLETT (exh. 1933-1950)**

Painter in oil and watercolour of flowers, still life and landscapes who lived in Great Yarmouth and was a member of the Ipswich Art Club. He was a regular exhibitor showing 32 works 1933-1950. The titles included 'Pewter and Petals' and 'Midsummer Mist' (both oils, 1935) and 'Tea Roses' (watercolour, 1936).

**Miss Lily MANN (exh. 1891-1893)**

Painter of landscapes and still life who lived at Earls Colne, Essex, and was a member of the Ipswich Art Club. She exhibited six works 1891-1893 and the titles included 'Colne Priory' and 'Fruit and Flowers' (both oils, 1893).

## William MANN A.R.C.A. (exh. 1950)

Landscape painter in oil and watercolour who lived in Plymouth and exhibited five works at the Plymouth Art Society Exhibition in 1950. The subjects were local views and a scene on the River Arun.

## Mrs. F.. MANNINGHAM-BULLER (exh. 1895-1898)

Painter of flowers and landscapes in oil and watercolour who lived in London and was a member of the Ipswich Art Club. She exhibited 12 works 1895-1898, mostly flowers but also landscapes including a view in Norway. The titles included 'Sweet Peas' (oil) and 'Christmas Roses' (watercolour) – both 1895, and 'The Gateway, Stokesay Castle' (watercolour, 1897).

## Philip MANSEL (exh. 1930)

Landscape painter who had a one-man exhibition at the Graham Gallery, London, in 1930. The modest typed catalogue showed 48 paintings, mostly Italian lake scenes and views of Venice and Rome.

## Douglas MAPPIN (fl. 1890-1920)

Watercolour painter of Egyptian scenes, landscapes and gardens who had an exhibition at the Prosser Gallery, London, in about 1890. The exhibition consisted of 62 watercolours – mostly scenes of Cairo and Luxor, but also 14 Venice views and a number of English landscapes.

## Miss M.. L.. MARGERISON (exh. 1912)

Painter in watercolour of landscapes and garden scenes who exhibited two works at the Winchester Art Society Annual Exhibition in 1912.

## Miss Theresa Rose MARRABLE (1862-1936)

Painter of portraits and figures in oil, watercolour and pastel who was born in 1862, the daughter of George Marrable, an H.M. Paymaster. She exhibited regularly with the Society of Women Artists c. 1903-1921, but as a portrait artist probably relied mostly on commissions. Her brother Cecil and her cousin Edith were artists and her uncle's wife Madeleine Marrable was the President of the Society of Women Artists. Theresa Marrable lived for many years at the family home in Onslow Square, London, and among her friends were the young Virginia Woolf and her sister Vanessa Bell.

## Miss Elizabeth B.. MARRIOTT (exh. 1924-1925)

Oil painter and watercolour artist who lived at Winchcombe, Glos, and exhibited a total of 12 works at the Cheltenham Art Group Exhibitions in 1924 and 1925. The pictures were mostly Cotswold landscapes and street scenes in watercolour.

## A.. MARSH (fl. c. 1900)

Painter in watercolour of river landscapes who was working around 1900. Most of the subjects were of the River Thames between Windsor and Goring including views of Cookham, Henley, Marlow and Bisham Abbey. It is surprising that this competent artist does not appear to have exhibited but the work was probably sold locally. The pictures were signed A Marsh in a printed script and sometimes inscribed with the location.

## Capt. J.. M.. MARSHALL (exh. 1929)

Painter of portraits and landscapes who exhibited four works at the Army Officers Art Society Exhibition in 1929. These were two portraits and two North African views.

## W.. D.. MARSHALL (fl. c. 1900)

Oil painter of coastal and moonlight scenes. This competent artist who painted in a typical Victorian style does not appear to have exhibited.

K. Marston        'The Farmyard, 1898' (w/c)

## Kathleen Mary MARSTON (1881-1923)

Painter in watercolour of rural landscapes who was the daughter of a farmer and born at Stoke Poges, Bucks, in 1881. Although an amateur artist, she studied under George Hiscox, a landscape painter, who lived at nearby Windsor. Many of her subjects were local farm and woodland scenes but she also painted views in France, Belgium and Switzerland. Most of her work dates from about 1896 until her marriage to James Wilkes in 1911. One of her sons E G M Wilkes (q.v.) became an artist and illustrator.

Kathleen Marston died after a short illness in 1923 aged 42. She signed her work K Marston or K M on small sketches, sometimes with a date and often inscribed with the location on the reverse.

## Miss E.. F.. MARTIN (exh. 1925-1926)

Painter of marines and landscapes who lived at Weston-super-Mare, Somerset, and exhibited a total of three works at the R.W.A. 1925-1926. The exhibits were entitled 'Sunshine and Shadow' (1925), and 'Dutch Fishing Boats' and 'Calm Waters' (1926).

## Miss F.. A.. MARTIN (exh. 1889-1891)

Painter of landscapes in watercolour who lived at Coddenham, and later Ipswich, and was a member of the Ipswich Art Club. She exhibited a total of 10 works at their exhibitions 1889-1891, most of the subjects were local scenes but also some London views.

## George Mayor MARTON (fl. 1940s)

Hungarian artist who was well known in his native land before the Second World War. He moved to London bringing his studio with him but most of his work was destroyed in a bombing raid in 1940.

Eva Maryon                    (Bourne Gallery)
'A Cottage Garden' (oil)

## Eva MARYON (1878-1954)

This was a pseudonym used by Eva Walbourn (q.v.) on some of her cottage and garden paintings. This signature often appeared on her better work. She may have used this inscription to prevent her pictures being mistaken for those of her husband, Ernest Walbourn (q.v.).

## Herbert W.. MASON (exh. 1906-1913)

Landscape painter in oil who lived at Sproughton, Suffolk, and was a member of the Ipswich Art Club. He exhibited 11 works 1906-1913, the titles included 'The Gipping at Sproughton' (1906) and 'Blakeney' (1910).

## Miss Olivia MASON (exh. 1916-1946)

Painter in watercolour of flowers and landscapes who lived at Felixstowe, Suffolk, and was a member of the Ipswich Art Club. She was a regular exhibitor there showing 48 works 1928-1946. Many of the subjects were flowers, but there were some local landscapes – 'Pin Mill' and 'Clopton Church' (1942) and a Yorkshire view 'White Wells, Ilkley Moor' (1946). Olivia Mason also exhibited at the Royal Academy in 1916 a portrait entitled 'Jack'.

## Charles MASTERS (fl. c. 1890-1920)

Painter in watercolour of landscapes and river scenes, particularly views on the Thames. This prolific artist was active from around 1890 but he does not appear to have exhibited.

## Miss M.. D.. MASTERS (exh. 1920-1929)

Painter in oil and watercolour of landscapes and garden scenes who lived at Clifton, Bristol, and later at Highworth, Wilts, and exhibited 20 works at the R.W.A. 1920-1929. The subjects included local landscapes and views in Cornwall, Yorkshire and Gloucestershire. There were also some flower and garden studies.

## George de Montfort MATHEW (exh. 1884-1933)

Painter in oil and watercolour of landscapes and some portraits who lived at Felixstowe, Suffolk, and was a member of the Ipswich Art Club. He was a regular exhibitor showing at least 126 works 1884-1933. The subjects were often local views, and the titles included 'Aldeburgh Lifeboat making for Harwich', (watercolour, 1894), 'Floodgates, Flatford Mill' and 'A Peep of the Orwell' (both watercolours, 1898).

James Matthews        'Thursley, Surrey' (w/c)        (Reid Gallery)

## James MATTHEWS (fl. c. 1900-1930)

Painter in watercolour of cottages and garden scenes. This good quality artist has largely escaped the reference books since he did not exhibit but relied on commissions to paint cottages and gardens in the South of England. He lived for many years at Rudgwick, Sussex, and then in the early 1930s moved to Eastbourne. James Matthews painted many scenes in Sussex, including subjects at Amberley, Fittleworth, Watersfield, and Bignor, as well as in Surrey around Clandon and Thursley. The quality and the popular subject matter has made his work increasingly sought after in recent years. (Illus. p.103).

## Miss R.. A.. MATTHEWS (exh. 1890-1893)

Landscape painter in oil and watercolour who lived at Earls Colne, Essex, and was a member of the Ipswich Art Club. She exhibited 12 works 1890-1893, mostly landscapes and coastal scenes in oil. The titles included 'Sunset Sizewell', 'Friday Street, Surrey' and 'Glendorgal Beach, Newquay' (all oils, 1890).

*Alex J Mavrogordato*        *(Angela Hone)*
*'A Cottage Hearth, 1924' (w/c)*

## Alexander James MAVROGORDATO (1868-1947)

Painter in watercolour and sometimes oils of landscapes and figures. Although he was a prolific exhibitor in London and the provinces, surprisingly little biographical information exists about this talented artist. It is known that he travelled widely, for the Fine Art Society held a one-man exhibition of his Russian views in 1896 and another in 1910 of Greek, Italian and English landscapes. Alexander Mavrogordato was an active member of the Brighton Arts Club and exhibited 96 works 1906-1925. In later life he lived at Edenbridge in Kent and died at the age of 78 on 16th February 1947.

## Thomas MAW (exh. 1886-1890)

Painter in oil of landscapes who lived at Needham, Suffolk, and was a member of the Ipswich Art Club. He exhibited 15 works 1886-1890, the titles included 'Old Pollards', 'A Weedy Pond' and 'A Shady Nook' (all 1890).

*Frances Maxwell-Lyte*    *'Venice' (w/c)*    *(Cdr. J. Morton-Lee)*

## Lady Frances Fownes MAXWELL-LYTE (1853-1925)

Watercolour landscape painter – born Frances Fownes Somerville at Wells, Somerset, in 1853. In 1871 she married Henry Maxwell-Lyte who was Deputy Keeper of the Public Records for over 40 years. A keen amateur watercolour artist, Lady Maxwell-Lyte painted many views on her frequent travels abroad in France, Italy, Switzerland, Turkey and Palestine. She did not sell her work but used to donate it to charity sales, and was an organiser for many years of the gift section of the Royal Amateur Art Society. Her watercolours are rarely signed but usually inscribed with the location and sometimes the date. Lady Maxwell-Lyte died on the 16th February 1925.

## Robert MAYES R.W.A. (1838-1918)

Landscape painter in oil and watercolour who lived at Downend, Bristol, and was a member of the R.W.A. and the Bristol Savages. Robert Mayes was a regular exhibitor at the R.W.A. showing at least 54 works 1867-1917. The subjects were local landscapes, views of the Thames and North Wales and some still life paintings of fruit. He also painted oils of Jersey – the titles included 'St Aubins Bay, Jersey' (1877) and 'At La Roque, Jersey' (1883). Robert Mayes was a friend of Arthur Wilde Parsons and Charles Brook Branwhite, to whom he was related by marriage. He was a keen entomologist and had a large collection of insects. The Bristol City Art Gallery have a local view in oil by Robert Mayes in their permanent collection.

## Lewis John MEAD B.W.S.
### (born 1888, exh. 1928-1937)
Watercolour landscape painter who lived at Cosham, Hants, and was a member of the B.W.S.. exhibiting two works at their Autumn Exhibition at Preston in 1928. He was also a member of the Portsmouth and Hampshire Art Society and exhibited 12 works 1935-1937. The titles included 'Inner Harbour, Brixham' (1935), and 'Clitheroe, Lancs.' and 'Red Roofs, Bosham'.

## Harry Halsey MEEGAN (fl. 1907-1912)
Painter in oil of moonlight and river scenes including Thames views. The similarities in the work suggest that he may have been related to Walter Meegan (q.v.) who also painted moonlight oils. Harry Meegan does not appear to have exhibited. 'Reflections on the Thames, Westminster' (1907) and 'Reflection on the Mersey' (1912) are typical titles.

W. Meegan          'Moonlight Scene' (oil)          (Sotheby's)

## Walter Linsley MEEGAN (c. 1860-1944)
Painter in oil of landscapes, river and coastal scenes usually by moonlight. He was born in Leeds in about 1860 and studied at the Leeds School of Art before moving to New York, where he only stayed for a short time before returning to Yorkshire. From Leeds he moved with his wife and large family to Scarborough and it was at this time that he started to paint his moonlight oils. He also had a cottage at New Brighton on Merseyside and painted some work around there. Some of his pictures are signed 'Walter Linsley' (q.v.) without the surname.

## Arthur Winston Dale MEGORAN (1914-1971)
Illustrator and marine artist in oil of yachting subjects. Winston Megoran's published work included some front cover illustrations for Yachting Monthly and Motor Boating magazines in the late 1930s. He also contributed work to the Illustrated London News in the 1940s and 1950s.

## Philip MENDOZA (born c. 1899)
Illustrator, designer and portrait artist. His father, of Spanish extraction, was a portrait painter and during Philip's childhood they lived in Cannes. On returning to England, around 1907, Philip Mendoza attended school in London before going to St Martins School of Art. He then moved to Yorkshire and worked briefly as a poster artist, before joining the Newcastle Sunday Chronicle as an illustrator. In the First World War he served as an infantryman in the Kings Own Yorkshire Light Infantry. By the early 1920s, Philip Mendoza had taken a studio in London and was working freelance for the Daily Mail and Sunday Dispatch under the names of 'Pip', 'Flam' and 'Spike'. He also showed a talent for portraits, exhibiting a study of his wife at the Royal Academy in 1939. A biography of Philip Mendoza appeared in The Artist magazine in December 1939.

## Percy W.. MEREDEW (fl. 1908)
A student at the Birbeck School of Art who won the 'Kings Prize' for figure drawing in 1908.

## J.. MERRETT B.W.S. (exh. 1928)
Watercolour landscape painter who was a member of the B.W.S. and exhibited three works at the B.W.S. Autumn Exhibition at Preston in 1928. These included a view on the River Severn at Bewdley and a harvesting scene.

H. S. Merritt          'Nether Wallop' (w/c)

## Henry Samuel MERRITT (1884-1963)
Painter in oil and watercolour of landscapes and Cornish harbour scenes. In his early years Henry Merritt lived in Essex and was a member of the Essex Art Club. He exhibited widely in London and the provinces, with one-man exhibitions at the Batsford Gallery in 1945 and 1947 and also at the Towner Art Gallery, Eastbourne. Henry Merritt was an Official War Artist 1939-1945 and sketches of London after the bombing are in the Imperial War Museum. He also contributed illustrations to 'Recording Britain' in the 1950s. He died in Bromley in 1963.

**Capt. K.. W.. MERRYLEES (exh. 1928-1937)**
Artist who lived in London and exhibited 15 works at the Army Officers Art Society Exhibitions 1928-1937.

**Mrs. Ada METCALF (exh. 1919-1938)**
Painter in oil of still life and landscapes who lived in Bristol and exhibited 21 works at the R.W.A. 1919-1938. Most of the subjects were oil still life with such titles as 'Wallflowers' (1919), 'Spring Flowers' (1923) and 'Poppies' (1926). She also exhibited some landscapes, including 'A View of Old Sodbury' (1923) and 'Old Houses at Caudebec-en-Caux' (1929).

**Mrs. Priscilla R.. MEWBURN (exh. 1925)**
Watercolour painter who lived at Daglingworth, near Cirencester and exhibited 10 works at the Annual Cheltenham Arts Club Exhibition in 1925. The subjects were mostly views of Tewkesbury and Cirencester.

**M.. MICHELSON-GORDON (fl. 1936)**
Painter in oil of landscapes and harbour scenes, whose work was reproduced in The Artist magazine in December 1936.

**Miss Maud L.. MILLER (exh. 1896-1907)**
Landscape painter in watercolour who lived in Ipswich and was a member of the Ipswich Art Club. She was a regular exhibitor and showed a total of 37 works 1896-1907. The subjects included local views and some Welsh landscapes – 'Torrent Walk, Dolgelly' and 'Sketch at Aberdovey' (both 1903).

**Mrs. M.. E.. MILLICAN (exh. 1936)**
Artist who lived at Henleaze, Bristol, and exhibited two works at the R.W.A. in 1936. These were entitled 'Port Gorey, Sark' and 'Trees, Isle of Sark'.

*J. Millington    'Dawn' (w/c)    (Cdr. J. Morton-Lee)*

**John MILLINGTON (1891-1948)**
Painter of marines and architectural subjects in ink and watercolour. John Millington worked for many years for Martins Bank in London but his spare time was spent painting marines, particularly tall clippers and tramp steamers. Many of his paintings were sold through Gladwell & Co, art dealers in the City. John Millington's work gained considerable popularity so he retired early from the bank to concentrate on the commissions. During the Second World War he painted many views in the City of streets and courtyards which were later destroyed by the bombs.

John Millington's pictures are not often seen on the market, but the quality and subject matter have made them collectable.

**Enid Sybil MILLS** R.M.S. **(1901-1985)**
Watercolour painter, illustrator and art teacher. She was born Enid Smith (q.v.) in London in 1901, the daughter of a consulting engineer, and was educated at the City of London School. She studied art at Westminster School under Bernard Meninsky and Walter Bayes and also at St Martins School of Art. Enid Mills exhibited at the R.I. and the R.W.S. in London and at the Pittsburg Art Gallery in the U.S.A. In 1961, she was elected a member of the Royal Society of Miniature Painters.

In addition to her painting and illustrating of children's books, Enid Mills was an illuminator and was commissioned to illuminate the Addresses for the Roll of Honour in 1945. Enid Mills lived for about 35 years near Witley, Surrey, and later moved to Alderley Edge, Cheshire, where she died in 1985.

**Arthur Edwards MILNE (1888-1981)**
Landscape, portrait and flower painter in oil, watercolour and pastel who was born in Edinburgh in 1888. He served in a Highland regiment during the First World War and also exhibited at the R.S.A. at that time. 'Hamish' Milne probably moved to the West Country in the 1930s and from 1931 to 1966 he was a regular exhibitor with the Bristol Savages, showing a total of 141 works at their exhibitions. The subjects were mostly still life, portraits and landscapes of local scenes and some of the Austrian Tyrol. Hamish Milne was President of the Savages in 1931, 1940 and 1951 and was made a life member in 1961. He was also a life member of the R.W.A. and after his retirement he worked at the R.W.A. restoring paintings. Hamish Milne lived at Weston-super-Mare and later Clifton, Bristol, where he died on 10th January 1981.

C. E. Milnes-Hey      *'Luz, Haute Pyrenees' (oil)*

### Charles Edward MILNES-HEY (fl. 1918-1939)

Painter in oil and watercolour of landscapes and coastal scenes who was working 1918-1939. He lived at Broadbridge Heath and later, Slinfold, near Horsham, Sussex. The subjects include views of the Isle of Wight, Dorset, Hampshire and Sussex, as well as continental scenes including Bruges, Florence and the Pyrenees. He signed his work 'MILNES-HEY' with a date, on oils, and usually with a monogram on the watercolours (see index).

### Herbert T.. MINETT (exh. 1901)

Artist who lived at Caversham, Reading, and exhibited two works at the Berkshire Art Society Exhibition of 1901. One was a portrait study and the other was entitled 'A Hot Day'.

### Jessie MITCHELL (fl. 1896)

Artist who lived at Sharrow, Sheffield, and won second prize for a Fairy Tale illustration in The Studio magazine competition of 1896.

### Frank MOLE (1892-1976)

Art teacher and painter in watercolour, pastel and pen and ink, who was born in Bedfordshire in 1892. He came to Bristol around 1923 to teach art at the East Bristol School. Frank Mole was a frequent exhibitor at the Bristol Savages' exhibitions showing a total of 226 works 1933-1975. The subjects included Cornish harbour scenes and some views in Brittany and Bruges. Frank Mole also exhibited at the R.W.A. – 38 works 1922-1936 and at the Walker Art Gallery in Liverpool. He was elected President of the Bristol Savages in 1937.

### Lt. Col. Francis A.. MOLONY (exh. 1929-1930)

Painter of landscapes and allegorical subjects who exhibited 13 works at the Army Officers Art Society Exhibitions of 1929 and 1930.

### Miss Maud MOLYNEUX (fl. 1908-1930s)

Painter in watercolour of landscapes and cottages. Maud Molyneux lived in Hove, Sussex, and exhibited two watercolours at the Royal Amateur Art Society Exhibition held there in 1908. The subjects were a 'Normandy Courtyard' and 'A Bit of Cuckfield'. She does not appear to have exhibited in London and it is likely that she sold most of her work locally.

### Ricardo MONTES (fl. 1906)

Illustrator who was a student at the Camberwell School of Art. He exhibited some illustrations for Don Quixote at the National Schools of Art Competition in 1906. These were reproduced in The Studio magazine.

### Miss Alswen MONTGOMERIE (fl. 1915-1928)

Painter in watercolour of English and continental landscapes who exhibited at the Modern Gallery, London, in July 1915. The exhibition consisted of 33 watercolours, mostly views on the Riviera, also some town scenes in wartime France and several English views. Alswen Montgomerie later had a joint exhibition with Mrs Esther Kerr at the Brook Street Gallery, where she showed 12 works, mostly landscapes and town scenes. She lived at Guildford, Surrey, for a number of years and her work is often found in that area.

W. A. Moody      *'Polperro Harbour' (oil)*      (Sheila Hinde)

### W.. A.. MOODY (fl. c. 1910-1930s)

Painter in oil and watercolour of Cornish street scenes and harbours. The work is of good quality, but the artist does not appear to have exhibited either in London or in the provinces. W A Moody lived at one time at Great Chesterford, near Saffron Walden, Essex.

*M. B. Moorcroft*       *'Roses, 1936' (w/c)*       *(Angela Hone)*

### Mary B.. MOORCROFT (fl. 1936)

Painter in watercolour of landscapes and flowers. This competent artist does not appear to have exhibited but she may have shown her work locally, in the Moss Side area of Manchester, where she lived.

### C.. G.. MOORE (exh. 1886)

Landscape painter in oil who lived at Lowestoft, Suffolk, and was a member of the Ipswich Art Club. He exhibited in 1886 – 'Swallow Falls, North Wales' and 'On the Yare, Gorleston'.

### Miss C.. S.. MOORE (exh. 1893-1895)

Watercolour landscape painter who lived in Ipswich and was a member of the Ipswich Art Club. She exhibited three works 1893-1895 and the titles were 'Neutral Bay – Sydney, N.S.W.' and 'Angel Inn – St Clements' (both 1893) and 'Cromer, Norfolk' (1895).

### Donovon M.. MOORE (exh. 1934-1949)

Artist who lived at Bishopston, Bristol, and exhibited three works at the R.W.A. 1934-1949. The titles were 'Studland Heath' and '435' (1934) and 'Interlude' (1949).

### Miss H.. Margaret MORCOM (exh. 1950-1960s)

Painter in watercolour of landscapes, coastal scenes and flowers who lived at Liskeard, Cornwall, and exhibited four pictures at the Plymouth Art Society Exhibition in 1950. The subjects were landscapes and a study of roses. She was also a member of the St Ives Society of Artists in the 1960s.

### Miss Mary E.. Taylor MORGAN (exh. 1896-1936)

Landscape and figure painter who lived at Sutton, Surrey, and later Clifton, Bristol. In the 1890s she exhibited 'Reverie' at the Royal Academy and also showed work at the R.C.A. and R.H.A. Some thirty years later, Mary Morgan was recorded as living in Clifton and exhibited nine works at the R.W.A. 1932-1936. The subjects were all landscapes, including views in Suffolk, Gloucestershire, Hampshire and one Swiss scene.

### J.. Bernard MORRALL (fl. 1911)

Artist who lived at Erdington, Birmingham, and won second prize in The Studio magazine pictorial art competition in 1912.

### Lt. Col. C.. O.. MORRIS (exh. 1930)

Artist who exhibited seven works at the Army Officers Art Society Exhibition in 1930.

*Garmon Morris*       *(J Collins and Son)*
*'Off Brixham' (w/c)*

### Garmon MORRIS (fl. c. 1900-1930)

Painter in watercolour of marines and coastal scenes. This prolific artist appears to have painted also under the name of G M Avondale (q.v.). The subjects were mostly fishing boats or shore scenes and were painted along the South Coast, with some Cornish and East Anglian views. Garmon Morris exhibited two watercolours at Elands Art Gallery in Exeter in 1906 and 1907, entitled 'The Coast near Ilfracombe' and 'St Michaels Mount'.

Some of his work was made into prints and C W Faulkner & Co. published some coastal scenes as postcards. The larger works are usually signed in full whereas the smaller sketches are often initialled.

*Bertram Morrish      'Yes Tor, Dartmoor' (w/c)      (J Collins and Son)*

## Bertram MORRISH (fl. c. 1900)

Watercolour painter of landscapes and, in particular, moorland scenes. He was the eldest son of William Snell Morrish (1844-1917) and his style shows the influence of his father's work. He was a prolific artist and many of the subjects were views in Devon where much of the work is found today.

Bertram Morrish exhibited two pictures at the Brighton Arts Club Exhibition of 1901, entitled 'The Old Cross' and 'The Cottage on the Hill".

## Mrs. A.. F.. MORSE (exh. 1906-1910)

Watercolour landscape painter who lived at Earlham, Norfolk, and was a member of the Norwich Art Circle. She exhibited 13 works 1906-1910, the subjects being mostly local views and some Scottish landscapes.

*G. Mortimer                              'The Roller' (oil)*

## Geoffrey MORTIMER (1895-1986)

Painter in oil of horse subjects, landscapes and portraits who was born in Norwich on 10th June 1895. Geoffrey Mortimer had no formal art training but, on leaving school, he joined his father's business in Norwich making and repairing stained glass windows. Although he did not exhibit Geoffrey Mortimer found a ready market for his work through a local art dealer, Butcher and Son, and also received several commissions for portraits. The Norwich Castle Museum has a portrait of a local Member of Parliament painted in 1928 and others by him hang in the City Hall and the Lads Club. Geoffrey Mortimer was a great admirer of Sir Alfred Munnings and this influence is seen in the working horse subjects that he mostly painted. For a time in the 1950s he lived in a gypsy caravan and cycled around the countryside sketching scenes for his paintings. Geoffrey Mortimer lived for many years at Old Costessey, near Norwich and died at the age of 90 on the 15th May 1986.

*L. Mortimer          'Brixham Harbour' (w/c)          (Bourne Gallery)*

## Lewis MORTIMER (fl. c. 1920-1930)

Watercolour painter of West Country harbour scenes and cottages. This artist is often confused with Thomas Mortimer who painted coastal scenes in a more Victorian style. The L Mortimer signature is difficult to read but the pictures are sometimes more clearly signed and inscribed on the reverse. The pictures show a similarity in style and colour to W H Sweet (q.v.) and most of the harbour scenes are St Ives or Newlyn. The popular subject matter has helped to make Lewis Mortimer's work increasingly collected in recent years.

## Miss Olive MORTIMER (exh. 1912)

Watercolour painter who exhibited two works at the Winchester Art Society Exhibition of 1912. The subjects were a view of Rouen and a study of roses.

*T. Mortimer*     *'A Harbour at Low Tide' (w/c)*     *(J Collins and Son)*

## T.. MORTIMER (fl. c. 1900)

Painter in watercolour of harbours, coastal scenes and continental town and lake scenes who was working around 1900. The watercolours are often beach scenes with figures and fishing boats and are usually found in pairs. The subjects include South Coast views, Dutch and French town scenes and, occasionally, Venice. This artist is sometimes confused with the 1930s West Country cottage and harbour scene painter L Mortimer (q.v.) who also signs with an initial but whose signature can be difficult to read.

## George MOSTYN (exh. 1934-1935)

Painter in oil of landscapes and still life who lived at Walberswick, Suffolk, and was a member of the Ipswich Art Club. He exhibited a total of six works 1934-1935 and the titles included 'Saw Mills, Beccles' and 'White Cyclamen'.

## Miss Florence H.. L.. MOTTS (exh. 1917)

Artist who lived at Clifton, Bristol, and exhibited two works at the R.W.A. in 1917, both were entitled 'Study of Scots Firs'.

## Miss L.. E.. MUMFORD (exh. 1886-1896)

Watercolour landscape painter who lived in Ipswich and was a member of the Ipswich Art Club. She exhibited 13 works 1886-1896 and the titles included 'A View of Bramford' and 'Hedgerow Elms, East Grinstead' (both 1893).

## Miss C.. D.. MURRAY (exh. 1906-1929)

Painter in oil and watercolour and etcher who lived at Holbrook, Suffolk, and later Bath and was a member of the Ipswich Art Club. She exhibited 22 works 1906-1923, including 'Peep of the Orwell' (oil, 1906), 'Barn Interior' (watercolour, 1914) and 'Old Granary, Ipswich' (etching, 1914). After she moved to Bath, she exhibited 'The Chapter House, Wells' and 'Bath Abbey' at the R.W.A. in 1929.

## David Knightly Wolfe MURRAY (1897-1970)

Painter and illustrator in watercolour of bird subjects who worked under the pseudonym of 'Fish-hawk' (q.v.). A one-man exhibition of his work was held at Stevens and Brown Gallery, London, in 1937 after which he concentrated on writing and illustrating bird books. David Wolfe Murray also exhibited at the Armed Forces Art Exhibitions and for many years showed work at the Annual Game Fair. He wrote and illustrated 'Birds Through the Year' and 'Studies of British Birds', as well as illustrating bird books for other authors. His work is not often seen on the market but the fine quality and subject matter would make the originals collectable.

*H. Murray*     *'Changing Horses' (w/c)*     *(Sotheby's)*

## H.. MURRAY (fl. c. 1920s)

This was most probably another pseudonym for the Birmingham artist and illustrator Horace Hammond who was working in the 1920s and 1930s. The artist had a distinctive style and is known to have worked under the pseudonym of J Barclay (q.v.) and A D Bell (q.v.). The watercolours signed H Murray are mostly hunting scenes and old coaching inns with figures and horses.

## Mrs. Katherine A.. MURRAY N.B.A. (exh. 1928)

Landscape painter who lived at Dedham, Suffolk, and was a member of the Ipswich Art Club. She exhibited three works in 1928 – 'A Creek at Flatford', 'Kimmaghame Bridge, Berwickshire' and 'Dunfermline Abbey'. She was also a member of the North British Academy of Arts.

## Marie Louise De M.. MURRAY (exh. 1950)

Oil painter of figure subjects who lived at Horrabridge in Devon and exhibited three works at the Plymouth Art Society Exhibition in 1950. The subjects were two portraits in oil and the 'Circus Players – Barcelona'.

## The Hon. Mrs. MYER (exh. 1920-1921)

Watercolour landscape artist who lived at Walberswick, Suffolk, and was a member of the Ipswich Art Club. She exhibited a total of five works 1920-1921, mostly local views and a study of Kew Gardens, London.

# N

### Frederick NAISH (exh. 1935-1936)

Artist who lived at Clifton, Bristol, and exhibited at the R.W.A. in 1935 and 1936. The titles were 'The Wharf, St Ives' and 'The Warren, St Ives'.

### Miss L.. A.. NEALE (exh. 1900)

Miniature painter who lived at Eastbourne, Sussex, and exhibited at the R.W.A. , in 1900, works entitled 'A Sea Nymph' and 'Jacqueline de Cordes'.

### Mrs. Hilda M.. NEATBY (exh. 1935-1960s)

Watercolour landscape painter who lived in Ipswich and was a member of the Ipswich Art Club. She was a regular exhibitor showing over 40 works 1935-1950 and was still active in the 1960s. Most of the subjects were local views including Walberswick and Aldeburgh. She was the wife of Edward M Neatby, a portrait, miniature and landscape painter.

*Phyllis Nelson*        'Tethered Goat, The Orkney Islands' (oil)

### Phyllis NELSON (born 1915)

Painter in oil and pastel of landscapes, animals and still life. A self-taught artist, most of whose work is oil on board and includes views in Surrey, Cornwall, The Orkney Islands and France. She lived at Hindhead, Surrey, for many years and later at Petworth, Sussex, where she now specialises in pastel portraits of teddy bears.

### E.. NEVIL (fl. c. 1890)

Painter in oil and watercolour of landscapes and continental town scenes who was working around 1890. The work is seen on the market but the artist does not appear to have exhibited. The continental scenes include views of Antwerp and Rheims.

### Miss B.. Amy NEVILLE (exh. 1901-1911)

Watercolour painter of landscapes, flowers and figures who lived at Sloley near Norwich and was a member of the Norwich Art Circle. She exhibited over 20 works 1901-1911.

### Miss E.. Kate NEVILLE (exh. 1906-1911)

Watercolour painter of landscapes and portraits, who lived at Sloley near Norwich and was probably the sister of Amy Neville (q.v.). She exhibited 17 works at the Norwich Art Circle 1906-1911, mostly watercolour landscapes including some Dutch views.

### Frederick 'Pat' NEVIN (born 1912)

Painter in oil and watercolour and illustrator, who was born in 1912 near Ballymena in Northern Ireland. He was interested in motor racing and the local Tourist Trophy races gave him the opportunity to draw racing cars at close quarters. His first exhibition was held at a local department store who put on a show of his racing car pictures. In 1937, Pat Nevin was appointed official motor racing artist for The Motor magazine and held that position until the outbreak of war in 1939. He painted racing cars in both oil and watercolour and his style shows some similarity to Bryan De Grineau whom he succeeded at The Motor. Pat Nevin now lives in retirement and still paints as a pastime, mostly seascapes and Cornish harbour scenes.

### Mrs. Leslia NEWALL (fl. 1912-1914)

Artist and illustrator who first studied at the Slade and then at the Byam Shaw School. A pen and ink figure study by her was reproduced in The Studio magazine in 1914. She signed her work 'Lesly' and with the date.

*A. E. Newcombe*        'Dinton Church, Bucks' (w/c)

### Albert E.. NEWCOMBE (fl. 1907-1915)

Artist and illustrator in pencil of landscapes and buildings. He lived in North London and exhibited an architectural study at the Royal Academy in 1907. The Studio magazine published 'Leaves from the Sketchbook' – seven views of Durham Cathedral by him in 1908 and 'East Anglian Sketches' – six landscape views in 1915. (Illus. p.111).

### E.. NEWLING (fl. 1920s-1933)

Portrait painter who specialised in Army, Navy and Air Force commissions and came to prominence after the First World War. He had studied at the St John's Wood School of Art. Several portraits by Newling are in the Imperial War Museum and a portrait of Sir Sefton Branker was commissioned for the Royal Aero Club.

### George NEWMAN (exh. 1883-1893)

Painter in oil and watercolour of landscapes who lived in Bristol and exhibited a total of 21 works at the R.W.A. 1883-1893. The subjects were mostly local views and also scenes in Berkshire and Gloucestershire. 'Haymaking, Westbury-on-Trym' (1890) and 'A Sunny Morning – Flax Bourton' (1891), both oils, are typical titles.

### J.. NEWMAN (exh. 1933-1938)

Landscape and figure painter who lived at Fishponds, Bristol, and exhibited 12 works at the R.W.A. 1933-1938. The subjects were mostly local and Yorkshire views and some foreign scenes – 'On the Jhelum River' (1936) and 'Rickshaw Boy' (1937).

### Frederick C.. NEWTON (fl. 1908)

Watercolour landscape painter of rural scenes and cottages. This competent artist does not appear to have exhibited. He signed his work with his initials monogrammed with his surname.

### Reginald Popham NICHOLSON (1874-1950)

Self-taught painter of landscapes and architectural subjects. His career in the diplomatic service meant that he spent much of his time abroad and many of the landscapes were foreign views. Reginald Nicholson's work was the subject of an article in The Studio magazine in 1930 and included several views of Cyprus where he was acting Governor. Later, he lived at Abinger Hammer in Surrey. He signed his work RN and with a date.

### Emily NICOLL (exh. 1935-1937)

Flower and landscape painter in oil and watercolour, who exhibited at the St Ives Society of Artists Exhibitions in 1935 and 1937. The titles were 'Pansies' and 'Wallflowers' (both 1935) and 'Lilies' and 'Loch Tay' (1937).

### R.. NICOLSON (exh. 1926-1927)

Landscape and figure artist who lived at Brislington, Bristol, and exhibited at the R.W.A. in 1926 and 1927. The exhibits were entitled 'The Toiler' and 'Kilconquhar, Scotland'.

### D.. A.. NIEL (fl. 1900s-1930s)

This was a pseudonym used by Reginald Daniel Sherrin (q.v.) for some of his paintings, being an adaptation of his Christian name, but it is not known how often this signature was used. He also signed work with the name of J. Whiteley (q.v.).

H. Nixon                    'St Ives, 1954' (w/c)

### Harry NIXON (1886-1955)

Painter in watercolour of landscapes often Cornish street and harbour scenes. He was born at Stoke-on-Trent on 7th October 1886 and at the age of 14 joined the Royal Doulton factory as an apprentice. Harry Nixon was to stay with the company for over 50 years, inaugurating the Doulton figurines in about 1913 and later taking charge of the 'Rouge Falmbe' department. He was also for many years on the part-time staff of the Burslem School of Art.

### Leslie Henry NORMAN (exh. 1936-1938)

Landscape painter who lived in Ipswich and was a member of the Ipswich Art Club. He exhibited seven works 1936-1938, and the titles included 'The By-Pass', 'Ipswich from the South-East' and 'Mudflats at Nacton' (all 1937).

## Stanley NORTH (exh. 1912)

Artist in tempera who studied at South Kensington under Prof. Lethaby. In 1912 his tempera painting 'St George and the Dragon' was a prize winner at the Crosby Hall Exhibition of Mural Decoration. He also worked as a stained glass artist and a collection of drawings of old English stained glass are in the South Kensington museum.

## Miss M.. L.. NOTT (exh. 1919)

Watercolour landscape artist who lived at Clifton, Bristol, and exhibited three works at the R.W.A. in 1919. The titles were 'On the Mendips', 'At Two Bridges, Dartmoor' and 'The Avon at Clifton'.

L. N. Nottage                    'Reading, 1905' (w/c)

## Lewis Nathaniel NOTTAGE (1867-1936)

Painter in watercolour of figure subjects and landscapes who studied at the Heatherleys School of Art and won the Roy Prize about 1900. Few details survive of his early life although he did travel to Norway where he sketched and painted. His best work was the fine quality genre watercolours of figures in elaborate costumes, often in gardens or interiors, which were painted in the early 1900s. Lewis Nottage lived in Hampstead and seemed to make little attempt either to exhibit his work or sell it. His pictures are not often seen on the market but the quality and subject matter would make them collectable.

## Miss Alexandra L.. NUNN (exh. 1884-1897)

Landscape painter in oil who lived in Ipswich and was a member of the Ipswich Art Club. She was a regular exhibitor showing 36 works 1884-1897. The subjects were mostly local views, but also some continental scenes such as 'Village on the Scheldt' (1889). Mrs. Lindley Nunn, Miss M C Nunn and Robert Nunn all share the same address and were members of the Ipswich Art Club.

## Mrs. Lindley NUNN (exh. 1893-1905)

Landscape painter in watercolour who lived in Ipswich and was a member of the Ipswich Art Club. She exhibited 18 works 1893-1905, including local scenes such as 'Old Houses, Coddenham' (1893) and some views of Windemere (1894). She was related to Alexandra, Robert and Miss M C Nunn.

## Miss M.. C.. NUNN (exh. 1886-1893)

Painter in oil of portraits and landscapes who lived in Ipswich and exhibited three works at the Ipswich Art Club 1886-1893. The subjects were local landscapes and a portrait. She was related to Alexandra, Robert and Mrs. Lindley Nunn.

## Robert Lindley NUNN (exh. 1880-1897)

Landscape painter in oil who lived in Ipswich and was a member of the Ipswich Art Club. He was a regular exhibitor showing a total of 54 works 1880-1897. As well as local views, the subjects included the Lake District, Cornwall and the Alps. He was related to Alexandra, Mrs. Lindley and Miss M C Nunn.

## C.. B.. NURSE (exh. 1903-1909)

Oil and watercolour painter who lived in Norwich and was a member of the Norwich Art Circle. C B Nurse exhibited 13 works 1903-1909 and the subjects were watercolour portraits and oil marines and landscapes.

A. Y. Nutt                    'Portisham Church' (w/c)

**Alfred Young NUTT (1847-1924)**

Painter in watercolour of landscapes and buildings. An architect by profession, Alfred Nutt was the Resident Architect to H.M. Office and Works at Windsor Castle. His watercolours are competently painted and have considerable charm. The pictures were usually small, sketched in pencil and finished with watercolour. Many were local Windsor or Thames Valley views but he also painted landscapes in Scotland, Yorkshire, Devon and on the Isle of Wight. He signed A Y Nutt indistinctly in pencil, and as a result the pictures are frequently miscatalogued. (Illus. p.113).

**Leonard B.. NUTTALL** B.W.S. **(exh. 1921-1928)**

Watercolour landscape painter who exhibited two pictures at the Derby Sketching Club Exhibition in 1921. He was a member of the B.W.S. and exhibited at Preston – 'A View of Knaresborough' in 1928.

**Henning NYBERG (exh. 1939)**

Swedish artist, who settled in England and studied at the Byam Shaw and Royal Academy Schools. An exhibition of his work was held at the Archer Gallery, London, in September 1939. Henning Nyberg lived at Uckfield, Sussex, in the 1980s.

## Maj. John B.. OAKES (exh. 1928-1950s)

Landscape and still life painter in oil who exhibited 10 works at the Army Officers Art Society Exhibitions in 1928 and 1929. The subjects included landscapes in Sussex, Hampshire and East Anglia as well as some garden scenes. By 1950 he was living at Bury St Edmunds and was a member of the Ipswich Art Club until the early 1960s. He exhibited two works in 1950 which were entitled 'Mudflats' and 'Chrysanthemums' (both oils).

## Herbert Colborne OAKLEY (1869-1945)

Painter in oil of portraits, figures and still life who lived in Southampton, Hants, and from the 1930s at St Davids, Pembrokeshire. Little is known of his early life but Herbert Oakley studied at the Hartley Institute, Southampton, and was among the prize winners for 1889. It is curious that this good quality artist did not exhibit, but he may have relied on his portrait commissions and selling his work locally. Herbert Oakley travelled abroad visiting France and Holland and appears to have lived for a time in Italy. He was a friend of the Bournemouth artist Douglas Snowdon (q.v.) and a cousin of the painter Elise D'Elboux. He signed his work Herbert Oakley in a printed script, often with a date.

F. R. Offer        'Harbour at Low Tide' (oil)

## Frank Rawlings OFFER (1847-1932)

Painter in oil, and occasionally watercolour, of coastal scenes and town views. Frank Rawlings Offer was born at Trowbridge, Wilts, on 15th August 1847, the son of William Offer, a draper and hatter. Little is known of his early life but it appears that he was employed in business as a traveller in Worsted cloth and around 1889 he moved to Southampton where he opened an artists materials shop and studio. He worked extensively in the Southampton area and

taught many students. About 1898, Frank Offer visited New York and is known to have painted there as some American landscapes still exist. In 1900, he moved from Southampton to the Manchester area where he continued to paint while living at various addresses in Warrington, Altrincham and Eccles. Pictures by Frank Offer have become increasingly collected in recent years as they are well painted and the subjects are often of local topographical interest. The Southampton City Art Gallery have works by him. The small oils were usually on board and if in the original frames, often glazed, so the protected paint can look very clean. He signed his work F R Offer in a printed script. Frank Offer died in 1932, but his daughter Alice Dawe (q.v.) continued to work as a watercolour artist and miniaturist.

## Miss Georgina E.. W.. OFFORD (exh. 1900-1911)

Watercolour painter of birds, flowers and landscapes who lived in Norwich and was a member of the Norwich Art Circle. She exhibited 75 works 1900-1911, mostly bird studies, local landscapes and flowers.

## Lt. E.. A.. OLDFIELD (exh. 1928-1930)

Watercolour painter of landscapes and portraits who exhibited 12 works at the Army Officers Art Society Exhibitions 1928-1930. The subjects included views of the North West Frontier and Greece.

## Col. H.. D.. OLIVIER (exh. 1929)

Artist who exhibited three works at the Army Officers Art Society Exhibition in 1929.

## Aina ONABOLU (fl. 1921)

A student from Lagos at the St Johns Wood School of Art, said to be the first West African to receive an art training in Europe. He was among the prize winners in 1921 and specialised in portraiture. It was his intention to return to West Africa to teach European methods of painting to his own people.

Sandison O'Neill    'Polperro Harbour' (oil)    (Market Street Gallery)

## Sandison O'NEILL (exh. 1952)

Painter in oil of Cornish harbour scenes who lived in Kew and was working in the early 1950s. Sandison O'Neill exhibited at the Royal Institute of Oil Painters in 1952 a work entitled 'The Outer Harbour Polperro'. His style and subjects are very similar to that of Hurst Balmford of whom he may have been a pupil. (Illus. p.115).

## Stanley ORCHARD (1904-1927)

Landscape painter and commercial artist who was born in Bristol on 18th August 1904. He was educated locally and studied at the Bristol College of Art before joining E. S. and A. Robinson who were commercial printers. Stanley Orchard exhibited four works at the R.W.A. 1925-1927 and seven at the Bristol Savages – the subjects being local scenes and views of Cornwall, Guernsey and Sark. Tragically he was killed in a motor cycle accident in Cornwall in 1927.

## Cecil ORR (born 1909, fl. 1928-1950)

Illustrator and cartoonist of books and magazines. Cecil Orr was born in Glasgow and spent his youth at Gourock, on the Firth of Clyde. He was educated locally and then studied for two years at the Glasgow School of Art. At this time he had his first illustration accepted for the Collins Boys Annual. From 1928 to 1941 Cecil Orr worked for Associated Scottish Newspapers and during the War joined the R.A.F. Cecil may have been related to the Orr brothers (Jack, Monro and Stewart) who were book illustrators living in Glasgow at the same time. He was the subject of a biography in The Artist magazine in June 1946.

## Caroline ORRIDGE (born. c. 1855)

Painter in oil of figure subjects. Works by Caroline Orridge seldom appear on the market although the quality of the work and the attractive genre subjects would make them collectable. Little is known about her early life although she did study under Albert Ludivici, lived in London and exhibited there in the 1890s.

## Philip OSMENT (fl. 1900s-1930s)

Painter in watercolour of marines and coastal scenes who was working from around 1900. The artist was quite prolific and the pictures were often painted in pairs, although he does not appear to have exhibited. He lived in Liverpool for many years and most of his work is found in that area. Many of his pictures are Welsh views but probably the most collectable works are his large studies of sailing yachts. Care should be taken to examine the condition of his work as some of the examples are now faded. He signed his work Phil Osment but the signature is difficult to read.

## C. W.. OSWALD (fl. 1890-1900)

Painter in oil of highland landscapes and rural scenes, often featuring cattle or horses. The artist lived in Liverpool and exhibited at the Walker Art Gallery in 1892. Some of the best work by C W Oswald featured working horses and these are more popular than the highland scenes.

## Joel OWEN (fl. 1900-1920)

Painter in oil of highland landscapes and rural scenes. The quality of the work of this prolific artist varies and he does not appear to have exhibited.

## Lt. Col. Robert Haylock OWEN (died 1927)

Painter in oil and watercolour who lived at Dursley, Glos, and exhibited four works at the R.W.A. 1923-1924. The titles were 'Old Port' and 'Oldbury from Kingston' (1923) and 'Where Waters Meet' and 'Kingsnympton Bridge, Lyme Regis' (both 1924).

# P

### Miss Katherine M.. PACKARD (exh. 1889-1949)

Landscape painter in watercolour who lived at Bramford, Suffolk, and later at Fleet, Hants, and was a member of the Ipswich Art Club. She was the daughter of Sir Edward Packard, one of the founders of the Club. Katherine Packard was a regular exhibitor showing at least 83 works at the Ipswich Art Club 1889-1949. The subjects were local scenes and views in Scotland and Cornwall as well as some Indian subjects. The titles included 'Boers Prison Camp, Bellary, India' and 'Monsoon Remeneny' (both 1901, 'Old Houses, Dedham' (1907) and 'November in Cornwall' (1920).

### Miss Winifred PACKARD (exh. 1894)

Watercolour landscape painter who lived at Bramford, Suffolk, and was the sister of Katherine Packard (q.v.). She exhibited at the Ipswich Art Club in 1894 a work entitled 'The River Ness'.

### Harold George PACKER (born 1908)

Painter in oil and watercolour and black and white artist who was born at Cotham, Bristol, in 1908. He was employed as a commercial artist by Mardon Son and Hall where he worked until his retirement in 1973. He was a member of the Bristol Savages and a regular exhibitor showing 79 works 1938-1978. The subjects included caricatures of fellow members and some landscapes and street scenes. Harold Packer was later made a life member of the Savages and the club still retain 30 of his figure studies.

### Arthur B.. PACKHAM (fl. 1896-1911)

Pen and ink landscape artist and illustrator who lived in Brighton, Sussex. He is first recorded as working in 1896, when he won second prize in The Studio magazine landscape competition. Arthur Packam contributed 40 illustrations to 'Off the Beaten Track in Sussex' by Arthur S Cooke published in 1911. Most of these were neat ink sketches of Sussex cottages and churches.

### Fred PADWICK (fl. 1917)

Watercolour landscape painter whose work has a pleasing bold impressionistic style. He does not appear to have exhibited.

### Miss B.. G.. PAINE (exh. 1918-1922)

Watercolour landscape painter who lived at Clifton, Bristol, and exhibited four works at the R.W.A. 1918-1922. The titles were 'In Ashton Park' (1918), 'Near Ashton, Bristol' (1919), 'The Two Trees' (1920) and 'Near Chelmick' (1922).

### John Lewis PALMER (exh. 1931-1950s)

Painter in watercolour and etcher of landscapes, figures and animals who lived in Ipswich, and later Colchester, and was a member of the Ipswich Art Club. He was a regular exhibitor, showing at least 30 works 1931-1950 and he continued to work after this date. Many of the works were etchings and the titles included 'The Plough' and 'The Ferret' (both 1932). He also exhibited landscapes including 'Fordham Church, near Colchester' and 'The Beach, Whitstable' (both watercolours, 1949).

### Lucas Shelton PALMER (exh. 1910)

Landscape painter in oil who exhibited two works at the Worthing Art Gallery Summer Exhibition in 1910. The paintings were entitled 'The Decoy Pond' and 'In Parham Park'.

### T.. PALMER (exh. 1909)

Watercolour landscape painter who lived in Ipswich and was a member of the Ipswich Art Club. He exhibited two works in 1909 – 'A View of the Gipping' and 'Evening on the Orwell'.

*H. Morley Park      'By Lake Windemere' (oil)      (Sotheby's)*

### Henry Morley PARK R.W.A. (1850-1919)

Painter in oil and watercolour of landscapes, figures and sporting animals who lived at Bristol and was a member of the R.W.A. He was a regular exhibitor showing at least 110 works at the Annual Exhibitions 1875-1919. Many of the subjects had a sporting theme – 'The Keeper' and 'Shooting Pony and Dogs' (1880) and 'Gordon Setter and Bird' (1919) are typical titles and he also exhibited several Scottish landscape views. Henry Morley Park exhibited some work at the Glasgow Institute.

## Col. John PARKER (exh. 1928-1938)

Watercolour landscape painter who lived at Clitheroe, Lancs, and exhibited 28 works with the Army Officers Art Society 1928-1938. The subjects included some foreign views of Madeira, Las Palmas and Lisbon.

## Miss J.. Hyde PARKER (exh. 1896)

Painter in watercolour of landscapes and still life who lived at Nairn, Scotland, and was a member of the Ipswich Art Club. She exhibited four works in 1896 – 'A Highland Bog', 'Loch Knochie . .', 'A Highland Loch in Stratt Errick' and 'Still Life Study'.

## Miss N.. M.. PARKER (exh. 1925-1930)

Watercolour landscape painter who lived in Bristol and exhibited five works at the R.W.A. 1925-1930. The titles included 'Dunster' (1925), 'Castle Coombe' (1927) and 'Wells Cathedral' (1930).

## Miss Kate PARKS A.R.W.A. (exh. 1896-1938)

Painter in watercolour, and occasionally oil, of landscapes and still life who lived in Bristol and was an associate member of the R.W.A. She was a regular exhibitor, showing over 100 works 1896-1938. The subjects included local scenes, Cornwall and Norfolk, as well as some views of Northern France and Spain. She painted some flower still life – 'Roses' (1900) and 'Hydrangeas' (1928) are among the titles.

F. Parr          'Bethesda Steps, St Ives' (w/c)          (J Collins and Son)

## Frederick PARR (fl. 1920s-1930s)

Painter in watercolour of moorland views, cottages, and moonlight scenes. The work shows a distinct similarity to that of F Beni (q.v.) which was probably a pseudonym. Many of the subjects were West Country views and the artist did exhibit in 1924 at Elands Art Gallery in Exeter.

## E.. PARRINI (fl. c. 1900)

Watercolour painter of river landscapes and coastal scenes who was active around 1900. The work is quite often seen on the market but the signature is difficult to read and the pictures are frequently miscatalogued. The subjects are well painted and include Thames views and Dutch coastal scenes.

## Ernest H.. PARROTT (exh. 1903-1933)

Painter in watercolour and pastel who lived at Portbury, near Bristol, and exhibited eight works at the R.W.A. 1903-1933. The subjects included portrait studies, landscapes and two foreign views – 'Luxor Temple' (1932) and 'Mont Blanc Ridge, Chamonix' (1933).

## Dorothy M.. PARSONS (fl. c. 1910)

Painter in oil and watercolour of portraits, figures, flowers and landscapes who lived at Rochester, Kent. Some student work indicates that she received a formal art training around 1910 when she was 23.

## Miss Pattie E.. PARSONS-NORMAN (exh. 1911)

Miniature portrait painter who lived in Norwich and was the daughter of G Parsons-Norman, a landscape and marine artist. She exhibited two works at the Coronation Exhibition of 1911 entitled 'Charles Dickens' and 'H.R.H. The Prince of Wales'. She was a member of the Society of Miniaturists.

F. H. Partridge          'View across the Marsh, 1907' (w/c)

## Frederick Henry PARTRIDGE (1849-1929)

Watercolour landscape painter who lived at Kings Lynn, Norfolk, and worked as a solicitor and Registrar of the County Court. This prolific artist, who was working from around 1900, painted many Norfolk coastal and landscape scenes which were sold locally. He is reputed to have painted up to six works in one day but these were probably the small studies rather than his larger more finished landscapes. The Kings Lynn Museum have three local scenes by Partridge – 'Holme next the Sea', 'Scolt Head' and 'Brancaster'.

## C.. T.. PASSMORE (fl. c. 1900)

Watercolour landscape painter who was working in the West Country around 1900. The work bears a close resemblance to that of Thomas Rowden and Passmore is thought to be a pseudonym for that Exeter artist. The subjects often feature horses and known works include 'Dartmoor Ponies' and 'The Logging Team'.

## Miss Marion F.. PATTESON (exh. 1901-1909)

Painter in watercolour of landscapes and buildings who lived in Norwich and exhibited 32 works at the Norwich Art Circle Exhibitions 1901-1909. The subjects were mostly local scenes but also included some views of Caudebec in Brittany (1901).

## Mrs. Edward C.. PAUL (exh. 1905-1906)

Painter in watercolour of flowers and landscapes who lived at Walton, Suffolk. She was a member of the Ipswich Art Club and exhibited 'A Corner of my Garden' (1905) and 'Peonies' (1906).

## Miss Ida PAUL (exh. 1897-1899)

Painter in oil and watercolour of figures and landscapes who lived in Ipswich and was a member of the Ipswich Art Club. She exhibited seven works 1897-1899 and the titles included 'Bramford Bridge' and 'A Coming Storm on the Seine' (both watercolours, 1898).

## Miss Lucie PAULI (exh. 1900-1902)

Landscape artist who lived in Bristol and exhibited four works at the R.W.A. 1900-1902. The titles were 'On the Avon' and 'Walton, Clevedon' (1900) and 'Bolton Gill, Yorks' and 'Redmore Gill, Yorks (1902).

*J. Paulman*          *'Safe on the Gate' (oil)*          *(Sothebys)*

## Joseph PAULMAN (exh. 1900)

Painter in oil of wooded landscapes and rural scenes, who was active around 1900. A work by him entitled 'Returning Home' was exhibited at the Spring Exhibition of 1900 at the Leeds City Art Gallery. His

pictures often feature figures in a rural landscape and the quality and subject matter have made Paulman's work increasingly popular.

*G. D. Paulraj*          *'Ox Carts, India' (w/c)*

## G.. D.. PAULRAJ (exh. 1935)

Painter of Indian landscapes and street scenes who was working in the 1930s. Pictures by this Indian artist are quite often seen on the English market and as such come within the scope of this book. He was a pupil of the Madras School of Art and exhibited at the Mysore Dasara Exhibition in 1935. The work has a pleasing impressionistic style and distinctive colours which should make it easy to recognise.

## Maurice F.. D.. PAVEY (exh. 1931-1951)

Artist who lived at Westbury, Bristol, and exhibited six works at the R.W.A. 1931-1951. The works were watercolour landscapes and coastal scenes and the titles included 'Craft at Sea Mills' (1947) and 'Fishing at Exmouth' (1949).

## W.. H.. PEARCE (exh. 1925-1927)

Landscape artist who lived at Thame, Oxon. and exhibited four works at the R.W.A. 1925-1927. The titles included 'On the River Thame' and 'Wheat in Stitch' (both 1926).

## Miss Edith E.. PEARSE (exh. 1919)

Watercolour landscape painter who lived at Stonehouse, Devon, and was a member of the Ipswich Art Club. She exhibited in 1919 – 'A Peep from a Cornish Garden' and 'Cawsand Beach at Low Tide'.

## Horatio G.. PEARSON A.R.W.A. (exh. 1904-1926)

Landscape painter who lived in Bristol and exhibited nine works at the R.W.A. 1904-1926. The subjects, including some watercolours, were local views and scenes of Dartmoor, Wales and Dorset.

**The Hon. Margaret PEASE (exh. 1940)**

Watercolour still life painter who was a member of the Darlington Art Society. A flower still life by her was illustrated in The Artist magazine in February 1940.

**Miss Cecily Edith PELLY (1891-1969)**

Watercolour landscape and figure painter who was born in 1891 at Witham, Essex. She was a cousin of the artist F I Clare Pelly (q.v.) and exhibited at the Walker Art Gallery, Liverpool, in the mid 1920s.

*F. I. C. Pelly*          *'A Tranquil River' (w/c)*

**Miss Florence Irene Clare PELLY (1884-1954)**

Painter in watercolour of landscapes and town scenes who was born at Tetbury, Glos, on 5th March 1884. During the First World War Clare Pelly did V.A.D. service in France. She had no formal art training, but did exhibit at the Walker Art Gallery, Liverpool, and at the Royal Cambrian Academy in the 1920s. Her subjects included views around Tetbury and Quenington, Glos., where she lived, and also some continental scenes. Clare Pelly died on 19th June 1954 at the age of 70.

**George Farquhar PENNINGTON (1872-1961)**

Painter in watercolour and sometimes in oil of buildings, landscapes and harbour scenes. George Pennington was an architect by profession and many of his pictures were studies of buildings around Pontefract, Yorks.

In the 1940s he lived at St Ives, Cornwall, where he painted street scenes in oil and watercolours of harbours. The Cornish oils show an influence of John Park, one of the leading St Ives painters of that time. George Pennington sometimes signed with a monogram (see index). (Illus. this page).

*G. F. Pennington*          *'A St Ives Street' (oil)*

**Mrs. A.. F.. PENRAVEN (exh. 1891)**

Watercolour artist who lived in Ipswich and was a member of the Ipswich Art Club. She exhibited two works in 1891 entitled 'Sunset Blackpool, April 1891' and 'Spring Flowers'.

*E. D. Percival*          *'Ilfracombe' (w/c)*          *(J Collins and Son)*

**Edward D.. PERCIVAL (fl. 1877-1905)**

Painter in watercolour of marines and landscapes who was working from the 1870s until about 1905. He was the son of Captain Percival who lived at Combe Martin and Ilfracombe in Devon and owned a small fleet of boats working out of Ilfracombe harbour. Little is known of his early life but Edward Percival did exhibit at the Glasgow Institute from a Crowborough, Sussex, address in 1892 but later returned to Ilfracombe where he had an art gallery and studio in the High Street. An old trade label of the gallery proclaims that he was 'Patronised by Royalty. Prize Medal Winner 1877/8. Hon. Mention, London, 1881'. Edward Percival's watercolours are well painted and often feature views of Ilfracombe harbour. He signed E. D. Percival with a flourish on the P and sometimes inscribed with the location.

**B.. W.. PERKINS** F.Z.S. **(fl. 1932)**

Painter of animals and an art teacher who offered tuition in animal drawing in the early 1930s.

**Arthur William PERRY (fl. 1908-1939)**

Painter in watercolour of landscapes and coastal scenes and postcard artist, who lived at Seaton, Devon. Arthur Perry did not exhibit widely but did show two works at the Royal Birmingham Society of Artists in 1908. His work was published by Worths Art Gallery, Exeter, in the form of hand coloured half tone postcards and the subjects included views of Seaton and Lyme Regis. Worths Art Gallery also sold the watercolours for the artist. He was still recorded as working at Seaton in 1939.

**Kathleen PERRY (exh. 1908-1913)**

Etcher and black and white artist, who lived at Iron Acton, Avon, and exhibited four works at the R.W.A. 1908-1913. These were probably etchings and the subjects were architectural views at Morlaix, Brittany (1908) and local scenes. The Bristol Central Library has 10 of her etchings of local street scenes.

**A.. W.. PETERS (fl. 1915)**

A fine quality artist in pencil who specialised in animal and bird studies. He illustrated 'The Zoo', published by A & C Black in 1915, with 20 studies of exotic animals and birds.

**Edwin R.. PHILLIPS (exh. 1950)**

Painter in oil and watercolour who lived in Plymouth and exhibited four works at the Plymouth Art Society Exhibition in 1950, which were mostly figure subjects. He worked as an illustrator of magazines, such as 'John Bull', in the 1950s.

**Mrs. March PHILLIPS (exh. 1907)**

Watercolour artist who had a joint exhibition at Baillie's Gallery, London, with the Earl of Plymouth (q.v.) in 1907.

**Roy PHILP (exh. 1950)**

Painter in oil and watercolour of landscapes and garden scenes who lived in Plymouth and exhibited four works at the Plymouth Art Society Exhibition in 1950.

**Harold PICKLES (exh. 1919)**

Artist who lived at West Bowling, Bradford, and exhibited three works at the Bradford Local Artists Exhibition in 1919. The subjects were 'The Duck Girl', 'Flight' and the 'Pennine Hills'.

**Miss L.. PICKTHALL (exh. 1909-1914)**

Landscape painter in oil and watercolour who lived in Ipswich and was a member of the Ipswich Art Club. She was a regular exhibitor showing 18 works 1909-1914 most of the subjects being local views. Typical titles were 'A Quiet Resting Place, Walberswick', 'Autumn, Butley Creek' and 'Dewy Harvest Field' (all watercolours, 1910). She also exhibited two Suffolk landscapes at the Winchester Art Society Exhibition in 1912.

**Walton S.. PIERPONT (exh. 1896-1927)**

Landscape painter in oil and watercolour who lived in Ipswich and was a member of the Ipswich Art Club. He exhibited 16 works 1896-1927, mostly local landscapes and river scenes. The titles included 'Sunny Afternoon, Pin Mill' (oil) and 'Old Cottage by the Orwell' (watercolour) – both 1897 and 'Ipswich Docks' (oil, 1927).

**M.. C.. PIGACHE** B.W.S. **(exh. 1928)**

Watercolour landscape painter who was a member of the B.W.S. and exhibited three works at their Autumn Exhibition at Preston in 1928. The subjects were landscapes and included a view of Goré Castle, Jersey.

**Miss Blanche A.. F.. PIGOTT (exh. 1902-1906)**

Watercolour landscape painter who lived at Sheringham, Norfolk, and exhibited 11 works at the Norwich Art Circle Exhibitions 1902-1906.

*Douglas Pinder      'Towarne Head, Newquay' (w/c)      (J Collins and Son)*

**Douglas Houzen PINDER (1886-1949)**

Painter in watercolour, and sometimes oil, of coastal views, moorland landscapes and desert scenes who was born in Lincoln in 1886. His mother was a school teacher in Newquay and in the early 1900s Douglas Pinder was articled to a local architect but later turned to painting full time. After the First World War, in which he was a conscientious objector, he was sponsored to visit Egypt where he painted a number of desert scenes during his stay at Port Said. Douglas Pinder lived for many years at Horrabridge, Devon, and from about 1940 at Newquay, Cornwall. While living at Horrabridge he painted some moorland scenes and these are usually signed 'Ben Graham' (q.v.). He is also believed to have used the pseudonym 'A P Shepherd' (q.v.). His work is frequently seen on the market, particularly the watercolours of coastal scenes of the Newquay area. He did not exhibit regularly but he did have a view of Polperro shown at the Plymouth Art Society in 1950 after his death. His early work is signed D H Pinder and the later works Douglas (H) Pinder in a printed script.

*L. Pinder*                          *'Too Deep' (w/c)*

## L.. PINDER (fl. 1908)

Humorous illustrator and watercolour artist who was working around the 1900s. His pictures often featured cars and horses and showed both imagination and humour, even if the draughtsmanship was sometimes lacking. His work is seldom seen but the unusual subject matter for the period would make the pictures collectable.

## John Dixon PIPER (exh. 1875-1886)

Landscape and figure painter in oil who lived in Ipswich and was a member of the Ipswich Art Club. He was a founder member of the Club and was elected their President in 1887. He exhibited eight works 1880-1886 which included local landscapes – 'The Post Office, Wenham' (1880) and 'Old Trees at Barnham' (1885) are typical titles.

## Florence Mary Sotheby PITCHER (1896-1982)

Painter of portraits, landscapes, still life and figure subjects who was born in London in 1896, the daughter of a marine engineer. After spending her childhood in Bexhill, Sussex, she went to London and worked for a time as a school art mistress. Florence had no formal art training until she met her husband Neville Sotheby Pitcher in the early 1920s. Neville was a well established marine painter and in 1925 they moved to Rye where they were to work until the outbreak of war. By the early 1930s Florence Pitcher was working in oil, watercolour and pastel, as well as showing a talent for woodcuts. She had also been elected a member of the Royal Drawing Society.

During the war Neville served in the R.N.V.R. and Florence moved to St Mawes, Cornwall. There she was able to develop her talent for portrait painting and exhibited two portraits at the Royal Academy in 1944. In 1945, Florence returned to Rye and, as well as showing again at the Royal Academy, exhibited at the R.B.A., P.S., N.S., R.S.M.A., and the Artists of Chelsea Exhibition. A Retrospective Exhibition of both artists work was held at the Rye Art Gallery in 1984. After Neville Sotheby Pitcher's death in 1959, Florence painted less but taught successfully until failing eyesight prevented her from doing further work. She died at the age of 85 in 1982.

Florence Pitcher's work showed considerable talent and versatility but is seldom seen on the market and has not received the recognition it deserves.

*Henrie Pitcher*                  *'Jovial Rustic' (oil)*

## Henrie PITCHER (fl. c. 1900-1910)

A painter in oil of figures, marines and landscapes who was working around 1900. His most common subjects were portrait studies of Scotsmen and rustic characters often shown drinking. Henrie Pitcher also painted a number of river landscapes with boats including some views on the Thames. This competent artist was quite prolific but does not appear to have exhibited. His work was usually signed 'Henrie Pitcher' scratched into the paint and dated.

## Lord PLYMOUTH (1857-1923)

Artist who held a joint exhibition at the John Baillie's Gallery, London, with Mrs March Phillips (q.v.) in 1907. The Studio magazine reported that his work showed 'considerable attainments as a painter'. He was the author of a book 'John Constable, R.A.' in 1903.

*Noel Pocock*                    *'Pudding and Pie' (w/c)*

## Ralph Noel POCOCK (1878-1949)

Humorous illustrator and landscape painter in watercolour. Ralph Noel Pocock was born in Hampstead in 1878, the elder son of Noel Pocock. He worked as an illustrator for A E Johnson in London and is recorded as working between 1907 and 1922. The books illustrated by Ralph Noel Pocock include 'Below Zero' (c. 1910) a humorous work on winter sports, 'Grimm's Fairy Tales' (1913), 'Austria and Hungary' (1914) and 'Robinson Crusoe' (1917). He also wrote and illustrated 'Pudding and Pie', a childrens story, in 1924, although this may not have been published. He was known as Noel Pocock and usually signed his work with an 'NP' monogram (see index) and this, in addition to the fact that he did not exhibit, has meant that this talented artist has slipped into virtual obscurity. He lived at one time at Linley near Bishops Castle, Shropshire, and died at the age of 71 on 26th June 1949.

## A.. POISSON (fl. 1890s)

This is the more common name used by the watercolour artist who also signed Madeline Hughes (q.v.) and E.. Collins (q.v.). The subjects are usually fisherfolk on a shore or peasants working in a field.

## Samuel George POLLARD (exh. 1900)

Artist who lived at Taunton, Somerset, and exhibited two works at the R.W.A. in 1900. The titles were 'Street at Fuenterrabia, Spain' (oil) and 'Tired Out'. This could be the same SG Pollard as the genre painter who exhibited in London in the 1870s.

## Nora POOLE (fl. 1940s)

Painter in oil and watercolour of figure subjects who was married to the artist George Poole. She lived in East Sussex and was working from the 1940s.

## Miss A.. V.. POOLEY (exh. 1895-1898)

Painter in oil of landscapes, figures and animals who lived at Stonham Aspal Rectory, Suffolk. She was a member of the Ipswich Art Club and exhibited 15 works 1895-1898. The titles included 'Felixstowe Donkeys – Gleam before the Storm', 'Buff – The Property of Miss Steward' (both 1895) and 'A Sketch of an Old Woman . . . Holland' (1896).

## R.. A.. PORTEOUS (exh. 1905)

Artist and illustrator who lived at Bolton, Lancs, and exhibited five works at the Bolton Local Artists Exhibition in 1905. The subjects were pen and ink sketches and portraits.

## Miss Isabel PORTER (exh. 1905-1920)

Watercolour landscape painter who lived at Rushmere, Suffolk, and was a member of the Ipswich Art Club. She was a regular exhibitor and showed 33 works 1905-1920. The subjects included views of Wylam, Northumberland (1905) and Sark in the Channel Islands (1910).

## Joseph POSFORD (exh. 1890-1898)

Watercolour landscape painter who lived at Felixstowe, Suffolk, and was a member of the Ipswich Art Club. He exhibited 17 works 1890-1898, mostly local scenes, and the titles included 'At Walton Ferry' and 'Harwich Harbour from Peewit Hill' (both 1898).

## Miss M.. A.. POSFORD (exh. 1921-1949)

Watercolour landscape painter who lived at Cheltenham, Glos., and was a member of the Ipswich Art Club. She was a regular exhibitor showing 55 works 1921-1949. The subjects were mostly views in Gloucestershire, East Anglia and the West Country. The titles included 'Swindon' and 'Gloucester Docks' (both 1927) and 'Bacton Beach' and a 'Norfolk Farm' (both 1937).

## Ernest POTTER (fl. c. 1900)

Painter in watercolour of cottage scenes who was working around 1900. The quality of the work varies but the popular subject matter would make the better examples collectable. The artist does not appear to have exhibited. He signed Ernest Potter in capitals with a flourish on the first and last letters.

*E. K. S. Powell*     *'Swans at Bruges' (w/c)*     *(J Collins and Son)*

**Elsie Kathleen Simpson POWELL (1895-1975)**

Painter in watercolour and pastel, illustrator and engraver of landscapes, animals and figure subjects. Elsie Powell was born in Aldershot, Hants, on 14th September 1895, the daughter of an Army doctor. She was recommended as a student for the Royal Academy School of Art by Sir Frank Dicksee, a family friend, but any opportunity to study was prevented by the Great War, when she served as a Red Cross nurse. In 1919 she resumed her studies by correspondence course with the John Hassall Art College and then in the late 1920s as a student at the Farnham School of Art. Elsie Powell travelled widely painting in Burma 1925-1928, where her married sister Hilda was living, and in Kenya 1947-1948. She also painted on holiday trips to Norway, France, Italy and Belgium. Elsie Powell showed work at local exhibitions but despite her obvious talent did not exhibit in London until the 1960s when she had work accepted by the Royal Institute of Painters in Watercolour. Elsie Powell lived with her sisters at Lower Bourne, Surrey, and later Dockenfield, near Farnham. She died on 5th October 1975, aged 80. An exhibition of her work was held at Jeremy Wood Fine Art, Petworth, Sussex, in November 1990. Some of the work is signed with a monogram (see index). (Illus. p.123).

**Joseph Arthur POWELL (1876-1961)**

Painter in watercolour of landscapes who was born in London in 1876, the son of the artist Alfred Powell. Joseph Powell studied art at the Slade School in London and also received tuition from his father whose work influenced his style. He was a regular exhibitor in London and Birmingham 1901-1914 and in April 1914 had an exhibition at the Modern Gallery in Bond Street entitled 'Canterbury, Surrey and Sussex'. In 1917, he moved to Plaistow, Sussex, where he was to live and work for over 40 years. As well as an accomplished artist, Joseph Powell was a skilled woodworker and model engineer and is known to have built two fine steam trains and a ship model. His sister Jane 'Florie' Powell also painted watercolours in a similar style and signed F. Powell. Many of Joseph Powell's landscapes were local Sussex views but he also painted in Kent, Surrey and Dorset. He signed Joseph Powell in printed letters but some of his early works are just signed J. Powell. Joseph Powell was elected President of the Association of Sussex Artists in 1947 and remained actively involved with the club to within a few weeks of his death at Steyning, Sussex, on 9th April 1961.

**W.. E.. POWELL (fl. 1900-1928)**

Watercolour painter and illustrator, particularly of bird subjects. The watercolours are of fine quality and are usually heightened with bodycolour which gives them a striking appearance. He is thought to have worked at the Royal Worcester Porcelain factory. Both a William and a Walter Powell were employed in the early 1900s as decorators specialising in bird designs. The quality and subject matter of W E Powell's work have made the pictures collectable, although they are not often seen on the market. He also painted some fairy pictures and desert scenes but these are quite rare. W E Powell illustrated some insect studies for a nature book 'I See All' around 1900.

**Miss Lucy POWER (1866-1898)**

Portrait and landscape painter in oil who lived in London. She exhibited at the Royal Academy two portraits (1893) and a landscape 'Parish Church, Whitby' (1898). This good quality artist was tragically swept from the pier by a wave and drowned at Whitby in 1898 cutting short a most promising career.

**Maud POWER (fl. 1908)**

Author and illustrator of 'Wayside India' published by Simpkin Marshall & Co. in 1908. The book contained 32 of her watercolour illustrations.

**Miss A.. J.. POYSER (exh. 1895)**

Artist who lived at Sydenham, Suffolk, and was a member of the Ipswich Art Club. She exhibited a portrait at their Exhibition in 1895.

**Miss Ianthe POYSER (exh. 1896-1897)**

Painter of portraits and miniatures in oil and watercolour, who lived at Sydenham, Suffolk, and was a member of the Ipswich Art Club. She exhibited four portraits 1896-1897 and the titles included 'The Errand Boy' (oil) and 'A Simple Child' (watercolour).

**William PRATER (exh. 1917-1923)**

Painter in oil and watercolour of Cornish landscapes and village scenes. William Prater came from a large family of Polish origin and was one of nine children of whom seven were artists. Three of his brothers Harry, Ernest and Joseph Prater exhibited at the Royal Academy. William Prater exhibited 10 works at the R.W.A. 1917-1923. The subjects were local scenes – 'Shipwright's Shop, Newquay Harbour' (oil, 1919), 'The Butcher's Cart, Crantock Village' (watercolour) and 'The Gannel, near Newquay' (oil, 1920) are typical titles. William Prater exhibited much of his work at the local tea shop at Crantock, painting in a small studio shack on the cliffs overlooking the bay.

**Miss Mary PRATT (exh. 1913-1915)**

Painter in watercolour of still life and landscapes who lived at Downend, Bristol, and exhibited three works at the R.W.A. 1913-1915. The works were entitled 'The Lonely Traveller', 'White Poppies' and 'Summer'.

G. Prelty      *'Sheep by a Shelter' (w/c)*      (Angela Hone)

### G.. PRELTY (fl. c. 1900s)

Painter in watercolour of landscapes and beach scenes often featuring animals. This good quality artist does not appear to have exhibited but is known to have worked in North Wales at one time.

### Miss G.. Minnie PRENTICE (exh. 1891-1893)

Painter in oil and watercolour who lived at Stowmarket, Suffolk. She exhibited three works at the Ipswich Art Club 1891-1893, and the titles included 'No Help for the Blind' (1893).

### H.. J.. PRENTICE (exh. 1935-1936)

Artist who lived at Westbury-on-Trym, Glos., and exhibited three works at the R.W.A. – 'The Severn Estuary . . .' (1935) and 'Silver Lining' and 'Sunshine and Shadow' (1936).

### Miss L.. May Manning PRENTICE (exh. 1895-1897)

Painter of landscapes and still life in oil and watercolour who lived at Stowmarket, Suffolk, and was a member of the Ipswich Art Club. She exhibited 14 works 1895-1897. The subjects included flowers 'Chrysanthemums and Eucalyptus' (oil, 1896) and landscapes – views of Dusseldorf and Holland.

### William Charles PRENTICE (exh. 1891-1934)

Landscape painter in oil who lived in Ipswich and was a member of the Ipswich Art Club. He was a regular exhibitor showing at least 184 works 1891-1934. Many of the subjects were local landscapes and the titles included 'Firs, Stowmarket', 'Bealings Church', 'Blakenham Mill' and 'Wortwell Marshes' (all 1901).

### W.. R.. PRENTICE (exh. 1912-1913)

Painter of landscapes and still life in oil and watercolour who lived in Ipswich. He was a member of the Ipswich Art Club and exhibited five works 1912-1913. The titles included – 'Blackhall Rocks, Castle Eden' (watercolour, 1912) and 'Gathering Clouds, Durham Coast' (oil, 1913).

### Mrs. L.. E.. PRESTON (exh. 1898-1915)

Painter in oil and watercolour of still life and landscapes who lived at Fishponds, Bristol, and was married to the artist J H T Preston. She exhibited seven works at the R.W.A. 1898-1915 – 'A Stormy Evening, Cleveden' (1903) and 'Primroses' (1913), both watercolours, were typical titles.

### Miss Muriel PRESTON (exh. 1903-1913)

Painter in oil and watercolour of still life and landscapes who lived at Fishponds, Bristol, and was probably the daughter of L E and J H T Preston. She exhibited four works at the R.W.A. 1903-1913, including 'A Study of a Chaffinch's Nest' (1904) and 'Linney Head, Pembrokeshire' (oil, 1908).

### Miss Maud PRETTY (exh. 1920-1933)

Watercolour landscape painter who lived at Felixstowe, Suffolk, and was a member of the Ipswich Art Club. She exhibited at least 52 works 1920-1933 and the titles included 'St Austell Bay' (1928), 'Chelsworth, Suffolk' and 'Polstead, Suffolk' (both 1930).

### Miss G.. M.. PRICHARD (exh. 1913-1924)

Artist who lived at Ramsgate, Kent, and exhibited at the Walker Art Gallery, Liverpool, in 1913. In 1924 she exhibited two desert scenes at the B.W.S. Exhibition in Cheltenham.

### Margaret PRIOR (fl. 1930s)

Oil and watercolour painter of portraits, figure subjects and landscapes. She studied art at the Slade under Franklin White and had an exhibition at the French Gallery, London, in November 1934. Margaret Prior showed a total of 17 works, mostly oils of circus scenes, interiors and portraits but also some watercolour landscapes.

### Alfred J.. PRITCHATT (exh. 1932-1950s)

Watercolour landscape painter who lived in Ipswich and was a member of the Ipswich Art Club. He was a regular exhibitor, showing at least 53 works 1932-1950, and was a member until the 1960s. Many of the subjects were local views and the titles included 'The River Alde, near Iken' (1932), 'Late October, Riddlesworth' and 'Evening at Rushmere' (both 1936).

### Col. Geoffrey Oliver Carwardine PROBERT (1892-1987)

Oliver Probert, born in 1892, was the son of Col. W. G. C. Probert. His mother, Mary Badcock, had been the model for Tenniel's original illustrations for Alice. Oliver Probert was educated at Eton and then at the Royal Military Academy, Woolwich, before being commissioned into the Royal Artillery.

His interest in art started at an early age. His father was a controller of the household of Princess Louise, the Duchess of Argyll, who was a keen amateur artist. Three of his aunts, Kate and Isabel Badcock (q.v.) and Ethel Davis, were also talented painters.

Oliver Probert was a self-taught artist and painted from his school days until the 1960s. Even during the First World War on active service he found time to paint and later he produced many works while serving in India 1929-1932. He was a regular exhibitor at the Army Officers Art Society and showed some 40 works 1928-1939. Most of his subjects were landscapes in oil painted in a free impressionistic style and were taken from his travels in this country and abroad. Oliver Probert died in April 1987 at the age of 95.

### Frank PROSSER (exh. 1932-1936)

Landscape artist who lived at Keynsham, Bristol, and later at Trowbridge, Wilts. He exhibited seven works at the R.W.A. 1932-1936 mostly West Country views and local scenes.

### Miss Winifred PROSSER (exh. 1915)

Landscape artist, who lived at Keynsham, Bristol, and was probably related to Frank Prosser (q.v.). She exhibited at the R.W.A. in 1915 a landscape entitled 'Poplars – Queen Charlton'.

### Thomas PROTHEROE (exh. 1881-1894)

Painter in oil and watercolour of portraits, genre, landscapes and still life. Thomas Protheroe was a successful portrait photographer with a studio in Wine Street, Bristol from 1871, and around 1897 he opened a second premises in Clifton. His patrons included Mr Gladstone and The Prince of Wales and he used his premises to display and sell his paintings of portraits and still life. Thomas Protheroe exhibited 60 works at the R.W.A. 1881-1894. The pictures, both oils and watercolours, were mostly portraits and figure subjects, but there were also some still life and local landscapes. 'Turkish Lady' (1881), 'The Old Sexton' (watercolour, 1885) and 'The Old Cobbler' (1891) are typical titles.

### Stuart W.. PROVERBS (fl. 1894-1911)

Figure and landscape artist in watercolour and pastel who lived in Wandsworth, South London. It is curious that this competent artist did not exhibit but Stuart Proverbs is listed in the 'Year's Art' as a craftsman and designer so he may have worked as a commercial artist. His landscapes included some views in Wales, painted in the 1890s.

Stuart Proverbs                'The Officer' (pastel)

### Lt. Col. G.. W.. T.. PROWSE (exh. 1930)

Artist who exhibited six works at the Army Officers Art Society Exhibition in 1930.

### Mrs. L.. D.. M.. PURSER (exh. 1926-1953)

Landscape painter who lived at Portishead, near Bristol, and exhibited 16 works at the R.W.A. 1926-1953. Most of the subjects were local landscapes, also some of Devon, and a continental scene 'Lake Lucerne' (1931).

### Tom PURVIS (1888-1959)

Painter and poster artist who was born in Bristol on 12th June 1888. His father, a retired Master Mariner, painted seascapes and Tom Purvis assisted him with the painting of skies. He studied at the Camberwell School of Art and kept himself by gaining a number of small commercial commissions. During the Great War he joined The Artists Rifles and was wounded in action on the Western Front. Tom Purvis is probably best known for his poster work. He was a leading poster designer for the London and North Eastern Railway as well as gaining commissions from many branches of industry. He was the Vice President of the Royal Society of Arts and helped organise the 'British Art in Industry' Exhibition in 1935. His work was the subject of an article in The Artist magazine in October 1934.

During the Second World War, Tom Purvis was employed by the Ministry of Supply on posters and propaganda work. In the 1950s as the demand for posters declined he turned to portrait painting and religious subjects and he exhibited at the Paris Salon in 1954 and 1958. Tom Purvis died on 27th August 1959. A sale of the remaining contents of his studio was held by Onslows in London on 6th February 1990.

## Walter PUTTICK (1851-1921)

Painter of landscapes in watercolour and black and white illustrator. He was a member of the Brighton Arts Club and the Hon. Secretary until a short time before his death. He was a regular exhibitor with the Club and his subjects included some views of Cornwall and the Isle of Wight (1912). Walter Puttick contributed 12 pen and ink illustrations for 'Off the Beaten Track in Sussex' by Arthur Stanley Cooke which was published in 1912. He lived in Hassocks near Brighton for a number of years and died on 10th December 1921.

## Miss Alice Muriel PYM (1891-1941)

Painter in watercolour, and sometimes oil, of rural scenes and landscapes who was born on 28th July 1891. She was the neice of Jessie Pym (q.v.) who influenced her style and she painted similar subjects. Alice Pym lived in Reigate for many years and does not appear to have exhibited although she was listed under 'Artists' in the local trade directories in the 1930s. She was the founder of the Reigate Scout movement around 1908 and during the First World War organised the local Women Volunteer Force, for which she was awarded the O.B.E. Sadly, Alice Pym suffered from diabetes and this precipitated her death at the age of 49 on 22nd April 1941.

and then in Paris with her cousin Hilda Chalk (later Lumley-Ellis). She exhibited in London and in the provinces from 1900 until the 1930s while living in Reigate. Jessie Pym travelled abroad painting in Italy, France and Holland. She retired to Selmeston, beneath the Sussex Downs, in the late 1930s where she painted many of her rural farming scenes. She was the aunt of Alice Muriel Pym (q.v.) who painted similar subjects. An exhibition of Jessie Pym's work was held at Jeremy Wood Fine Art, Cranleigh, in May 1979. Her watercolours have a distinctive 'wet' impressionistic style and the popular subject matter have made them collectable. She usually signs J. Pym in a sloping script but many of the studies are unsigned.

## Miss K.. A.. PYNE (exh. 1897)

Watercolour landscape painter who lived at Highgate, London, and was a member of the Ipswich Art Club. She exhibited seven works in 1897 and the titles included 'A Wiltshire Lane', 'The Downs at Wroughton, Wilts' and 'The Apple Orchard'. Miss M F Pyne (q.v.) of the same address was probably her sister.

## Miss M.. F.. PYNE (exh. 1897)

Watercolour landscape painter who lived at Highgate, London, and was a member of the Ipswich Art Club. She exhibited seven works in 1897 and the titles included 'Trafalgar Square', 'The Viaduct at Highgate' and 'The Mill Stream at Wroughton'.

*Jessie Pym*          *'Ploughing on the Downs' (w/c)*

## Jessie PYM (1868-1946)

Painter in watercolour of rural landscapes often featuring working horses, Jessie Pym, born in Reigate on 3rd October 1868, studied art at the Slade School

# R

## Edward RABY (exh. 1924-1926)

Painter in watercolour of birds, still life and flowers, who lived in Worcester and exhibited at the Cheltenham Arts and Crafts Society in 1924 and 1926. The subjects included 'Young Magpies and Apple Blossom' and two flower studies.

## S.. F.. RAHAMIN (fl. 1900-1925)

Indian portrait painter who had an exhibition at Arthur Tooth & Sons in June 1925 entitled 'Paintings of India'. The artist was usually known as S. F. Rahamin Samuel (q.v.).

*A. Ramus       'Shipping off the Coast' (w/c)       (Marble Hill Gallery)*

## Aubrey RAMUS (fl. c. 1900-1930)

Painter in oil and watercolour of landscapes and marine subjects. This prolific artist, whose work was mostly rural landscapes and highland scenes in oil similar to F E Jamieson (q.v.), does not appear to have exhibited. The watercolour marines signed A Ramus are of better quality than the oils and should be more valuable. The subjects are usually fishing boats in the Channel or off the French coast.

## Miss Lillian E.. RANDS A.R.W.A. (exh. 1895-1923)

Painter in oil and watercolour of portraits, landscapes and coastal scenes, who lived in Northampton and moved to Bristol in the 1900s. She exhibited at Birmingham and the Society of Women Artists and, from 1908, became a regular exhibitor at the R.W.A. showing over 19 works there until 1923. The subjects included portraits in oil – 'Eileen' and 'A Franciscan Monk' (1908) and coastal scenes and landscapes – 'Floods, Porlock' and 'Gurnards Head, Cornwall' (1923).

## Miss E.. RANKIN (exh. 1890)

Painter in oil and pastel of landscapes and coastal scenes who lived at Rochford, Essex, and exhibited four works at the Ipswich Art Club in 1890. The titles were 'A Bit of Western Sky' and 'On the Roach' (both oils) and 'When the Tide comes in' and 'The Departing Day' (both pastels).

## Capt. Robert RANSHAW (exh. 1889-1890)

Painter in oil of landscapes and still life, who lived at Louth, Lincs., and was a member of the Ipswich Art Club. He exhibited four works 1889-1890 and the titles were 'Old Books' (1889) and 'The Wetterhorn', 'Left by the Tide', 'Before the Season' (1890, all oils).

## Mrs. D.. E.. A.. RASH (exh. 1924-1928)

Watercolour landscape painter who lived at Wortham, Norfolk, and was a member of the Ipswich Art Club. She exhibited eight works 1924-1928 and the subjects included views of Norwich, and a harvesting scene.

## Frederick H.. RAY (fl. 1897-1907)

Landscape painter in oil who lived in Norwich and exhibited 23 works with the Norwich Art Circle 1901-1907. The subjects were mostly local views and scenes on the Broads. He was also a member of the Ipswich Art Club in 1897, but did not appear to exhibit there.

## Miss Noel READ (exh. 1927-1950s)

Watercolour landscape and flower painter who lived in London and later Salcombe, Devon, and was a member of the Ipswich Art Club. She was a regular exhibitor showing at least 57 works 1927-1950 and was active until the mid 1950s. The titles included local landscapes – 'Ufford Church' (1930) and 'Canvey Island from Lee-on-Sea' (1932) and still life subjects – 'A Basket of Primroses' and 'Wallflowers' (both 1932).

## T.. L.. REES (exh. 1910-1915)

Landscape painter and illustrator who lived in Ipswich and was a member of the Ipswich Art Club. He was a regular exhibitor showing 30 works 1910-1915 mostly rural scenes in watercolour. The titles include 'Ripe for Harvest' (1911), 'Near Martlesham' and 'A Suffolk Farmyard' (both 1915).

## Miss E.. K.. REEVES (exh. 1910)

Watercolour landscape painter who exhibited a view of Lancing College, Sussex, at the Worthing Art Gallery Exhibition in 1910.

## Miss Charlotte D.. RENNARDS (exh. 1921-1930)

Watercolour landscape painter who was a member of the Ipswich Art Club. She exhibited nine works 1921-1930, mostly local scenes and some Italian views. The titles included 'View on the Orwell' (1924), 'Roman Theatre, Fiesole' (1928) and 'Morning, Tuscany' (1930).

## Lt. Col. William John Kerr RETTIE (1868-1939)

A former officer in the Royal Artillery who exhibited a total of 15 works at the Army Officers Art Society Exhibitions 1930-1931.

## James Crabtree RHODES (exh. 1936-1938)

Artist in watercolour and pen and ink who lived at Ipswich and was a member of the Ipswich Art Club. He showed nine works 1936-1938 and the titles included – 'Lilac Trees' and 'Ploughed Land' (both 1938).

G. Rhys-Jenkins                    'Glory Hole, Lincoln' (w/c)

## G.. W.. RHYS-JENKINS (born 1872, fl. 1900-1929)

Painter and illustrator in watercolour, architect and designer who worked extensively in England and the U.S.A. until the late 1920s. Rhys-Jenkins illustrations were reproduced in The Sphere, The Tatler and The Studio magazines and some of his middle eastern market scenes were published as prints. He signed Rhys-Jenkins in block letters with a flourish on the J.

## Albert RICH B.W.S. (exh. 1928)

Watercolour landscape painter who was a member of the B.W.S. and exhibited at the B.W.S. Autumn Exhibition at Preston in 1928. The picture was entitled 'The Orange Mill, Zeeland'.

## W.. RICH (fl. c. 1900s)

Humorous illustrator in black and white of animals who was probably working c. 1900.

## Frank T.. RICHARDS (exh. 1950)

Painter in oil, watercolour and gouache who lived in Plymouth and exhibited three local views at the Plymouth Art Society in 1950.

## L.. RICHARDS (fl. c. 1920s)

This is generally accepted to be one of the pseudonyms adopted by the artist Daniel Sherrin (q.v.). A wide range of subjects and styles, usually in oil, appear under this signature, including coastal scenes, harbours and landscapes.

## W.. RICHARDS (fl. c. 1900s-1930s)

This was a pseudonym for F.. E.. Jamieson (q.v.) who specialised in painting oils of Scottish lochs and highland landscapes. The pictures are usually inscribed on the back of the canvas with the location.

H. O. Richardson                    'Pepper' (w/c)

## Harry Oliver RICHARDSON (born 1863, fl. 1890-1897)

Painter in watercolour of horse portraits who was born at Fenny Stratford, Bucks., in 1863. Harry Richardson was a prolific painter of horse portraits who lived in Rugby, Warks., and was known to have been working between 1890 and 1897. The pictures have considerable charm and their quality and subject matter should make them collectable. He signed his work H. O. Richardson in a disjoined script usually dated and inscribed 'Rugby' and some also have the name of the horse.

## Mrs. Ellen RICKETTS (exh. 1932-1938)

Landscape and flower painter in oil and watercolour who lived at Sproughton, Suffolk, and was a member of the Ipswich Art Club. She was a regular exhibitor showing 16 works 1932-1938 and the titles included 'The Old Lockgates, Sproughton' (1935) and 'Fir Trees' (1936).

*Fred Rider*                         *'Near Steyning, Sussex' (w/c)*

*Sidney Robbins*           *'Portrait Study' (pencil)*

## Fred RIDER (fl. 1920s)

Painter in watercolour of landscapes and river scenes. This good quality artist does not appear to have exhibited. Most of the subjects were South of England scenes and he often signed the work neatly in ink.

## Miss F.. M.. RIGNALL (exh. 1884)

Painter in oil of still life who lived at Halesworth, Suffolk, and was a member of the Ipswich Art Club. She exhibited two works in 1884 entitled 'Dead Game' and a 'Basket of Flowers'.

## Richard RIMMER (exh. 1905)

Artist who lived in Bolton, Lancs, and exhibited two flower studies at the Exhibition of Local Artists at the Merehall Art Gallery in 1905.

## Miss F.. A.. RINGER (exh. 1924)

Landscape painter in oils who lived in Cheltenham and exhibited three works at the Cheltenham Art Gallery in 1924. The subjects were landscape views in Wales and Gloucestershire.

## N.. L.. RIPLEY (exh. 1935)

Painter in oil of landscapes and still life who exhibited four works at the French Gallery, London, in 1935. This was an exhibition of 'Weekend Work' by industrial artists employed by the advertising agency J.. Walter Thompson.

## R.. C.. RISELEY (fl. 1904-1918)

Painter in watercolour of landscapes and cottages. This competent artist does not appear to have exhibited but the work is usually dated and examples have been seen spanning 1904 to 1918.

## Sidney John ROBBINS (1879-1965)

Portrait and figure artist in pencil and red chalk. Sidney Robbins was educated at St Mark's, Chelsea, and studied art while working as a graphic designer for the family business in Church Road, Chelsea. During the First World War he served as a Corporal in the Signals in France and Belgium. Most of his work was pencil studies of figures and portraits drawn in the 1920s. Sidney Robbins lived in Tooting for a number of years and died on 14th August 1965. He signed with initials (see index).

## Nina ROBERTS (exh. 1924)

Watercolour painter who exhibited a view of Whitby at the B.W.S. Exhibition at Cheltenham in 1924.

## Mrs. Ethel Lilley ROBERTSON (1873-1953)

Miniature portrait painter who lived at Tulse Hill, South London, and had earlier exhibited under her maiden name of E L Hovenden (q.v.). She exhibited eight works at the Royal Academy, mostly miniatures of her family, and at the Royal Society of Miniature Painters. Ethel Robertson died on 5th August 1953.

## Arnold W.. ROBINSON (1888-1954)

Stained glass artist and occasional painter who was born in Bristol in 1888. He exhibited 21 stained glass designs at the R.W.A. 1918-1938 and also over 45 designs at the Bristol Savages Exhibitions 1921-1953. He was President of the Bristol Savages in 1927. After the Second World War Arnold Robinson was responsible for reinstating the stained glass in Bristol Cathedral.

**Boardman ROBINSON (exh. 1922)**

Artist and illustrator who had a one-man exhibition at Macleans Gallery, London, in November 1922. The exhibition was entitled 'Drawings and Characters' and consisted of 56 works – mostly portrait sketches of political figures.

**Cyril E.. ROBINSON (exh. 1912)**

Landscape painter in watercolour who was a member of the Winchester Art Society and exhibited three Scottish landscapes at the 1912 Exhibition.

**Lt. Col. E.. H.. ROBINSON (exh. 1923)**

Watercolour landscape painter who lived at East Bergholt, Suffolk, and was a member of the Ipswich Art Club. He exhibited three works in 1923, entitled – 'Dedham Lock', 'Reina Christina, Water Tower' and 'A Moorish Backyard'.

**Julius ROBINSON (exh. 1914-1917)**

Artist who lived at West Kensington in London and exhibited eight works at the N.B.A. 1914-1917.

**Mrs. Mary G.. ROBINSON (exh. 1910)**

Watercolour landscape painter who exhibited three works at the Worthing Art Gallery Summer Exhibition in 1910. The subjects included a Yorkshire stream and a view near Petersfield.

**Miss Leila ROBSON (exh. 1885)**

Painter in oil who lived at Beccles, Suffolk, and exhibited a work at the Ipswich Art Club in 1885 entitled 'French Partridge'.

**Miss Dorette ROCHE (exh. 1908-1910)**

Painter in oil and watercolour of portraits and landscapes. Dorette Roche lived in South West London and was a student at the Lambeth School of Art. In 1908 she was a prize winner for an oil landscape and received an Hon. Mention for a watercolour at the Lambeth Art Club Exhibition. In 1909 she exhibited a watercolour portrait at the National Schools of Art Competition and 1910 she exhibited at The Royal Institute of Painters in Watercolour.

**Miss Muriel Gordon ROE (exh. 1906-1909)**

Landscape painter in oil and watercolour who lived in Kings Lynn and exhibited 14 works at the Norwich Art Circle Exhibitions 1906-1909. The subjects included some local views in watercolour and Cornish landscapes in oil.

**Delamark Banks ROFFEY (exh. 1875-1884)**

Painter in oil of figure subjects who lived in South Kensington, London, and was a founder member of the Ipswich Art Club. He exhibited at the opening exhibition in 1875 and between 1880 and 1884 showed 12 works. The titles appear to be mostly figure subjects and included 'My Bird, I think', 'Lady Susan at Home' (both 1882), 'On Guard' (1883) and 'The Blue Ribbon Movement' (1884).

**Samuel Enoch ROGERS (born 1890, exh. 1926-1931)**

Landscape painter, who lived at Pill, Somerset, and exhibited nine works at the R.W.A. 1927-1931. The subjects were local views – 'The Post Office, Avonmouth' (1927), 'Portbury' and 'Old Pill Harbour' (1929) are typical titles.

**R.. W.. ROGERSON (exh. 1886-1889)**

Landscape painter in watercolour and sometimes oil who lived in Bristol and exhibited nine works at the R.W.A. 1886-1889. The titles included 'Old Highland Smithy' (oil, 1888) and 'Near Sodbury, Glos' (watercolour, 1889).

**F.. Arthur ROLFE B.W.S. (exh. 1928)**

Watercolour landscape painter who was a member of the B.W.S. and exhibited 'Uphill Church, Weston-super-Mare' at the Autumn Exhibition at Preston in 1928.

**Joseph A.. ROLL (exh. 1913)**

Watercolour landscape painter who lived at Elmswell, Suffolk, and was a member of the Ipswich Art Club. He exhibited two works in 1913 – 'The Railway Bridge, Gorleston' and 'Beach at Evening, Gorleston'.

**Maurice ROMBERG (exh. 1913)**

Watercolour landscape painter who had an exhibition at the Dowdeswell Gallery, London, in January 1913 of views in Morocco and Algeria.

**Paul ROMNEY (died c. 1900)**

This was the pseudonym adopted by Carl Holder, the son of Edward H Holder and brother of Edith Holder (q.v.). Carl painted in oils and the work included some portraits. He was reputedly killed in the Boer War.

**Pat ROONEY (fl. 1930-1950s)**

Illustrator and caricaturist, particularly of R.A.F. personnel, who was working from 1930 until the 1950s. He exhibited at the Royal Scottish Academy in the 1930s, but apparently nothing later, when he probably relied on his portrait commissions. Pat Rooney toured R.A.F. messes around the country to sketch the portraits usually in pastel and charcoal. The work is signed Pat Rooney and often inscribed with the sitter's name.

**George F.. ROSE (fl. 1890-1932)**

Painter in watercolour of landscapes and harbour scenes who lived at Richmond, Surrey, and was working c. 1890-1930. This competent artist does not appear to have exhibited, but known work indicates that he painted in the Channel Islands (Creux Harbour – 1890) and in Sussex (Houghton Bridge – 1932).

*Nina Rothney*       *'Terrier Study' (oil)*

## Nina ROTHNEY (1877-1970)

Painter in oil and watercolour of dog portraits, figures and landscapes. She was born Georgina Emma Rothney on 20th September 1877 at Barrakpore, Culcutta, India, where her father James Rothney was a successful businessman. The family returned to London around 1890 and lived in Upper Norwood. Nina Rothney studied at the Crystal Palace School of Art winning the Scholarship and Silver Medal for 1897. The first decade of the 20th Century was to be one of her most productive periods. She exhibited at the Society of Women Artists and was a member and exhibitor at the Society for the Preservation of Art 1900-1904. Nina Rothney joined and exhibited at several of her local art clubs including The Surrey Art Circle, The Croydon Art Society and The Stanley Art Club. Much of her work at this time was dog portraits and she received commissions from dog clubs, breeders and private owners. As well as animals, Nina Rothney painted landscapes in Scotland, Devon, France, Belgium and Holland. In 1910 she married Thomas Hill and appears to have done little painting until the 1920s when she exhibited as 'Nina Hill' (q.v.). A retrospective exhibition of her work was held at Jeremy Wood Fine Art, Cranleigh, in November 1979. The early work is signed Nina Rothney and the small sketches sometimes with a monogram (see index).

*W. Ednie Rough*       *'The Harbour' (w/c)*

## William Ednie ROUGH S.S.A. (1892-1935)

Painter in watercolour of landscapes and harbour scenes who was born in Kircaldy, Fife, in 1892. He was educated locally and at the Edinburgh College of Art where his studies were cut short by the outbreak of the First World War. William Rough saw active service throughout the conflict, first in Gallipoli and later as a commissioned officer in France. After the War he returned to the Edinburgh College of Art and was awarded a Diploma in Drawing and Painting in 1920. William Rough, like many artists, chose to enter the teaching profession, joined the George Heriot School as assistant art master and later became the Principal Teacher in Art at Dumfries Academy. In 1931 he was appointed Art Master at Daniel Stewart's College, Edinburgh. William Rough regularly showed work at the Royal Scottish Academy and at other principal Scottish exhibitions 1926-1935. In 1934 he was elected a member of the Society of Scottish Artists. Sadly, William Rough died at the early age of 42 on 19th February 1935. A memorial exhibition of his work was held later that year.

William Rough's work is not often seen on the market but has a most appealing and distinctive 'wet' impressionistic style. The subjects include Scottish highland scenes, harbours and Breton landscapes. He signed the work 'W Ednie Rough' in a printed script underlined.

## Douglas E.. ROW (exh. 1924)

Watercolour painter of marines and landscapes who exhibited two pictures at the B.W.S. Exhibition at Cheltenham in 1924 – 'The Cutty Sark' and a 'Guernsey Garden'.

*Leeson Rowbotham*       *'Summer Landscape, Sussex' (w/c)*

## Leopold Charles Leeson ROWBOTHAM (1889-1977)

Leeson Rowbotham, the son of the well-known watercolour artist Charles Edmund Rowbotham, was born in Brighton in 1889. He studied at the Brighton School of Art but he decided to follow the more secure career of banking. During the First World

War, Leeson Rowbotham saw active service in France where he was severely wounded. He took up painting again the late 1920s and painted landscape views in Cornwall, Suffolk and local scenes in his native Sussex. He also painted some South of France and Italian lake scenes but these were usually based on pictures by his father. His work was at its best in the 1930s and showed some of his father's vibrant colouring but without the highlights in bodycolour.

Leeson Rowbotham did much to support the local art community and for 25 years was the Chairman of the Brighton Seafront Art Council. After retiring as the manager of a local bank, he continued to paint as a pastime to within a few years of his death in 1977.

### Walter George ROWNEY (1862-1947)

Artist member of the famous painting materials company who was born in London in 1862. An obituary in The Artist magazine in September 1947 described him as . . . 'an exceptionally good amateur painter, many of his pictures comparing favourably with much of the professional work of his day'.

### Miss Irene ROWSELL (exh. 1902-1909)

Painter in oil of flowers and still life who exhibited nine works at the Norwich Art Circle Exhibitions 1902-1909. She lived at the Rectory in Beccles and was the daughter of the Rev. T N Rowsell who also exhibited at Norwich and in London.

### Hugh RUDBY (1855-1954)

This was the adopted name of the artist Walter Hugh Wright, who painted landscapes in watercolour from about 1890 until 1930. The work was signed either Hugh Rudby or Hugh Wright-Rudby (q.v.). He adopted the name in order to distinguish himself from other artists called Wright who were working in the area.

### Miss Florence RUEGG (exh. 1900-1908)

Landscape painter who lived in Clifton, Bristol, and exhibited 12 works at the R.W.A. 1900-1908. The subjects were mostly Bristol street and harbour scenes together with a study of 'Fishing Boats, Looe, Cornwall' (1904).

### F.. S.. RUSSELL (exh. 1950)

Painter in oil and watercolour who lived in Plymouth and exhibited three works at the Plymouth Art Society Exhibition in 1950. The subjects were Scottish Loch scenes and a Dartmoor view.

### Mrs. Marjorie RUSSELL (exh. 1950, died c. 1989)

Painter in oil of still life and interiors who was the daughter of the artist Henry George Cogle. She lived at Holmbury St Mary, Surrey, for many years and exhibited three works at the Plymouth Art Society Exhibition in 1950.

### William Smart RUSSELL (1849-1930)

Painter in watercolour and sometimes oil, of rural scenes and buildings particularly of Horsham, Sussex, where he lived. He was the son of Julius Russell of Chiddingly, Sussex. He was in business with his father as a grocer in West Street, and then The Bishopric, Horsham, from about 1907. William Russell painted a number of watercolours of local views, and some were published as coloured postcards by J. Salmon of Sevenoaks. The work is occasionally found in the Horsham area and is of local historical interest. William Smart Russell died on 15th July 1930 at the age of 81.

Harold Ryder                    (Nick Cotton)
'Place de la Gare, Ostend" (w/c)

### Harold RYDER A.R.C.A. (fl. 1911-1915)

Painter in watercolour of figures and landscapes who studied at the Royal College of Art 1911-1915. This talented artist had a studio at one time in Barons Court, West London, but does not appear to have exhibited. He may have been related to George Ryder who studied at the Royal College of Art at the same time. Some French subjects by Harold Ryder are known to exist. He signed his work Harold Ryder in block letters with a flourish on the L.

# S

### Henry James SAGE (1868-1953)

Painter in watercolour of landscapes and old buildings. Henry Sage was born on 4th October 1868 in London where he studied under an artist, Mr Montague, before moving to Guildford, Surrey. Most of his work was painted in the Guildford area depicting views of old streets and cottages. Henry Sage did some illustrations for E A Judges book 'Some West Surrey Villages' (c. 1900) but these black and white views do not show the artist's true ability. His best work was his cottage and street scenes and the popular subject matter has made these increasingly collectable. Henry Sage continued to paint into old age and died on 22nd July 1953. The Guildford Borough own a collection of his work which was exhibited at Guildford House in June 1994.

E. St John    'Italian Lakeside Town' (w/c)

### Maj. Gen. Richard S.. St. JOHN (1876-1959)

Artist who exhibited six works at the Army Officers Art Society Exhibition in 1929.

### Miss F.. M.. SALDANHA (fl. 1930s)

Painter of portraits and ecclesiastical subjects and designer who lived in South West London. She was working in the early 1930s.

H. J. Sage    'A Surrey Lane' (w/c)

### Miss R.. G.. A.. SAGE (exh. 1927-1936)

Landscape and coastal scene painter who lived in Bristol and exhibited 14 works at the R.W.A. 1927-1936. The subjects were mostly local scenes and Devon and Cornwall views, including Brixham, Exmouth and Babbacombe.

### Edwin St. JOHN (fl. 1876-c. 1910)

Painter in watercolour of landscapes including continental lake and town scenes. His work shows considerable similarity to that of the Earp family and he may well have been connected with these Brighton artists. Edwin St. John's watercolours were often large and depicted lake and town scenes in France, Switzerland and Italy – his best work usually dating from the 1870s and 1880s. He does not appear to have exhibited in London but his work was shown at Elands Art Gallery, Exeter, in 1907. This artist seems also to have painted under the pseudonym of F. Catano (q.v.).

R. H. Sams   'Cloudy Evening, Wular Lake, Kashmir' (w/c)

### Lt. Richard H.. SAMS (fl. 1927-1970s)

An Officer in the Royal Engineers who exhibited 26 works at the Army Officers Art Society exhibitions 1928-1936. His work was mostly landscapes in watercolour including several views in India. Later, Richard Sams was to exhibit at the Royal Society of Marine Artists in the 1970s.

## S.. Rahamin SAMUEL (fl. 1900-1925)

A good quality Indian portrait painter who also appears to have worked under the name of S Rahamin (q.v.). He took up painting around 1900, first studied at the Slade and then at the Royal Academy Schools. He later returned to Bombay where he found many willing subjects for portrait commissions. Rahamin Samuel exhibited two portraits at the Royal Academy in 1903 and 1910 and had an exhibition at Arthur Tooth & Sons Gallery in 1925 under the name of S Rahamin. His work was also featured in The Studio magazine in 1910.

*A. E. Sanders       'Evening Calm' (w/c)       (J Collins and Son)*

## Alfred E.. SANDERS (fl. c. 1911)

Painter in watercolour of sunset landscapes, beach and coastal scenes. He does not appear to have exhibited but a dated watercolour indicates that he was working before the First World War. His work was reproduced as postcards by Henry Moss & Co. and C W Faulkner & Co. including views on the Norfolk Broads and the coast of Cornwall. He signed his work A E Sanders in capitals, sometimes with a date.

*W Sands       'Clovelly' (w/c)       (John Horton)*

## W.. SANDS (fl. c. 1930s)

Painter in watercolour of West Country views particularly Devon and Cornwall harbour and street scenes. The name is believed to be a pseudonym for the artist T H Victor (q.v.) who painted a large number of similar views at around the same time. Thomas Victor lived at Mousehole and many of his subjects were views of Newlyn, St Ives and Clovelly. The quality of W Sands work varies but the better examples are becoming popular. (Illus. this page).

## Maj. Gen. Harry Neptune SARGENT (1866-1946)

A former officer in the Royal Army Service Corps who exhibited 14 watercolours at the Army Officers Art Society 1928-1932. The subjects were mostly landscape views of the West Country including Torquay and Dartmoor scenes.

## Maj. A... J... SAUNDERS (exh. 1928-1931)

A former officer in the Royal Artillery who exhibited 14 watercolours at the Army Officers Art Society 1928-1931. The subjects included English landscapes in Kent and Sussex, a Dorset harbour scene and also some foreign views

## Miss Elaine SAVAGE (fl. 1927-1934)

Artist who lived at Sutton, Surrey, and is listed in the local trade directory as working between 1927 and 1934.

## Frederick SAVERY (exh. 1900-1901)

Landscape painter who lived in Bristol and exhibited three works ath the R. W. A. 1900-1901. The titles were 'Wickham Bridge, Stapleton' (1900) and 'Clack Mill Cottages, Stoke Bishop' and 'St Brelades Bay, Jersey' (both 1901).

## Miss Mabel SAW (exh. 1899-1921)

Watercolour landscape painter who lived at Dereham, Norfolk, and was a member of the Ipswich Art Club. The exhibits give her address as the Secondary School for Girls where she was probably a teacher. Mabel Saw exhibited 36 works at the Ipswich Art Club 1899-1921, mostly local landscapes and some Cornish scenes such as 'At Looe' (1919).

## D.. J.. SAWYER (fl. c. 1920s)

Black and white illustrator, who may have done work for books and magazines. The subjects include First World War aeroplanes in 'dogfights'. There is no record of the artist exhibiting any work.

*Zue Sayers*       *'Old Cottages, Rye' (w/c)*

## Mrs Zue SAYERS (1870-1952)

Watercolour landscape painter who was born in Gloucestershire in 1870 but at an early age moved to Sussex where her father was to farm. Born Zue Goodrich, she married the watercolour artist Richard Sayers and they lived in Brighton and later at Peasmarsh, near Rye, Sussex. Her watercolour style was much influenced by her husband and could on occasion be mistaken for his work. Her best paintings were her detailed building studies in Sussex villages but she also painted more open rural landscapes. Zue Sayers died at the age of 81 on 6th January 1952. She signed with a monogram (see index).

## Spiro SCARVELLI (fl. c. 1890-1910)

Painter in watercolour of desert scenes, views on the Nile and sometimes Corfu, which appears to be his island of origin. Spiro Scarvelli had a one-man exhibition of his watercolours at the Macleans Gallery in London in the 1890s and must have sold his work widely as it is often seen on the market. The Greek connections have resulted in his work becoming increasingly popular in recent years.

## G.. Forrester SCOTT (fl. 1898)

Artist in pen and ink of architectural subjects who studied at Heatherleys and later at South Kensington. Some charcoal studies of street scenes in Normandy are illustrated in The Studio magazine in 1899.

## E. A.. SEABORNE (exh. 1925-1930)

Landscape artist who lived in Bristol and exhibited nine works at the R.W.A. 1925-1930. Most of the subjects were West Country views, including three of St Ives, also some of Oxford and Reading and two Swiss scenes – 'Interlaken' (1926) and Lucerne (1927).

## Miss Mabel SEAGER (exh. 1903-1915)

Watercolour landscape and coastal painter who lived in Ipswich and was a member of the Ipswich Art Club. She exhibited 15 works 1903-1915, mostly local views. The titles included 'The Creek, Walberswick', 'By the River Blythe' and 'The Sea against the Cliff doth daily beat' (all 1903).

## R.. SEAGER (exh. 1895-1905)

Landscape painter in oil and watercolour who lived in Ipswich and was a member of the Ipswich Art Club. He exhibited 24 works 1895-1905 and the titles included 'A View on Oulton Broad', 'Evening View, Lake Lothing' (both watercolours, 1900) and 'A Bit of Lowestoft Harbour' (1903).

## William John SEARLE (exh. 1923-1950)

Landscape and marine artist who lived in Bristol and was a regular exhibitor at the R.W.A. showing 42 works 1923-1940. The subjects were mostly West Country views including Polperro, Brixham, Falmouth and St Ives – also local scenes and studies of old buildings.

## Miss M.. Josephine SEDGWICK (exh. 1919-1937)

Landscape and flower painter, miniaturist and sculptor, who lived at Ipswich and was a member of the Ipswich Art Club. She exhibited 13 works 1919-1937, the titles included 'Autumn Sunshine', 'Gladioli' and 'Italian Girl' – a Bas Relief figure (all 1936).

## Miss A.. I.. SEED (exh. 1924-1929)

Artist who lived at Clifton, Bristol, and exhibited at the R.W.A. in 1924, 1928 and 1929. The exhibits were entitled 'St Ives', 'Piazza Colonna, Roma' and 'Arch of Titus, Rome'.

## Joseph SEEL (exh. 1905)

Painter of animal subjects who lived at Broughton, Lancs., and exhibited six works at the Local Artists Exhibition at the Merehall Art Gallery, Bolton, in 1905.

## Louise M.. SENGEL (fl. c. 1920)

Watercolour landscape painter who painted in a wet impressionistic style similar to Helen Sengel, to whom she may have been related. Her subjects included some views of Bruges.

## Capt. Heywood W.. SETON-KARR (1859-1938)

A former Captain in the Gordon Highlanders, who exhibited five works at the Army Officers Art Society in 1930. He was a working member of the Society for the Preservation of Art in 1900 and the author of several books on travel and big game hunting.

Dorothy Sexton          'Caught' (w/c)

Miles Sharp     'Autumn Ploughing, 1907' (w/c)     (Angela Hone)

maker in Bristol and was a self-taught artist, but a regular exhibitor at the R.W.A., showing over 57 works 1910-1937. The subjects, mostly etchings, were street scenes and studies of buildings. Edward Sharland exhibited three local Bristol views at the Royal Academy in 1911, 1923 and 1925. Frost and Reed published a series of his etchings of local streets and views in Venice and Toledo (1934) and later the Gloucester Galleries, Bristol, published his work. About 1950, Edward Sharland moved to Cornwall and he died in Truro in 1967 at the age of 83.

## Miss Dorothy H.. SEXTON (fl. c. 1910-1920)

Watercolour painter of still life and illustrator. This good quality artist does not appear to have exhibited, although she did receive a formal art training in about 1915. Her student work shows a particular talent for still life and illustrations.

## Miss E.. M.. SEXTON (exh. 1886-1893)

Landscape painter in oil who lived in Ipswich and was a member of the Ipswich Art Club. She exhibited 21 works 1886-1893, mostly local landscapes. The titles included 'Stutton Rectory' (1889), 'A Quiet Stream' (1890) and 'Morning on the Orwell' (1893).

## Miss Annie Foster SHAPLEY R.W.A.
## (exh. 1895-1930)

Landscape painter in oils who lived at Sea Mills, Bristol, and exhibited at least 37 works at the R.W.A. 1895-1910 and then one in 1930. The subjects were mostly Welsh landscapes and Devon village and moorland scenes. 'The Path to Idwal, North Wales', 'The Village Street, South Zeal, Devon' (1900) and 'Dartmoor' (1901) were typical titles.

## Edward W.. SHARLAND (1884-1967)

Etcher of street scenes and architectural subjects, also sometimes oil painter and watercolourist, who lived in Bristol. Edward Sharland worked for a cabinet

## Miles SHARP (fl. 1907)

Watercolour landscape painter who was active around 1900. His work is usually attributed to Miles B Sharp ARCA, the painter and engraver who was born in 1897, but dated examples of his work are too early for them to be the same artist. It is most likely that the watercolour landscape painter was the father of Miles B Sharp and that he lived and painted near Brighouse, Yorks.

G. Shaw          'Moorland Landscape' (oil)

## George SHAW (1843-1915)

Painter in oil of moorland and coastal scenes. George Shaw was born in Derby on 8th February 1843, the son of a general trader and pawnbroker. The family moved to Worcester and George worked as a pawnbroker, but later described himself as a dealer in 'Rare China, Antiques, and Works of Art'. After a brief spell in the U.S.A. he returned to England in the 1890s and the following decade appears to have been his most active period as a painter. George Shaw found a ready market for his work in Devon where he lived and he exhibited regularly at Elands Art Gallery, Exeter, and at W F Dyer's Gallery in Exmouth. In 1896, a large oil landscape of the Doone Valley was accepted by the Royal Academy, but not hung, and the Exmouth Chronicle reports it was sold to 'a gentleman at South Kensington for twenty five guineas'. Many of his subjects were Dartmoor and Exmoor scenes, but he also painted coastal and sea studies. George Shaw lived at Exmouth, Torquay, Exeter, and finally Rewe, Devon, where he died on 2nd July 1915. He signed his work G Shaw in red sometimes with a date.

## Miss M.. Olive SHAW (exh. 1925-1927)

Painter in oil of figures and portraits who lived at Woodbridge, Suffolk, and was a member of the Ipswich Art Club. She exhibited six works 1925-1927, mostly portrait studies in oil. She was probably the daughter of Mrs A M Shaw who exhibited from the same address.

## S.. T.. SHAW (exh. 1927)

Landscape artist who lived at Bishopston, Bristol, and exhibited two works at the R.W.A. in 1927. The titles were 'Westbury' and 'Shadowed Valley, South Downs'.

## Harry SHELDON (fl. 1947)

Painter in watercolour of landscapes and interiors. He wrote and illustrated a series of articles in The Artist magazine in 1947 entitled 'Watercolour Painting as I see it'. The article was illustrated with some fine quality watercolours of Italy and Burma and a portrait study. It is curious that this competent artist is not better known.

## William Arthur SHELDON (1868-1960)

Landscape painter in oil and watercolour who lived in Bristol and exhibited at the R.W.A. and the Bristol Savages, of which he was made a life member. A teacher by profession, he was art master and then headmaster of two schools in Bristol until his retirement in 1931. William Sheldon was a prolific artist, exhibiting over 280 works with the Bristol Savages 1907-1960. These were mostly views of Cornwall, Devon, Somerset and Wales. He also exhibited over 30 works at the R.W.A., the titles included 'Burnham Jetty, Low Tide' (1898) and 'Porthminster Beach, St Ives' (1925). William Sheldon continued to paint into his nineties and he died on 6th July 1960.

## Miss Florence Ada SHEPHERD (exh. 1900-1902)

Landscape painter who lived in Bristol and exhibited at the R.W.A. 1900-1902. The subjects included a Welsh landscape and a woodland scene.

## H.. C.. SHEPPARD (exh. 1915-1916)

Artist who lived at Weston-super-Mare, Somerset, and exhibited at the R.W.A. in 1915 and 1916. Later he moved to Shaldon, near Teignmouth, Devon.

## Isaac SHEPPARD (c. 1842-1899)

Painter in oil of landscapes who lived in Ipswich and was a member of the Ipswich Art Club. He was a regular exhibitor showing 76 works 1880-1898. Many of the subjects were local landscapes and these included several moonlight and winter scenes. Among the titles were 'A View of Mildenhall – Winter', 'Moonlight on the Orwell' and 'The Gipping' (all 1890). Examples of his work were included in the Centenary Exhibition of the Ipswich Art Club in 1975.

## E.. J.. SHERMAN (exh. 1895)

Landscape and coastal scene painter in oil who lived at Felixstowe, Suffolk, and was a member of the Ipswich Art Club. He exhibited four works in 1895 entitled 'Suffolk Scene, Kersey', 'Bawdsey Ferry', 'Felixstowe Beach' and 'Dovercourt from the Sea'.

*Daniel Sherrin*     *'Riverside Church' (w/c)*     *(Reid Gallery)*

## Daniel SHERRIN (1868-1940)

Daniel Sherrin was born in Brentford, Essex, in 1868, the son of John Sherrin R.I., the well-known flower and still life painter. There is no record of him receiving a formal art training but it is probable that he studied with his father. Most of Daniel Sherrin's work is in the style of several popular artists of the time. He painted rural landscapes after the style of Benjamin W Leader, marines after Montague Dawson and river scenes in watercolour after Stuart Lloyd. He did not exhibit in London, but preferred to work directly under contract for a gallery painting the subjects (and styles!) that they required. He also painted under the pseudonym of L Richards (q.v.) and these are quite often seen on the market. The family moved to Ramsgate, when Daniel was a young boy, and his father died there in 1896. Daniel Sherrin later moved to Seasalter, near Whitstable, Kent, and died there on 26th January 1940. The artistic talent was carried to a third generation for his son Reginald Sherrin (q.v.) also became an artist.

*R D Sherrin*     *'Belstone Moors, Dartmoor' (w/c)*     *(J Collins and Son)*

## Reginald Daniel SHERRIN (1891-1971)

Painter in watercolour, gouache and sometimes oil of landscapes and coastal scenes. Son of the artist Daniel Sherrin, Reginald was born at Seasalter, near Whitstable, Kent, on 5th April 1891. He served in the First World War and during the Second World War worked at a munitions factory in Rochester. Like his father before him, Reginald Sherrin did not find a need to exhibit since there was a ready market for his pictures. A few oils exist of cottages, but most of his work was coastal and moorland scenes in gouache in a style made popular by F J Widgery. Reginald Sherrin moved to Devon in 1953 and died there on 26th March 1971. Some of his work was signed with pseudonyms which include J Whitely (q.v.) and D A Niel (q.v.).

## Winifred Norton SHILLINGFORD (1882-1963)

Painter in oil of portraits, genre and landscapes, who lived at Etchinghill, near Folkestone, Kent. Little is known about her early life, but Winifred Shillingford studied at the Slade School of Art in 1901 and 1902 where she obtained a certificate for figure drawing and a prize for anatomy. She returned to Folkestone where she became an active member of the Folkestone Art Club exhibiting there regularly 1907-1911. Winifred Shillingford does not appear to have painted after about 1914. Throughout her life, Miss Shillingford was involved with her village and for more than 40 years was president of the local Womens Institute. She died at the age of 81 on 15th February 1963. An exhibition of her work was held at the Roland Goslett Gallery, Richmond, Surrey, in March 1985.

*G A Short*     *'Pub Gossip' (w/c)*

## George Anderson SHORT (1856-1945)

Painter in watercolour of hunting scenes and related subjects who was born at Bellingham, Northumberland, in 1856. This prolific artist specialised in painting hunting scenes, interiors of inns and studies of keepers and huntsmen. Many of the pictures were painted in the Yorkshire area and the work is most frequently found there today. The quality of the work varies but some of the interiors have considerable charm. He signed his work G A Short usually with a date. (Illus. this page).

*Major Shortspoon*     *(Burlington Paintings)*
*'In the Burn, St Andrews' (w/c)*

## Major SHORTSPOON (fl. 1868-1890s)

This was the pseudonym adopted by the golfing artist and author Francis Powell Hopkins (q.v.). His golfing watercolours which can command high prices are signed 'Major S' or sometimes just 'Shortspoon'.. Many of the subjects were of his local course at Westward Ho! in Devon. He also wrote regular articles on Golf for The Field magazine.

*Thomas Sidney*     *'Venice' (w/c)*     *(Sheila Hinde)*

## Thomas SIDNEY (fl. 1900s)

A painter in watercolour of landscapes, coastal and beach scenes. The work of this prolific artist is frequently seen on the market but he does not appear to have exhibited. Many of the watercolours are scenes on the South Coast of England and are usually inscribed with the location and dated. Thomas Sidney also painted a number of Venetian views.

## Lt. Col. W.. A.. SIMMONDS (exh. 1928-1933)

Watercolour landscape painter who exhibited 28 works at the Army Officers Art Society Exhibitions 1928-1933. The subjects included castles and landscapes in Wales and Kent and some continental scenes.

*Eyres Simmons*     *'West Appledore, Devon' (w/c)*   · *(J Collins and Son)*

## Charles Eyres SIMMONS (died c. 1955)

Painter in watercolour of landscapes, harbours and coastal scenes. Charles Eyres Simmons studied art under Hubert Coop who influenced his style of painting. He lived in Herefordshire, Cornwall, Devon, The Channel Islands and finally at Hastings, Sussex. Eyres Simmons exhibited at the Dudley Gallery, Piccadilly, and in Liverpool, 1902-1914. His work had a pleasing wet impressionistic style but his watercolour signature is difficult to read and is frequently miscatalogued in the saleroom.

## Mrs. K.. E.. SIMON (exh. 1927-1930)

Painter of flowers and still life who lived at Bishopston, Bristol, and exhibited at the R.W.A. 1927-1930. The works were entitled 'Scabious', 'Russets and Grapes', and 'The Garden Steps'.

## Henry SIMPSON (exh. 1926-1936)

Landscape painter who lived in Bristol and exhibited 11 works at the R.W.A. 1926-1936. Most of the subjects were landscapes and town scenes, including views in Brittany 'Caudebec' (1926), 'Old House, Liseux' (1927) and the Italian lakes 'Gandria, Lake Lugano' (1932) and 'Early Morning, Lake Maggiore' (1935). He also painted some English landscapes in Kent and North Wales.

*Jackson Simpson*     *(J Collins and Son)*
*'The Fly Fisherman' (w/c)*

## Jackson SIMPSON (1893-1963)

Etcher and watercolour artist of landscapes, rivers and fishing subjects. This artist is often confused with Joseph Simpson, a well-known etcher of figure subjects, whose signature is equally difficult to read. Jackson Simpson lived in Aberdeen and etchings by him are in the Aberdeen Art Gallery.

*Marjorie E Sinclair*     *'Siamese Cat' (w/c)*

## Mrs. Marjorie Edith SINCLAIR R.B.S.A. (1908-1969)

Watercolour painter who lived in Birmingham and was elected an associate member of the R.B.S.A. in 1956 and a full member in 1959. Her twin sister Dorothy Lockwood R.W.S. was also a successful artist. Marjorie Sinclair died suddenly on 26th December 1969. (Illus. p.140).

## Max SINCLAIR (fl. 1881-1898)

Painter of landscapes and marines in oil and watercolour. This prolific artist does not appear to have exhibited, although much of the work was inscribed and dated giving some indication of the period of his work and the location of the subjects. Most of the landscapes are views in Wales and Scotland and the majority date from the early 1880s.. The marine subjects include views of the London and Liverpool docks. Many of his paintings were signed with a monogram (see index).

*W. M. Skeens*　　　　　*'The Armed Knight, Lands End' oil)*

## Walter Morgan SKEENS (1886-1969)

Painter in oil and etcher of landscapes and coastal scenes, who was born in Portsmouth on 23rd December 1886. He lived at Redland, Bristol, and later at Westbury-on-Trym and was the art master at two local schools. Walter Skeens was a regular exhibitor with the Bristol Savages showing over 200 works 1928-1968. The subjects were mostly local views with some of Cornwall, the Lake District, and France. He was elected President of the Savages in 1953. Walter Skeens also exhibited 39 works at the R.W.A. 1921-1948 again mostly local landscapes. The Bristol City Art Gallery have three oils and an etching by him.

## Miss M.. SKELTON (exh. 1900)

Artist who lived in Norwich and exhibited with the Norwich Art Circle in 1900.

## Miss Rose SKIDMORE (exh. 1900-1902)

Artist who lived in Bristol and exhibited three works at the R.W.A. 1900-1902. These included 'Rocks, Ladys Bay, Cleveden' and 'Moorend, near Bristol'.

## Cyril Leslie SKINNER A.R.W.A. (1908-1970)

Painter and etcher of landscapes, buildings and flowers who lived at Bristol and later in Luton, Beds. He exhibited 15 works at the R.W.A. 1928-1936, mostly local scenes but also some views in Bruges. Cyril Skinner was a member of the Bristol Savages and exhibited 48 works 1931-1945. These were mostly flower studies, local buildings and landscapes. In 1938 he moved to Luton and was Headmaster of the Arts and Crafts School until his retirement. The Bristol City Art Gallery have four etchings and a drypoint by him. He died on 23rd August 1970.

## Mrs. G.. SKIRROW (exh. 1920-1922)

Watercolour artist who lived at Clifton, Bristol, and exhibited four works at the R.W.A. 1920-1922. The subjects were mostly studies of local churches.

## Gertrude SLADE (fl. 1903)

Book illustrator and designer who was a student at the St Albans School of Art. Her work was illustrated in The Studio magazine in 1903.

## Martin J.. SLATER F.R.I.B.A. (exh. 1924-1945)

Watercolour landscape painter who lived in Ipswich and was a member of the Ipswich Art Club. He exhibited nine works 1924-1945 and was active until the 1970s. The titles included 'Woodbridge', 'Claydon', 'Ufford' and 'Firle, Sussex' (all 1927) and 'Fishing Boats' (1945).

## Bert SMALE (fl. 1897)

Artist who lived in St John's Wood, and was a prize winner in The Studio magazine 'Humorous Figure Subject' competition in 1897.

## Miss Ada SMALL (exh. 1892-1910)

Painter in oil, and sometimes watercolour, of flowers, still life and landscapes who exhibited over 25 works at the R.W.A. 1892-1910. The majority of the works were flowers and still life, including fruit and birds nests. 'Tempting Fruit', 'Iris' (1900) and 'Fresh from the Garden' (1904) are typical titles. She lived at Cheddar, Somerset.

## Reginald H.. SMALLRIDGE (fl. 1938-1939)

Etcher and pen and ink artist who was active in the late 1930s. At this time he had a studio at Looe, Cornwall. His work included some coloured etchings of Venice.

## Miss Ellen Casterton SMELT (exh. 1896)

Watercolour landscape painter who lived in Ipswich and was a member of the Ipswich Art Club. She exhibited eight works in 1896 mostly continental scenes. The subjects included views of Venice, Norway, Switzerland and a 'Fjord in the Arctic Circle'.

## Allan SMITH (1889-1963)

Painter in watercolour of landscapes and coastal scenes, art teacher and author of several books on painting and craft design. Allan Smith lived at Barnstaple, Devon, and was the art master at the Barnstaple Grammar School from 1924 until 1954. Many of his pictures were West Country landscapes and local coastal views. He died on 7th November 1963 at the age of 74.

*Austin Smith*                    *'Off Scarborough, 1919' (w/c)*

## Austin SMITH (fl. 1919-1928)

Painter in watercolour of marines and coastal views in a style similar to T B Hardy. The subjects were mostly Yorkshire views including Whitby and Scarborough. The work is usually signed Austin Smith and dated.

## Alex. F.. SMITH (exh. 1919)

Artist who lived at Keighley, Yorks, and exhibited three works at the Bradford Local Artists Exhibition in 1919. The subjects were an interior and two local landscapes.

*A. T. Smith*                    *(pen and ink)*

*'Er-If you see a Bowler 'at on the way, Miss
it's mine an yer might bring it back'*

## Maj. Alfred Talbot SMITH (1876-1968)

Humorous illustrator, cartoonist and black and white artist who was born in Canton, China, in 1876 the son of Frederick Smith, a merchant. He was brought up in England, being educated at the Whitgift School and then studied at the Croydon School of Art. Alfred Smith specialised in humorous drawings for Punch, The Humorist and London Opinion as well as many books and magazines. He lived for many years at Chipstead, Surrey. An exhibition of his illustrations was held at J. Collins and Son Gallery, Bideford, Devon in 1986. (Illus. this page).

## A.. W.. SMITH (exh. 1936)

Artist who lived in Bristol and exhibited two works at the R.W.A. in 1936 entitled 'Spring Flowers' and 'The Flowing Tide'.

*Enid Smith*                    *'The Spell' (w/c)*

## Miss Enid SMITH (fl. 1920s)

This was the maiden name used on the early work of the artist who was better known as Enid Sybil Mills (q.v.). The work signed Enid Smith included some early book illustrations and dates from the 1920s.

## Harold Gilead SMITH (exh. 1933-1938)

Watercolour landscape painter and craftworker who lived at Hacheston, Suffolk, and was a member of the Ipswich Art Club. He exhibited 12 works 1933-1938 and the titles included 'On the Medway' and 'Sunset, Wickham Market' (1936) and some views in the Dordogne.

Vivian Smith          'Homeward' (w/c)          (Barry Keene)

Douglas Snowden          'Low Tide' (w/c)

## Capt. Vivian Norman SMITH (1885-1916)

Painter in watercolour and oil of heavy horses. Vivian Smith lived at Holt, Norfolk, and was a teacher at Gresham School. He exhibited four watercolours at the Royal Academy 1912-1915 and also showed an oil of a horse and cart at the Royal Institute of Oil Painters. This talented artist's career was cut short when he joined the Wiltshire Regiment in 1915 and was killed in action in France on 13th November 1916. His paintings are seldom seen on the market but the quality and subject matter make them highly collectable.

## Frederick John SNELL (1862-1935)

Author and artist who lived at Tiverton, Devon, and was working around 1900. Frederick Snell was the author of several books including 'A Book of Exmoor', 'The Blackmore Country' and 'North Devon'. Most of his paintings were moorland landscape or cottage scenes. Frederick Snell exhibited at the Brighton Art Gallery in 1901 a work entitled 'Winter Tor-Dartmoor'. He died on 25th May 1935.

## Arthur SNOW (exh. 1934-1936)

Landscape painter in oil and watercolour who lived at Wendon, Essex, and was a member of the Ipswich Art Club. He exhibited 'Willows' and 'A Sunny Farmstead' (both 1934) and 'Walberswick', 'Duck Street, Wendon' and 'Old Norwich' (all 1936).

## Mrs. Grace E.. SNOW (exh. 1934-1936)

Landscape and portrait painter in watercolour who lived at Wendon, Essex, and was a member of the Ipswich Art Club. She exhibited four works – 'Wendon Willows' and 'Above St Ives Harbour' (both 1934), and 'Rocks at Mawgan Porth' and a portrait (1936). She was probably the wife of Arthur Snow (q.v.) who exhibited at the same time.

## Douglas SNOWDEN (fl. 1897-1926)

Painter and illustrator in watercolour of landscapes. He was first recorded as a member of the R.C.A. Vacation Sketching Club in 1897 where he exhibited two works which were highly praised by The Studio magazine art critic. Douglas Snowden also exhibited a work at the Royal Academy in 1919 which was the Interior of a Church at Ypres, Belgium. In 1926 he illustrated 'Unknown Hampshire' by Clive Holland with 12 colour plates and 34 black and white sketches. His work is not often seen but the quality would make a good example collectable.

## Miss Kate SOARES (fl. c. 1910)

Landscape painter in watercolour who lived at Queens Gate, Kensington, and was working around 1910. The work is of good quality and includes some Exmoor views similar to Charles Brittan. She signed her work 'K. Soares'.

D. H. Somerfield          'Outwood Mill, 1949' (w/c)

**Denis Hugh SOMERFIELD (1911-1986)**

Painter in oil and watercolour of landscapes and portraits who was born at New Malden, Surrey, on 18th April 1911. He was educated privately and studied at the Kingston School of Art where he was awarded a scholarship. In 1934, Denis Somerfield joined the Daily Mail and during the Second World War was in the Navy where he worked on instructional drawings and also painted portraits of his naval colleagues. He exhibited once at the Royal Academy in 1941, an oil entitled 'The Home Front' which depicted a kitchen interior. From 1951 until his retirement in 1976, Denis Somerfield worked in the art department of Joe Lyons in Fleet Street, London. He lived for many years at Send, near Woking, Surrey. He signed his work D H Somerfield and sometimes with a date. (Illus. p.143).

**Brig. Gen. Charles Wyndham SOMERSET (1862-1938)**

Landscape painter in watercolour who exhibited 18 works at the Army Officers Art Society 1928-1933. The subjects included English landscapes and views in India and Kashmir.

**Miss Maude SOUTH (exh. 1888-1895)**

Landscape painter in oil who lived at Stutton, Suffolk, and was a member of the Ipswich Art Club. She was a regular exhibitor showing 23 works 1888-1895, the titles included 'Gun Hill, Dedham', 'A Glimpse at Stutton Rectory' and 'Pin Mill' (all 1890).

*Rubens Southey     'Fingle Bridge, Dartmoor' (w/c)    (J Collins and Son)*

**Rubens A.. J.. N.. SOUTHEY (1881-1933)**

Painter in watercolour of landscapes and coastal scenes who was born at Wellington, Somerset, in 1881. He does not appear to have exhibited widely, but may have shown nine works at Elands Art Gallery, Exeter in 1906 and 1907 under the name of Robert Southey. The subjects were typical including 'The Coast near Bude, Cornwall' and 'Dartmoor, High Tor'. The work is of good quality and the West

Country locations make the pictures popular. A number of large coloured prints of his work were published particularly of the coastal subjects. Rubens Southey died at Newton Abbott in 1933 at the age of 53.

**Ethel J.. SOWELS (exh. 1902)**

Artist who lived at Thetford, Norfolk, and exhibited two works at the Norwich Art Circle Exhibition in 1902.

**Miss B.. J.. SPENCER (exh. 1929-1930)**

Landscape painter who lived at Weston-super-Mare, Somerset, and exhibited three works at the R.W.A. 1929-1930. The titles were 'Sand Dunes, Brean, Somerset' (1929) and 'In Willow Land, Colnbrook' and 'Pathway to the Vine, Hampton Court' (1930).

**Miss C.. M.. SPROTT (exh. 1909)**

Painter in oil of animals who exhibited horse studies at the First Exhibition of the Calderon Art Society in 1909. She was a student at the Calderon School of Animal Painting at the time and became treasurer of the Society.

*Fred Stafford          'D H Four-Engined Express' (w/c)*

**Frederick STAFFORD (fl. 1910-1930s)**

Painter and illustrator in oil, watercolour and gouache. Fred Stafford appears to have worked as a commercial artist in the 1930s doing illustrations for railways, aircraft companies and breweries. He also painted a large number of watercolour landscapes which are often seen on the market but frequently uncatalogued as the signature is difficult to read.

*H. W. Stagg*         *'Horsey Mill, Norfolk, 1910' (w/c)*

### Harold William STAGG (1882-1918)

Painter in watercolour of landscapes and river scenes who lived at Beckenham, Kent, and exhibited two river landscapes at the Royal Academy in 1912. His work has a pleasing wet impressionistic style similar to that of Wilfrid Ball and the subjects include views of the Norfolk Broads and the Channel Islands. Harold Stagg's work is of excellent quality but quite rare as he was killed in action at an early age in 1918.

### Miss L.. Frances STAINS (exh. 1890)

Painter in oil of landscapes and still life who lived at Ipswich and was a member of the Ipswich Art Club. She exhibited at the two exhibitions in 1890 – 'Walberswick, Windy Day' and 'Apples – a Study'.

### G.. J.. STANFIELD (exh. 1921)

Landscape painter who exhibited three works at the First Admiralty Art Club Exhibition in 1921. The subjects were Somerset and Dorset views.

### Joseph Morewood STANIFORTH (1863-1921)

Painter in watercolour, illustrator and cartoonist. Joseph Staniforth was born in Gloucester in 1863 and became a leading cartoonist for the Cardiff Evening Express and the Western Mail. Examples of his work were reproduced in The Studio magazine in 1898 and 1903 and his cartoons appeared in Punch. Later, Joseph Staniforth moved to Lynton, Devon, where he painted watercolour landscapes and coastal scenes. He died in Barnstaple in December 1921.

### Lancelot Norman STANILAND R.W.A. (1899-1970)

Painter of landscapes in oil and watercolour and black and white artist who lived in Bristol and later at Winscombe, Somerset. He was a member of the R.W.A. and a regular exhibitor showing a total of 71 works 1925-1969. The subjects were mostly watercolour landscapes – West Country views and moorland scenes and several of Pembrokeshire and the Gower Peninsula. Lancelot Staniland was a regular exhibitor at the Bristol Savages showing 147 works 1928-1968, again mostly West Country and Welsh views. Both the Bristol Savages and the Bristol City Art Gallery own examples of his work. He died on 26th August 1970 aged 70.

### Col. Edward Alexander STANTON (1867-1947)

Artist who exhibited five works at the Army Officers Art Society Exhibition in 1928.

### Vincent STEADMAN A.R.I.B.A. (exh. 1900)

Architect who lived at Clifton and exhibited two building studies at the R.W.A. in 1900.

### Miss Beatrice M.. STEEL (exh. 1919-1931)

Painter in oil and watercolour and etcher who lived at Crowfield, Suffolk, and was a member of the Ipswich Art Club. She was a regular exhibitor showing at least 41 works 1919-1931. The subjects were building studies, local landscapes and some garden scenes. The titles included 'A June Garden' (oil, 1923) and 'Hemingstone Church' and 'Old Houses at Coddenham' (both watercolours, 1927).

### Miss Gertrude STEEL (fl. 1903)

Student at the Lambeth School of Art whose design illustration for the National Competition is illustrated in The Studio magazine in 1903.

### Mrs. L.. M.. C.. STEPHENSON (exh. 1934-1936)

Painter of flowers and still life who lived at Redland, Bristol, and exhibited four works at the R.W.A. 1934-1936. The titles were 'Phlox' (1934), 'The Spode Jug' (1935) and 'Zinnias' and 'Delphiniums' (1936).

### Russell STEPHENSON (fl. 1865-1925)

Landscape painter who had a loan exhibition of his work at the Gieves Gallery, London, in 1925. The artist was entirely self-taught and although he lived in Canada for many years he painted widely on the Continent and in England and Scotland 1893-1922.

### Richard L.. R.. STEVENS (exh. 1950)

Painter in oil of landscapes and coastal scenes who lived in Plymouth and exhibited three works at the Plymouth Art Society in 1950.

### Miss S.. STEVENS (exh. 1930)

Landscape painter who lived at Shirehampton near Bristol and exhibited five works at the R.W.A. in 1930. The exhibits were entitled – 'Elms', 'Sutton, Cambs', 'Silence on the Stairs', 'Solemnity' and 'Mary Le Port Street'.

### Lt. Col. A.. F.. STEWART (exh. 1928-1934)

An Officer in the Indian Army who lived in Jersey and exhibited 24 works at the Army Officers Art Society Exhibitions 1928-1934. The subjects in both oil and watercolour included views in Jersey and Kashmir.

*W Stewart*      *'Fishing Smacks off the Coast' (w/c)*

### W.. STEWART (fl. c. 1910-1930)

Painter in watercolour of marines, usually of fishing smacks, but also some Venice lagoons. This artist's work shows a striking resemblance to that of Frederick Aldridge, a popular marine artist of the time and it is possible that he was a pupil. It appears that W Stewart also painted under the names of J.. Hill (q.v.) and F.. Grayson (q.v.) both of whom have similar styles and subjects. The artist painted many small marine studies and these are sometimes just signed with initials.

### Harry STINTON (1883-1968)

Landscape painter in watercolour who was born in 1883, the son of John and nephew of James and Walter Stinton. He worked at the Worcester Porcelain Factory from the age of 13 as a decorator and designer. Harry Stinton painted a large number of birds and animals in landscapes similar to his porcelain designs. This competent artist does not appear to have exhibited but probably found a ready market for his work in the Worcester area. He signed his work 'H Stinton' in a printed script.

*Oliver Stockman*      *'Donkey Rides' (oil)*      *(Sotheby's)*

### Oliver STOCKMAN (fl. c. 1900s)

Painter in oil of interiors and genre scenes. This competent artist does not appear to have exhibited although his work appears on the market. The style suggests that the artist may have worked as an illustrator. Typical titles are 'Blind Man's Buff' and 'Donkey Rides' and the more important examples of his work can command quite high prices.

### Elizabeth STONE A.R.W.A. (exh. 1937-1974)

Painter in watercolour, pen and ink artist and etcher who lived near Bristol and was an associate member of the R.W.A. She exhibited 67 works at the R.W.A. 1937-1974. The pictures were mostly watercolour, or ink and wash and some etchings. The subjects were flower studies, figures and a few landscapes.

### Harold STONE (exh. 1932-1934)

Artist who lived in Bristol and exhibited at the R.W.A. 1932-1934. The works were entitled 'Host Street, Bristol', 'Ye Llandoger Trow, King Street' and 'Old Cottages, Chipping Campden'.

### Jack D.. STONE (exh. 1950)

Painter in oils of figures who lived in Plymouth and exhibited five works at the Plymouth Art Society Exhibition in 1950.

*M. A. Stone*      *'Roses' (oil)*

### Mrs. Marguerite Agnes STONE (1885-1972)

Painter in oil and occasionally watercolour of flowers, still life and gardens. She lived for many years at Cranleigh, Surrey, and sold her work locally, relying on commissions for her flower studies. She is believed to have painted some flower illustrations for a seed packet company. The work is signed M A Stone or just with initials on small sketches. She died on 30th August 1972 aged 87.

*W. R. S. Stott      'Off Portugal, 27th June 1911' (oil)*

*Fred Stratton      'Portrait Study' (w/c)*

## William Robertson Smith STOTT (1870-1939)

Painter and illustrator of portraits, figures and landscapes in oil who lived in Aberdeen and later moved his studio to Chelsea, London. W R S Stott exhibited regularly at the Royal Academy, showing a total of 22 works 1905-1934. These were mostly landscapes but also some genre subjects and portraits. He did not exhibit often outside London but did show some work at Glasgow and Liverpool. Despite a long painting career Stott's work is not often seen on the market but the quality of the pictures and the subject matter would make them collectable.

## Miss Annie STOW (exh. 1928-1933)

Watercolour artist who lived at Ipswich and was a member of the Ipswich Art Club. She exhibited two works entitled 'Ipswich Docks from Stoke Bridge' (1928) and 'Kersey Street' (1933).

## Lt. Col. Richard John STRACHEY (1861-1935)

Watercolour landscape painter who lived at Abingdon, Berks. An Officer in the Rifle Brigade, he exhibited 10 works at the Army Officers Art Society 1928-1933. The titles included 'From my Window' and 'The Garden' (1932).

## George Harry STRAIN (1888-1965)

Painter in oil and watercolour and metalworker who was born in Oldham, Lancs., in 1888. He won the Kings Award at the Royal College of Art, where he studied in 1912. He was a friend of the artist Sidney Tushingham and they went on sketching trips together. Most of his pictures were painted prior to

## Fred STRATTON (1870-1960)

Fred Stratton was born in Lincolnshire on 22nd March 1870, the son of a farmer. Very little is known about his early life but by the 1890s he had a studio in London and he was married in 1897. Fred Stratton moved to Amberley, Sussex, around 1900 and along with several other notable artists came under the influence of Edward Stott who had settled there in 1889. Fred Stratton exhibited widely in London and in the provinces but it was largely as a portrait painter that he made his living. He found many patrons for his work and these commissions may have caused him to move his studio back to Chelsea in the late 1920s. At the outbreak of the Second World War, Fred Stratton was visiting Peru and he was to remain there until his death in Lima on 6th May 1960. Although most of his portrait commissions were painted in oil this talented artist also worked in pastel and watercolour. An exhibition of his watercolours was held at Jeremy Wood Fine Art, Petworth, Sussex, in November 1987. He signed his work 'F Stratton' or 'F. S.' and a date on small sketches.

## Allan STRAWBRIDGE (fl. 1930s)

Artist and teacher who lived at Much Hadham, Herts. He held painting classes at his studio and took students on painting trips to Bruges in Belgium. Contemporary advertisements describe him as 'Consultant Artist to the British Museum and the Royal Family of Sweden'

## A.. W.. STROUD (exh. 1930-1936)

A student at the Central School of Arts and Craft, London, in the 1920s who later lived at Saltford, Somerset, and exhibited 12 works at the R.W.A. 1930-1936. Many of the subjects were Sussex landscapes but there were also views of Herefordshire, Shropshire and Suffolk. His wife Mrs G Stroud (q.v.) also exhibited. An aquatint by A W Stroud was reproduced in The Studio magazine in 1921.

## Mrs.. G.. STROUD (exh. 1930-1936)

Artist who lived at Saltford, Somerset, and exhibited seven works at the R.W.A. 1930-1936. The exhibits were all landscapes and the titles included 'The Weir, Saltford' (1931), 'Near Arundel, Sussex' (1934) and 'Iford Bridge, Wilts' (1936). She was married to the artist A W Stroud (q.v.).

## Emily STRUTT (exh. 1913)

Watercolour landscape painter who held a one-woman exhibition at the Modern Gallery, London, in June 1913 entitled 'South Africa, Scotland and Elsewhere'. This consisted of 74 watercolours, mostly of the countries entitled, but also some landscape views in Ireland, Normandy and Essex.

## Mrs. Margaret STRUTT-DAVIES (exh. 1934)

A painter in oils who was a member of the Reading Guild of Artists and exhibited at the Reading Art Gallery in the mid 1930s.

Ernest Sutton                    'A Village Street' (w/c)

## Ernest E.. SUTTON (fl. 1914-1926)

Painter in watercolour of landscapes, beach scenes and some figure subjects. This competent artist was active c. 1914-1926, but does not appear to have exhibited. The subjects are quite varied and examples are known to exist of beach scenes (Cromer, 1926), a Japanese tea party and some village streets. The work is usually signed Ernest E Sutton in a disjoined script and dated.

## Miss I.. M.. SWAINE (exh. 1920)

Watercolour artist who lived in Bristol and exhibited two works at the R.W.A. in 1920 entitled 'Cattybrook Brickworks' and 'At Old Passage'. She was the sister of Agnes K Swaine who was also an artist and illustrator.

W. H. Sweet                    (David Steer)
'Newlyn Harbour' (w/c)

## Walter Henry SWEET (1889-1943)

Painter in watercolour of Devon and Cornish landscapes, cottages and harbour scenes. Walter Sweet was born on 11th April 1889 and studied at the Exeter School of Art under the guidance of his friend John Shapland. He worked locally and exhibited work at the Devon and Exeter Annual Exhibition at Elands Art Gallery in the 1900s. At the outbreak of the First World War Walter Sweet joined the Devonshire Regiment and saw active service abroad. After the War, he moved to Dundee, Scotland, and was employed by James Valentine and Sons as a commercial illustrator. He married and had two sons, one of whom studied at the Dundee College of Art. Walter Sweet died in Dundee on 12th February 1943 at the age of 53.

Walter Sweet's watercolours are decorative and the popular West Country subject matter has made them increasingly collectable.

## Lt. Col. E.. L.. SWIFTE (exh. 1929)

Artist, who exhibited four works at the Army Officers Art Society Exhibition in 1929.

**Warwick T.. SWINBANKS (exh. 1938-1949)**

Watercolour landscape painter who lived in Ipswich and was a member of the Ipswich Art Club. He exhibited eight works 1938-1949, mostly local scenes such as 'Boats – Ipswich Docks' and 'A Barn at Foxhall' (both 1938). Other titles were ethereal subjects including 'Origins of Life' and 'Cycle of Events in the Universe' (both 1949). Warwick Swinbanks held an Art Teachers Diploma.

**W.. SWINDELL (exh. 1921)**

Artist who exhibited three works at the Derby Sketching Club Exhibition in January 1921.

**Mrs. J.. O.. SYMES (exh. 1929-1934)**

Artist who lived at Clifton, Bristol, and exhibited at the R.W.A. in 1929 and 1934. The titles were 'At Marhamchurch, Cornwall' and 'Country Cottages'.

*J Ayton Symington      'A Shady Lane, Stanmore' (oil)      (Sotheby's)*

**J.. Ayton SYMINGTON (fl. 1898-1914)**

Painter in oil of landscapes and rural scenes. This competent artist does not appear to have exhibited but he was recorded as living in Putney in 1898. In 1904 he illustrated 'Edinburgh and its Story', published by J M Dent, with plates in colour and black and white. Ayton Symington painted mostly in the Home Counties and he was still active in 1914.

# T

## Mrs. R.. TALLACK (exh. 1889-1909)

Watercolour landscape painter who lived in Norwich and was a member of the Norwich Art Circle. She was a regular exhibitor and showed 49 works 1889-1909. These were mostly local views in watercolour but also some black and white illustrations. She signed her work R. Tallack with the date.

W. Tanner                    'Moonlight Harbour,' (oil)

## W.. TANNER (fl. c. 1900-1915)

Painter in oil of figures, landscapes and harbour scenes who had a pleasing impressionistic style which should make his work collectable. He does not appear to have exhibited although his work was reproduced in Colour Magazine in 1915. This painting of a child in a flower filled landscape shows some influence of Charles Sims R.A., a popular painter of the time. Tanner also painted landscapes and harbour scenes, probably in the West Country, more in the style of the Newlyn and St Ives Schools.

## Wilfrid Burnet TAPP A.R.W.A. (exh. 1919-1951)

Painter of landscapes, still life and figure subjects who lived at Thornton, Bradford, and exhibited six works at the Bradford Local Artists Exhibition in 1919. In the early 1920s he moved to Bristol and became a regular exhibitor at the R.W.A. showing 31 works 1923-1951. The subjects were mostly local landscapes – 'Lacock', 'The Severn at Almonsbury' and 'The Courtyard, Norton St Philip' (all 1928) are typical titles. Wilfrid Tapp was elected an associate member of the R.W.A. in 1927.

## E.. W.. TARVER (fl. 1904-1905)

Painter in watercolour of landscapes and coastal scenes. This good quality artist does not appear to have exhibited but dated examples exist from 1905 giving an address in St Johns Wood, North London. The subjects included a beach scene at Minehead, Somerset.

## Miss D.. T.. TAYLOR (exh. 1931-1932)

Landscape artist who lived at Clifton, Bristol, and exhibited at the R.W.A. 1931-1932. The exhibits were entitled 'Beeches at Alfoxden, Somerset' and 'Helford River'.

F. P. Taylor          'H.M.S. Impregnable at Devonport, 1909' (w/c)

## F.. P.. TAYLOR (fl. 1905-1909)

Painter in watercolour of ship portraits and marines who was working in the early 1900s. The work was of good quality and often featured warships. If the pictures are found in the original frames, they are usually titled and copiously inscribed on the reverse. The artist did not appear to have exhibited but may have painted many of the pictures as commissions.

## Miss Kathleen E.. TEMPLE (exh. 1898-1954)

Painter in oil and watercolour of landscapes and portraits who lived at Blakenham, Suffolk, and was a member of the Ipswich Art Club. She was a regular exhibitor showing 45 works 1898-1911. The titles included 'Venice – St Giorgio Maggiore', 'In an Old Garden' (both oils) and 'The Mill Blakenham' (watercolour) all 1907. Later, she exhibited widely under her married name of Temple-Bird including six works at the R.A. 1930-1954.

## William Percival C.. TENISON (1884-1983)

Still life painter in oils and illustrator who was born on 25th June 1884. William Tenison was educated at Marlborough and Sandhurst and, after active service in the Great War, he retired as a Lieutenant Colonel in the Indian Army. After the Second World War he worked at the Natural History Museum, London, where he specialised in illustrations of fish and reconstructing a mammoth. He died in 1983 just short of his hundredth year.

### A.. B.. THATCHER (exh. 1927-1932)

Artist who lived at Redland, Bristol, and exhibited at the R.W.A. in 1927 and 1932. The titles were 'A Load of Mischief' and 'Carnival'.

### R.. F.. THATCHER (exh. 1925-1931)

Landscape painter who lived at Brislington, Bristol, and exhibited nine works at the R.W.A. 1925-1931. Most of the subjects were local views of Bristol, Lacock and Wells and there were also three French landscapes and 'A Bullock Cart, Madeira' (1925).

### Miss Janet THIRTLE (exh. 1906-1908)

Painter in oil of figure subjects who lived at Bungay, Suffolk, and was a member of the Ipswich Art Club. She exhibited five works 1906-1908, the titles included 'Grandmother's Friends', 'Just Arrived' and 'The Jailers'.

### Alfred THOMAS (exh. 1924)

Oil landscape painter who lived at Cheltenham and exhibited at the Cheltenham Art Gallery Exhibition in 1924. The picture was a landscape view in the New Forest.

### Charles William THOMAS (1884-1958)

Artist, illustrator and cartoonist who was born at Portishead, Somerset in 1884. After the First World War, he ran a tobacconists shop before turning to journalism and becoming a cartoonist and column writer for the Bristol Evening Post. Charles Thomas was an active member of the Bristol Savages and exhibited over 300 works 1905-1958. Many of these exhibits were pen and ink cartoons or caricatures. He was President of the Bristol Savages in 1920, 1932 and 1941. Charles Thomas died at Portbury in March 1958 aged 74. The Bristol City Art Gallery has a watercolour by him in their collection and the Bristol Savages have several examples of his work.

### Joan Gale THOMAS (fl. 1935)

Black and white artist who studied at the Chelsea School of Illustrators. She designed song covers and wrote and illustrated childrens verse.

### Rev. Lindsay J.. THOMAS (exh. 1914-1916)

Watercolour landscape painter who lived at Swilland Rectory, near Ipswich, and was a member of the Ipswich Art Club. He exhibited 10 works 1914-1916 and the titles included 'The Last Sheaves', 'The Kiss of Dawn' and 'Gathering Light'.

### Margaret THOMAS (1843-1929)

Painter of portraits, figure subjects and landscapes who exhibited widely including 11 works at the Royal Academy 1868-1880. This good quality artist, although well recorded, has largely escaped the attention of collectors because her work often goes unrecognised. Many of the subjects are finely detailed Middle Eastern scenes and these were often signed with an indecipherable monogram (see index). She travelled widely in Europe, North Africa and the Middle East and wrote and illustrated several books on the subject.

### Stuart J.. G.. THOMAS (exh. 1922-1938)

Painter, etcher and sculptor who lived in Bristol, and later moved to Cornwall. He exhibited five works at the R.W.A. 1922-1928, mostly landscapes and a sculpture. The titles included 'Old Houses, Veere, Holland' (1928). Stuart Thomas also showed 29 works with the Bristol Savages 1928-1938 including marines and Cornish and Dutch landscapes. In 1931 he moved to St Ives, Cornwall, and lived on his houseboat 'Hero'.

*W. B. Thomas 'Boston, Lincs' (w/c) (Barnes Gallery)*

### William Bartol THOMAS (1877-1947)

Watercolour landscape painter who lived at Boston, Lincs, and painted local views. He was the eldest son of William Thomas, an architect, and was educated locally at the Boston Grammar School. An artist by profession, 'Billy' Thomas was also a keen amateur skater and shooter. He died on 25th May 1947 just short of his 70th birthday.

The work of this artist is always of good quality and often features views across the River Witham with the familiar landmark of Boston Stump in the distance. Relatively unknown, W B Thomas has not yet received the recognition he deserves.

**Miss G.. THOMPSON (exh. 1940)**

Watercolour still life painter who was a member of the Darlington Art Society and a prize winner at their exhibition in 1940.

**Murray THOMPSON (1859-1924)**

This was one of the pseudonyms used by Norris Fowler Willatt when painting his English watercolour landscapes. These are not seen very often, since most of his work was Dutch canal scenes and these were usually signed with his other pseudonym L. Van Staaten (q.v.). The subjects for his English landscapes were often Surrey views close to his home at Pyrford, near Woking.

**William E.. THORN B.W.S. (exh. 1928)**

Watercolour painter who was a member of the B.W.S. and exhibited two works at the B.W.S. Autumn Exhibition at the Preston Art Gallery in 1928. The subjects were a view of Cambridge and 'A Shower in Berkshire'. He lived at Whetstone, near Barnet, Herts.

**Cyril W.. THORNE (exh. 1931-1948)**

Landscape artist who lived in Bristol and exhibited six works at the R.W.A. 1931-1948. The subjects were views at Bibury, Glos., 'Norwich, Norfolk' (1931), 'Lynmouth Harbour, Devon' (1932) and 'The River Coln, near Fairford' (1948).

**W.. THORNTON (fl. 1930s)**

This was a pseudonym adopted by William Thornton Brocklebank (q.v.) and occasionally signed on some of his oils probably in the 1930s. Most of the work was fully signed.

**Col. F.. M.. THRUPP (exh. 1928-1939)**

Watercolour painter who lived at Oxted, Surrey, and exhibited regularly with the Army Officers Art Society showing 55 works 1928-1939. These included English landscapes and buildings and a few Far Eastern views.

**Fred C.. THURLEY B.W.S. (exh. 1928)**

Watercolour landscape painter who was a member of the B.W.S. and exhibited at the B.W.S. Exhibition at Preston in 1928, a work entitled 'Autumn's Gold'.

**E.. Temple THURSTON (1879-1933)**

A well-known Edwardian novelist who exhibited eight landscapes at the 'Authors and Artists Exhibition' at the Little Art Rooms, Duke Street, London, in 1918.

**Mrs. Percy TIBBENHAM (exh. 1925-1950s)**

Painter in oil and watercolour of flowers and landscapes who lived at Ipswich and was a member of the Ipswich Art Club. She was a regular exhibitor showing at least 28 works 1925-1950. The titles included 'Sproughton' (1925), 'The Meadows at Martlesham' (1928) and 'Early Roses' (1932) – all watercolours.

**Miss Mary TIDBURY (exh. 1883-1886)**

Painter in oil of flowers and still life who lived in Ipswich and was a member of the Ipswich Art Club. She exhibited six works 1883-1886 and the titles included 'Sunflower', 'Poinsettia' (1883) and a birds nest study in 1885.

Otto Tilche                                   'Arab Dhows' (w/c)

**Otto TILCHE (fl. 1920s)**

Painter in watercolour of desert and eastern scenes. This prolific artist usually painted small pairs of watercolours often showing Bedouins and camels in the desert or Nile scenes. He also painted under the name of 'A. Calvert' (q.v.). He signed his work O. Tilche or with the initials on small sketches.

**Herbert M.. TIMBERS (exh. 1926-1930)**

Landscape painter in oil and watercolour who lived in Woodbridge, Suffolk, and was a member of the Ipswich Art Club. He exhibited 16 works 1926-1930, mostly local scenes and also some views at Newquay, Cornwall.

**William Vivian TIPPET (1833-1910)**

Landscape painter in oil and sometimes watercolour who lived in Bristol. He was a prolific exhibitor at the R.W.A., showing 132 works at the Annual Exhibitions 1856-1892, and a further 63 works at the Winter Exhibitions. Most of the subjects were rural landscapes featuring cattle, sheep and horses and also some views of South Wales. He exhibited several river landscapes and the titles included 'On the Avon' (1870) and 'On the Frome at Yate' (1888). The Bristol City Art Gallery owned a view of

'Winterbourne Church' (1898) and his work was featured in the 'Ten Bristol Artists' Exhibition at the Gallery in 1934.

*W. S. Tomkin     'Sail and Steam, 1917' (ink and w/c)     (Falcon Gallery)*

## William Stephen TOMKIN (1861-1940)

Marine painter in watercolour who was born in 1861 at Boughton Monchelsea, Kent. At first it was thought that he might study to be an architect, but William Tomkin was more interested in becoming an artist so he took the opportunity to work as a draughtsman for General Pitt Rivers who was Inspector of Ancient Monuments. He was to accompany the General throughout the country recording the ancient sites and he also illustrated two of Pitt Rivers' books on archaeology. In 1889 he joined the artists department of Waterlow & Sons as a designer and illustrator and he was to remain with that firm for over forty years.

William Tomkin was a talented painter of marines who was equally able to portray both steam and sail. His work found favoured patrons such as Sir Thomas Lipton but Tomkin never really exploited his art commercially. He only exhibited once in London, 'Wind against Tide' at the Royal Academy in 1909. He died at Chingford, Essex, on 7th April 1940.

William Tomkin's work is not often seen on the market today and a fine example should command a high price.

## Gerald William TOOBY (1893-1984)

Painter of portraits, figures, animals and landscapes in oil, watercolour and chalk, also lithographer and sculptor. Gerald was born in Munich on 11th March 1893, the son of Charles Tooby, a well-known animal painter.

The young Gerald Tooby spent his childhood in Germany, but being a British National he was interned in a prisoner of war camp during the First World War. This ordeal was ended when he was among those who were exchanged for German prisoners held in Britain. He then travelled to Holland where he spent six months at the Dutch Art Academy before coming to England.

Gerald Tooby settled in Chelsea and soon started to make a reputation for himself as a portrait painter

and also worked as a sculptor's assistant. He showed work at an exhibition for ex-prisoners of war at the Westminster Hall, London, and some of his paintings were bought by George V and Queen Mary. Gerald Tooby also exhibited at the Chenil Gallery and had his work reproduced in Colour Magazine in the 1920s.

In 1940, Gerald Tooby moved to Reading, Berks, where he continued to paint and also teach art. He was a member of the Reading Guild of Artists and work by him is in the collection of the Bath Museum and Art Gallery. He died in Reading at the age of 91 in 1984.

## Arthur E.. TOOPE (1884-1954)

Landscape painter and commercial artist who worked in the artists department of the Bristol commercial printers Mardon, Son & Hall. He was a founder member of the Bristol Savages and their President in 1931. He was a regular exhibitor showing a total of 148 works 1906-1932. Many of the subjects were rural life scenes – 'Carting Hay' (1920), 'Ploughing' (1922) and 'The Day's Ploughing Over' (1924) are typical titles. An oil painting by Arthur Toope is in the Bristol City Art Gallery, and the Savages own a number of his sketches.

## Thurston TOPHAM (exh. 1921)

Landscape painter in oil who exhibited four works at the Derby Sketching Club Exhibition of 1921. These were local subjects and also a view in Canada.

*H. S. Tozer     'By the Fireside, 1906' (w/c)     (Sotheby's Sussex)*

## Henry Edward Spernon TOZER
## (born 1864, fl. 1888-1938)

Painter in watercolour and oil of interior scenes and figure subjects who was born at Sheppey, Kent, in 1864. His work is of good quality and most frequently features old cottage interiors with seated figures. Typical titles are 'Humble Fare' (oil, 1888), 'Rustic Lunch' (watercolour, 1904), 'A Cosy Evening' (oil, 1921), and 'Village Gossip' (watercolour, 1929). Henry Spernon Tozer was listed in the local trade directories as an artist 1890-1924 at Thursley, Surrey, although dated work suggests that he was working at least until 1938. He does not appear to have exhibited but is sometimes confused with the Cornish seascape artist Henry E Tozer who showed work at the Royal Academy in 1892. The quality and the popular subjects have made Henry Spernon Tozer's work command high prices in recent years.

### Miss Agnes L.. TRACY (exh. 1880-1895)

Watercolour landscape painter who lived in Ipswich and was a member of the Ipswich Art Club. She was a regular exhibitor showing 34 works 1880-1895. Many of the subjects were local views and the titles included 'A Winters View – Tuddenham Church' (1883) and 'Harwich from Felixstowe Pier' (1893). Her sisters Isabel and Jessie (q.v.) also exhibited.

### Isabel M.. W.. TRACY (exh. 1880-1882)

Watercolour painter of flowers and landscapes who lived in Ipswich and exhibited at the Ipswich Art Club. She exhibited 10 works 1880-1882, mostly flower studies but other titles were 'Treasures' and 'In the Fog' (both 1880). She lived with her sisters, Agnes and Jessie (q.v.), who also exhibited.

### Miss Jessie F.. TRACY (exh. 1880-1893)

Painter in oil and watercolour of landscapes and flowers who lived in Ipswich and exhibited at the Ipswich Art Club. She exhibited 10 works 1880-1893 and the titles included 'Pink Azaleas' (1890), 'November Sunset – Butter Market' (1891) and 'Framlingham Castle' (1893) – all watercolours. She lived with her sisters, Agnes and Isabel (q.v.), who also exhibited.

### Maj. Lionel J.. TRAFFORD (1855-1900)

Painter in oil and watercolour of landscapes and figure subjects including eastern scenes. He was born in Hereford, the son of C Guy Trafford, an artist who had accompanied David Cox on sketching expeditions. Lionel Trafford was brought up in Hereford but later lived in Ross-on-Wye. He worked from a studio in Chelsea and exhibited once at the Royal Academy in 1899. Lionel Trafford was represented by two works at a loan exhibition of Deceased Hereford Artists at the Hereford Museum and Art Gallery in 1928. One of these was 'The Somnambulist', his Royal Academy exhibit, which was still owned by the family and presumably had not sold. He died on 20th September 1900.

### Lt. Col. Henry Paul TREEBY (1858-1935)

Painter in oil of still life, flowers and landscapes who exhibited 23 works at the Army Officers Art Society 1928-1934. Most of the pictures were flowers and fruit still life and also some landscapes. He lived at Worplesdon, Surrey.

### Lt. Col. F.. C.. TREGEAR (exh. 1928-1938)

Watercolour landscape painter who was an Officer in the Indian Army and became a regular exhibitor at the Army Officers Art Society. He showed a total of 18 works 1928-1937, mostly landscape views in Devon, Cornwall and Suffolk.

G. Trevor                                    'Brig O' Balgownie' (w/c)

### G.. TREVOR (fl. 1920s-1930s)

Watercolour landscape painter who was probably working 1920s-1930s. The pictures were well painted and often heightened with bodycolour which gave them an attractive and colourful appearance. The subjects included views of the Lake District, Wales and Scotland. The artist signed G Trevor in an indistinct script and as a result are frequently miscatalogued.

### G.. E.. TREWEEK (exh. 1927-1937)

Painter of coastal scenes in oil and watercolour who lived at Stowmarket, Suffolk, and was a member of the Ipswich Art Club. He exhibited a total of five works 1927-1928 including views of Kynance, Cornwall, and the Devon coast. He also exhibited a watercolour at the St Ives Society Winter Exhibition in 1937 of 'Porth Headland, Newquay'.

E. W. Trick                                 'Lynmouth, North Devon' (w/c)

**Edward William TRICK (1902-1991)**

Painter in watercolour of landscapes and buildings who was born in Exeter on 23rd January 1902. Edward Trick, who was deaf and dumb, studied art under John Shapland, the former Headmaster of the Exeter School of Art. His subjects included cathedrals and old cottages but most of his work was landscapes including Dartmoor and Exmoor views. He knew several of the West Country artists including W H Sweet (q.v.) and Wycliffe Eggington. Edward Trick exhibited at the local Exeter Art Society exhibitions. He signed his work 'E W TRICK' in capitals. (Illus. p.154).

**Egbert Ware TROTMAN (exh. 1900-1904)**

Landscape painter who lived in Bristol, and exhibited five works at the R.W.A. 1900-1904. The titles included 'Early Evening, East Devon' (1900), 'A Bit of Lyme Regis' (watercolour, 1901) and 'Branscombe, Devon' (1904).

**F.. G.. TROTT (exh. 1935-1937)**

Painter of landscapes and street scenes in oil who lived in Clifton, Bristol, and exhibited four works at the R.W.A. 1935-1937. The titles were 'Westbury Village' (1935), 'Hazy Morning, Mevagissey' (1936), and 'St Mary, Redcliffe' and 'The Sloop Inn, St Ives (1937).

**William TRUE (fl. 1903)**

Illustrator and caricaturist who was associated with the London Sketch Club. A portrait sketch by him of John Hassall was illustrated in The Studio magazine in 1903.

**Miss Adrien TRUSCOTT A.R.C.A. (exh. 1950)**

Watercolour and black and white artist who lived in Plymouth and exhibited five works at the Plymouth Art Society Exhibition in 1950. These included local landscapes, figure subjects and portraits.

**Col. M.. A.. TUITE (exh. 1928-1939)**

Painter in oil of landscapes, portraits and figure subjects. A former officer in the Indian Army who lived at Swiss Cottage, London, and exhibited 68 works at the Army Officers Art Society Exhibitions 1928-1939. Most of the subjects were South of England views, figures and portraits.

**Miss E.. R.. TURNER (exh. 1884-1889)**

Painter in oil of landscapes who lived in Ipswich and was a member of the Ipswich Art Club. She exhibited six works 1884-1889 and the titles included 'Near Bramford' and 'Pin Mill' (both 1886) and the 'Corner of the Old River' (1889).

**H.. Vane TURNER (fl. c. 1916)**

Landscape painter in watercolour who was working around 1916. The subjects were often small sunset scenes and included views on the Thames and in East Anglia.

**Leonard TURNER (exh. 1881-1908)**

Landscape painter in watercolour who lived in Ipswich and was a member of the Ipswich Art Club. He exhibited 28 works 1881-1908, mostly local landscapes. The titles included 'Old Mill, Walton-on-the-Naze' (1903), 'Rainclouds, Southwold' and 'Dunwich Marshes' (both 1906).

**Miss Margaret L.. TURNER (exh. 1891-1893)**

Oil painter who lived at Colchester, Essex, and exhibited three works at the Ipswich Art Club. The titles were 'Grannies Treasures' (1891), 'Reflected Glory' and 'Cut off in their Prime' (both 1893).

**Arthur A.. TURNEY B.W.S. (born 1896, exh. 1928)**

Watercolour landscape painter who was a member of the B.W.S. and exhibited at the B.W.S. Autumn Exhibition at Preston in 1928.

**C.. TURNLEY (exh. 1934-1935)**

Landscape painter who lived at Cotham, Bristol, and exhibited three works at the R.W.A. 1934-1935. The exhibits were entitled 'Near Mangotsfield, Glos' (1934), 'Near Stapleton' and 'October' (1935).

**Miss B.. N.. TUTHILL (exh. 1901-1903)**

Landscape painter in oil who lived at Fakenham, Norfolk, and was a member of the Norwich Art Circle. She exhibited three local views 1901-1903.

**Miss Eirene M.. TYNDALE (exh. 1920-1934)**

Watercolour landscape artist who lived at Bristol, Melksham and, later, Bath and exhibited 25 works at the R.W.A. 1920-1934. The subjects were mostly landscapes including views of Bath and Windsor Castle. She also exhibited some portraits.

*F. H. Tyndale     'A Lakeside Cottage' (w/c)     (Marble Hill Gallery)*

**F.. H.. TYNDALE (fl. c. 1900-1920)**

Painter in watercolour of cottages and rural landscapes who was working c. 1900-1920. The surname might suggest a connection with the well-known Walter, or Thomas Tyndale (q.v.) but this could not be established. The work varies in quality but the subject matter would make a good example collectable. (Illus. p.155).

*T. N. Tyndale      'Coombs Farm, Worthing' (w/c)      (John Sheppard)*

**Thomas Nicolson TYNDALE (1858-1936)**

Painter in watercolour of cottages, landscapes and some Venice scenes. He was the cousin of Walter Tyndale (1855-1943), the well-known watercolour painter and illustrator. Thomas Tyndale lived in Acton, West London, and was a regular exhibitor with the Dudley Gallery Art Society at the Egyptian Hall in Piccadilly. He also exhibited in the provinces, including at least nine works at the R.W.A. 1903-1908. The subjects were mostly Surrey and Sussex cottage scenes – 'Cottage near Haslemere, Surrey' (1903) and 'Near Horsham' (1907) are typical titles.

Thomas Tyndale also worked as an illustrator and painted 20 watercolours as illustrations for the book 'Worcestershire' published by A & C Black in 1909. Most of his watercolours were cottages and rural landscapes, but he also painted abroad in Bruges and Venice. Thomas Tyndale later moved to Worthing and died there at the age of 78 on 15th December 1936. The quality of the work and the popularity of the subject matter has made the cottage scenes, in particular, increasingly sought after by collectors.

# U

## Viscount ULLSWATER (1855-1949)

Watercolour landscape painter who lived at Campsea Ashe, near Woodbridge, Suffolk, and was President of the Ipswich Art Club 1933-1945. He was a regular exhibitor, showing 29 works 1931-1945. The subjects were mostly local views and also some scenes in Mallorca (1933) and Madeira (1936).

## Sidney UPTON (exh. 1935)

Painter in watercolour of industrial landscapes. He exhibited three works at the French Gallery in 1935 at an 'Exhibition of Weekend Work' by industrial designers of J Walter Thompson.

## May UREN (fl. c. 1900s)

Painter in watercolour of coastal scenes who was probably related to the Cornish marine artist John C Uren. Her pictures are not often seen on the market, but are found in the West Country.

## Miss M.. F.. URMSON (exh. 1912)

Watercolour painter who, although not a member, exhibited two works at the Winchester Art Society Exhibition in 1912. The pictures were entitled 'The College Gateway' and 'A Storm on the Itchen'.

## Reginald B.. URQUHART (fl. 1909)

Landscape artist in pencil who lived at Honor Oak, South London. He won second prize in The Studio magazine competition of 1909 for 'A Street in Messina' which was also reproduced.

# V

### Miss E.. F.. VAGGERS (exh. 1900)

Flower painter who lived in Bristol and exhibited at the R.W.A. in 1900. The titles of the pictures were 'Geraniums' and 'Still Life' and these were shown in the amateur section.

Florence E. Valter                    'Terrier Study' (w/c)

### Florence E.. VALTER (1869-1947)

Painter in watercolour of dogs and horses whose work was of fine quality but is not often seen on the market. Her style is similar to Eugenie M Valter, a Birmingham animal painter, who had pictures reproduced as postcards in the 1920s. Florence Valter also had her dog and horse portraits reproduced as postcards in the 1930s by Valentine & Sons of Dundee. She died in Leeds in 1947 at the age of 78.

### Winifred A.. De VANY (exh. 1950)

Painter in oil who lived in Plymouth and exhibited five works at the Plymouth Art Society Exhibition of 1950.

### E.. VAN JONES (exh. 1950)

Portrait and landscape painter in oil who lived in Kingsbridge, Devon, and exhibited four works at the Plymouth Art Society Exhibition of 1950.

### L.. VAN STAATEN (1859-1924)

This was a pseudonym adopted by the artist Norris Fowler Willatt (q.v.) and used by him for his Dutch canal scenes. He found that they sold more quickly with a foreign sounding name, although there are some Dutch scenes signed Fowler Willatt, but these are not common. He used this pseudonym for the three works that he exhibited at the Royal Academy 1908-1914. (Illus. this page).

L. Van Staaten                    'Dutch Canal Scene' (w/c)

### Miss E.. VAN ZYL (exh. 1912)

Watercolour artist who exhibited a street scene and a cottage painting at the Winchester Art Club Exhibition of 1912.

### Miss M.. L.. VAUGHAN (exh. 1912)

Painter in watercolour of landscapes and coastal scenes who exhibited three works at the Worthing Art Gallery Summer Exhibition in 1912. The works were entitled 'Stormy Sunlight', 'Ever Fleeting Waves, North Cornwall' and 'An Old House, Norfolk'.

Hugh Verrall        'A Sussex Cottage' (w/c)        (Peter Gardner)

### Hubert Gerard Washington VERRALL (1894-1940)

Painter in oil and watercolour of portraits, rural scenes and cottages. Hugh Verrall spent much of his childhood at Warninglid, Sussex. He was called up in 1915 and served as a machine gunner and in the Signals in France until his discharge in 1919. After the War he worked on the family farm and in 1932 went to the Central School of Art in Kingsway, London. The 1930s were to be Hugh Verrall's most productive period. He showed three works at the Royal Academy – 'The Newborn Calf' (oil, 1934), 'The Egoist' (watercolour, 1938) and 'Moonlight at Hobshorts' (1940). He had an exhibition 'Sussex Rural Life' at the Brook Street Art Gallery in 1935 which included 42 watercolours and eight oils. The titles included landscapes – 'Loading the Elevator, Poynings', 'The Windmill, West Chiltington' and some figure subjects, such as 'The Old Hedge Trimmer' and 'The Cowman'.

Hugh Verrall also held a show in Lewes around 1939 of 'Tone Paintings' being 44 sepia wash sketches mostly rural Sussex scenes and cottages. His commercial work included some illustrations for The Field in 1937 and a poster for London Underground. Hugh Verrall's work would probably be better known had he not been killed at an early age in a railway accident at Wembley in 1940. He signed his work 'Hugh Verrall' in an ink script on the wash drawings.

T. H. Victor (J Collins and Son)
'Mousehole, Cornwall' (w/c)

## Thomas Herbert VICTOR (1894-1980)

Painter in watercolour of West Country views, mostly harbours and street scenes, who was born at Penzance on 6th September 1894. This prolific artist painted many small studies often of Mousehole or Clovelly which are sometimes signed with the pseudonym W Sands (q.v.). He had a shop in Mousehole during the 1960s and died on 10th March 1980 aged 85.

## Mrs. Constance Mary VILLIERS-STUART (fl. 1911-1913)

Author, journalist, and painter in watercolour of garden scenes. She illustrated her book 'Gardens of the Great Mughals' (A & C Black 1913) with 15 colour sketches mostly executed in 1911 and 1912. Constance Villiers-Stuart was interested in garden history and design and was a Fellow of the Royal Horticultural Society. She lived at Beachamwell Hall, Swaffham, Norfolk.

## Mrs. Dorothy VINCENZI (exh. 1938-1946)

Watercolour landscape painter and illustrator who lived at Earl Soham, Suffolk, and was a member of the Ipswich Art Club. She exhibited four works 1938-1946, the titles included 'From the Beach, St Jean de Luz' and 'First Pony' (both 1946).

## Francis VINGOE (fl. 1900-1914)

Painter in oil of houses. This prolific artist painted pictures of houses on commissions particularly in Surrey and Sussex where many of his paintings are to be found today. There are also some similar studies of early motor cars, which may earn him the dubious distinction of being the first 'car portrait' artist. In 1902, Francis Vingoe exhibited a work entitled 'The Village Street, Arborfield Cross' at the Berkshire Art Society Exhibition in Reading. He signed his work F Vingoe and often with a date.

# W

### A.. Cecil WADE (fl. 1911-1935)

Illustrator and commercial artist who wrote a series of articles for The Artist magazine entitled 'Commercial Art as a Career' in 1935.

### Albert WAIN (exh. 1933-1934)

Landscape artist who lived at Clevedon, Somerset, and exhibited at the R.W.A. 1933-1934. The titles were 'Sunset in the Woods' and 'Hillside Pines'.

A. L. Walbank                    (Vi Preston)
'The Old Mill, 1911' (w/c)

### Arthur Lee WALBANK (1871-1940)

Watercolour painter of landscapes and rural scenes who was born in Keighley, Yorks, in 1871. In the 1890s Arthur Walbank moved to Barnes where he lived and worked until just before his death on the 1st September 1940. Many of his subjects were local views of Barnes and Richmond, although he did some work in France. He sometimes signed his pictures with a monogram (see index).

### Ernest WALBOURN (1872-1927)

Painter in oil of rural landscapes and cottages who was born at Dalston, Middx., on 16th February 1872. The family owned property in Tasmania which provided an income and enabled Ernest to have a formal art training. From 1895 he exhibited regularly

Ernest Walbourn    'Driving Home the Flock' (oil)    (Sotheby's Sussex)

at the major exhibitions including nine at the Royal Academy and among the titles were – 'In the Orchard' (1900), 'Summertime' (1917) and 'The Mill' (1920). In 1906, Ernest married Eva Knight who assisted him with the backgrounds of his larger pictures and later became an accomplished painter in her own right. Ernest Walbourn painted widely in England but only rarely abroad. In 1902 he visited Australia and some sketches exist of his port of call, Capetown, and in 1923 he spent a holiday in Brittany where he painted some landscapes and town scenes. Most of his work was sold to dealers – usually W W Sampson and Louis Woolfe in London. Several prints were made of his paintings and this helped to make the work popular and reproduction rights were bought by Raphael Tuck and Stelhi Freres of Zurich. Ernest Walbourn died on 29th July 1927 at the age of 55. For the next 60 years the work of this artist had largely gone unnoticed and was not often seen except for some larger paintings. However, in April 1987 a major exhibition of 122 works from the artist's studio was held at Bourne Gallery in Reigate, Surrey.

Eva Walbourn    'A Garden Border' (oil)    (Sheila Hinde)

### Eva Maryon WALBOURN (1878-1954)

Painter in oil of cottages and garden scenes. Born Eva Knight on 7th October 1878 she married, in 1906, Ernest Walbourn (q.v.), a well-known Victorian landscape painter. She accompanied him on his painting trips and would assist him by painting in the backgrounds on some of the larger works. Eva Walbourn had talent and soon started painting cottages and garden scenes by herself. The pictures show considerable influence of her husband's style and at their best could be mistaken for his work. Many of the subjects were gardens near their Essex home. Eva Walbourn did not exhibit her work but sold much of it through the art department at Harrods. Her work is mostly signed Eva Walbourn but sometimes Eva Maryon (q.v.). She died on 23rd July 1954 at the age of 75.

### Catherine WALBROTH B.W.S. (exh. 1928)

Watercolour landscape painter who was a member of the B.W.S. and exhibited a French landscape at the B.W.S. Autumn Exhibition at Preston in 1928.

### Miss Beatrice A.. WALDRAN (fl. 1898-1903)

Watercolour landscape painter and craftworker who was working around 1900. She lived at various North London addresses from 1898 until 1903, including Islington and Lower Edmonton. A competent watercolour artist who sometimes signed with initials.

H. Walford          'A Country Cottage' (w/c)          (W. F. Wilson)

### Howard Neville WALFORD (1864-1950)

Watercolour painter of cottages, landscapes and garden scenes who was born at Charlton Musgrove, Somerset in February 1864. He was educated at Sherbourne School, but had no formal art training being entirely self-taught. He was a great admirer of Harry Sutton Palmer and some of his landscapes show that artist's influence. Howard Walford's paintings have a most attractive style and colouring and with the present popularity of cottage scenes, have become increasingly collected. His work was used by Raphael Tuck & Sons for calendars, mostly the cottage and garden landscapes. Howard Walford was a keen amateur photographer and invented a colour photography process which he patented and sold before the First World War. Most of the watercolour landscapes were painted in Surrey, Sussex and Hampshire where he lived. Later he moved to Bovey Tracey, Devon, where he died at the age of 86 in 1950. His work is usually signed H Walford and is sometimes wrongly attributed to H Louisa Walford, a Victorian flower painter.

### Maj. John Colquhoun WALFORD
### (born 1882, fl. 1914-1918)

War artist in watercolour. John Walford was commissioned into the Royal Artillery, went to France in 1914 with the 119th Battery R.F.A. and finished the war after distinguished service as an acting Lt. Colonel. His watercolours of field gun batteries in action in France are well drawn and delicately coloured. A folio of these watercolours were left by the artist to the Royal Artillery Institution.

### Raymond WALKER (exh. 1923-1948)

Landscape artist in watercolour and pastel who lived in Bath and exhibited 10 works at the R.W.A. 1923-1948. The subjects were West Country scenes and a view in the Lake District and the titles included 'Bathers at Warleigh' and 'Porlock Weir' (1935), 'Mevagissey' (1947) and 'The Dorset Sea' and 'Houses at Polperro' (1948).

### Miss Lucy WALLER (exh. 1880-1895)

Painter in oil and watercolour of landscapes, portraits, animals and flowers who lived at Newton Longville, Bucks, and was a member of the Ipswich Art Club. She was a regular exhibitor, showing 83 works 1880-1895. The titles included 'The Farmer's Enemy' and 'Great Blakenham Mill' (both watercolours – 1880) and 'A Meditative Little Dog' (oil, 1891).

### Rev. A.. R.. WARBURTON (exh. 1912)

Watercolour painter who was a member of the Winchester Art Society and exhibited a landscape in 1912.

### Miss Katherine A.. WARBURTON (exh. 1912)

Watercolour landscape and coastal artist who was a member of the Winchester Art Club and exhibited four works at the 1912 Exhibition. These were mostly views of Studland Bay.

### Dudley WARD (fl. c. 1920s)

Watercolour painter of rural scenes and river landscapes. Very little is known of the artist but he may have worked as an illustrator.

**Dr. Francis WARD (exh. 1931)**

Landscape painter in watercolour who lived at Nayland, Suffolk, and was a member of the Ipswich Art Club. Although a member of the Club for many years he exhibited only four works, in 1931, the titles included 'On Barton Broad', 'Devils Elbow, Dartmoor' and 'Gallipoli, 1915'.

**Miss Hester E.. WARD (exh. 1880-1907)**

Painter in oil of flowers, still life and landscapes who lived in Ipswich and was a member of the Ipswich Art Club. She was a regular exhibitor, showing 82 works 1880-1907. The titles included 'Fresh from the Woods', 'Harvest Time' and 'Poppies' (all 1883) and 'At Pin Mill' and 'The Orwell from Freston' (both 1907).

**Brig. Gen. Walter Reginald WARD (1869-1952)**

Watercolour landscape painter who lived at Newton Ferrers, Devon, and exhibited two works at the Plymouth Art Society Exhibition in 1950.

**A.. M.. WARREN (exh. 1924)**

Painter of landscapes in watercolour who exhibited three works at the B.W.S. Exhibition at Cheltenham in 1924. These included 'On the Thames, Teddington' and 'Passing Clouds, Lake of Thun'.

**Miss B.. WARREN (exh. 1912)**

Watercolour artist, who exhibited 'Offington Mill' at the Worthing Art Gallery Summer Exhibition in 1912.

**Miss P.. WASHBROOK (exh. 1919-1921)**

Watercolour artist who lived in Bristol and exhibited at the R.W.A. in 1919 and 1921. The titles were 'Fir Trees' and 'Frenchay Glen'.

**Mrs. Arthur WATERFIELD (exh. 1902-1905)**

Watercolour landscape painter who lived at Great Yarmouth and exhibited 11 works at the Norwich Art Circle 1902-1905. These included some views at Dalhousie and other Indian subjects.

**Mrs. E.. WATERFIELD (exh. 1924)**

Still life painter in oil and watercolour who lived at Cheltenham and exhibited two works at the Cheltenham Arts Exhibition in 1924.

**Miss D.. WATKIN-WILLIAMS (exh. 1927-1930s)**

Artist who lived at Honiton, Devon, and exhibited at the R.W.A. from 1927. She is still recorded in the 1930s and she may have exhibited later.

**Alfred John WATSON (1858-1927)**

Painter and etcher who was born in London and studied art at South Kensington. In 1886 he came to Bristol and taught at the Bristol Municipal School of Art, a position he was to hold for 39 years. Alfred Watson was also Head of the drawing department of Bristol University. He exhibited five works at the R.W.A. 1904-1913, mostly views of Minehead, and 11 works at the Bristol Savages 1910-1922. The exhibits at the Bristol Savages were mostly etchings of landscapes and included views of Minehead and Newquay. Alfred Watson retired to Portishead, Somerset, and died on 20th January 1927 at the age of 69.

*Alfred S. Watson*        *(J Collins and Son)*
*'Richmond Old Bridge, 1916' (w/c)*

**Alfred Sale WATSON (fl. 1898-1928)**

A good quality painter in watercolour of river scenes and landscapes who lived in Birmingham and exhibited at the R.B.S.A. in 1898. Many of his subjects were views on the Thames and date from the early 1900s to about 1928. He has a distinctive highly detailed style, which combined with the subject matter have made his pictures sought after in recent years.

**E.. J.. WATSON (exh. 1923-1930)**

Landscape artist who lived in Bristol and exhibited four works at the R.W.A. 1923-1930. The subjects included views of Jerusalem, Warsaw and a castle in Bohemia.

**Miss F.. Lawson WATSON A.R.W.A. (exh. 1903-1919)**

Painter in watercolour of landscapes and street scenes who lived in Bath and was an associate member of the R.W.A. She was a regular exhibitor, showing at least 29 works 1903-1919. The subjects were mostly foreign views including Jerusalem, Holland, Bruges and Brittany. 'A Street in Bruges' (1917), 'A Wet Day, Brittany' (1918) and 'Interior

Volendam' (1918) are typical titles. She also exhibited two coastal scenes at the Winchester Art Society Exhibition in 1912.

scenes. She also showed work with the St Ives Society, at the Paris Salon and had a joint exhibition at Walkers Gallery, London, in 1949.

*Geoffrey Watson*        *'Formation Flight' (etching)*

*J. Millar Watt*        *(Church Street Gallery)*
*Willows at Flatford, 1937' (oil)*

## Geoffrey WATSON (fl. 1919-1949)

Painter, etcher, illustrator and poster designer specialising in aviation subjects. Geoffrey Watson worked on aviation posters in the First World War and in 1919 he contributed the 15 illustrations to Wade's 'The Aeroplane of the Great War'. He exhibited 1919-1949 including seven works, mostly flowers, at the Royal Academy. Geoffrey Watson had a one-man exhibition at the Cooling Gallery and at the Brook Street Art Gallery in July 1920 entitled 'Aircraft in War and Peace'. Examples of his work were reproduced in The Studio magazine in 1930 and the Fine Art Society published a number of his etchings. Although not often seen on the market, the quality and the unusual subject matter have made his pictures collectable.

## George WATSON (1856-c. 1937)

Painter in oil and pastel of landscapes and marines who lived in Bristol and later in Cirencester, Glos. He was a regular exhibitor at the R.W.A. showing over 22 works 1899-1936. The subjects were mostly coastal scenes in oil including views in Wales, Cornwall and Jersey, and also a number of moorland landscapes.

## Amy Millar WATT (1900-1956)

Painter in oil of flowers and landscapes. Born Amy Maulby Biggs, she married the artist John Millar Watt (q.v.) whom she met while a student at the St. Martins School of Art in London. She was a regular exhibitor at the Royal Academy showing 19 works 1929-1953, mostly flower still life and some harbour

## John Millar WATT (1895-1975)

Painter in oil and watercolour, illustrator and cartoonist. John Millar Watt was born on 14th October 1895 near Greenock, Scotland, educated in Ilford and studied art at the Sir John Cass Institute. He worked briefly for an advertising agency, but with the outbreak of the First World War, he joined the Artists Rifles and later the Essex Regiment seeing action on the Western Front. In 1919, John Millar Watt resumed his art studies at the Slade and while he was there he submitted cartoons and illustrations to magazines. In 1921 his cartoon 'Pop' first appeared in the Daily Sketch – it was a resounding success and ran for over 25 years. John Millar Watt and his wife Amy (q.v.), also a talented artist, lived at Dedham for many years, later Windsor, St Ives in Cornwall and London. He was a member of the Ipswich Art Club where he exhibited 39 works 1923-1935, he showed three pictures at the Royal Academy and was a member of the St Ives Society of Artists in Cornwall. He later concentrated on commercial work and illustrated for Readers Digest, The Sphere and the Illustrated London News. He died at Lavenham, Suffolk, in 1975. A retrospective exhibition of John Millar Watt's work was held at the Church Street Gallery, Lavenham, in 1989 and again in June 1991.

## Arthur H.. WATTS (exh. 1898-1902)

Painter in oil of portraits, figures and still life, who lived in Gorleston, and later in Great Yarmouth, and was a member of the Ipswich Art Club. He was a regular exhibitor showing 25 works 1898-1902. Most of the subjects were figures – 'Girl Reading', 'Sweet Seventeen' and 'Digging for Rabbits' – (all 1901) are typical titles.

*Sidney Watts*      *'On the River' (oil)*      *(Bourne Gallery)*

### Sidney WATTS (fl. 1900s)

Painter in oil and watercolour of rural landscapes, including some Scottish Loch scenes, who was working around the 1900s. The similarity of the style and the subject matter with a number of other artists, such as Daniel Sherrin, suggests that this may be a pseudonym. The work was quite competent and although not usually dated was often inscribed with the location on the reverse.

### Duncan WEBB (fl. c. 1930s)

Painter in gouache of Eastern street and market scenes in the style of Noel H Leaver. This competent artist does not appear to have exhibited but probably worked in the 1930s.

*E. G. Webb*      *'Buckland on the Moor' (w/c)*      *(J Collins and Son)*

### Ernest George WEBB (1876-1951)

Painter in watercolour and occasionally oil of landscapes and cottage scenes. Ernest Webb was born in Plymouth in 1876 and studied at the Plymouth School of Art from 1890 where he received the Silver and Bronze Queen's Medals. He trained as a stained glass artist and joined Fouracres in Plymouth who supplied windows for many churches and houses in the West Country. Many of his watercolours were scenes of Dartmoor and the Plymouth area. He was a founder member of the Plymouth Society of Artists and works by him are in the City of Plymouth Art Gallery. An exhibition of his work was held by J. Collins and Son, Bideford, in November 1986.

### Mrs. Florence WEBB (exh. 1936-1964)

Painter in oil of flowers, still life and figure subjects, who lived in Bristol, and exhibited 14 works at the R.W.A. 1936-1964. The subjects were mostly still life and figure studies and the titles included 'Girl having Tea' (1954), 'A Girl Painting' (1958) and 'The Green Dress' (1964).

### Miss Mildred WEBB (exh. 1913)

Landscape artist who lived in Portishead, Somerset, and exhibited two works at the R.W.A. in 1913. The titles were 'Mariner's Path, Portishead' and 'The Woods, Portishead' (both oils). Later, she moved to Weston-super-Mare.

### Walter Noel WEEDON (fl. 1922-1938)

Artist who lived in Croydon, Surrey, and is listed in the local trade directories between 1922 and 1938.

### R.. Jasper WEIRD (fl. 1906-1911)

Former Punch illustrator and cartoonist who exhibited at the Coronation Exhibition, London, in 1911.

### Miss Mia WELHAM-CLARKE (exh. 1900-1907)

Painter in oil and pastel of landscapes who lived in Harleston, Norfolk, and was a member of the Norwich Art Circle. She was a regular exhibitor, showing a total of 34 works 1900-1907.

### A.. J.. WELSBY (exh. 1925-1927)

Landscape artist who lived in Redland, Bristol, and exhibited at the R.W.A. in 1925 and 1927. The titles were 'A Corner of Oxwick Bay' and 'Coast Guard's Cottage, Worms Head'.

### Violet B.. WENNER (born 1886)

Portrait painter in oil who was born in Manchester and studied at the Manchester School of Art where she first showed her talent. She also had skills as a harpist but decided to follow a painting career and then studied in Vienna under Professor H. Angeli. Her commissions have included portraits of the Duchess of Teck and her family. An example of her work was reproduced in The Studio magazine in 1908.

*Alice L. West*             *'Long Tailed Tits' (w/c)*

### Alice Lizzie WEST (1853-1941)

Painter in watercolour of flowers and birds and illustrator of calendars and postcards. She studied art at the Bloomsbury School in Queens Square, London, under the tuition of her aunt who was the Principal. After qualifying as a drawing teacher, Alice went to Mussoorie in the Himalayas where she taught art and exhibited at the Simla Exhibition of 1876. She returned to England in 1879 and worked in London before finally moving to Tunbridge Wells, Kent, around 1900. Alice West exhibited at the major exhibitions in London and the provinces including six works at the Royal Academy but much of her time was taken up with her illustration work. She illustrated postcards for Faulkners and Hildesheimer, as well as notelets, calendars and seed packet designs for Suttons. Alice West painted animals at the London Zoo and also travelled the South of England with fellow artists who became known as the 'Daub Club', painting landscapes. She was also an accomplished portrait painter. The studio sale of her work was held at Michael Newmans, Plymouth, in November 1987.

### Marian May WEST (1871-1947)

Painter of landscapes as an amateur, in the South of England and Cornwall. Younger sister of Alice and Maud West (q.v.) who showed considerable talent but did not follow an artistic career.

### Maud Ashley WEST (1858-1943)

Painter in watercolour and illustrator of landscapes, gardens and flower studies. Sister of Alice Lizzie West (q.v.) and Marian May West (q.v.). Maud West studied art at the Bloomsbury School in Queens Square, London, and then took up teaching at the Plymouth High School for Girls. The boisterous environment of the girls school did not suit her quiet temperament so she gave up teaching to concentrate on her art. Most of her work was flower studies and she exhibited three works at the Royal Academy as

well as at The Society of Women Artists. Her designs were sold for greeting cards and she illustrated a book entitled 'Through Woodland and Meadow' published in 1891. She lived for many years in Tunbridge Wells, Kent, with her elder sister Alice.

### Thomas WESTCOTT (exh. 1900-1903)

Marine painter in oil who lived in Ipswich and was a member of the Ipswich Art Club. He exhibited 14 works 1900-1903 and the titles included 'Off the Doggerbank', 'Beating to Windward' and 'Wrecked on the Shipwash Sands' (all 1901).

### H.. C.. WESTGATE (exh. 1884-1901)

Watercolour artist and designer who lived in Ipswich and was a member of the Ipswich Art Club. He was a regular exhibitor showing a total of 28 works 1884-1901. The titles included 'Autumn Afternoon' a cover design (1899) and 'Fitting Out' (1901).

### Mrs. Jessie Marian WETHERED (1877-1956)

Painter in watercolour of rural landscapes and alpine scenes who studied art under John Hardwicke Lewis. She lived in Clifton, Bristol, and exhibited seven works at the R.W.A. 1907-1928. The titles were 'Grisedale, Ullswater' (1907), 'Baveno, Lake Maggiore' (1907) and 'Bristol Harbour' (1908) but then no exhibits until 1927 and 1928 when she showed four views around Zermatt, Switzerland. An exhibition of her work was held in Bristol in the 1970s.

### Miss Minnie WHALLEY (exh. 1919-1928)

Landscape and still life painter, mostly in watercolour, who lived in Redland, Bristol, and exhibited 13 works at the R.W.A. 1919-1928. The titles included 'Moorland, Zennor', 'Old St Ives' (both 1923), 'Pink Roses' (1925) and 'Marigolds' (1927).

### Mildred F.. WHEELER (exh. 1923-1924)

Watercolour painter who exhibited two works at the B.W.S. Autumn Exhibition in 1924 entitled 'The Vegetable Barrow' and 'The Balloon Man'.

### A.. E.. A.. WHEREAT (exh. 1908-1936)

Painter in oil and watercolour of landscapes who lived in Bristol and exhibited regularly at the R.W.A., showing at least 62 works 1908-1936. The subjects included local views, moorland scenes and Devon and Cornwall landscapes. The titles included 'Nocturne - Shirehampton', 'Cornish Breakers' and 'Peaceful England – Dunster' (all 1918).

### Mrs. E.. M.. WHISH (exh. 1913)

Artist who lived in Shepton Mallet, Somerset, and exhibited three works at the R.W.A. in 1913.

*Hector Whistler*                    *'Architectural Study' (w/c)*

### Reginald Hector WHISTLER (1905-1976)

Painter in watercolour and oil of portraits and landscapes, illustrator, decorator and mural painter. Hector Whistler was born on 22nd January 1905 in Jersey and he was brought up and educated there at the Victoria College. He trained initially as an architect before attending the Slade School of Art in London. From 1925 to 1928 he was a Lieutenant in the Royal Jersey Light Infantry and during the War, an acting Squadron Leader in the R.A.F., where his artistic training proved useful for camouflage work.

Hector Whistler was first cousin to Rex Whistler, the artist and illustrator who was killed in 1944 during the Normandy Invasion, and also cousin to Laurence Whistler, the glass engraver and author.

After the War, Hector Whistler spent much of later life in Jamaica, in the West Indies, but he exhibited regularly in London as well as at the Paris Salon and Venice. He exhibited work at the R.B.A. and R.H.A., and held several one-man exhibitions including one at the Building Centre in London (1957) and at the Brighton Art Gallery (1959). Hector Whistler undertook many commissions including murals for the liner Queen Elizabeth and the Dorchester Hotel and decorated glass panels for the Liverpool Philharmonic Hall.

His early work, up to the 1930s, was signed R. H. Whistler in a manner that is sometimes mistaken for his cousin Rex, but later works were signed 'Hector Whistler' the name by which he has always been known.

Hector Whistler was both a talented and versatile artist, but his most productive years were after the Second World War - a period of art that has not yet received its true recognition.

### Frank WHITBURN (fl. 1950s)

Painter in oil of landscapes and town scenes, who seems to have worked in Sussex and painted several views of Arundel. He does not appear to have exhibited.

### Mrs. J.. W.. WHITBY (exh. 1910-1912)

Painter of landscapes and buildings in oil and watercolour who lived at Raydon, Suffolk, and was a member of the Ipswich Art Club. She exhibited 13 works 1910-1912, and the titles included – 'A Suffolk Harvest Field', 'Harvest Sunset' and 'The Building of Tower Bridge, 1900' (all watercolours – 1910).

### Miss Alice E.. WHITE (exh. 1901)

Artist who lived at Mortimer, Berks, and exhibited two works at the Berkshire Art Society Exhibition at Reading in 1901. The titles were 'Bray Almshouses' and 'A Street in Vitre'.

### C.. WHITE (fl. 1885-1900s)

Painter and illustrator in watercolour of birds. This artist does not appear to have exhibited but painted a number of bird illustrations at the end of the 19th Century.

### Ernest WHITE (fl. 1901-1908)

Pen and ink artist and illustrator of architectural subjects. Ernest White studied first as an architect, but gave it up due to ill health, and then attended the Herkomer School of Art at Bushey. He worked in Italy and Switzerland and an example of his work was reproduced in The Studio magazine in 1908.

### Cyril WHITEHEAD (fl. 1930s-1950s)

Painter in oil of landscapes and moonlight scenes including some West Country views. He lived in Cheddington, near Leighton Buzzard, and later in Eversholt Street, London. His work is attractive and quite competent but he does not appear to have exhibited at the major exhibitions.

*R. H. Whitehead*                    *'Venice, 1888' (w/c)*

### Richard Henry WHITEHEAD (fl. 1882-1888)

A painter in watercolour of landscapes who lived at Hollinwood, Manchester, and exhibited locally in the 1880s. He travelled in Italy and many of his subjects were Venetian scenes. Richard Whitehead's work was of good quality and he would probably be better known if he had not died at the early age of 37, in Capri. (Illus. p.166).

### J.. WHITELEY (fl. 1930s)

This was a pseudonym used by R D Sherrin (q.v.) for some of his West Country coastal and moorland scenes. The work, painted in gouache, was in the style of F J Widgery, a popular artist of the time.

### Miss Bessie M.. WHITWILL (exh. 1913-1929)

Watercolour landscape painter who lived at Clifton, Bristol, and later in Bath and exhibited regularly at the R.W.A., showing 26 works 1913-1929. The subjects were mostly Devon views and moorland scenes and the titles included 'The Road from Lyme Regis' (1915) and 'On the Holn Moor, South Devon' (1921).

George Whyatt    'Petworth, Sussex' (w/c)    (John Sheppard)

### George Henry WHYATT (1885-1945)

Painter in watercolour of rural landscapes, cottages and village street scenes. Surprisingly, little is known about this good quality artist, although he did exhibit once at the Royal Academy 'At Bosham, Sussex' in 1910. He also exhibited at the R.I. and occasionally in the provinces but appears to have relied on selling his pictures locally. Much of his early work, when he lived at Worthing, was Sussex village scenes and cottages but in the early 1920s he moved to Wolverhampton. Here he advertised in the directories as a 'Painter of watercolours for exhibitions, landscapes, sheep and figures included' – clearly a man with an eye for a saleable picture.

### A.. WHYMPER (exh. 1907)

Landscape painter in watercolour who specialised in Dartmoor scenes. He exhibited six watercolours of Dartmoor at the Annual Devon and Exeter Exhibition at Elands Art Gallery, Exeter, in 1907.

### Charles A.. WIDLAKE (exh. 1900-1907)

Artist who lived in Clapham, South London, and exhibited three works at the R.W.A. 1900-1907. The titles were 'St Michaels Hill, Bristol' (1900) and 'Harvest Time, Bideford' and 'Evening on the River Wandle' (both watercolours, 1907).

### G.. A.. WIDMANN (exh. 1927-1928)

Artist who lived at Sea Mills, Bristol, and exhibited at the R.W.A. in 1927 and 1928 – 'Paxton Church, Somerset' and 'King Street, Bristol'.

### E.. WIGGLESWORTH (fl. 1945)

Watercolour landscape artist. A work by the painter was reproduced in The Artist magazine in April 1945.

R. T. Wilding    'Queensbro' (w/c)

### Robert Thornton WILDING (fl. 1910-1921)

Painter in watercolour of marines and coastal scenes. R. T. Wilding was quite prolific and his work is often seen on the market. He does not however seem to have exhibited. Both the style and subject matter is similar to Thomas Bush Hardy and R T Wilding's best work could be mistaken for that artist. He was living in Wimbledon, South London, in the early 1920s.

*B. H. Wiles*     *'The Smithy' (oil)*     *(Falcon Gallery)*

## Bernard Harper WILES (1883-1966)

Painter in oil and watercolour of landscapes and rural scenes. Bernard was the youngest son of Henry Wiles (1838-1930) a well-known sculptor who lived in Cambridge. He studied with his father and later trained as a photographer in London. In 1906, he was sent to Burma on photographic work but stayed on to paint and worked in Rangoon selling his pictures to tourists. On the outbreak of War in 1914 Bernard Wiles joined the Indian Army and served in the Middle East until 1918. He was commissioned as an official war artist and work by him is in the Imperial War Museum.

He married in Cambridge and then lived for a while on Exmoor before returning to East Anglia in 1921. Bernard Wiles continued to paint and sell pictures but also turned to fruit farming to help supplement his income. In the 1930s he was a friend of the artist J C Harrison and they went on painting trips together. An exhibition of his oils was held at the Assembly Rooms, Norwich, in September 1959 and a further retrospective exhibition was held after his death in 1966. Two of his brothers were also artists, Frank Wiles (1881-1963) was an illustrator and portrait painter and Walter Wiles became a well-known landscape painter in South Africa.

*E. Wilkes*     *'Monoposto Alfa Romeo' (w/c)*

## Edward George Marston WILKES (born 1914)

Watercolour painter of marines and pre-1940 motor racing scenes. Born 12th May 1914 at Egham, Surrey, Edward Wilkes was educated at Berkhampstead School and studied at the Watford School of Art, In 1932 he joined Temple Press as a staff artist illustrating for 'The Motor' and 'The Light Car'. He became a keen amateur racing driver, building and racing his own specials in sprints and hill climbs. Later he joined Rootes Group and was in charge of their Coventry car styling department from 1945 to 1952. He left to form his own successful industrial design partnership. Edward Wilkes is a member of the Association of Sussex Artists. He signs his work E. Wilkes or E.W. in a box on some small sketches. (Illus. this page).

## Gilbert WILKINSON (born c. 1890)

Illustrator, cartoonist and watercolour painter. Gilbert Wilkinson was born in Liverpool, studied at the Liverpool School of Art under Robert Fowler and then later at the Camberwell School of Art in London. He started illustrating for the 'Morning Leader' while he was apprenticed to Nathaniel Lloyd. At the outbreak of the First World War, Gilbert Wilkinson joined the London Scottish Regiment and served for four years. When he was wounded he spent much of the time in hospital drawing cartoons. His most productive period was the post war years – he illustrated every cover for 'Passing Show' 1921-1934 and worked for 'London Mail', 'Pan' and the American 'Judge' magazine. He painted front covers for 'Drawing and Design' and later for 'John Bull'. In addition to his illustrations and cartoons, Gilbert Wilkinson was a keen watercolourist but most of his work was confined to holidays.

*N. Fowler-Willatt*     *'A Surrey Common' (w/c)*

## Norris Fowler WILLATT (1859-1924)

Watercolour landscape painter who lived at Pyrford, near Woking, Surrey, and specialised in painting Dutch canal and town scenes. A self-taught artist, Norris Fowler Willatt first painted the Dutch scenes under his own name but soon realised that they sold better with a Dutch pseudonym and thus he adopted 'L Van Staaten' (q.v.). He appeared to have found a ready market for his work and did not exhibit widely although he did show three watercolours at the Royal Academy under the name of Louis Van Staaten. His first exhibit, from a Wimbledon address, was a view of Dordrecht in 1908 and then he showed two further works in 1913 – another Dordrecht view and 'The Interior of an old Surrey Farmhouse'. As well as the Dutch scenes Norris Willatt painted some English landscapes and these are usually signed under his own name or sometimes 'Murray Thompson' (q.v.). These were mostly Surrey landscapes and heath scenes, often featuring a shepherd and sheep. The pictures were usually large in size and the competent style and pleasing subjects have made his work increasingly sought after in recent years.

## Robert WILLCOX (exh. 1922-1935)

Landscape painter in watercolour who lived at Stoke Bishop, Bristol, and exhibited 13 works at the R.W.A. 1922-1935. The subjects were West Country views and local scenes and the titles included 'Early Morning, St Ives' (1924) and 'The White Hart, Keynsham' (1931).

## M.. H.. WILLFORD (exh. 1922-1924)

Artist who lived at Marple, Cheshire, and exhibited three works at the R.W.A. 1922-1924. The artist was still recorded at that address into the 1930s and may have painted later.

Ada M. Williams        'The Sorrel Horse, Ipswich' (w/c)

## Ada Mary WILLIAMS (1872-1949)

Painter in watercolour of landscapes and old buildings who lived in Acton, West London, and was a member of the Ipswich Art Club. Ada Williams was one of the longest exhibiting members of the Club showing over 260 works 1895-1949. Many of these were local views and building studies with some London subjects and Gloucestershire scenes, where she lived after the First World War. As well as a watercolourist, she was an accomplished artist in pen and ink and was a regular entrant for The Studio magazine landscape competitions and was often among the prize winners. Ada Williams did not exhibit in London frequently but she did show some work at the Society of Women Artists in 1901 and 1902. It is curious that the work of this artist who was active for over 50 years is not often seen on the market. The quality of the watercolours and the appealing subject matter should make her work collectable.

## A.. Ruth WILLIAMS (exh. 1900-1904)

Painter in oil of still life and landscapes who lived at Redland, Bristol, and exhibited six works at the R.W.A. 1900-1904. The titles include three studies of Roses, 'The Old Mill, Lynton' (1900) and 'On the Thames' (1901).

## Miss E.. C.. WILLIAMS (exh. 1922-1928)

Painter who lived at Frome, Somerset and exhibited 11 works at the R.W.A. 1922-1928.

## F.. WILLIAMS (fl. c. 1920s)

Watercolour landscape painter whose work shows a striking similarity to that of Albert Haselgrave (q.v.) for whom it may be a pseudonym. The subjects are often rural scenes at sunset with figures and sheep.

J. W. Williams        'Whitby Harbour' (w/c)

**J.. W.. WILLIAMS (fl. c. 1900-1920)**

Painter in watercolour of harbours, town scenes and landscapes who was working around 1900. Most of the subjects were Yorkshire views including harbour scenes and old buildings in Whitby and Scarborough. Some of the work was reproduced as postcards by J T Ross (Whitby), Taylor Thomas and Son and F T W Dennis (both of Scarborough). He signed J W Williams in a disjoined script. (Illus. p.169).

**Mrs. Norah H.. WILLIAMS (exh. 1933-1943)**

Landscape and figure painter who lived at Ipswich and was a member of the Ipswich Art Club. She exhibited five works 1933-1943 and was active until the 1970s. The subjects were portraits, and landscapes 'The Holy Loch, near Dundoon' (1933), 'Boats at Pin Mill' (1937) and 'Weeping Willows' (1943).

**Oliver WILLIAMS (exh. 1902-1905)**

Watercolour landscape painter who lived at Sheringham, Norfolk, and exhibited 12 works at the Norwich Art Circle 1902-1905. Most of the pictures were local views including Cley and Sheringham Mills.

**A.. D.. WILLIAMSON (exh. 1928-1934)**

Watercolour landscape painter and etcher who lived at Woodbridge, Suffolk, and was a member of the Ipswich Art Club. He exhibited a total of 23 works, mostly local views 1928-1934. The titles included 'The River Deben, Woodbridge' and 'Coddenham' – an etching (both 1930).

**W.. H.. WILLIAMSON (exh. 1924)**

Watercolour landscape painter who exhibited a view near Sheffield and another of Whirlow, Derbyshire, at the B.W.S. in 1924. This artist is not to be confused with the marine painter of the same name who was active in the 1860s.

**Miss C.. F.. WILLIS (exh. 1880-1895)**

Painter in watercolour of flowers, still life and landscapes who lived at Trimley St Mary, Suffolk, and was a member of the Ipswich Art Club. She was a regular exhibitor showing a total of 25 works 1880-1895. The titles included 'Berries' and 'Young Thrush' (both 1880) and also some local landscapes, including views of 'Eye Church' and 'Harwich' (both 1893).

**N.. WILLIS-PRYCE (fl. 1920s)**

Landscape painter in oil who was working around the 1920s. The artist was probably related to George Willis-Pryce who was working in Birmingham in the 1880s. His subjects included Welsh landscapes and were usually signed Willis Pryce in a printed script.

**M.. A.. Hilliard WILLSON (fl. 1913-1936)**

Portrait and landscape painter, who lived originally in Leeds, and from about 1925 at Windemere in the Lake District. He does not appear to have exhibited but may have shown some work locally.

**Lt. Col. L.. Worthington WILMER (exh. 1882-1883)**

Watercolour still life painter who lived in London and was a member of the Ipswich Art Club. He exhibited a still life of fruit in 1882 and another in 1883.

**Alfred J.. WILSON (1906-1963)**

Landscape and poster artist who was born in Hull in 1906, came to Bristol in 1936 and worked as a commercial designer for Mardon, Son and Hall. He was a member of the Bristol Savages and a regular exhibitor showing a total of 96 works at their exhibitions 1936-1962. The subjects were mostly landscape views in Cornwall, Devon, Surrey, Kent and the Isle of Wight. In 1948 Alfred Wilson moved to Putney, where he worked as a freelance artist, and died in Surrey in August 1963.

**Col. C.. L.. WILSON (exh. 1928-1933)**

Painter in watercolour of landscapes, moorland and river scenes. Late of the Royal Artillery, Colonel Wilson lived at Fleet, Hants., and exhibited 22 works at the Army Officers Art Society 1928-1933. Most of the watercolours were West Country views – 'Gratton Bridge, Yelverton' and 'A Devon Trout Stream' being typical titles.

**Edith M.. WILSON (fl. 1904)**

Watercolour flower and still life painter who lived at Leamington Spa, Warks. This good quality artist does not appear to have exhibited.

**Lt. F.. A.. Holmes WILSON (exh. 1930)**

Artist who exhibited seven works at the Army Officers Art Society Exhibition in 1930.

**Lt. Col. R.. H.. W.. WILSON (exh. 1928-1932)**

Artist who lived at Folkestone, Kent, and exhibited four works at the Army Officers Art Society in 1928. He was made an Honorary Member of the Society in 1932 but does not seem to have exhibited after that date.

J. Wilton        *'Cottage by the River' (w/c)*

**J.. WILTON (fl. 1890s)**

This appears to be a pseudonym sometimes used by the watercolour landscape painter John Wilton Adcock (q.v.). (Illus. p. 170).

**J. Miller WINCH (exh. 1891-1914)**

Painter in oil of landscapes, figures and animals who lived at Colchester, Essex, and was a member of the Ipswich Art Club. He exhibited 30 works 1891-1914. The titles included 'The Hermit' (1894), 'Sleeping Mischief – Puppy' and 'Cat's Head' (both 1900) and 'Old Roofs, Colchester' (1914)

**David WINDER (exh. 1905)**

Watercolour landscape artist who lived in Bolton and exhibited at the Marehall Art Gallery Exhibition of Local Artists in 1905.

**Miss Lillie WINDER (exh. 1905)**

Painter in watercolour of flowers and still life who exhibited three works at the Local Artists Exhibition in Bolton in 1905. She was related to David and Madeline Winder (q.v.) who share the same address.

**Miss Madeline WINDER (exh. 1905)**

Artist who lived in Bolton and exhibited two watercolours at the Local Artists Exhibition in 1905. Related to David, Lillie and S.P. Winder (q.v.).

**S.. P.. WINDER (exh. 1905)**

Watercolour artist who lived in Bolton and exhibited two works at the Local Artists Exhibition in 1905. Related to David, Lillie and Madeline Winder (q.v.).

**C.. Lewis WINDSOR (exh. 1915-1921)**

Watercolour landscape painter who lived in Bristol and exhibited eight works at the R.W.A. 1915-1921. The titles, mostly rural landscapes, included 'Fleeting Shadows', 'Ungarnered Corn' (both 1915), 'The Open Heath' (1916) and 'A Bend in the River Chew' (1917).

**Mrs. M.. E.. WINDSOR (exh. 1916-1919)**

Watercolour painter who lived at Cotham, Bristol, and exhibited five works at the R.W.A. 1916-1919. The titles included 'The Foxglove' (1916), 'Shadow Entertainment' (1917) and 'A Feathered Visitor in the Garden' (1919).

**Miss M.. E.. WINTERTON (exh. 1927-1937)**

Landscape painter who lived at Eye, Suffolk, and was a member of the Ipswich Art Club. She exhibited 16 works 1927-1937 which included local views, 'Stonehaven, Aberdeen', 'Damholme, Goathland, Yorks', and some London scenes.

**Edward J.. T.. WITHNALL (fl. 1900-1923)**

Painter in oil of landscapes and for many years a member of the Reading Art Club. The artist had a pleasing impressionistic style of painting and most of his subjects were views in the Thames Valley. An appreciation of Edward Withnall's work with

illustrations was featured in The Studio magazine in 1923, written by the fellow Reading artist Ernest Lumsden.

**Miss May J.. WOODFORD (exh. 1912)**

Watercolour artist who exhibited a picture entitled – 'A Cornfield Blakeney, Norfolk' at the Winchester Art Society Exhibition in 1912. She was not a member of the Society.

**Harry WOODS (exh. 1893-1905)**

Landscape painter in watercolour who lived at Needham Market, Suffolk, and was a member of the Ipswich Art Club. He was a regular exhibitor showing 57 works 1893-1905. The titles included 'Waning of the Day', 'Wind in the Lowland', 'Month of June' and 'The Sexton's Garden' (all 1901).

**C.. M.. WOODWARD (fl. 1920)**

Poster artist and illustrator who was working in the early 1920s. He lived at Solihull, Birmingham.

**G.. Pewtress WOODWARD (exh. 1889-1891)**

Artist who lived in Clifton, Bristol, and exhibited four works at the R.W.A. 1889-1891. The titles were 'Fresh from the Briny Waves' (oil, 1889), 'Autumn' (watercolour) and 'Fishermans Cottage' (oil, 1890) and 'In the Woods' (oil, 1891).

**Walter WREN (exh. 1901)**

Artist who lived at Woolhampton, Berks., and exhibited two works at the Berkshire Art Society Exhibition of 1901. These were landscapes entitled 'On the Mole, Leatherhead' and 'On the Surrey Hills'.

**Charles Edward WRIGHT (exh. 1876-1904)**

Landscape and portrait artist who lived at Weston-super-Mare, Somerset, and exhibited 33 works at the R.W.A. 1876-1904. The subjects were mostly local landscapes in oil and scenes in Devon and Wales. Charles Wright also exhibited portraits and some continental views including 'Lucerne' (1876) and 'Mont Blanc from Chamonix' (1883).

**Miss Marjory WRIGHT (exh. 1903)**

Watercolour and black and white artist who lived in Norwich and was a member of the Norwich Art Circle. She exhibited two works at the 1903 Exhibition.

**Walter Hugh WRIGHT-RUDBY (1855-1934)**

Painter in watercolour of landscapes and coastal scenes. Born Walter Hugh Wright in 1855, he was the fifth son of the Rev. Charles Wright and was educated at Oundle School. For 14 years he worked in a local bank before taking the bold decision to earn his living as an artist. There were many painters in the district named Wright so he decided to adopt the surname Rudby after a town Hutton Rudby in North Yorkshire that had family associations.

H. Wright-Rudby          'Wareham Bridge' (w/c)

## Miss H.. M.. WRINCH (exh. 1891)
Landscape painter who lived at Harkstead, Suffolk, and exhibited at the Ipswich Art Club in 1891 an oil entitled 'By Quiet Waters'.

## John H.. WRINCH (exh. 1891-1898)
Watercolour landscape painter who lived in Ipswich and was a member of the Ipswich Art Club. He showed eight works 1891-1898, the titles included 'Road by the River' (1893), 'The First Sign of Dawn' and 'Departing Day' (both 1897).

## Edgar N.. WYBROO (exh. 1926-1928)
Watercolour landscape painter who lived at Woodbridge, Suffolk, and was a member of the Ipswich Art Club. He exhibited 10 works 1926-1928, all alpine views – 'The Jungfrau from Egersletscher' and 'The Leissigrat' (both 1928) are typical titles.

## Mrs. R.. F.. WYKEHAM-MARTIN (exh. 1911)
Miniature portrait painter who exhibited a portrait at the Coronation Exhibition, London, in 1911. She was a member of the Society of Miniaturists.

## Miss Aileen Doreen WYLLIE (1903-1988)
Aileen Wyllie, the youngest daughter of William Lionel Wyllie R.A., was born in Rochester, Kent, on 26th October 1903 and studied art under her father and at the Municipal College, Portsmouth. She did not exhibit often at the major exhibitions but did show a portrait of her father at the Royal Academy in 1928 and a painting of the Cenotaph Ceremony at the Walker Art Gallery, Liverpool. However she exhibited regularly with the Hampshire Art Society. In 1929, Aileen Wyllie assisted her father with a huge panorama of the Battle of Trafalgar which was painted for the Victory Museum to help preserve the ship. The work took a year to complete and was so large that it had to be painted in situ. After spending the War in East Africa, Aileen returned to Scotland where she exhibited for seven years with the Perth Art Society. She later returned to Portsmouth where she was elected President of the Hampshire Art Society, a position she was to hold for 12 years.

## Maj. R.. WYMER (exh. 1931)
Painter in watercolour of military uniforms. This artist held an exhibition at Fortnum and Masons, London, in 1931 entitled 'Regiments and their Old Time Uniforms'. This consisted of 186 miniature watercolours and 33 larger works covering most uniforms of the regiments of the British Army. He does not appear to have exhibited elsewhere.

A.Wynne          'A Country Lane' (oil)          (Bourne Gallery)

## A.. WYNNE (fl. 1890s-1900s)
This was a pseudonym used by the landscape painter Henry Maidment (q.v.) for some of his river and rural scenes. Henry Maidment did not exhibit at the major exhibitions but sold his work on commission and through smaller galleries. It is possible that the 'Arthur Wynne' who exhibited once at the R.B.A. in 1897 from a Putney address is the same artist. The works signed A Wynne were rural landscapes or river scenes in oil and included views on the Thames at Sonning and Henley.

## Miss Ada M.. WYNTER (exh. 1907)
Watercolour artist who exhibited two works at Elands Art Gallery, Exeter, in 1907.

# Y

## Mrs. B.. A.. YABBICOM (exh. 1889)

Artist who lived at Bristol and was the wife of T H Yabbicom (q.v.). She exhibited an oil 'Apples and Oranges' at the R.W.A. in 1889.

## T.. H.. YABBICOM (exh. 1879-1888)

Landscape painter in oil who lived at Clifton, Bristol, and exhibited five works at the R.W.A. 1879-1888. The titles included an 'Old House in Strasbourg' (1879), 'Welsh Views' (1886), 'A Reverie' (1887), and 'On the Yorkshire Coast' (1888). His wife B A Yabbicom (q.v.) also painted.

## H.. F.. YELF (exh. 1889-1890)

Landscape artist who was a member of the Norwich Art Circle and exhibited three local views 1889-1890.

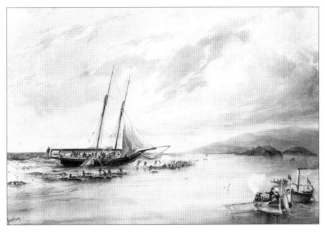

*K. A. Yockney    'A Wrecked Slaver off the Coast' (oil)    (Bourne Gallery)*

## Kenneth Alington YOCKNEY (1881-1965)

Painter in watercolour, and occasionally oil, of marines and landscapes. Kenneth Yockney was born on 6th November 1881, the eldest son of Algenon Yockney R.N., and his mother was the daughter of Admiral Alington. He was brought up at the family home in Ryde on the Isle of Wight, and then studied art at the Slade School in London. He lived on the Island for much of his life and the proximity of the sea must have given him inspiration for his marine paintings. Kenneth Yockney did not exhibit his pictures at the major exhibitions but preferred to sell them locally, and through Percy Beer, an art dealer in Portsmouth. Many of his best works are small detailed watercolour ship portraits and studies of the fleet at Spithead. Kenneth Yockney scorned wealth

and had no ambition to promote his work, which may be why this talented artist is comparatively unknown. He died in 1965 at the age of 83.

## Percy Howard YORKE (1876-1955)

Painter in watercolour of landscapes and cottages. This competent artist, who exhibited at the Walker Art Gallery in the 1890s, was still working in 1950. He lived in Liverpool and was probably related to William Howard Yorke, a well-known marine painter. He signed his work P H Yorke often with a date.

## Mrs. D.. Chilton YOUNG (exh. 1927-1938)

Painter in oil and watercolour of flowers and still life who lived at Bradfield, Essex, and was a member of the Ipswich Art Club. She exhibited 28 works 1927-1938, mostly flower studies in watercolour, and the titles included 'Apple Blossom', 'Butterfly Bush' and 'Japanese Anemones' (all 1930).

## Ralph YOUNG (exh. 1924)

Pastel artist who exhibited at the 1924 British Watercolour Society Exhibition at Cheltenham. The titles were 'Sunset' and a 'Crowded Christmas Street'.

## Miss Ada C.. YOUNGMAN (exh. 1884-1889)

Landscape painter in oil who lived at Kelvedon, Essex, and was a member of the Ipswich Art Club. She exhibited three works, entitled 'A Castle in the Rhine' and 'Now comes Still Evening on' (both 1884) and 'An Afternoons Sport on the Blackwater' (1889).

# INDEX OF ARTISTS

Cotterell, A N
Couche, A J
Coulson, Constance J D
Coulson, J
Coupe, Fred
Courtice, R W A
Cowell, Bertha
Cowley, Florence
Cowper, Cecil
Cox, O S
Craddy, Eric H
Craig, V P
Craven, Helen 35
Creed, E Mercy
Cripps, Clara
Crook, Sylvester
Crosley, William
Cross, E Mary
Croston, Joseph A
Crowther, T S C
Crump, P P
Crute, H E
Culley, Mabel
Culverwell, M E
Cumming, R H Neville 36
Cundall, Florence T
Curtis, K B
Curtis, S J
Cutting, A Margaret

# D

Dade, Fred 37
Daintrey, Alice S
Daintrey, C M
Dale-Glossop, E M
Dalley, C F
Dalton, Percival G
Damant, P S
Daniell, Sophie
Darbyshire, H
Darley, J F
Davey, Geo 38
Davey, Kate H
Davey, W
Davidson, K M
Davie, K M
Davies, G B
Davis, A Mollie
Davy, G M O
Dawe, Alice G
Dawkins, J 39
Day, R J
Deakin, F
Dellis, W O
Dennes, Katherine
Denny, Alexander
Denny, Mrs E
Denton, P M
De Paris, G
De Tivoli, Arthur
Dickins, F J
Diplock, Joseph
Disney-Roebuck, B 40
Dixon, C M
Dixon, C W
Dixon, L M
Dobbs, Frank
Dolan, Philip
Dollery, Percy N
Dollond, W Anstey 41
Dollond-Hulke, H
Dolton, Vere G F
Donnelly, Norman
Dorey, Frederick K
Doria, James
Douglas, J C
Douglas-Willan, Ethel
Dowding, E
Dowes, A S
Dowling, T H
Down, K Thornton

Drane, H Cecil
Drew, Arthur 42
Drew, J E
Drew, Nora L
Drummond, Algernon
Drummond, F B H
Drummond, Hon. Mrs
Ducker, Jack M
Duckett, I N
Duckett, Lewis
Duckett, M M
Durman, Alan
Dutton, Wilfred
Dyer, Rachel M
Dyer, W H 43
Dyke, Beatrice
Dymond, Fred
Dymond, R J D

# E

Eames, W 44
Earl, Kate
Earle, M Peploe
Earp, Edwin
Earp, E M
Earp, M
Earp, W A
Earp, W H
East, H
Eccles, W
Eden, Philip L
Edgcombe, F J H 45
Edmonds, Roland W
Eldridge, Elsie G
Eliot, R Granville
Eliott, James
Eliott, P W
Ellis, Gordon
Ellis, H G Venn 46
Ellis, J
Elson, E John
Elton, Ambrose
Elton, H
Emeny, A
Emeny, J
Endacott, L 47
Endacott, S
England, Daphne K
English, H
Ennion, E A R
Evans, F
Evans, Vivien
Everard, Dorothy
Eyres, Edward 48
Eyton, J W

# F

Fabian, Ena H 49
Fabian, Ernest F
Faint, Frank R
Fairclough, Mary
Fairlie, F A
Fairs, John T
Faning, M L
Fare, A C
Farley, Charles W
Farquharson, John 50
Farrer, R N
Faulks, Jack M
Feilden, C M
Fellowes, Gwendoline
Fenson, R
Ferrier, Arthur
Fidler, H 51
Field, Arthur

Field, Violet
Filmore, Sidney
Finch, Bessie
Finch, W H
Fisher, W C
Fish-Hawk, 52
Fiske, G G
Fiske, W G
Fison, Kathleen M
Fitch, F W
Fitchew, Edward H
Fitchew, Evangeline E M
Fitzgerald, V
Fitzroy, Cyril D 53
Fleming, Winifred J
Flexen, Ernest W P
Flexen, Mrs. E
Flight, Elizabeth G
Florance, H
Flowers, Alfred
Floyd, Donald H
Floyd, E
Floyd, J F M
Follett, John
Foote, Leonard L
Forbes, Leyton 54
Forester, M
Forman, Robert
Forster, C M
Forster, Harold
Fosbery, F C W
Foster, Walter C
Fowell, M
Fowler, Alice
Fox, H C 55
Foxell, John T
Foxwell, Mabel
Francis, T E
Frank, Mary
Frank, W A
Fraser, Cecil
Fraser, F G
Fraser, J D
Freeman, William 56
French, Fred
French, Geoffrey M
Fringes, B
Frost, George L
Fry, Edward R
Fry, Priscilla A
Fuller, J V
Fuller-England, G
Furneaux, Florence

# G

Gaffron, Horace C 57
Galloway, Patience
Gardiner, Edith
Gardini, Theo L
Gardner, G
Gardner, J
Gardner, N
Garrett, Elsie
Garrington, Arthur W
Garstin, A A
Gaussen, C de L
Gay, Arthur W
Gell, E A S 58
Genge, Hilda K
Genge, Stella
George, Harold K
Gerity, Ethel
Gerity, K M
Gibb, N J
Gick, Reginald W
Gill, Charles L
Gill, Edmund W
Gill, G R
Gill, Marion 59
Gill, William
Gill, W W

Gilliard, Walter
Gleb, Marion
Goaman, W Doris
Goddard, Amelia
Goddard, Walter W
Godwin, L C
Goldney, Ruth
Gooddy, Edward C
Goodge, Marjorie J 60
Gooding, Thomas H
Goose, Miss
Gordge, Jack
Gordon, Arthur
Gordon, F
Gordon, Harold
Gordon-Cumming, C F
Gore-Browne, D
Gosling, Edward
Gossop, R Percy
Gower, Alice L
Gowers, Albert R 61
Gowers, Arthur
Gowers, Percival B
Gow-Stewart, Marjory
Gozzard, J W
Grace, F M
Graham, Ben
Grant, Ellen L
Grant, M W
Grayson, F
Greaterex, A E
Green, E M 62
Green, Henry G
Green, I F
Green, T W M
Greene, Miss Taylor
Greenhill-Gardyne, A D
Greenwood, Bertie
Greenwood, Lydia D
Gregory, Victor A
Grey, Sydney
Gribble, S D
Griffiths, Dorothy B
Grimes, Leslie 63
Grimsey, Miss
Grotowski, Marian
Grove, W J
Gulley, M E
Gunter, Clarence P
Gunton, Kit
Gurney, Agatha
Gurney, Gerard H
Gurney, Helen
Gutch, Judith E
Guy, D L
Guyatt, Henry C

# H

Hacksley, M V 64
Hale, E Maud
Hall, Albert
Hall, E M
Hall, S E
Hallett, Hylda
Hamilton, Beamish
Hamilton, C F
Hammersley, G H
Hammond, C Eaton
Hammond, R
Hancock-Heate, C P
Hand, Thomas H 65
Handoll, T H
Hanford, Henry
Harcourt, A F P
Harding, B M
Harding, F A
Harding, M J
Harding, M L
Harding, S A
Hardy, Cyril
Hardy, Mary L 66

Harford, Alfred
Hargrave, Gordon
Harker, Joseph
Harker, Thomas H
Harle, E T
Harlock, H
Harms, Edith M
Harmsworth, H 67
Harmsworth, Maud
Harper, T Laurence
Harrington, E R
Harris, George
Harris, Henry
Harris, Henry (Clifton) 68
Harris, Josephine M
Harrison, A D
Harrison, Brook
Harrison, Frank W
Harrison, J Clifford
Hart, Claud M 69
Hart, T Dyke
Harvey, G Garstin
Haselgrave, A
Haswell, Violet M
Hatchard, Dora J
Hatherley, E A A
Hattersley, C G
Hattersley, F W 70
Hattersley, G P
Hatton, W Scarlett
Havell, Ernest B
Havell, Joyce
Havers, Ethel
Havers, Gladys M
Hawes, W O
Hawkes, Violet E
Hawkins, H L
Hawley, E Stretton 71
Haxell, Winifred
Haxton, Elaine
Hayes, G R
Hayward, Ruby G
Head, Basil
Heading, R
Healey, Edward
Healey, Mary
Heap, B Lanta
Heard, Hugh P 72
Heath, Jessica F
Heath, Sidney
Heathcote, Arthur
Heaviside, Ethel
Heelas, Alice
Heir, J Allister
Hellicar, E
Helps, Herbert
Hempson, E 73
Hempson, K
Hemsworth, L
Hennessey, Richard
Heriz-Smith, L M
Herrmann, H Z
Heseldin, J
Hewitt, Robert J
Hibbs, Catherine M
Hicks, H W 74
Hicks, Victor
Hider, Frank
Hider, George
Hill, E D
Hill, J
Hill, Nina
Hillier, H D 75
Hine, Frank
Hinkins, Frank R
Hips, Phil
Hirst, H C M
Hitchcock, Laura S
Hobson, C I
Hocknell, Lilian
Hodges, Charles M
Hodges, W W
Hodgkinson, Winifred
Holden, Beatrice
Holden, Douglas H
Holder, Carl
Holder, Edith 76

Holding, A L
Holland, Evered
Hollyer, W P
Holman, R W
Holmes, Gerald
Holmes, Harold J
Holmes, Margaret
Holmes, Wilfred 77
Holsner, Emily F
Home, Emily G
Homfray, J R H
Hony, May
Hood, Eileen
Hooper, E Horace
Hooper, Millicent L
Hooper, Miriam M
Hope, D K E
Hopes, Reginald F
Hopking, Nöel H 78
Hopkins, Francis P
Hopkins, G C
Hopper, M
Horley, Fred
Horstmann, A
Houghton, Stanley
Hounsell, Stanley R
Hovenden, Ethel L 79
Howell, Jamison
Howell-Baker, George
Howells, Frederick W
Howes, Kate A
Howitt, S F
Hoyer, Maria A
Hoyland, Mrs Stanley
Hubner, H
Hudd, Alfreda T
Hudd, D A
Hudson, Cyril A
Hudson, M U
Hugh-Jones, Rose K
Hughes, Madeline 80
Hughes-Richardson, H
Huitt, A E
Hulk, Claude
Humphries, E
Hunnibell, Annie L
Hunnibell, Charles F
Hunnibell, F C W
Hunnybun, Mary H
Hunt, H Millson
Hunt, Jessie
Hurlstone, Henry
Husey, Edgar E
Hutchings, Albert S
Hutt, H R M
Hyde, George 81

# I

Ingall, Frank 82
Ingerson, C F
Inglis, M Leslie
Ingram, Leslie
Ingram, M
Isaac, Jessie M
Isbell, W
Izard, Eileen

# J

Jack, Evan M 83
Jackson, Maud H
Jackson, R D
James, A E
James, H L
James, S S
Jamieson, F E

Jarrett, Dudley
Jarrett, Mabel
Jauncey, Eleanor V
Jay, Florence 84
Jeens, E Maud
Jenkins, G H
Jervis-White-Jervis, Mary
Jervoise, Mrs E
Jezzard, Edith
Jillard, Hilda
Joel, H B
Johnson, Beatrice 85
Johnson, S Y
Jones, G D
Jones, R B Hooper
Jones, Winifred J
Jordon, Phyllis T
Joy, Ruth
Jump, Annette

# K

Keenan, John 86
Keer, N
Kellar, Walter D
Kelly, S E
Kendal, I A
Kennaway, May
Kennedy, C
Kennett-Barrington, A G 87
Kerly, Fred R
Kerr, Alfred
Kerr, Mark
Kettlewell, Annie I
Keyworth, W
Kilpack, S L
King, George A 88
King, G Hartley
King, M
King, V A
Kingston, Thos
Kingwell, Mabel A
Kinnaird, Wiggs
Kinsella, E P 89
Kinsella, Katherine
Kirk, T C
Kitchingman, Dawson
Kitson, Ethel M
Knight, Bertha W
Knight, Frank H
Knox, W

# L

Lacon, Caroline H 90
Lacy, Leonard
Lane, C de Wynter
Langford-Reed, Joan
Langley, W
Larcombe, Ethel
Larner, George
Latham, Molly M
Law, Denys 91
Lawrence, Sidney
Leach, Edith
Leather, F
Leathes, M K
Le Boueff, Pierre
Lee, Frank H
Lee, Norman
Leefe, R H
Leggett, Rowley
Leigh, Henry J 92
Leighton, George W
Leipner, Helen
Leith, M C I
Lennard, Hilda

Leonard, Edward A
Lewcock, K M
Lewin, F G
Lewis, Ada I 93
Lewis, Alfred
Lewis, J
Lewis, L
Lewis, Lowry
Lewis, L C
Lewis, Percy
Leyman, Alfred 94
Leyton, F
Lillie, Arthur
Lindley, Constance
Lineham, Wilfred J E
Lingford, George
Linsley, W
Lintott, W H Bernard
Little, Norman
Littlewood, P M A 95
Lloyd, Stanley
Lloyd-Jones, Conway
Lock, C F
Lockwood, Lucy
Lockwood, W
Long, Margaret
Longe, L R 96
Long-Holloway, Arthur
Longmate, Edith M
Longmate, Ernest
Loring, W
Lothian, B J F
Lovegrove, A Vernon
Lovell, E H
Lovell, John
Lowe, Lydia P 97
Lownds, May
Loxton, S J
Loy, Mina
Loyd, E W
Lucas, C Vera P
Ludlow, Mary S
Ludlow, W H
Lugg, R J
Lummis, Victor
Luton, E M
Luttrell, Hugh F
Lynch, Ethel M 98
Lynton, H S

# M

Macauley, R 99
McAllister, F
McCheane, M W H
McConnel, Jessie F
McCracken, F W N
Macdiarmid, John
McDonald, Gertrude
Macdonald, R J
Macdonald, W Alister 100
MacGeorge, J B
Macgregor, Helen
MacGregor, R
McInnes-Millar, J
Mack, Miss
McKaig, D I
Mack-Smith, Margery
McLeish, Annie
McLeish, Phoebe
Macleod, Mary
McNish, Bertha 101
McPherson, Irene
Macpherson, Isabel L
Maggs, C W
Maidment, Henry
Makgill, George
Malan, L N
Malcolm, Thalia
Mallenda, J M
Mallett, Wilfrid T
Mann, Lily

Mann, William 102
Manningham-Buller, F
Mansel, Philip
Mappin, Douglas
Margerison, M L
Marrable, Theresa R
Marriott, Elizabeth B
Marsh, A
Marshall, J M
Marshall, W D
Marston, K M
Martin, E F 103
Martin, F A
Marton, George M
Maryon, Eva
Mason, Herbert W
Mason, Olivia
Masters, Charles
Masters, M D
Mathew, George de M
Matthews, James 104
Matthews, R A
Mavrogordato, Alex J
Maw, Thomas
Maxwell-Lyte, Frances F
Mayes, Robert
Mead, Lewis J 105
Meegan, Harry H
Meegan, Walter L
Megoran, Winston
Mendoza, Philip
Meredew, Percy W
Merrett, J
Merritt, H S
Merrylees, K W 106
Metcalf, Ada
Mewburn, Priscilla
Michelson-Gordon, M
Miller, Maud L
Millican, M E
Millington, J
Mills, Enid S
Milne, Arthur S
Milnes-Hey, C E 107
Minett, Herbert T
Mitchell, Jessie
Mole, Frank
Molony, Francis A
Molyneux, Maud
Montes, Ricardo
Montgomerie, A
Moody, W A
Moorcroft, Mary B 108
Moore, C G
Moore, C S
Moore, Donovan M
Morcom, H Margaret
Morgan, Mary E T
Morrall, J Bernard
Morris, C O
Morris, Garmon
Morrish, Betram 109
Morse, A F
Mortimer, G
Mortimer, L
Mortimer, Olive
Mortimer, T 110
Mostyn, George
Motts, Florence H L
Mumford, L E
Murray, C D
Murray, D K Wolfe
Murray, H
Murray, Katherine
Murray, Marie Louise De M
Myer, The Hon. Mrs.

# N

Naish, Frederick 111
Neale, L A
Neatby, Hilda M

Nelson, Phyllis
Nevil, E
Neville, B Amy
Neville, E Kate
Nevin, E
Newall, Leslia
Newcombe, A E 112
Newling, E
Newman, George
Newman, J
Newton, Frederick C
Nicholson, Reginald P
Nicoll, Emily
Nicholson, R
Niel, D A
Nixon, H
Norman, Leslie H
North, Stanley 113
Nott, M L
Nottage, L N
Nunn, Alexandra L
Nunn, Mrs. Lindley
Nunn, M C
Nunn, Robert L
Nurse, C B
Nutt, A Y 114
Nuttall, Leonard B
Nyberg, Henning

# O

Oakes, John B 115
Oakley, Herbert C
Offer, F R
Offord, Georgina E W
Oldfield, E A
Olivier, H D
Onabolu, Aina
O'Neill, Sandison 116
Orchard, Stanley
Orr, Cecil
Orridge, Caroline
Osment, Phil
Oswald, C W
Owen, Joel
Owen, R H

# P

Packard, Katherine M 117
Packard, Winifred
Packer, Harold G
Packham, Arthur B
Padwick, Fred
Paine, B G
Palmer, John L
Palmer, Lucas S
Palmer, T
Park, H Morley
Parker, John 118
Parker, J Hyde
Parker, N M
Parks, Kate
Parr, F
Parrini, E
Parrott, Ernest H
Parsons, Dorothy M
Parsons-Norman, Pattie
Partridge, F H
Passmore, C T 119
Patteson, Marion F
Paul, Mrs Edward
Paul, Ida
Pauli, Lucie
Paulman, J
Paulraj, G D
Pavey, Maurice F D

Pearce, W H
Pearse, Edith E
Pearson, H G
Pease, Margaret 120
Pelly, C E
Pelly, F I C
Pennington, G F
Penraven, A F
Percival, E D
Perkins, B W 121
Perry, A W
Perry, Kathleen
Peters, A W
Phillips, Edwin R
Phillips, Mrs March
Philp, Roy
Pickles, Harold
Pickthall, L
Pierpont, Walton S
Pigache, M C
Pigott, Blanche A F
Pinder, Douglas H
Pinder, L 122
Piper, John D
Pitcher, Florence
Pitcher, Henrie
Plymouth, Lord
Pocock, Noel 123
Poisson, A
Pollard, Samuel G
Poole, Nora
Pooley, A V
Porteous, R A
Porter, Isabel
Posford, Jospeh
Posford, M A
Potter, Ernest
Powell, Elsie K S 124
Powell, Joseph
Powell, W E
Power, Lucy
Power, Maud
Poyser, A J
Poyser, Ianthe
Prater, William
Pratt, Mary
Prelty, G 125
Prentice, G Minnie
Prentice, H J
Prentice, L May M
Prentice, William C
Prentice, William R
Preston, L E
Preston, Muriel
Pretty, Maud
Prichard, G M
Prior, Margaret
Pritchatt, Alfred J
Probert, G O C
Prosser, Frank 126
Prosser, Winifred
Protheroe, Thomas
Proverbs, Stuart W
Prowse, G W T
Purser, L D M
Purvis, Tom
Puttick, Walter 127
Pym, Alice M
Pym, Jessie
Pyne, K A
Pyne, M F

# R

Raby, Edward 128
Rahamin, S F
Ramus, A
Rands, Lilian E
Rankin, E
Ranshaw, Robert
Rash, D E A

Ray, Frederick H
Read, Noel
Rees, T L
Reeves, E K
Rennards, Charlotte D 129
Rettie, W J K
Rhodes, James
Rhvs-Jenkins, G W
Rich, Albert
Rich, W
Richards, Frank T
Richards, L
Richards, W
Richardson, H O
Ricketts, Ellen
Rider, Fred 130
Rignall, F M
Rimmer, Richard
Ringer, F A
Ripley, N L
Riseley, R C
Robbins, S J
Roberts, Nina
Robertson, Ethel L
Robinson, Arnold W
Robinson, Boardman 131
Robinson, Cyril E
Robinson, E H
Robinson, Julius
Robinson, Mary G
Robson, Leila
Roche, Dorette
Roe, Muriel G
Roffey, Delamark B
Rogers, S E
Rogerson, R W
Rolfe, F Arthur
Roll, Jospeh A
Romberg, Maurice
Romney, Paul
Rooney, Pat
Rose, George F
Rothney, Nina 132
Rough, W Ednie
Row, Douglas E
Rowbotham, Leeson
Rowney, Walter G 133
Rowsell, Irene
Rudby, Hugh
Ruegg, Florence
Russell, F S
Russell, Marjorie
Russell, W S
Ryder, Harold

# S

Sage, H J 134
Sage, R G A
St John, E
St John, R S
Saldanha, F M
Sams, R H
Samuel, S Rahamin 135
Sanders, A E
Sands, W
Sargent, H N
Saunders, A J
Savage, Elaine
Savery, Frederick
Saw, Mabel
Sawyer, D J
Sayers, Zue 136
Scarvelli, S
Scott, G Forrester
Seaborne, E A
Seager, Mabel
Seager, R
Searle, William J
Sedgwick, M Josephine
Seed, A I

1. Outdoor life class, Bushey 1930s

2. John Farquharson

5. Charles F Dalley

6. Tom Purvis

8. Indoor life class, Bushey 1930s

9. James F Darley